ISBN: 9781407748061

Published by:
HardPress Publishing
8345 NW 66TH ST #2561
MIAMI FL 33166-2626

Email: info@hardpress.net
Web: http://www.hardpress.net

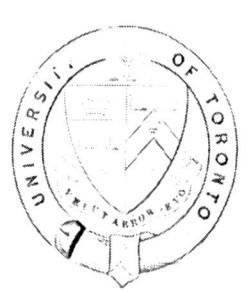

THE HON. LIEUT.-GENERAL JAMES MURRAY.

From a print of about the year 1773.

By kind permission of the Clarendon Press, Oxford.

LIFE OF GENERAL
THE HON. JAMES MURRAY
A BUILDER OF CANADA

WITH A BIOGRAPHICAL SKETCH OF THE FAMILY
OF MURRAY OF ELIBANK BY HIS DESCENDANT

MAJOR-GEN. R. H. MAHON, C.B., C.S.I.

WITH ILLUSTRATIONS

LONDON
JOHN MURRAY, ALBEMARLE STREET, W.
1921

PREFACE

ANCESTRY as a basis for biography is legitimised by custom, but it is often uninteresting! Yet the founders of the House of Elibank belong to a period that still lives in song and story, and so I have ventured a chapter on James Murray's progenitors—partly in the hope that my estimate of his character may receive a certain confirmation therefrom.

His connection with Canada, however, forms my chief reason for writing. There has been no small controversy regarding the campaigns of 1759–60—"the struggle for Canada "—and I have endeavoured to bring out the truth, and to indicate the leading part which fell to him. His government of Quebec for seven years, and his efforts to secure justice for the French inhabitants, has been obscured by the effects of the convulsion that was even then brewing in America, yet as a founder of the Canadian constitution as we know it now, Murray's work was remarkable and enduring.

The story of Minorca and its heroic defence, which forms the concluding episode of his active career, is perhaps of minor interest to us in these days, shadowed by memories of the Great War; but even in this case it is of interest to recall the gallantry of soldiers of other times under conditions not less trying than those we have experience of.

My thanks are especially due to Viscount Elibank, who generously placed at my disposal a large number of family papers; to the Hon. Dudley Murray, who gave me much time and labour at the Public Record Office; to my aunt, Mrs. James Murray, and my cousin, the Rev. James Arthur

Murray, for the loan of the collection of the General's papers, often referred to as the "Bath Papers"; to Dr. Doughty and Mr. H. P. Biggar, of the Archives Department in Ottawa and London, for much kind assistance; to Mr. Charles Lane-Sayer, for the extensive information contained in the "Collier Letters"; to Sir Archibald Lamb, now of Beauport, the Mayor of Hastings, and Mr. Meadows, for their assistance in reading the town's records; and to many others who have kindly procured information on my subject.

Commenced before the outbreak of the Great War, this story would in all probability have remained unpublished but for the generosity and enthusiasm of Colonel Thomas Cantley, of New Glasgow, Nova Scotia. His admiration of the character of "Old Lion Heart," as he so aptly dubbed my hero, and his desire to preserve for Canada a memoir of one who loved her so well, is the mainspring of what now appears in print—for his sake I hope it may be successful.

CONTENTS

CHAPTER   PAGE

I. THE MURRAYS OF ELIBANK 1

II. THE WAR WITH SPAIN, 1739 27

III. PEACE AND WAR, 1744–57 40

IV. THE CAPTURE OF LOUISBURG, 1758 57

V. NEW FRANCE 74

VI. QUEBEC, 1759 90

VII. QUEBEC, CONTINUED 121

VIII. THE MYSTERY OF THE ANSE AU FOULON . . . 170

IX. THE FIRST WINTER IN QUEBEC, 1759–60 . . . 188

X. THE SECOND BATTLE OF THE PLAINS, 1760 . . . 219

XI. THE CONQUEST OF CANADA, MONTREAL, 1760 . . 250

XII. PUBLIC OPINION AND HOME LETTERS 268

XIII. THE MILITARY GOVERNMENT OF QUEBEC, 1761–62 . 276

XIV. THE FIRST BRITISH GOVERNOR OF CANADA . . 298

XV. THE GOVERNMENT OF QUEBEC, 1764–66 . . . 318

XVI. THE GOVERNMENT OF QUEBEC, CONCLUDED . . . 352

XVII. MINORCA, 1774–81 372

XVIII. THE DEFENCE OF FORT ST. PHILLIPS, 1781–82 . . 397

XIX. THE REWARD OF CONSTANCY 417

XX. CONCLUSION 435

INDEX 443

LIST OF ILLUSTRATIONS

FACING PAGE

GENERAL THE HON. JAMES MURRAY . . . . *Frontispiece*

FACSIMILE OF THE LAST PARAGRAPH OF THE BRIGADIERS' "REPLY"
TO GENERAL WOLFE, WITH THEIR SIGNATURES 128

SHIELD, FORMERLY AN ORNAMENT OF THE GATES OF QUEBEC AND
NOW IN THE TOWN HALL OF HASTINGS 189

THE MANSION HOUSE OF BEAUPORT NEAR BATTLE, SUSSEX . . 436

MAPS

SKETCH MAP OF THE QUEBEC BASON 105

THE ST. LAWRENCE RIVER FROM QUEBEC TO ST. AUGUSTIN . . 111

THE ST. LAWRENCE RIVER FROM ST. AUGUSTIN TO PTE.-AUX-TREMBLES 123

THE HEIGHTS OF ABRAHAM, WITH APPROXIMATE CONTOURS . . 231

LIFE OF GENERAL THE HON. JAMES MURRAY

CHAPTER I

THE MURRAYS OF ELIBANK

" Every Scottish man has a pedigree. It is a national prerogative as inalienable as his pride and his poverty." I commence these memoirs, as the Author of *Waverley* commenced his autobiography, for I think that a sketch of the ancestry of James Murray, which I hope may not in itself want in interest, cannot fail to aid in forming a true estimation of the man himself. Heredity counts for much even in our day, and was more marked in its effect at the time of which I am writing. In Scotland, particularly, the continuance of the feudal system up to a late date of the eighteenth century made the line dividing the scions of the noble houses from those who were their dependents more clearly defined than can be easily pictured to-day, and could not fail to induce a sense of command in those brought up in such a school.

The " Scottish man " who treasured the history of his family was imbued with its traditions and bore himself accordingly. A highland chief in those days was a law unto himself, subject to the central authority of the Crown in so loose a fashion, that government consisted more in producing a balance of power in a series of minor states than in authoritatively ruling them. In the lowlands, with which I am immediately concerned, the Sovereign's power extended further, but here also the legacy of border warfare

1

and of blood feuds between various families had served to maintain the idea, even when the fact had vanished, that the strong man armed keepeth his house in peace.

The family of Blackbarony, of which our family of Elibank is a branch, claim descent from the same source as the noble family of Atholl, and if William de Moravia ranks in relation to a number of Scottish families in somewhat similar degree as Brian Boroihme to as many in Ireland, I have no intention of bringing reproof on my head from descendants of either hero (the more so. as I claim both myself!) by casting any doubts on the authenticity of the pedigree. I therefore propose to skip various generations of Moravia, Moray, and Murray, and come at once to Sir Andrew Murray of Blackbarony, who was the head of that ancient family in the first half of the sixteenth century.

Sir Andrew succeeded to the family honours as an infant in 1513, when his father fell on Flodden side; and during his lifetime maintained his rights in the good old simple plan, like most of his neighbours. By his second wife, Grizel Bethune, he became the father of Gideon Murray, his third son, who was first of Elibank, and with whom this history properly commences; but before parting with Sir Andrew and his wife I cannot forbear, at the risk of a digression, from putting in my record some recollections of the romantic history which this union brought into the ancestry of my hero.

Grizel Bethune was one of the younger daughters of John Bethune or Beaton of Criech, in Fifeshire, and the name brings us at once into close touch with the tragic story of Mary of Scotland. Her two elder sisters were Janet, and Margaret, Lady Forbes of Reres, and about these a host of memories arise. Janet was a lady of matrimonial proclivities, her third husband being Walter Scott of Buccleugh, known to fame as "Wicked Watt," for, indeed, nearly all Scotts were Walters, and it was very necessary to bestow on them distinctive epithets. Wicked Watt was murdered in Edinburgh in 1552, and Janet as his widow, whose " burning pride and high disdain forbade the rising tear to flow," is the heroine of the *Lay of the Last Minstrel;* but her claim to historic fame rests rather on her connection with Mary Stuart than on the poet's licence of Sir Walter Scott. It was she who was known as the " Auld Witch of Buccleuch," she who was alleged to have cast love spells round the unfortunate queen to encompass the marriage with Bothwell, a story we may reject right off as originating in the evil tongues of the day which were many and sharp, for it is at least certain that she parted in anger from her Royal mistress immediately after the disastrous event ; she to whom scandalous tongues attributed love affairs with Bothwell himself, though she was quite old enough to be the mother of that " glorious, rash, hazardous young man," nevertheless it is curious that both she and Bothwell had the reputation of dabbling in " black magic," and the lady at least was credited with powers to call " the viewless forms from air." It was Janet, too, from whom originated the story in the *Reiver's Wedding*, that she laid before her hungry retainers a dish containing just a pair of silver spurs, as a delicate hint that it was time to be up and doing, and Cumberland beef was to be had for the taking. No doubt she was a redoubtable lady, quite capable of leading her Scotts on a foray, and of showing the truth of the maxim that " nothing came amiss to a Scott that was not too heavy or too hot." *

Lady Forbes of Reres was a close companion of Mary's, and fortunately we can dismiss as mere scandal the stories retailed by that prince of ungrateful liars, Master George Buchanan. She was the " fat massy old woman " that Buchanan alleges was let down by a " string " over the wall of the Exchequer House at Edinburgh when on a disgraceful errand to Bothwell—though why she should not have taken the more reasonable method of going through the gate by which Bothwell returned with her is not

* It is likely enough that it was the queen herself who applied this epithet to her unruly Scotts, for Mary, no doubt, had read her Rabelais from cover to cover, and remembered that to the followers of Picrochole, " Rien ne leur fut ny trop chaud ny trop pesant."

explained. When Buchanan embellishes his story with the detail that the " string " broke and the " massy old woman " fell the rest of the way, one wonders how it comes that some historians of repute have quoted him to " prove " the case against poor Mary.

Lady Forbes, too, figures in that famous " casket letter," which it is falsely alleged was addressed by the Queen to Bothwell, wherein the supper party is described and much made of Mary's description of it ; how Lord Livingston " thristit her in the body " and made a remark which has been interpreted by her enemies much to her disadvantage. After all " thristit " only means nudged, and Livingston's remarks are capable of a perfectly innocent rendering.

Then there were many other Beatons in the story. James, Mary's faithful ambassador in Paris ; John his brother, who devoted his life to her, and died in her service during her captivity in England ; and Mary, who lives in song as one of the four Maries—all were faithful to their sovereign.

With all these interesting personalities our Sir Andrew became connected by his marriage with Grizel Bethune, and at the same time with the house of Buccleuch, for Grizel when he married her was the widow of William Scott—the strange fact being that the sisters Janet and Grizel were the wives respectively of father and son. Thus it came about that when Grizel became the mother of Gideon Murray, afterwards of Elibank, the young stranger found himself nephew to the famous ladies referred to above, and half-brother to the Lord of Buccleuch, another Walter Scott. I like to picture the young Gideon at Branxholm, when that famous stronghold was rebuilt by his half-brother after its destruction by Sussex, and to think that he saw the chiselling of that inscription over the arched doorway—

In varld is nocht nature has vrought yat sal lest ay
Therefore serve God keep veil ye rod thy fame sal nocht dekay.*

---

* Which may be rendered :
In the world is nothing wrought by nature that shall endure,
Therefore serve God, keep watch, that thy fame shall not decay.

and no doubt found it a good motto to remember, and one which we may be sure was well known to his descendants.

Perhaps it was here that he acquired that taste for architecture that enabled him many years later to repair the king's palaces at Holyrood and Falkland at small cost, which mightily pleased his Majesty, who examined his expenditure with all the care of a canny Scot.

Gideon Murray was intended for the Church, and even got so far as to be " presented " to the parish of Auchterles in 1582, an office which carried with it the position of " Chantor " of Aberdeen. However, his spiritual career was cut short by an " accident," for it is recorded that " Mr. Gideon Murray, Chantor, quha cannot be comptit ane of the Chapter, because for slauchtir he was fugitive out of the North and never returned ther agane." The accident was the killing of a man named Aicheson, though how our Gideon came to forget his cloth so far is not recorded. However, the fact drove him to seek another outlet for his energy, and we next find him in the capacity of guardian to the son of his deceased half-brother, still another Walter Scott, and particularly in a famous skirmish between the Wardens of the Marches, known in border story as the " Lockerbie Lick," in which the Scotts and Johnstons were victorious over the Maxwells. However, though more successful as a soldier than as a cleric, Gideon had still to find his real vocation, and throughout the succeeding years he appears as the faithful and trusted councillor of King James VI.

It is said that he owed his advance in the favour of his Sovereign to the influence of his " near relation," Robert Ker, afterwards Earl of Somerset, but family tradition holds that his advancement was due to the king observing his faithful discharge of his duties in connection with Buccleuch, and his being desirous of utilising his ability and honesty, the latter being a qualification not very readily obtainable at the time. This latter version is more acceptable, having in view the somewhat unsavoury character of Somerset, and indeed the " near relationship " referred to by Sir Walter of Abbotsford was not so very near after all, for Somerset was the son of Janet Scott, a half-sister of Buccleuch's, and no blood relation at all to our Gideon. Be that as it may, his advance was rapid. Knighted in 1605, he was Justiciary of the border in the same year, and in 1607 the Privy Council passed an Order approving of his services in preserving the peace of the Marches.

But the old Adam was not dead, and I must refer to the remarkable story, which has been so often repeated that it stands a good chance of becoming true, wherefore I repeat it again for the express purpose of running a tilt at it. According to Sir Walter of Abbotsford, the incident, which must have occurred in 1610, if it occurred at all, concerned the Scotts of Harden, the head of which family was Sir Walter, commonly known as " Auld Watt." It appears that Auld Watt cast the eyes of desire on Sir Gideon's fat cattle, and evidently having little respect for the worthy knight's position as guardian of the peace, sent his son William to annex as many of the said cattle as he conveniently could. Sir Gideon, however, happened to be at home, and no doubt with a good experience in similar ventures was not to be caught napping, and having captured the adventurer, was about to hang him on the " doom tree," which we are to suppose was handy at the castle gate, when his more considerate and far-seeing dame interposed saying, (I quote Sir Walter), " Haut na, Sir Gideon, would you hang the winsome Laird of Harden, when ye have three ill-favoured daughters to marry ? " The Baron " catched at " the idea, and replied, " Right, he shall either marry our daughter mickle-mouthed Meg or strap for it." Upon this alternative being proposed to the prisoner he at the first view of the case stoutly preferred the gibbet, but, to shorten the story, finally consented and married the young lady.

And now for my tilt ! To begin with, Sir Gideon had only one daughter, and her name was Agnes ; and to go on with, her marriage with William Scott of Harden took place in 1611 under the most leisurely of legal and contractual formalities. The marriage contract, which is preserved by her descendant, Lord Polwarth, is, I believe, seven feet long and *minutely written ;* and to end up with, Sir Gideon provided what was a more than usually handsome " tocher " of 7000 merks Scots, and more also, the lady had a " curious hand at pickling beef," a very desirable art when " consignments " came in in quantity at irregular intervals ! I leave the impartial reader to judge how much truth there may be in the aspersions cast on the personal attractions of my collateral ancestress, but should the judgment be adverse, and in mitigation of sentence, let me mention that her new-found mother, " Auld Watt's " wife, was the beautiful Mary Scott, renowned on the border as the " Flower of Yarrow," so let us hope Agnes's descendants, who were both numerous and distinguished, found, if necessary, a corrective as to their personal appearance on the paternal side. They had odd nicknames in those days. Agnes's sister, in her new family, was known to fame as Meggie Fendie, and it was her fate to marry " Gibby " Elliott of the " Gowden Garters," and to become the ancestress of the noble house of Minto.

But to return to Sir Gideon. In 1612 he was appointed Treasurer Depute, and Controller and Collector Depute of the Kingdom, and as Somerset, who was Lord High Treasurer, was very much engaged elsewhere, and paid very little attention to his business, it can be safely assumed that Sir Gideon conducted the duties of the office entirely. In 1613 Sir Gideon was appointed a Lord of Session, with the title of Lord Elibank.*

In 1618 he was a member of that momentous assembly at Perth which passed the Five Articles.† Whether he

* Reg. Privy Council Scotland, vol. x. p. 164. The title was for life only.

† The Five Articles were rules of ecclesiastical procedure framed in direct opposition to the form of worship maintained by the Presbyterian majority in Scotland, originating that open opposition to Royal prerogative which was a principal cause of the Civil War.

was one of those who advised the king to follow a moderate course in respect of the Articles is not recorded. His early connection with Aberdeen, and the habit gained by contact with the king, makes it certain that he belonged to the Prelatic party, and there were few among them who foresaw the cataclysm that followed, which ultimately destroyed the throne and affected the fortunes of his son and his descendants disastrously. Whether or not his action in this and other similar matters was the cause, Sir Gideon did not arrive at his present position without creating enemies. " Neither the wealthy, the valiant, nor even the wise, can long flourish in Scotland ; for envy obtaineth the mastery over them all." So it was with Sir Gideon ; in the year 1621 an information was laid against him for abusing his office to the king's prejudice. An account of the circumstance is given by Archbishop Spottiswood in his *History of the Church in Scotland*, from which it appears that the information was laid by James Stuart of Ochiltree, who, it appeared, had been treated with too much strictness by Sir Gideon in connection with certain revenues for which he was responsible, and the matter was submitted for trial. Sir Gideon,

" being of great spirit, and taking impatiently that his fidelity, whereof he had given so great proof, should be called in question on the information of a malicious enemy, by the way, as he returned from Court did contract such a deep melancholy as neither counsel nor comfort could reclaim him . . . and so after he came to Edinburgh within a few days departed this life. It was not doubted if he should have attended the trial, but he had been cleared, and the accusation proved a mere calumny ; nor was it thought that the king did trust the information, but only desired to have the honesty of his servant appear. . . . By his death the king did lose a good servant as ever he had in that charge ; and did sore forethink that he should have given ear to such dilations,"

and, finally, as Spottiswood quaintly puts it, " The gentleman alwaies died happily and had his corps interred in the Church of Halerudhouse."

With that conspicuous quality of being too late, which characterised the Stuarts, the king made " amends " by the issue of a letter under the Great Seal,

" making mention that His Majesty, calling to mind the true and faithful service done to His Majesty by Umquhile Sir Gideon Murray of Elibank, Knycht . . . and to make an honourable remembrance that others by his example may be moved by the like care and fidelity, and therefore His Majesty of certain right and proper motion, with advice and consent of the Lords of His Majesty's present Council, finds and decrees that said Umquhile Sir Gideon Murray . . . during the whole time and period thereof from his first employment to his decease behaved himself therein faithfully and diligently as became a loyal subject and dutiful servant . . . and declares him and his heirs free of all imputations, calumnies, or aspersions whatsoever, whereby his person, name, fame, goods, lands or posterities may in any sort be taxed, scandalised, or endangered. . . ."

With this eulogy of the character of Sir Gideon we will leave him. If ancestry be a sound basis for biography, I can have no better foundation for my subject than this sketch of the life of the founder of the House of Elibank, and in much that has been said of Sir Gideon, and much more that might be said, there are similarities to the character and history of him whose life will be written here. Like his ancestor, he served his king doggedly, and did what he had to do without fear, favour, or affection, and like him it was his fate to suffer from the effect of religious controversy, and like him, too, his reward for distinguished service was to be dragged before a public tribunal on the " information of a malicious enemy," in order that his " honesty might appear." " Virtute Fideque "—by courage and faithfulness—was the motto bestowed on the house by King James and James Murray worthily maintained the tradition.

During the latter years of Sir Gideon's lifetime a new spirit had found place in the Scottish home life, the effect of which should be briefly noticed here. The death of Elizabeth and accession of James to the dual Crown brought to lowland Scotland the beginnings of two remarkable changes : the one, which tended to peace, was the gradual suppression of the border warfare ; the other, which had the opposite effect, was the disturbance of the religious equilibrium of the people. In a sense the one reacted on the other; the border and family feuds were, it is true, replete with tragedy, but they had a kind of grim humour which suited the temper of the combatants, and at least left them ready to combine in the face of a common enemy, and a sufficient devotion to the Sovereign whose power was not exercised at too close quarters. They acted as a kind of safety valve to a people whose aspirations were confined in narrow channels. For the Scot there were few questions of foreign politics. Colonisation projects did not demand his thought and energy. Scottish fleets were not to be found in every sea providing the news-sheets with tales from the world beyond ; trade was of meagre dimensions, and in the hands of a few ; communication between different parts of the country scarcely existed. It is true that many of the young men found congenial employment in the foreign armies, but until the closing scenes of the Thirty Years' War, not many of them returned to bring a new spirit of militarism, and when they did, it was to find that a new order of things had arisen demanding their employment in a controversy not very dissimilar to that they left behind them on the Continent of Europe.

And yet in the soul of this people lay, as yet unborn, a genius for trade, manufacture, invention, and agriculture ; a fixity of purpose, an indomitable perseverance, which has since made them known the world over. Looking backwards, with history crystallised before us, it is easy to see what the Stuarts might have done. What they did was to stifle the awakening life of the people and to sow in it, and force into unnatural growth with an insane tenacity of purpose, the seed of bitter religious controversy, which divided the nation sharply into two parties and alienated the majority from the old allegiance which was at one time their heritage ; a controversy into which the opponents entered with astonishing vehemence, partly because a fanatical obstinacy was part of their nature, but chiefly because other and more advantageous outlets for their instincts were denied them.

Thus it came about that when Gideon's eldest son, Patrick Murray, reached manhood he found a stormy horizon, and the necessity for choosing a side. It is scarcely necessary to say that with his inherited instinct he became a king's man and followed the fortunes of the unfortunate monarch who afterwards succeeded to the throne. It is not certain in what capacity he rendered his first services, but a document is preserved showing that as early as 1615 King James had bestowed a " pension " on him for " true and faithful service," and " to give him better occasion to do the like in time coming," words which almost seem to contain a prevision of the approaching storm. At that Session of the Estates held in 1621, which ratified the famous " Five Articles " already accepted by the General Assembly, Patrick, now Sir Patrick, voted with the majority, and no doubt took a part in that too eager enforcement of the " Innovations," the effect of which I have already referred to. In 1628, the year in which the king's action to resume the Church revenues came before the Estates, Sir Patrick was advanced to the dignity of baronet, doubtless for services in connection therewith.

It is a matter of history that the king's intention was never carried to finality. Ostensibly, at all events, it was to provide funds for the better endowment of the clergy, schools, and hospitals, but while the Presbyterian party saw in it a design to increase the power of the Prelacy, it had the further effect of estranging a number of the great families who had been granted ecclesiastical lands or tithes, and had no intention of parting from them without a struggle. Sir James Balfour * calls it that revocation which " was the ground stone of all the mischief that followed after, both to this king's government and family."

* I quote from Burton, *History of Scotland*.

I must here introduce another name in my story, that of John Stuart, Earl of Traquair, with whose fortunes Sir Patrick of Elibank and his son and successor were closely connected. Traquair was throughout, for good or evil, an ardent supporter of the Royal cause. He was descended in the female line from James II. of Scotland, and again directly from Joan, the Queen Dowager * of James I., who, as granddaughter of John of Gaunt, was of the Royal line of England, and thus Traquair could claim the Royal blood of both kingdoms. Aristocratic, and without sympathy for those whose views differed from his own, he was little fitted as an instrument to carry out schemes which met with vehement protest, except by the application of force, which was difficult in the face of a united opposition.

" I sal either mak the service be read heir in Edinburgh or I sal perishe by the way. Nothing proves more pre-judiciall to your Maties. service than to prosecute yr commandments in a half or halting way "—thus he wrote to the King; and again, " From which sect (the Presby-terians) I have seldom found any motioun proceid but such as did smell of sedition and mutiny."

Holding such views it is little likely that he would succeed in persuading a proud and obstinate people to adopt a course they abhorred.

The connection between Traquair and Sir Patrick Murray may have originated in the fact that he succeeded Sir Gideon as Treasurer Depute (with, I think, one intermediate holder); at all events, they were officially of the same view and privately on intimate terms, which were cemented by the marriage of Sir Patrick's eldest son with his daughter Elizabeth Stuart † The

---

* By her re-marriage with James Stuart, " The Black Knight of Lorne."

† I presume that, correctly, the augmentation of the " Double Tressure " in the Elibank arms was introduced by the son of this marriage, Patrick, third Lord Elibank ; though I believe this is not held by the Lyon King-at-arms; Porny, in his *Heraldry*, states that this " Ordinary was anciently given to none but such as had matched with or were descended from some of the daughters of the Royal Family."

history of Scotland at this period was decided in the Cabinet of the English Primate, and in Traquair, Laud found a willing instrument, and Murray became involved by the acts of his friend.

In 1643 Sir Patrick was raised to the Peerage of Scotland as Lord Elibank, in consideration of his " worth, prudence, and sufficiency, and of the many worthy services done to His Majesty, our late dearest Father in his Council, Session and Exchequer by the late Sir Gideon Murray." The patent was issued from Oxford, where the king then maintained his government. Sir Patrick had, indeed, devoted himself and his goods to the Royal cause, and had raised a troop of horse which accompanied the Scots convoy sent to Oxford in this year. In 1647 he was one of the six Peers of Scotland who opposed the decision to hand over the person of King Charles to the English Parliament, and in the final step, when the next year Scotland attempted to retrieve her lost honour, Traquair, who had staked his all, was followed by Lord Elibank, who became deeply involved. The family papers give some insight into the extent that the estates were burdened, and it appears probable that the voluntary contributions to the Royal cause were supplemented by involuntary levies enforced by the Covenanters, for the principal estate of Ballencrief, being situated in the midst of country which was the cockpit of the opposing forces, was naturally placed under contribution by the " War Committee " of the Scots Estates.

Lord Elibank did not long survive his royal master. He died in 1650, almost within sound of the long drawn-out conflict at Dunbar, which proclaimed the end of Scotland as an independent power. More fortunate than Traquair, who lived to see his estates pass into other hands, and who died in penury—of starvation, it is said—the final crash came after his death, and it was the lot of his eldest son, Patrick, now second lord, to see it decreed that the family property should pass into the hands of his creditors. This was in 1658, and little more than two years later the second

Lord Elibank died. There is nothing on record to give details of his life. He was but forty when he died, but it is not difficult to imagine that the son-in-law of Traquair, ruined by the ruin of the Royal cause, would meet with little sympathy in the country under the iron heel of Cromwell and dominated for the moment by the triumphant Covenant.

The third lord, also Patrick, was a lad of twelve years of age when he succeeded to the family honours. It appears from the records that the breaking up of the estates had been avoided by a family arrangement. A statement exists which shows that they continued in possession, but with a mortgage of 85,400 merks, the advent (interest) on which, together with the necessary outgoings, absorbed two-thirds of the revenue and left but a slender income to the noble owner. His education was finished at Edinburgh in 1666, not, we may be certain, on a luxurious scale, for a receipt exists for " the sum of 35 pounds Scots for a high Chamber in the College possessed by my Lord Elibank and his servants from Michaelmas, 1664, to Michaelmas, 1666." That is an annual rent of about thirty shillings sterling !

Lord Elibank married in 1674 the daughter of Archbishop Burnet,* and left one son, Alexander, who succeeded, aged nine, to the title, and was the father of General James Murray, the subject of this memoir.

An inventory of the " goods, geir, and plenishings " of the house at Ballencrief exists, taken by the " tutors " of the minor, which give a good idea of the home in which my hero was born some thirty-four years later. In the great hall and dining-room, besides many hangings of arras, some described as " pictured," used no doubt to cover the bareness of unplastered walls, were three carpets, twenty two " Rushie leather chairs and one resting chair," a clock in a " fir case." The " Lady's Chamber and a little dark room off the same " contained a good equipment ; the " Chamber above the dining-room " had,

* Elizabeth Burnet, widow of Lord Elphinstone.

among other things, a "fashionable bedstead" and a "looking-glass." There were also the "Dames Chamber," "Maiden-head Chamber," and the "Picture Chamber," the last containing, *inter alia*, "a chest full of old accompts and papers belonging to the deceased Sir Gideon, most thereof anent the Treasury"; here were also four pictures. My lord's closet contained four guns, and my lady's a "posseline cup set in gilded silver," also two looking-glasses. The linen closet was no doubt the pride of its owner, it contained what must have been an unusually good equipment, 19 pairs of sheets, 13 tablecloths, 6 dozen and 4 napkins, etc., etc., and "ane English blanket"! Judged by the standard of the time, such a mansion must be classed as well found, the possession of three carpets in the Great Hall was an uncommon luxury, for Graham, in his interesting work on *Social Life in Scotland*, tells that more than fifty years later not more than two carpets existed in the whole town of Jedburgh. There was evidence of refinement, too. What would not a collector give to-day for the "posseline cup set in gilded silver"; genuine of at least the Kang He period and probably much older!

Young Alexander completed his education at the college at Edinburgh, and an important result of his college career was that the young lord fell in love, and married, aged twenty, Miss Elizabeth Stirling, the daughter of an eminent surgeon of Edinburgh, and afterwards a member of the Scots Parliament. The young lady at an early age displayed the possession of independent character, which sometimes led her into eccentricities, and she transmitted to her family more than a usual share of those traits which impel men to keep clear of the well-worn grooves of life, and to strike out lines of their own. John Ramsay, in his *Scotland and Scotsmen*, relates an anecdote which shows that Miss Betty possessed a masterful character. An incautious minister, when undertaking "public examinations," addressed her as "Betty Stirling," and drew down on himself a scathing rebuke from the young lady, who stated, not without adjectives, that "Mistress Betty," or " Miss Betty " was the style of address she was accustomed to, but certainly not " bare Betty "—and as Bare Betty she was generally known afterwards ! But this side of her was not the best ; she was a tender-hearted mother and adored by her somewhat unruly family. In 1739, then a widow, she wrote to her eldest son, under orders to join Lord Cathcart's expedition to the West Indies, " If ye have any comfort to give me for God's sak writ soon, for I'm in the utmost distress : oh, thes wars will brack my heart " ; and, again, her son George, writing to his brother shortly after the battle of Quebec, " I wish our good mother had lived to a been witness of the praises so deservedly bestowed on you."

Reading between the lines of the letters it is not hard to see that the difficult task of keeping the family above water in times of great financial stress was in her capable hands. And when in 1720, a year when all England went crazy with the speculative mania, of which the most remarkable episode was the great financial catastrophe known as the South Sea Bubble, Lord Elibank lost heavily, we may be sure that his lady had an addition to her anxieties which must have tried her to the utmost. The sequel is best told in a letter to Lady Elibank a few weeks later.

" I am infinitely more vexed that you should torment yourself so much, which I assure you is more galling to me than any misfortune that has yet befallen me . . . as I shall answer God I have never bought a farthing's worth of stock but that third subscription, nor you may depend on it will I venture a groat more that way, for now the South Sea has fallen to its primitive 110 this day, so * that it seems now past all recovery ; what parliament will be able to do with it I cannot tell."

Lord Elibank was a heavy loser ; he returned to Scotland to face the situation. In 1723 he was one of the founders of the " Society of Improvers in the knowledge of Agriculture in Scotland," of which it is stated in the *Life and Writings of Lord Kames,* " Before it commenced we

* It stood at 1000 a few days before.

seemed to be several centuries behind our neighbours in England, now I hope we are within less than one of what they are either with regard to husbandry or manufacture." To-day the Scots farmer is accounted the best in Great Britain!

To Alexander Lord Elibank and his wife was born a numerous family of fifteen sons and daughters, of which five sons and six daughters survived them. And as these brothers of my hero reappear in this story, it is convenient that I should here briefly indicate their history, the more so that, as will be seen, their action had a very marked influence on James Murray's fortunes.

The eldest son, Patrick, afterwards fifth baron, was at first in the military service, and it is a curious illustration of the strange regulations of the day, to find his "commission" as captain of a company in Colonel Alexander Grant's regiment, signed by Queen Anne in 1706. The gallant captain being then just three years old! Not less strange is it to find in 1711 two records relating to the same officer, the one a bill for his board while at school in Edinburgh, and the other a statement of his regimental pay, including "Flanders Arrears" for himself and three servants. The recipient being then aged eight!

Soldiering, though he subsequently saw a good deal of service, was not the line to which his inclinations bent him, and a few years after his marriage with the widow of Lord North and Grey in 1735, he left the army and followed that literary career which was more to his taste.

"Nothing was wanting to make him an admired writer but application and ambition 'to excel,'" writes John Ramsay. "For a number of years Lord Elibank, Lord Kames, and Mr. David Hume were considered as a literary triumvirate, from whose judgment in matters of taste and composition there was no appeal. At his house the youthful aspirant to fame saw the best company in the kingdom, and drank deep of liberality and sentiment. . . . During the reign of King George II. Lord Elibank kept aloof, being a professed Tory if not a Jacobite in his talk."

Lord Elibank was a founder of the " Select Society " of Edinburgh, which included among its members the most brilliant wits in Scotland. He was said to have the " talent of supporting his tenets by an inexhaustible fund of humour and argument," and Dr. Johnson, who paid a visit to Ballencrief in 1773, put on record his opinion that Lord Elibank was " one of the few Scotchmen whom he met with pleasure and parted from with regret," and the learned doctor was not as a rule complimentary, certainly not to Scots As a member of the famous Cocoa Tree Club, at which it was said the coach of a Jacobite invariably stopped of its own accord, Lord Elibank gave some ground for Horace Walpole's opinion that he was a " very prating and impertinent Jacobite ! "

George Murray, the second son, entered the Navy in 1721, and, after seeing service during the war of 1740 in the West Indies, accompanied Lord Anson (then Commodore) in his famous voyage round the world, but a full share of the perils and successes of that expedition was denied to him, as his was one of the two vessels disabled during the great storms which were met with when rounding Cape Horn. In 1744, in command of the *Revenge*, he was present at the naval action off Toulon, and in 1756 he retired as a rear-admiral. His impatient character unfitted him for a successful career in the service. He succeeded to the Barony of Elibank on the death of his brother, and died in 1785, leaving no male heirs.*

Gideon, the third son, entered Holy Orders from Oxford in 1733, and even in this profession he had some of the warlike experiences of his brothers, having served as chaplain to the Earl of Stair during the operations in Germany in 1743. After filling several posts of importance in the Church, he was finally appointed to the rich canonry of Durham. It is said that his chance of a bishopric was lost on account of the part taken in politics by his brothers.

Alexander, the fourth son, was the *enfant terrible* of the

* He married Lady Isabella Mackenzie; Ann, afterwards Duchess of Sutherland, descended from this union. The forfeited Earldom of Cromartie was revived in her person.

family, and whatever judgment may be passed on his actions, it must be at least admitted that he displayed strong independence of character, the results of which unfortunately reacted adversely on the more law-abiding members of his family at a period when the House of Brunswick, with every desire to deal moderately with the adherents of the Stuarts, could not afford to pass over such open antagonism as was displayed by him. Horace Walpole, in 1737 (Journal of Geo. II.), wrote of him and his brother (Patrick, Lord Elibank) that they were " both such active Jacobites that if the Pretender had succeeded they would have produced many witnesses to testify their zeal for him."

Walpole was, perhaps, not an impartial witness, but unquestionably Alexander Murray made himself an object for the resentment and persecution of the Whig ministers, and by a strange irony of fate the popular cry of " Murray and Liberty," which was raised by the mob on more than one scene of tumult, was separated by but a short interval of time from that of " Wilkes and Liberty," which the same mob used to greet the man who set himself to be the bitter enemy of all the Murrays, and whose trenchant and powerful pen did much to hinder their success. After a period of imprisonment in Newgate, by order of the House of Commons, it was resolved to bring Murray to the bar of the House, there to receive admonition on his knees ; but on the Speaker requesting him to kneel, he replied, "Sir, I beg to be excused; I never kneel but to God." It was thereupon resolved that he was guilty of a high and most dangerous contempt of the authority of the Commons and was recommitted to Newgate. After the prorogation of Parliament he was released by the sheriffs of London, and went in triumphal progress to Lord Elibank's house in Henrietta Street. Murray became a popular hero, and the political pamphleteers and verse makers were busy in exciting the passions of the people.

Before Parliament met again in November, 1751, Murray had gone to France, and while there was much in

C

evidence at the Court of Prince James Stuart, from whom it is said he received a patent as Earl of Westminster—at all events, he was known later as Count Murray, and finally received letters of recall under the Privy Seal, dated 1771.

The fifth and youngest son was James Murray, the subject of this memoir. He was born at Ballencrief on January 21, 1721, old style. The time of his advent was not a convenient one, coming as it did immediately after the South Sea smash, and though I have only negative evidence to go on, the almost complete absence of mention in the letters of the family tends to indicate that young James was not very warmly welcomed, and it is pretty certain that he shared in few of the advantages which Lord Elibank did his utmost to bestow on his other sons. It is probable that his early youth was not a very happy one, and at least the impoverished condition of the estate at this time permitted few luxuries for the fourteenth child ! As to luxury, however, it is difficult for us of the twentieth century to form a conception of the conditions of life in Scotland in the early years of the eighteenth century. Since to the Scot born and bred in these surroundings the conditions presented nothing abnormal, and gave to one ignorant of anything better no cause for complaint, there would be no point in referring to them here, were it not that in the preceding pages I have endeavoured, by sketching the ancestry and immediate relatives of my hero, to give some insight into the characteristics with which he was likely to start the battle of life. So by a brief sketch of the surroundings of his youth I would emphasise the reason why so many young Scots, when carving for themselves names which adorn the history of the Empire, commenced their career with that contempt of hardship, or, if you prefer it, that ignorance of luxury, which formed the best possible equipment for the pioneer and for the soldier.

It is true that in England the amenities of life were very far behind our standard, but Scotland was very far behind England in everything that connotes comfort.

The country was miserably poor. Measured by English standards, a " rich " man in Scotland lived from hand to mouth, in the most literal sense. Dependent almost entirely on the fruits of agriculture, carried on by the most obsolete methods, the landlord and his dependents were always at the mercy of the season. What would be thought of a noble lord in England who, so late as 1728, wrote, " Nothing but want of wind in the barn doors these two or three days by gone hath hindered the barley coming to you " ? and though Henry Fletcher of Saltoun, the friend and neighbour of Lord Elibank, had brought over the invention of barley mills and fans from Holland, this method had evidently not been taken up at Ballencrief !

Even had the methods of agriculture enabled crops in proper proportion to the land cultivated to be garnered, they would have been of little use, for the means to carry them were wanting. " There was no such convenience as a waggon in the country," says Tobias Smollett, when he started under the pseudonym of Roderick Random to seek his fortune in England, nor, had they existed, were there any roads on which they could travel. Produce, baggage, even coals were carried in small quantities at a time on horse-back, and travellers of all degrees were obliged to ride or be carried in chairs. A fifteen-year-old lad of to-day would think himself asked to undertake a big thing if obliged to write, as young Gideon Murray did in 1726, to his father, . . . " If you please you may send horses for me on Saturday, one for myself and another for my trunk and cloathes." To be whirled home for the holidays by express train and motor is a different affair altogether to facing a twenty-mile ride on execrable roads none too well secured from attack by thieves.

The difference of nearly two hundred years has, however, altered the schoolboy very little in one respect, and I cannot forbear quoting again from the same letter.

" My lord, you cannot expect but that I may be in some little debt now in this time of year, when the bowls and other such diversions are in hand.   Half-a-crown or three shillings or anything will serve my turn. . . . I pray you don't forget ye money with ye first occasion ! ''

However, as I have said, the comparison as to luxury of travel or other things is not fair.   The young Scot was used to it, and " use is everything," as was said on another occasion ; but the training had its advantages, and started the youth of that period with a self-reliance and power of command which the young gentleman of to-day has not got, and perhaps requires in less degree.   The astonishing age at which men succeeded to high places in those days may have been due to this early training.   Can any one suppose that the younger Pitt would have been a prime minister at twenty-five if he had lived a century and a half later, or Napoleon an emperor at thirty-five if he had been born in the nineteenth century ?   Wolfe was but thirty-two at Quebec, and our James Murray was governor of a province and commander of an army at thirty-nine. Wellington was but thirty-four at the close of the Mahratta War.   It was the century of young men !

If the circumstances of the landowner in Scotland were bad, those of the peasantry were infinitely worse.   Even Andrew Fletcher, the apostle of liberty, was forced to advocate serfdom as the best means of ensuring that a large number of the population should not want for the necessaries of life.   Within a few miles of Ballencrief the labourers in the salt and coal mines were in fact slaves, and in his boyhood James Murray must have been well used to witness scenes of horrible misery, which cannot but have left an indelible picture in his mind.   To this we may, with some certainty, trace the firmness with which he subsequently, to his own personal detriment, protected the French Canadians from oppression.

Thus the daily life and the daily scenes tended to form the character and produce that stern gravity which in boyhood, as in manhood, left its stamp on the Scot.   Hardship, even danger, was the common experience of all ;

pride, poverty, and self-reliance were the hall marks by which the pupils of the school might be recognised.

I have described the ancestry of James Murray, and I have said something about the conditions which formed his experience; am I wrong if to both these factors I attribute the successes and the failures which were his lot? That he was generous and high-minded we shall have ample evidence. Gifted with a wide and statesmanlike insight of his opportunities and his responsibilities, where he built he laid solid foundations, and did not desire to run up a gaudy structure that might have won for him greater reward from short-sighted governments incapable of appreciating work by its durability. He followed his ideal consistently, looking neither to the right hand nor the left, and perhaps too indifferent to the obstacles which stood in his way to pay enough heed to the manner in which he removed them. The " national prerogative " of pride he possessed is well illustrated by his writing to the Duc de Crillon,* that he had attempted to assassinate the character " of a man whose birth is as illustrious as your own."

Possibly he carried this " prerogative " to excess, and was somewhat autocratic, and it may be intolerant, with his subordinates, yet to the rank and file and to the people whose government was in his hands he was lenient, approachable, and beloved. No general could have got out of his troops more than he did. " Old Minorca," as they christened him afterwards, was a soldier's general. If on suspicion of incapacity or neglect he acted strongly, perhaps harshly, yet my history will show that the occasion demanded promptness and vigour, and Murray was no respecter of persons. To those who showed devotion to duty, no man was more ready to award praise and recommendation, nor did failure meet with his condemnation if honest endeavour accompanied it. " A man of the most ardent and intrepid courage, passionately desirous of glory," † he was ever ready to admire bravery in others,

---

* This incident is referred to at p. 399.
† *Annual Register*, 1760.

and there was no hardship and no adventure which he was not ready to share when his duty permitted him. His equally generous and intrepid leader, Wolfe, wrote of him after the capture of Louisburg, " Murray has acted with infinite spirit. The public is indebted to him for great service." * He was modest withal, and displayed no desire to figure in public, which was perhaps uncommon at the time. When the painter West approached him to allow his portrait to be included in his picture, " The Death of Wolfe," he refused, saying, " I was not there, I was commanding the troops in my charge."

It is characteristics such as these that it is my duty to portray, and the measure of my readers' approval will be the degree of my success.

Of the boyhood of James Murray there is, as I have already said, but little record. His education apparently commenced at Haddington,† but in January, 1734, he was a pupil at the school of Mr. William Dyce in Selkirk, where he remained until August, 1736. His holidays, it appears, were spent partly at Ballencrief and partly at Westerhall, with his sister Barbara (Lady Johnston), and, indeed, it appears that both she and her husband took a warm interest in the lad, for there is an entry in the school account showing that his " pension " (pocket money) was increased from 3d. to 6d. a week " by Sir Jas. Johnston's orders."

It was during his residence at Selkirk that his father died in 1735, when the young scholar was but fourteen years old, and we may be sure that this event added to the difficulties which he had to face in making his start in life. It is a family tradition, for which I can find no definite confirmation, that the lad was destined for the Law—possibly this was his father's intention, for he had already given two sons to the Army, one to the Navy, and one to

---

* Wolfe to Lord Geo. Sackville, *Hist. Doc. Commn.*, vol. ix.

† His brother George, writing in after years, says, " You cannot think how much the folks in Haddington value themselves for your being, as they pretend (claim), educated there."

the Church, but his early death, combined with the inclinations of the lad himself, caused a change in this plan.

Among the visitors to Ballencrief was Colonel William Murray, who had made for himself a distinguished career in the Dutch Service, in that famous fighting force known as the Scots Brigade. Like Uncle "Toby" Shandy, William Murray had been a hero at the Siege of Namur, where he was promoted for his service, and like him, too, there is little room to doubt that he was full of stories of the "Barrier Towns"—of sieges, assaults, and forlorn hopes—which young James drank in with avidity. It is probably due to the tales of this veteran of the wars in the Low Country, who ended his career with the resounding title of "Sergeant-Major-General of Infantry," that James imbibed that strong taste for arms which decided his choice of a profession. He was not without influence to attain his desire, for his brother Patrick had married in 1735 the widow of Lord North and Grey, a lady of Dutch extraction, daughter of Cornelius de Yonge, Receiver-General of the States of the United Provinces. Whether the tradition, that James took the law into his own hands and " enlisted " in the Scots-Dutch, is true, or whether, and I think this is more probable, his family influence procured for him a more legitimate method of beginning his career as a soldier, cannot now be said with certainty; but at all events he became a " cadet " in the 3rd Scots Regiment, then stationed at Ypres in West Flanders, on December 6, 1736. It was in this regiment that his cousin, William Murray, had served, and in it was also serving a Major Boyd, who had been known to his father and whose name appears more than once in the letters.

This event took place during what was known as the " Period of Peace," when after years of continuous war the brigade had nothing more exciting on hand than garrisoning the frontier towns and a constant readiness to repel French aggression. But although the times were peaceful, no better training ground for a young soldier could be found. The corps which had fought throughout

Marlborough's wars, on whose colours the laurels of Ramillies and Malplaquet were still fresh, and which maintained a pride of discipline and place which not infrequently led to disputes as to precedence with other troops in the allied armies, was, we may be sure, a good school. The three years which James Murray passed in these circumstances must necessarily have been years of soldierly education, in which the cadet, while still retaining a species of commissioned rank, yet performed all the duties of a soldier in the ranks, a circumstance which our hero used to allude to in later years, laughingly saying " he had served in all ranks except that of *drummer*." * Nevertheless, the prospect at the moment in the Dutch Service was not one to commend itself to an ambitious aspirant to military fame. Promotion was slow, and no doubt to those soldiers of fortune serving in a foreign legion the principal causes which ensured their sympathy, namely, plenty of fighting, quick promotion, and if fortune favoured, a share in the spoil of war, were for the time being wanting. Thus it came about, when England plunged hot headed and all unprepared into war with Spain, that not a few of the younger officers serving in foreign corps sought commissions in the regiments about to be raised in England, and among them was James Murray, who, apparently from his brother's influence, was offered a second-lieutenancy in the English army.

Thus it was in the year 1740 that Murray, then nineteen years old, received his first commission from George II., and commenced his military career under the Union Flag at the beginning of a period which offered opportunities which surely were unequalled by any other in English history.

* In the parlance of the day a " drummer " was one who extolled his own wares.

CHAPTER II

THE WAR WITH SPAIN OF 1739

For three-quarters of a century a state of war constantly existed, and the " face of Europe changed like that of a fine lady," as was said at the time. " No former period was of a more transitional character than the first eighty years of the eighteenth century. The unhappy wars had almost continuously changed the territorial frontiers without being able to settle them permanently," * and to this might be added, that in the great colonial empires of France and Spain, the wars resulted, after a succession of failures and successes, in the birth of the British Empire as we know it now.

Throughout the year 1739 the opposition in Parliament, led by Pulteney, and aided by the rising genius of Pitt, had done their utmost to precipitate war with Spain. Walpole, with clearer insight and greater knowledge of the resources of the kingdom, was content to acknowledge that the injuries complained of were by no means confined to one side, and steadfastly refused to rupture negotiations by which he hoped to preserve an honourable peace. In this case, as happened not infrequently, he failed to accomplish his object, for the reason that *British Trade* was affected : British merchants saw sources of profit in the hands of the Spaniards for which they claimed a monopoly, and in every action of Spain, a determination to maintain treaty rights which limited the trading facilities of England

* *Napoleon*, by H. P. Geerke.

27

with South America and gave the Spaniards right of search on British vessels suspected of infringing them. The City was inflamed, and pressure brought by powerful interests proved irresistible. In the words of Horace Walpole, " Ambition, avarice, distress, disappointment, and all the complicated vices that tend to render the minds of men uneasy are got out of Pandora's box and fill all places and all hearts in the nation."

In August the national clamour forced the government to extremities ; naval reinforcements were sent to the West Indies under Admiral Vernon, and an ultimatum was sent to the Court of Madrid, claiming immediate renunciation of the right of search, a claim that was refused at once, as was expected. In December the City bells pealed joyously to proclaim the declaration of war, and " universal and rapturous joy and exultation spread from man to man." * Walpole, whose hands had been forced, could not be expected to take the same view. " They may ring the bells to-day," he exclaimed, " before long they will wring their hands " ; and so it came about.

It was one of the strange results of the political situation that the very party which cried aloud for war placed every obstacle in the way of providing means to carry it on. The most vehement " little Englander " or the most pronounced " anti-militarist " of to-day could not have been more strenuous than the party, which, while desiring all the benefits which come from strength, were yet disposed to tie the hands of the minister in that consistent preparation which can alone procure success in war. The navy was ill-manned and ill-found. The standing army quite insufficient for home defence, with schemes for colonial aggrandisement superadded. The king, denied the means of raising fresh battalions for the land forces, was driven to the expedient of raising new corps of marines, which by some occult quibble apparently did not come within the parliamentary veto. Thus on the outbreak of war hasty orders were issued to get together a force for the

* *Hist. England,* Lord Mahon.

conquest of Spanish America, and six fresh battalions of marines were ordered to be formed to reap that triumph which in an evil hour the nation considered within its grasp.

It was in the fourth of these battalions, commanded by Colonel John Wynyard,* that our hero received his commission as second-lieutenant on February 2, 1740. His brother, Lord Elibank, was appointed lieut.-colonel of the regiment, a post which gave little satisfaction to his mother, who regarded it as a job to get a person, whose political views had been too freely expressed, out of the way. " Ye are not much obliged to thos that has put you in such a situation," she wrote; " but I hope you are not such a fool as to risk your life in so desperat a way." The force assembled in the Isle of Wight in the spring of 1740, composed to a considerable extent of drafts from old regiments, probably not of the best quality, and also largely of raw recruits, " the product of the hard winter," and the result was " remarkable neither for drill nor discipline."

Lord Cathcart was appointed to the command, and his opinion of the efficiency of the force is summed up by the remark, " They may be useful a year hence, but at present they have not strength to handle their arms." At Lord Cathcart's urgent request, which in fact he made a condition of continuing his command, two old regiments, the 15th Foot (Harrison's) and the 24th Foot (Wentworth's), were added to the command, and the colonel of the latter, Brigadier-General Wentworth, was appointed second in command in the expedition. Later on, a further addition of 3000 men, recruited from the British colonies of Virginia, Pennsylvania, Maryland, Rhode Island, Connecticut, and New York, was agreed to, to join the force, under Colonel Blakeney (of the 27th Foot), at Jamaica. Strenuous work

* The remaining battalions were commanded by Colonels Wolfe (father of the victor at Quebec), Robinson, Lowther, Douglas, and Moreton. The six battalions were later re-numbered as the 44th to 49th of the line, but were disbanded in 1748. The battalions now bearing those numbers, except the 49th, were raised in 1741, and originally numbered 55th to 59th. The present 49th Regiment being raised in 1743 from companies formed in Jamaica and numbered 49th in 1748.

fell to the commanders of this raw force before any semblance of training could be imparted to it, but by August
Cathcart reported it fit to embark, and indeed this was
the latest date which all information indicated as that on
which the expedition should have sailed to enable its operations to be carried on during the healthy season in the West
Indies.

Unfortunately further delays occurred, partly, it is said,
due to unfavourable winds; but other evidence seems to
indicate that this cause was less the deciding factor than
the unprepared state of the fleet to undertake operations
of the magnitude which it was soon apparent must be faced.
The extensive preparations going forward in England were
well known at the Spanish Court. Much blame was attached to the government for its want of secrecy, and by
some accident even the proclamation intended to be
published by Lord Cathcart in Spanish America became
public ; probably secrecy would, in any case, have been
impossible, and only swift and energetic action would have
found the enemy unprepared, and this, as has been said,
was impossible. The breathing time given to Spain was
fully utilised, and reinforcements were sent, and, what is
of more importance, assistance from France, then nominally
at peace with England, was invoked and granted. A
French fleet sailed from Brest and necessitated a corresponding augmentation of the English preparations.

" I need not tell you," writes Sir Charles Wager to
Admiral Vernon, " how much time it takes to prepare
and victual so large a squadron for a voyage to the West
Indies, nor how difficult it very often is to get them out
of the Channel when they are ready to sail, as this year we
have experienced, and I thought it would not be amiss
for both French and Spaniards to be a month or two in
the West Indies before us . . . that they might be half-
dead and half-roasted before our fleet arrived." *

Sir Charles Wager's anticipations were, indeed, fulfilled,
for the French fleet returned without effecting anything,

* Lord Mahon, *Hist. England,* vol. iii.

decimated by disease. But it appears strange that no foreboding of a similar disaster to our own forces occurred to him, and his own experience in the West Indies in earlier years * should have been sufficient to warn him of the great danger of delay.

To return, however, to Lord Cathcart, it was not until September 2 that he could report " the wind is at last favourable," but on the 14th he was still at Spithead, and writes—

" The troops having now been six weeks on board, and upon salt provisions, and the prospect we have of being so much longer here, obliges me to represent to your Grace † of what consequence it would be to the men's health if during our stay here they were ordered to be furnished with fresh provisions."

Comment on such a disclosure is scarcely necessary ; as a preparation for young soldiers to face an unhealthy climate nothing worse could be imagined, and already sickness began to make its appearance before ever the expedition left harbour.

Throughout October the luckless troops were still kept on shipboard, always on the point of starting, and it was not until November 1 that the Armada sailed, consisting of 27 ships of the line and 143 transports and attached ships for the army, the whole land force being some 7000 men. There can be little doubt that the enthusiasm of the army had ebbed during the long period of waiting and the practical demonstration of the inefficiency of those responsible for preparing the expedition ; moreover, the constant bickerings in Parliament, in which neither side spared the vilest accusations, led to a widespread feeling that the expedition, prepared under the pressure of popular clamour, was not receiving the whole-hearted support of the Government. An open letter, published in the style of the day by a member of the force, voices this general

* Sir Charles Wager commanded at the first capture of Cartha-gena in 1708.
† The Duke of Newcastle.

feeling, and purports to be addressed to some one who had the good fortune to be left behind.

" Give me leave to congratulate you on your deliverance from amongst us. I sincerely rejoice as well on your account as that it is no small satisfaction to find that there is one person likely to escape who is qualified to tell our unfortunate story. . . . Never forget that you owe it as a duty to your friends, to yourself, and to your country, to represent the execrable villainy of those at home, who, from avarice, and perhaps envy, have sacrificed us and the honour of their country, remember that you were destined for a victim, and that it is incumbent on you to show yourself worthy of a milder sentence than was pronounced against you . . ."

and much more to the same effect, which if, no doubt, exaggerated, exhibits the current of opinion that the shocking mismanagement had aroused.

Delayed and scattered by tempestuous weather, the ships began to assemble in St. Rupert's Bay, Dominica, on December 19, 1740. Scurvy and dysentery had already made terrible inroads on the strength of the force, and the day after arrival the commander-in-chief himself fell a victim to the epidemic.* The condition of the transports described in the *Adventures of Roderick Random* enables us to imagine the state of affairs. In the ship in which Smollett served as a surgeon's mate the hospital is thus described :—

" Fifty miserable distempered wretches, suspended in rows, so huddled upon one another that not more than fourteen inches of space was allotted for each with his bed and bedding, and deprived of the light of day, as well as of fresh air ; breathing nothing but the noisome atmosphere of the morbid steams exhaling from their own diseased bodies, devoured by vermin hatched in the filth that surrounded them, and destitute of every convenience necessary for people in that helpless condition."

---

* Lord Cathcart was buried at St. Dominica, and a tomb on the beach of St. Rupert's Bay was erected to mark the place. The body was, however, afterwards removed to England.

And this, be it noted, was the case while the fleet lay at anchor at Spithead! Add to this description, tropical heat and the horrors of an epidemic of dysentery, and a condition of affairs can be imagined which must have constituted a veritable hell.

Major-General Wentworth, second in command of the expedition, succeeded Lord Cathcart, and this change was in itself another serious blow to success. The new commander had shown energy in organising the force with the means at his disposal, but in the field he proved irresolute and incapable of taking responsibility or of adapting himself to circumstances. Although every day was of importance, it was not until January 9 that the fleet finally assembled at the rendezvous at Jamaica, and here they were met by the levies from the British-American colonies raised by General Blakeney—3500 men, " illequipped, ill-disciplined, and already very sickly." " We have buried nine officers and about 100 men," writes Blakeney, even before Wentworth's arrival, and before the end of the year out of the whole force, 17 officers and 600 men were dead and 1500 were on the sick list. With extraordinary fatuity, although the unhealthy rainy season was rapidly approaching, the fleet lay at anchor at Port Royal for more than a month. It was decided, chiefly at the dictation of Vernon, that Carthagena should be the first objective. Vernon had failed against this place in the previous year, and was burning to retrieve his laurels. Wentworth had not force of character to resist him, and thus this heterogeneous levy, principally of raw recruits, was brought against " the strongest and best fortified place of any that belonged to Spain in America," * to gain its first experiences of war.

Delays, in part due to apprehension of the French fleet, which was, however, found to have returned to Europe, prevented the arrival of the expedition off Carthagena until March 4, 1741. The town, which lies at the head of an inland lake, although itself strongly fortified,

* Tindal, *History*, vol. xx.

had the additional protection of the narrow and difficult approach from the sea to the lake, known as the Bocachica, defended on each side by forts, one being of considerable strength known as St. Louis.

It is unnecessary to detail the preliminary operations following the first landing, they are sufficiently described by *Roderick Random* and in Lord Elibank's Journal, preserved in the Public Record Office. They were so far successful that by April 5 the march on the main objective—Carthagena, and its key, Fort. St. Lazarus—began. A small body of Spaniards was met with who fled; but Wentworth, who went in constant dread of ambuscades and surprises, decided to halt and form a camp a " small mile " from Fort St. Lazarus, though it remained the fixed belief of the Admirals Vernon and Ogle, who had watched the slow and clumsy movements of the land forces with unconcealed disgust, that a more energetic and capable commander should have advanced at once to Fort St. Lazarus, the key to the city, on the heels of the retreating enemy.

During this halt the troops, exposed as they were without shelter to the unhealthy miasmas arising from the surrounding swamps, and moreover already unfitted by their long imprisonment on shipboard to resist disease, fell ready victims to the terrible scourge of yellow fever, which had already made its appearance, but now assumed a violent epidemic form. Wentworth completely lost his head, and urged by the taunts of the admirals, as well as by the patent fact that his army was rapidly melting away, decided on the desperate plan of assaulting Fort St. Lazarus without waiting for artillery to be brought up. The fort itself was a square structure mounting six guns on each face, and situated at the top of a considerable eminence overlooking the city, and, though a comparatively small place, was the key of the position, and almost impregnable against infantry attack.

According to the diary left by Captain Watson,* the army was drawn out for the attack in the early hours of

* State Papers.

April 9, 1741, in two columns, the design being to attack simultaneously the north and south sides of the fort.   The first column, with nine companies of Grenadiers and the 15th Foot, under Colonel Wynyard, being told off to attack the southern face, while Colonel Grant, with the 24th and a mixed company of the 34th and 36th, attacked the northern.   Colonel Daniel commanded a reserve of Wolfe's Marines completed to 400 men.*   The Americans were in charge of the scaling ladders and woolpacks for filling the ditches.   With each column a Spanish deserter acted as guide.

In his comprehensive work on the British army, Fortescue has given a vivid and eloquent description of the affair.

" At four o'clock the march began, the fireflies still flickering overhead against the darkness.   The air close and still, alive with the chirping, whistling, and croaking of the noisy tropic night.   Within the camp men lying in scores under the scourge of yellow fever, some tossing and raving in delirium, some gasping in the agonies of the last fatal symptoms, some prostrate in helpless ghastly collapse, waiting only for the dead hour before dawn when they should die. . . . Before long Wynyard's men reached the foot of the hill and began the ascent, the ground being so steep that they were forced to climb on their hands and knees.   The officers began to doubt that the guides had played them false.   Still the Grenadiers scrambled on almost to the top of the hill, and then suddenly, at a range of thirty yards, the Spaniards opened a deadly fire."

The shortness of the range made every shot effective, and the ranks were torn by grape and round shot, and though the soldiers advanced steadily firing at the flashes of cannon and musketry that blazed from the ramparts, direction of their efforts was wanting, the confusion resulting from the darkness and the climbing, combined with want of experience, prevented a lead being given which might possibly have succeeded.   The defection of the

* Lord Elibank's Journal.

Americans, who threw down the ladders and woolpacks and fled in all directions, brought the men to a standstill, though they still maintained their position undauntedly. On the northern attack a like tragedy occurred. Grant was shot down early, and after his fall confusion reigned, but officers and men held on grimly with infinite heroism. At dawn the guns of Carthagena added to the carnage ; such light artillery as was available had been left by Wentworth in rear of the columns and was useless for reply. The complete incapacity of Wentworth prevented any movement of the reserves to the aid of their unfortunate companions, and it was not until a column of Spanish infantry was seen issuing from the city with intention to cut off the retreat that orders to retire were given at eight o'clock, and the remnant drew off in good order, covered by a party of 400 men under Lord Elibank.

Perhaps, taking into consideration the conditions in which the troops had passed the months preceding the attack on Fort St. Lazarus, the long period of inaction on the ships, with bad accommodation and worse food, the hourly fight with disease that had faced them during most of the time, and the nerve-shattering effect of the epidemic raging at the moment, combined with the incessant labour and hardship in a tropical climate since the first landing at Bocachica, it is not too much to say that no greater exhibition of undaunted courage has ever been displayed by the British army than that of these young soldiers on the fatal April 9 before Fort St. Lazarus. The Spanish commander pronounced their eulogy, " C'etait dommage d'envoyer des hommes contre des murrailles, ils etaient de braves gens et ils ont merités un meilleur sort." Wentworth was not so generous ; in his despatch of April 26, 1741, he discusses the disastrous night attack in a few lines which do not even accurately describe the event, and nowhere does he yield any tribute to the gallantry of his soldiers. Out of 1500 men engaged, 43 officers and 600 men were killed or wounded, and the remnant of the army in terrible straits from the fatal results of the epidemic, and disheartened by defeat were in no way fit to renew the conflict. The force was literally rotting with disease, and of the 8000 men landed at Bocachica a month previously not 1500 remained fit for duty.

A council of war, held on April 23, determined to abandon the enterprise and return to Jamaica, and thus ended in utter failure this phase of the great expedition, which had caused consternation in Europe, and of which the English had felt so assured of success that medals commemorating the fall of Carthagena had been struck ! *

Details of the part taken by James Murray are wanting. He was present during the siege and attack of Fort St. Louis, of Bocachica, and also during the assault on Fort St. Lazarus, and escaped unscathed on both occasions. At St. Lazarus he was probably attached, or perhaps definitely appointed, to the 15th Foot, which, it will be remembered, formed part of the southern attack under Colonel Wynyard. That he bore himself well through all this long period of trial is certain, for we find that on November 20, 1741, his commission as a captain in the 15th Foot is confirmed, and it is probable that he had held that position by local appointment for some months previously;—it must be remembered that at this time appointments to the subaltern ranks of officers were almost invariably made on the recommendation of the commanding officers.

It was on May 19, 1741, that the fleet convoying the shattered remnant of the army arrived at Port Royal, and from there Vernon sent home seven ships and several frigates with a number of sick officers, among whom was Lord Elibank. James Murray, however, stayed with his new battalion, and saw the campaign through to the end, returning to England in December, 1742.

Crowded in the small transports, with improper treatment, the dead, the dying, and the sick literally heaped together in horrible surroundings, it is only possible to suppose that human nature must have vastly changed

* Mahon, *Hist. Eng.*

if the young soldier of the day was other than terribly tried to preserve his equanimity. Murray faced these conditions for three years, and it is not too much to draw from the fact that he was of an exceptionally hardy and enduring constitution; and although his subsequent career afforded plenty of the excitement of the soldier's life, there can be no doubt that no later experience could have equalled this one in demanding the highest qualities which a man can be called upon to exhibit. While his contemporaries were earning laurels in the leisurely continental wars, the force in this forgotten corner of the globe was showing greater claims to enduring fame by patient courage under unparalleled misfortunes.

The 15th Regiment of Foot, in which Murray passed the remainder of his regimental service, suffered severely in this campaign. It is of interest to note the losses amongst the officers by an examination of the *Army Lists* preserved in the Royal Artillery Institution and in the Record Office, for the years 1740 and onwards to 1743. Nothing can more clearly demonstrate the ordeal through which the survivors must have passed.

CASUALTIES AMONGST THE OFFICERS OF THE 15TH FOOT, 1739–41.

Lieut.-Col. Samuel Daniel	.. ..	Died June, 1741
Major Simon Loftus ..	.. ..	,, June, 1740
Captain Robert Thompson ..	..	,, June, 1740
,, Henry Delaune (afterwards distinguished at Quebec) ..		—
,, Chas. Campbell	.. ..	—
,, Geo. Dawson ..	.. ..	,, April, 1741
,, John Dennett ..	.. ..	,, ,,
,, Arthur Mainwaring ..	..	,, ,,
,, Wm. Selbie ..	.. ..	,, March, 1741
Lieut. George Sharples..	.. ..	,, May, 1740
,, Wm. Strachy ..	.. ..	,, June, 1740
,, John Bell * ..	.. ..	—
,, Gabriel Sedieres..	.. ..	,, April, 1741
,, John Grant ..	.. ..	—

Lieut. John Maitland *	..	..	—
,, Andrew Pringle ..	..	..	Died May, 1741
,, Thomas Gregson	..	..	., April, 1741
,, John Morris ..	..	..	,, (no date)
,, Theophilus Johnston	..	..	,, April, 1741
Ensign Robert Bell * ..	..	..	—
,, Musgrave Briscow *	..	..	—
,, John Allenson ..	..	..	—
,, Daniel Richardson	..	..	—
,, Job Walker ..	..	..	,, April, 1741
,, Allan Horde * ..	..	..	—
,, Robert Holley *	..	..	—
,, Justly Watson *	..	..	—
,, Thos. Davenport Davies	..		—

NOTE.—In December, 1742, the only names of the original list remaining are those marked with an asterisk, some of the others may have been transferred to other battalions.

The dates given are those of the filling up of the death vacancy, and may not be the actual date of death.

The majority of the death vacancies occurred in April, 1741, and doubtless most of them should read " Killed in action " during the attack on Fort St. Lazarus; but the record does not distinguish between death from wounds or disease.

The name of James Murray does not appear, as he was not officially appointed to the regiment until November, 1741. It is shown in lists later than that date.

It is remarkable that among the younger officers there were many fewer casualties. It is possible that in some cases these officers had not joined during the operations in the West Indies, or at all events during the worst period.

CHAPTER III

PEACE AND WAR, 1744–57

IN 1744, shortly after his return from the West Indies, we find Murray's first recorded connection with the town of Hastings, a connection which continued with intervals of absence during the rest of his life. Hastings, like most other towns on the English coast, was a centre of " preventive " service. Smuggling then, and for many years afterwards, was carried on on a scale and with an audacity which we of the free-trade persuasion can scarcely imagine. Gangs of armed men frequently assisted at the unloading of contraband goods and conveyed them openly by road to London. The country people were in the know and assisted them, and the gentry were not always free from suspicion. Here is a description of a band, extracted from a letter * of the period : " A gang of smugglers of twenty-one horses laden, and about fourteen or fifteen men openly armed with pistolls and blunderbusses (particularly one of them had a great brass blunderbuss slung over his shoulder) passed on the road to London." To deal with these bands, detachments of infantry and dragoons were stationed at various centres along the coast, and very frequently had active service of a dangerous and difficult nature to perform. It was to this service that James Murray was attached for his first soldiering in England.

The service was apparently one in which the officers were attached to the corporation, for I find from the town

* Collier Letters.

records that in July, 1744, James Murray, together with other gentlemen, and also one John Hide, master and commander of H.M sloop *Swift*, were severally sworn in and handed their certificates of—

" having received the sacrament of the Lord's Supper according to the usage of the Church of England, and they severally took the oath of allegiance and supremacy and also the abjuration oath and subscribed the same and also made the Declaration concerning transubstantiation and subscribed it according to law."

All of which must have been somewhat of a mouthful to Captain Murray, even though his prelatic upbringing helped him, to say nothing of a certain broadmindedness in matters of religion which he had acquired as a visitor to foreign countries.

In this year, too, he first made acquaintance with Mr. John Collier * and his family. Mr. Collier was at the time one of the jurats, that is, a justice, of Hastings, whose duties seem to have combined that of alderman with some more particular functions as magistrate. At all events, he was a power in the land, and his assistance was of immense benefit to my hero, as will be seen. Politically, Collier's influence was considerable. The Duke of Newcastle, who manipulated the parliamentary candidates from a number of boroughs, was firmly seated at Hastings, and had secured one of his relatives, Thomas Pelham, as one of the sitting members.† Henry Pelham, afterwards Prime Minister, had written to the Duke some years previously—

" As to Collyer, you can't do too much, for I judge that town (Hastings) absolutely depends on him, and perhaps if he were cool, would leave you. I desire therefore you will, from me, tell Sir Robert Walpole, if he has a mind to have two Whigs chosen at Hastings, he must provide handsomely for Collyer."

* Mr. Collier had been mayor of Hastings before this date, and was so many times subsequently.
† The other was Andrew Stone, the Duke's secretary.

Thus in attacking, or perhaps I should say attaching, a Whig stronghold, James Murray, with his Jacobite ancestry and personal leanings, performed no small feat, and, as I have said, laid the foundation of a friendship with the Colliers which soon ripened into something more. Of the Collier family I need only refer to two, James Collier, who was just Murray's age, and Cordelia, who was a year younger. The former evidently was warmly attracted to the young soldier, and the latter—well, it seems quite clear that the young soldier was very warmly attracted to her from the first, the first symptom of which may be divined from a letter of James Collier to his father in November, 1744, wherein he refers to some earrings being purchased for his sister, which " Captain Murray says should be blue ! " And, again, a month or two later a certain Dr. Thorp gave vent to some malicious sneers and envious insinuations (evidently regarding Miss Cordelia) which were checked " by the just chastisement from Captain Murray," which indicates that our young Scot was developing not only a taste in ladies' trinkets, but was also prepared to whip any one who disagreed with him as to the merits of his lady !

The events of the year 1745 brought Murray face to face with a conflict between his duty to the King, whose uniform he wore, and that other king " over the water," to whom, in common with his house and his traditions, he felt his natural allegiance was due. His brothers were certainly Jacobites, and Horace Walpole has left on record that " if the Pretender had succeeded they would have produced many witnesses to testify their zeal for him." James himself at twenty-four years of age was probably neither more nor less romantic in the cause of Prince Charlie than were so many other young Scotsmen of quality, but whatever his feelings were he kept them to himself. Family tradition says that he was inclined at this period to place his sword at the Prince's disposal. I confess I am unable to find any confirmation of the story, nor any ground why the author of the article in the *Sussex Archæological*

Journal should describe him as " Captain Hon. James Murray, a suspected Jacobite." I think that he was at the moment more concerned with the welfare of the ladies of the Collier family, or at least of one of them, than with any question of Stuart or Hanover.

It was on July 23 that the French brig *Doutelle* conveying Prince Charles Edward arrived at the island of Eriskay, and the adventurous expedition began which ended in the following April on the bloody field of Drummossy Muir (Culloden). Whether James would have found the unfurling of the Prince's banner too great a demand on his allegiance was fortunately not put to the test. The victorious Marshal Saxe was carrying everything before him, and now threatened Ghent and Ostend. The Quadruple Alliance with the States-General of Holland, the King of Poland, and Maria Theresa, had been formed, and England agreed to send reinforcements to Ostend—four battalions were agreed upon, though I can only find that two were sent, and of these one was Harrison's (15th Foot),* and Murray, of course, went with it, thus removing him, for the time at all events, from temptation. The battalion sailed for Ostend in July, 1745, and can only just have arrived when the town was invested—and surrendered after a short resistance on August 23.

In this operation, which shed little lustre on the British arms, Murray was severely wounded, from which circumstance we may at least infer that he was as usual in the front line.

War was, at least by comparison with our days, a gentlemanly occupation, and the French gave the usual terms to the garrison, viz. to march out with military honours, and in this case with the additional privilege of being conducted to Mons, which was still held by the Allies. Murray, whose wounds did not permit of active service, was left at Ghent.

The progress of the Scotch campaign began to alarm the Ministry at home, and in October eight battalions were

* The other was Handasydes' (16th Foot).

recalled from Flanders, among them the 15th Foot, which arrived in the Thames on the 25th of that month.

In the following year (1746) Murray had an opportunity of forgetting his ambitions, if he had any, in the matter of Prince Charles Edward, though it must be confessed that the expedition on which he proceeded had no more of military glory than that of the preceding year, and did not add to the reputation of any of the senior officers concerned.

The plan was to capture and destroy the town of L'Orient, which formed the depôt of the French East India Company, and contained merchandise believed to be of immense value. This episode, happily almost forgotten, ended without success. Six battalions, including the 15th Foot,* commanded by General St. Clair, and convoyed by a squadron under Admiral Lestock, who, it is stated by Tindal (*History*, vol. ix.), "was by this time grown old and infirm for enterprise," landed unopposed at Quimperle Bay in Brittany.

It is interesting to note, as being a foreshadowing of coming events, that both Murray and Wolfe were members of the expedition, and that the original idea of assembling the troops was (according to Tindal) † in accordance with a plan of reducing Canada, which the capture of Louisburg in the previous year by Sir Wm. Pepperel had brought within the views of the British Ministry. Chiefly because peace was believed to be in prospect the expedition to Canada was postponed, and the troops which had assembled at Portsmouth in May, and been kept in idleness there, were diverted in September for the purpose above referred to.

The force landed on September 20, ten miles from the objective of Port L'Orient, and on the march thither there were ugly stories of pillage of the villages and want of

---

* The other battalions were 1st, 28th, 36th, 39th, 42nd (Fortescue). Tindal adds two battalions of footguards (in all 5800 men).

† This is confirmed in a letter from James Collier to his father, dated April 10, 1746. " Mr. Randoll told me that the Highland regiment and Harrison's with four others was under orders to go to Cape Breton to conquer Canada, to be on board by May 1."

discipline of the troops. On the 21st they arrived before L'Orient and summoned the place to surrender, which apparently the French commander was quite prepared to do, provided guarantee against plunder and for the safety of the East India Company's magazines and storehouses was given. Such a guarantee was obviously out of the power of the British commander to give, and the general demanded two million livres and a four-hours' pillage. Probably he calculated within that time his unruly crew would have been able to effect the object of the expedition !

However, in grasping at too much he lost all, for the French, who had gained considerable time during the parley, succeeded in obtaining a reinforcement and now refused to surrender at all. The English force had only been provided with ten pieces of light artillery, and finding it impossible to batter the walls, and being, moreover, in danger of being surrounded by the rapidly increasing French army, the general began to think discretion the better part of valour, in which decision he was much aided by the admiral, who threatened to sail for England if he did not re-embark at once, which he accordingly did, thus ending one of several very inglorious episodes of which I say, happily, very little is known.

Inglorious though it was, Murray found an opportunity to distinguish himself, and the following record appears in the regimental history of the 15th Foot—the incident occurred on the march to L'Orient :—

" The French militia fired on the troops from the woods and put the men of one or two corps into some confusion, when Captain Hon. James Murray led the Grenadiers of the 15th forward with great gallantry and dispersed the enemy."

It is said, too, with what truth I cannot say, that Murray was the last man to embark. One can imagine that he was not well pleased with the feeble display of which he had been a witness.

The year 1747, though it contained plenty of military movement, did not bring Murray any chance of active service, as his regiment remained in garrison in England. The nations were becoming exhausted, but were unable to agree on terms of peace, and in England the Commons voted the " enormous " grant of 9½ millions for the service of the country, which by the way included subsidies to the Queen of Hungary, the King of Sardinia, for the Hanoverian and Hessian auxiliaries and the electors of Cologne, Mainz, and Bavaria. The battle of Lauffeldt was fought on June 20, and the Maréchal * was successful as usual. Bergen-op-Zoom fell in July, notwithstanding the heroism of the " Scots-Dutch," and the fate of the United Provinces of Holland seemed to be about to follow that of the Austrian Netherlands already in French hands. But then, as now, the British sea power held the winning card.

Anson and Warren had destroyed a powerful French fleet off Finisterre. Hawke had done the same off Belleisle. The British cruisers in every sea harried the enemy merchant shipping so severely that ruin faced the trading section of the community, and the French monarch had the " mortification to see the commerce of Britain flourish in the midst of war " (Smollett, *Hist. England*). France was forced to treat for peace, not because they lacked victory on land, but because want of victory at sea strangled the life of the nation. In England it is interesting to note that the heavy charges brought forth by the war were met in part by the imposition of " poundage exacted from all merchandise imported into Great Britain," and manufactures on which hitherto we had been dependent on enemy nations were encouraged within the British dominions. So does history repeat itself.

To return to my subject. If 1747 was not a year of war with James Murray, he managed to make it a year of importance to himself. His lady spent a good part of the year in London, staying with her Uncle William Cranston, and James was apparently in close attendance. Society does not seem to have been much affected by the war, and in her letters Miss Delia Collier describes what seems to be

* Saxe.

a fairly continuous succession of entertainments. The theatre absorbs a good deal of time, and we hear of Mrs. Cibber as Polly Peachum in the *Beggar's Opera*, and Garrick in the *Provoked Wife*. The hour for opening was five o'clock, with dinner at three ! The young lady and her sister were somewhat concerned about their " cloaths," which at first were apparently not quite up to the mode in London. " We will get our things as soon as possible, but do a sure you our stays was tried on but yesterday, and have not got a hoop yet which frets us very much, and am forced to go in our old cloaths to morrow."

Uncle William Cranston had apparently a soft corner in his heart for the young people, but not so the father of Miss Delia, for by the end of the year affairs had reached a climax, and John Collier requested his brother-in-law to signify to our gallant captain, in regard to a certain " tender affair," that " our correspondence must now cease " ; and later he wrote : " I told him I could never think of marrying my daughter to the uncertain situation he was in." James was, however, too good a soldier to be discouraged by any single failure to carry the fortress, and in May following (1748) he visited Hastings again to make a personal application, which appears, either then or soon after, to have had some result. In August Cranston writes, " I read him (Murray) your three querys—he proposes to take a house and furnish it ; he says he has £2000 . . ."

This modest fortune, which I suppose was inherited, was not considered enough " for the expenses of a married life in a manner suitable to a man of quality and his high notions of it " ; but, as I have said, William Cranston was rather inclined to help. " I could heartily wish," he writes, " that matters had a more promising aspect, because I am persuaded within myself that there is such an attachment between 'em, that I doubt cannot be got the better of (at least by one of the parties)." John Collier apparently found himself in a dilemma. Miss Delia had been delicate from her youth and was obviously rather spoilt by her family, and I think the fear of the effect that would be caused by separation from the man of her choice must have been the deciding factor; at all events, James won his point, and writes on December 17, 1748 :

" I have the pleasure to inform you " (Mr. Collier was in Bath) " that this day I had the happiness of being made your son at St. Bride's Church.   Mr. Cranston is a great deal better, but was not able to go to church, so Mr. Cole acted for him as father.   We dined with him afterwards and went to the play, so I have only time to beg you'll accept Mrs. Murray's and my duty, and be assured that nothing can add more to our happiness than the news of your recovery."

The regiment was under orders for Ireland, and the young couple tried to get an exchange, as Cordelia was very " averst " to going; but when this fell through she made up her mind to be contented.   " Certain it will be my own fault if I am not happy, for Mr. Murray has shown ye greatest regard and tenderness for me about this affair that was possable," and in another letter to her mother :

" You seem to think in your letter that I was low-spirited, but I am not, for I have myself a better opinion of Mr. Murray now than ever I had before, and am sure he would do anything in ye world to make me happy, and I am really so.   I assure you he is not that fickel man you thought him."

Evidently Mrs. Collier was the leading member in the opposition !

In January, 1749, James informed his father-in-law that he was taking his majority in his own regiment for £1100, besides the price of his own company.   And this, no doubt, was a serious haul out of his fortune.   His wife had received £3000 on marriage, but this was to be settled on her in real estate.   John Collier was evidently not disposed to trust too much in his son-in-law's economy.

It seems clear from the letters that Lord Elibank did not approve of his brother's marriage, and a considerable estrangement resulted.   His lordship evidently was at no pains to conceal his disapproval; probably at the bottom of his feelings lay the fact that the Collier family were whole-hearted Whigs. But apart from the question of fortune, which by the way was far from being a small one, there is no doubt that by his marriage James Murray counteracted, in a great degree, the pernicious influence on his career of his brother's overt acts against the government. In many of her letters Mrs. Murray complains of the treatment of the Elibanks, but James was in no way influenced by it, though it is quite clear that he felt it more than a little. Mrs. Collier, too, having decided in her own mind that her son-in-law was extravagant and "fickel," was foolishly inclined to persuade her daughter to the same view, but Cordelia, to her credit, would have none of it.

"I am sorry you should still think Mr. Murray has no regard for me, when I have all ye reason in ye world to believe he loves me as well as I do him. You are sensible he is warm in his temper, and says a thing then that he is sorry for directly." And again, "As to Mr. Murray being thought an extravagant man, I know he was in ye country; but if I may be a judge of his temper, I think him quite the reverse"

In April (1749) Mrs. Murray fell ill of the small-pox, a disease which was then almost a constant spectre in the home life and very much feared. As a trait of Murray's character, without suggesting that he did more than he should, I quote Mrs. Murray's letter to her mother after her recovery. "Mr. Murray hardly ever stirred out of ye room from me ye whole time, so that I had no use for a nurse." For her better recovery our young couple went into the *country !* "On Tuesday we go to Nightsbridge (*sic*) for air, asses milk (recommended for the invalid), and a vew of the fireworks."

The "fireworks" were the outward and visible sign of the national rejoicings at the peace of Aix-la-Chapelle. All London went mad with rejoicings, as they had done before when the war commenced ! But the "peace" was merely a truce of exhaustion, and except the King of Prussia, who retained Silesia, none of the belligerent powers gained anything. So far as England was concerned, the question of " right of search," which commenced her participation, was not mentioned, and, what is of more importance to this story, Cape Breton Island and Louisburg, then in the hands of the New Englanders, were restored to France. The " fireworks " were, indeed, a failure, and were fairly symbolic of the peace itself. Our Murrays admired the rockets, but the grand set piece was spoilt, " one of ye wings taking fire preatty soon, which made great confusion."

In June (1749) they left for Ireland. Mrs. Murray mentions that she is told that the voyage, which she greatly dreaded, was " seldom more than forty-eight hours with ye wind tolerably fair," which gives one a little insight into travelling 170 years ago ! In July they are settled at Waterford, where the regiment was first stationed. Living here was cheap, and it will interest housekeepers in this year of grace 1921 to know that beef was 2*d.* a pound, mutton 1*d.*, and chickens 2*d.* apiece ; moreover, three bedrooms, a dining-room, and a kitchen were rented at £18 per year. Murray was constantly busy with his regimental duties, and found in Colonel John Jordan, who now commanded the 15th, a chief very much to his liking. The Colonel is thus described :

" A true soldier indeed, for the officers have not an hour to themselves. He ferets them out every morning at five, and so to continue till they are quite masters of ye Duke's exercise, for he is quite determined to make a good regiment at last."

Irish manner of life and Murray's, too, are described in a little word picture :

" Mr. Murray is grown quite the married man, and as drunkenness is ye chief delight of ye gentlemen in this country, he spends no time from home but in the field, and indeed has made all ye inconveniences of this country sit very light upon me by his kind behaviour."

Mistress Murray was evidently something of a social success, which no doubt made up in part for the " inconveniences." We are told that her " hoops and caps " were much in request as patterns by the Waterford ladies. There was plenty of society apparently, and a *certain* degree of decorum was insisted on, for at the balls no dancing was allowed " after tea, which is to be made at twelve o'clock, and nobody to dance in a night gown,* as they have done all this summer at ye card rooms ; " but with regard to this latter relaxation, it is fortunate that the letters tell us that Murray abstained from card playing, and we may therefore hope that dancing in night attire did not form part of the amusement of my hero and his wife ! However, *autre pays autre mœurs*, possibly it was not so bad as it sounds.

The political notoriety which Alexander Murray attained by his action at the Westminster elections in the winter of 1749 has already been referred to, and though it cannot fail to have harmed James's prospects in the army, it is satisfactory to find that he had adopted, without reserve, the service of King George and his government, and I do not think any incident in his later life gives reason to suppose that the old leanings had, any longer, weight with him. He was, in truth, as he frequently expressed himself, thoroughly loyal to the government he served. Thus in December, 1749, writing to his father-in-law, he says :

" I am glad the Independents † have been worsted at Westminster, for tho' Sir George Vandeput is my particular acquaintance, the obligations I ly under to the Duke of Newcastle's family must always make me wish for success to them in everything they attempt."

It was, no doubt, fortunate too that in the Primate of Ireland, who was brother to Andrew Stone, member for

---

* Presumably a dressing-gown is meant !
† The Independent electors of Westminster who, headed by Alexander Murray, opposed the election of the government candidate, Lord Trentham.

E

Hastings and friend of Mr. Collier, Murray had a friend at Court, and this interest, combined with that of Lord George Sackville * and the strong recommendation of Colonel John Jordan, led to his obtaining the lieut.-colonelcy of the 15th Foot in January, 1751. I think I am justified in saying that with the disabilities under which he suffered at a time when politics had a finger in every detail of life, it is a strong argument of Murray's worth as a soldier that he succeeded in getting on so quickly. Mr. Collier's influence and generosity were certainly greatly instrumental in this success, and Murray was thoroughly sensible of it and proportionately grateful. Writing in December, 1752, he says :

" I can't express how sensibly I am obliged by yr application to Mr. Pelham, and how I am vexed to the soul that you should be put to the blush on my account, for his objection to my family is plausible. I am sure time and opportunity, if fortune favours me with any, will convince all the world that I have no share in their guilt, tho' I am likely to have the whole punishment of it unless protected by your influence. Hitherto I am very sensible it has been that alone that has procured my rank and good fortune, and if it pleases God to spare my life I am farr from dispairing of success in my profession, as I shall ever study to behave as your son ought to do ; and should the blind goddess deprive me of her smiles, it will always be a consolation to have done my utmost to deserve them."

The routine of Irish service continued without much incident.† In 1753 the regiment is at Limerick, " a large populace (*sic*) place and governed quite by ye military," says Mrs. Murray. Here James is in the position of commanding officer, being " ye oldest (senior) colonel of ye three regiments." In 1755 the regiment is rumoured to be for foreign service, and this has brought about a crisis in Murray's affairs, for it appears that life in Ireland,

* Son of the Duke of Dorset, and Secretary for Ireland.
† A contemporary opinion describes Ireland thus : " A country where law has lost its energy, magistracy all authority, and nothing but military force could restrain the subject within due obedience " (Bedford to Pitt, December, 1759.)

cheap though it was, has not been accomplished without debts, and the probability of foreign service has brought out a number of creditors. Murray is faced with the possibility of having to sell his commission and enter the Queen of Hungary's service. His own family, says Mr. Cranston, " so far from giving him any help, t'would be a matter of triumph to them to see him undone." However, Mr. Collier stepped into the breach and advanced the money.

In April (1755) the regiment landed at Bideford, and the Irish exile was over. A little later Murray is in great hopes of being made Lieut.-Governor of Stirling Castle, but is informed that his brother's conduct is too recent to admit of this. If this was a disappointment at the time it was no doubt ultimately a benefit, as he would probably have missed the active service which was now coming.

On May 17, 1756, the inconclusive peace of Aix-la-Chapelle was formally broken, and England declared war. There is perhaps nothing more extraordinary than the state of belligerency which existed for several years previously, and which constituted a kind of recognised piracy on both sides. In America war of the most overt kind had been in progress for at least two years. Armies were on the move, posts had been captured ; at sea Boscawen had scattered the French supply squadron which sailed from Brest in May, 1755, and captured two of their ships. Hawke was at sea with orders to take what he could find, and by the end of the year 300 vessels had been taken to England. A French squadron with 15,000 troops had left Toulon, and in May, 1756, had captured Minorca. It was not until this culminating act was in progress that war was declared, and the Seven Years' War, which was indeed two years old already, was textually announced—a war which left England mistress of the seas and of an empire.

The first acts in the drama with which we are immediately concerned was the so-called " secret " expedition to Rochefort ; but, unfortunately, as in so many other cases, long before the expedition left to execute its purpose, all

question of secrecy was at an end. Pitt had planned the
expedition, and had set a high importance on its success ;
but even Pitt was unable to control the deliberate movements of the navy.

The orders were issued in July, 1757, for the assembly of
ten battalions * and a train of artillery in the Isle of Wight.
Murray was in command of his battalion, the 15th Foot,
and he wrote on August 16, 1757 :

" For my own part I am in great health and vigour,
and never knew myself fitter to undergo the fatigues and
hardships my profession is liable to in time of service.   I
have the honour to command a glorious regiment of my own
training, and am confident of acquiring a little reputation,
at least, which in due time may procure preferment."

James Wolfe was quartermaster-general of the troops.
The general in command was Sir John Mordaunt, ap-
pointed on August 3, and the instructions issued to him
were brief—to make a descent on the French coast near
Rochefort ; to destroy the docks, arsenals, and shipping,
and after this to consider the possibility of attacking Port
L'Orient and Bordeaux.   There were two brigadiers—
Major-Generals Conway and Cornwallis.

The fleet did not, however, get under way until
September 8, the troops having embarked on the 6th, and
appeared off the French coast on the 20th.   It was obvious
to Mordaunt that surprise would be no longer possible, for
undoubtedly the French would have received ample warning,
and he wrote to Pitt asking for instructions as to what
course he should take if he should find it impossible to effect
an early landing.   The minister, who was evidently not
pleased with the general conduct of the affair, replied by
snubbing the general, telling him it was no part of his
business to tell him how to carry out his orders.

*	3rd	Foot,	Howard's.	24th	Foot,	Cornwallis'.
	5th	,,	Bentinck's.	25th	,,	Hume's.
	8th	,,	Wolfe's.	30th	,,	Loudon's.
	15th	,,	Amherst's.	50th	,,	Hodgeson's.
	20th	,,	Kingsley's.	51st	,,	Brudenal's.

The wind being unfavourable, the fleet was unable to make the passage between the islands of Rhé and Oleron, and it was not until September 23 that the island of Aix was attacked and easily captured; but here the success of the venture ended. The ships could not approach within two miles of the shore—observations of the enemy's dispositions were difficult. The general was diffident about venturing an attack, estimating that possibly 40,000 regular troops besides militia could have been assembled to dispute the landing. The coast was obviously alarmed, and smoke from signals observed. A council of war was held on board the *Neptune* on September 25. On the 26th the admiral, as so often happened, announced his intention of leaving if action was not taken. On the 29th it was decided to return to England. Nothing more feeble than the whole affair can well be imagined, and Pitt was furious. Grub Street excelled itself, and pamphlets purporting to detail the true causes of the failures with " replies " and " answers " abounded, written by armchair critics, who knew nothing of the difficulties encountered.

So far as this work is concerned we should probably have known little of Murray's part in the affair but for the fact that Pitt resolved on bringing Sir John Mordaunt before a court martial, and two of the principal witnesses called were James Wolfe and James Murray, the former for the prosecution, the latter for the defence. Perhaps Wolfe was an unwilling witness, for he had received much kindness from Mordaunt, and had been a frequent visitor at his house; but reading the evidence, one derives the opinion that a full statement of his observations was not brought out in his replies. Murray's evidence, on the other hand, though his information was gained under the same conditions as was Wolfe's, brought out many details in Mordaunt's favour, and in the end the general was acquitted.

But greater matters were now afoot, and we will pass from what may be called Murray's minor experiences to a consideration of the greater parts that he played on the world's stage. Yet it will be proper to note here the promise which the young soldier had shown, though his opportunities had so far not been great, and his lot had been cast in affairs for which the promoters had good reason to desire oblivion, yet he had managed to obtain distinction in all of them and to show that he was a stout soldier, worthy of the name he bore.

CHAPTER IV

THE CAPTURE OF LOUISBURG, 1758

WHEN in June, 1757, Pitt returned to the Ministry as Secretary of State, with full control of the foreign policy of the country, a new life was infused into the nation which was felt to its farthest limits. He assumed control not only of the army, but of the navy. He was supreme, and proceeded to utilise his power with characteristic genius and energy. It is with his plans for the conquest of Canada that we are for the moment concerned, and for this the plan of campaign included, as a principal objective, the capture of Louisburg.

In those days, no less than at present, a naval base, from which to control operations at sea within a given area, was essential, and in the North Atlantic the English possessed only Halifax from which action to cover the Gulf of the St. Lawrence could be taken. Louisburg, then in French hands, was some 180 miles nearer, and was the true key to the position. Time and again the difficulty of keeping great fleets at sea at a distance from a harbour had frustrated the attempts to prevent the French carrying reinforcements and supplies into Canada. Thus the capture of Louisburg, dominating a secure haven and commanding the approach by sea to the French North American possessions, became the first object of what may be termed the eastern section of Pitt's * plan for the

* It cannot be said that this was a new conception. As far back as 1745, when Louisburg was captured by Sir William Pepperel, a similar idea was put forward. For an interesting chapter on the importance of Louisburg to the French, see Colonel Woods' *Logs of the Conquest of Canada.*

reduction of Canada, which involved the termination of French control over the hinterland of New England, and the security and expansion of the English colonies.

Since the peace of 1748 vast sums and the best engineering talent had been expended on the fortress, which was styled the Dunkirk of America, and no effort had been spared to make it an impregnable position commensurate with its strategical importance. It is said that in some respects the fortifications were defective and not completed to the original design, but it is not probable that this had any important effect on the result. The fortress was isolated, the garrison was insufficient, consisting of 6000 men, including the 3000 seamen manning the squadron lying in the harbour, a part of which, escaping the vigilance of Admiral Hardy, had recently arrived, carrying considerable supplies for the garrison.

No effective succour could be expected either from Canada, then preparing to resist the English advance on Montreal via Lake Champlain, or by sea, where the English fleets held the undoubted superiority. Thus the best defence of Louisburg, other than its own ramparts, was the open and dangerous coast, rock-bound and continually swept by storms, which rendered it a difficult task to assemble and maintain in position a great fleet of transports and war vessels, and a still more hazardous undertaking to land an army in the face of opposition from the French. Had Drucour * commanded a sufficient garrison to enable him to hold all the defences of the harbour as well as to maintain a considerable movable force in the open, it is doubtful how the affair would have ended, and even as it was, the astonishment expressed by Montcalm, when later he heard of the English landing, seems to have had good ground.

" Why," wrote Montcalm, " did not the troops, whose duty it was to defend the entrenchments at this point, march after the first discharge of artillery and musketry, with bayonets fixed, upon the English, whom they ought

---

* Chevalier de Drucour, governor and commander of Louisburg.

to have destroyed? Why did not those of other entrenchments advance also?" *

To encompass this formidable undertaking orders were issued for the assembly of a large force at Halifax.

Including the four battalions of the Royal Americans (60th Foot), there were twenty-one battalions of the regular army in North America, and of these the assembly of twelve battalions † at Halifax was ordered two additional battalions, the 15th Foot, commanded by Lieut.-Col. the Hon. James Murray, and the 58th Foot, were sent out with the fleet of twenty-three vessels of the line which sailed from St. Helen's on February 19, 1758. The 15th was apparently included at the urgent solicitation of Amherst, who was its colonel, backed up by all the influence which James Murray could bring to bear through his interest with the Pelhams.‡ Five companies of New England Rangers were added, and about 300 artillerymen. In all a force of some 14,800 men.

The command was given to Amherst, whose substantive rank as colonel dated from May, 1756, but who, for the purpose of this venture, received the local rank of major-general, the commission being dated March 1, 1758.

The three brigadiers appointed under Amherst were Edward Whitmore, appointed December 30, 1757; Chas. Lawrence, appointed December 31, 1757; and James Wolfe, appointed January 23, 1758. Of these, the two first

---

* Journal under date June 26, 1758.

† 2nd 1st Foot.

	35th Foot.	48th Foot.
17th ,,	40th ,,	2nd 60th ,,
22nd ,,	45th ,,	3rd 60th ,,
28th ,,	47th ,,	78th ,,

‡ There is a letter from Mr. Andrew Stone, secretary to Newcastle, and a friend of Mr. Collier, Murray's father-in-law, regretting that Colonel Murray is under any uneasiness on account of the disposition of the troops designed for America, and promising to take the first opportunity to mention the affair to the Duke. This is dated January 2, 1758.

The 15th Foot was in garrison at Maidstone with a detachment guarding French prisoners at Sissenhurst when they were ordered to Southampton for embarkation on December 31, 1757.

A letter from Lord Barrington to Murray, dated January 23, 1758, details arrangements made to collect the parties of the regiment which were still in Ireland.

concern this story but slightly. Wolfe, however, was, as has already appeared, connected on more than one occasion with Murray, and his name is so closely woven with the events of the years 1758 and 1759 that some details regarding his personality find proper expression here, and, indeed, though in some respects they differed widely, there are many similarities in the character and life-history of the two which are of interest.

In both the martial spirit was strongly developed. To follow " the profession of arms " was the absorbing occupation of their time and their thoughts. Glory, personal honour, the military ambition to lead, their dread of any stain on their name, or on that of the troops they commanded, were to them ingrained principles which found expression in a shibboleth that fills many of their letters, whether private or official, and the very fear that their claims to advancement might be overlooked, and thereby reduce their prospects of leadership, led both into hasty acts which in these days would be called insubordination, but which are justly to be regarded as indications of their superlative desire to participate more closely in the honour of the campaigns they engaged in, and in no sense to mere material advantage.

On the other hand, Murray, strong and robust of body, controlled his natural tendencies, and was more equable in temperament than Wolfe. Defeat did not depress him, but set his energy into fresh action to secure what remained. He gloried in a tight corner, and depended on himself to come through, at least with honour if victory was impossible. Wolfe battled constantly against ill-health, and even his gallant spirit was unable always to preserve its constancy under the exhausting effect of the complaints from which he suffered ; tortured by rheumatism, and frequently suffering from gravel, he was also consumptive, and had to endure the intermittent depression which accompanies that disease. His brother Edward had died of it, and it appears certain that he himself had but a few months to live when he fell gloriously in action at Quebec. His physical incapacity explains much that is otherwise incomprehensible ; it gave him a sense of detachment which caused him to regard himself as one apart, and on a different level, and endued him with a vanity which led him into strange excesses of self-assurance. " The world could not expect more from him than he thought himself capable of performing," wrote Horace Walpole, and if this attitude of mind, combined with his undoubted gift of organisation, had procured for him phenomenally rapid advancement to the rank of lieut.-colonel, under the ægis of the Duke of Cumberland, it could hardly be expected that his personal views would receive the same favour from superiors not of royal rank, to whom he did not hesitate to express his opinions as to their proper movements with a freedom that he showed no disposition to permit when in turn he came to command.* It is only necessary to compare his letters to Amherst containing his advice to that general as to future movements, with his reply to Brigadier Monckton during the operations before Quebec ; when the brigadier asked for more definite instructions he was informed that it was not usual for " inferior officers " to ask questions. And it is easy to see that the fears which he himself expressed, that command had a bad effect on character, were not groundless. Yet this was but one mood of a man of many moods, who was " happy or ruined by my last night's rest, or from sunshine or from light or sickly air." † At other times he was nobly generous in his commendation of his officers and troops, and never behindhand in assuming blame for his mistakes.

In the quaint language used by Wolfe, he and Murray were old " antagonists," and it is quite clear that he uses the word not in the sense usually applied to it, but as meaning " comrades," ‡ or, perhaps, " friendly rivals," though how

* " Some of his contemporary and succeeding officers were not disposed to give him as much credit for military talent as his country in general. This was certainly the case with Lord Amherst."—*Memoir of the Rev. Joshua Parry.*

† Letter to his father, quoted by Wright.

‡ *Cf.* his letter to his friend Rickson, quoted by Wright, in which he refers to himself as " Your Antagonist," and there are other

he succeeded in twisting it into this sense is not easy to explain.   In 1740 they had met when the troops assembled at the Isle of Wight prior to the disastrous West Indian expedition.   Wolfe, a lad of thirteen, had been attached as a volunteer to his father's regiment of marines, but fortunately for him his delicate constitution gave out before the expedition started, and he was landed at Portsmouth and sent back to school, while Murray, as we know, went through three years of a campaign full of horrors.

In 1745 Murray and Wolfe were together in Flanders, and in the same year both returned to England—Wolfe to take part in the campaign against the Scots " rebels," which ended in the massacre of Culloden, and added very little to his military experience.   They did not meet during the campaign abroad of 1746–47.   Wolfe was wounded in the hardly-contested battle of Lauffeld, while Murray had been employed in the far less glorious attack on L'Orient. From the peace of 1748 both were employed at home, and from 1750 were in command of battalions exercising their utmost ability to bring their commands to perfection. Murray and Wolfe were both enthusiastic regimental officers, and they each received high praise for the · efficiency to which they brought their respective battalions. In 1757 they served again together in the expedition to Rochfort, as we have seen, and in 1758 and again in 1759 were together at Louisburg and Quebec.   Thus the war services of Wolfe and Murray were, on the whole, very similar, and they had been in frequent contact.   Wolfe had a warm admiration for his " antagonist," and expressed it on several occasions, and it is certain that if Murray was occasionally irritated with Wolfe's vacillation in their last campaign, he nevertheless held Wolfe in high estimation as a gallant and intrepid soldier.

Although Pitt used every means to hurry the despatch from England of the fleet intended to support the Louisburg operations, Boscawen's squadron of twenty-three sail of the

equally strange perversions of the meaning of words, *e.g.* " illustrate " =render illustrious.

line, accompanied by numerous transports, sailed from St. Helen's considerably later than was intended, and, delayed by contrary winds and much bad weather, made an extraordinarily slow voyage. Wolfe, who accompanied the fleet, writing to his former colonel, Lord George Sackville, describes the arrival at Halifax on May 8:

" From Christopher Columbus' time to our days there was never a more extraordinary voyage ; . . . a fleet of men of war . . . has been eleven weeks on its passage ; . . . we found Amherst's regiment * in the harbour in fine order and healthy. Fraser's and Lawrence's battalions were here (78th and 3rd 60th), both in good condition. The Highlanders, very useful serviceable soldiers, and commanded by the most manly corps of officers I ever saw. Webb's, Otway's, and part of Monckton's battalions from Philadelphia came in with us (48th, 35th, and 2nd 60th) . . . about 500 Rangers are come, which in appearance are little better than *cannaille*. Brigadier Whitmore is expected every day with the artillery, and the troops from New York and Boston, Bragg's (28th Foot) from the Bay of Fundy, and Anstruther's (58th) from Ireland."

On June 2 the fleet, with about one-third of the troops, anchored in Gabarus Bay,† and on the same afternoon Amherst, Lawrence, and Wolfe reconnoitred the coast in boats from the fleet. On the 3rd most of the transports had assembled, but the surf ran too high to permit the boats to venture near the shore. On the 4th, 5th, and 6th fog and a heavy swell hindered action, and the admiral declared against making the attempt. It is said ‡ that considerable doubt existed among the sea officers as to the practicability of landing on a well-defended coast, with the difficulties superadded of a rocky and surf-bound shore, but that one of the captains, Fergusson by name, commanding the *Prince of Orange*, alone adhered to the advice of landing at all costs, and of not calling a council

* The 15th Foot, commanded by Lieut.-Col. James Murray. This regiment had sailed with Boscawen, and apparently arrived just before him.
† Cape Breton Island, near Louisburg.
‡ Entick, *Hist. Late War*, vol. iii.

of war, and this advice Boscawen determined to adopt. It was not until the 8th that the weather moderated. By break of day the troops were in the boats. A furious cannonade was opened by the ships of the line stationed along the coast of the bay, and under its cover the flotilla pushed for the shore in three divisions, that on the left commanded by Wolfe, with the Grenadier companies of the 1st, 15th, 17th, and 22nd under Col. James Murray, and a mixed battalion of light infantry, commanded by Major Scott of the 40th, who was brigade-major of the force, together with a company of Rangers, and supported by the 78th and remaining Grenadiers. This division headed for the left of Kennington Cove,* where the New England troops had effected their landing thirteen years previously. The centre division, under Lawrence, with 15th, 40th, 35th, 22nd, 3/60th, 45th made for the cove to the right of Wolfe's division, while the right attack, under Whitmore, including the 1st (2nd Batt.), 47th, 2/60th, 17th, 58th, 48th, made for White Point some two miles to the right, in order to induce the enemy to divide his force.† The 28th Foot had already been sent in sloops with some artillery to L'Orembeck on the east of the harbour, there to threaten a landing.

The approach of the boats containing the left and centre divisions was the signal for a heavy fire from the French, who were in force at this point, and well protected by entrenchments covered in front with spruce and fir trees laid on the ground with the tops outward. It is said by Drucour in his Journal that 985 soldiers under St. Julian were stationed here, besides some Indians, and that the rugged steep approach to the position was at least fifteen feet above the beach line. To Wolfe, who apparently disapproved ‡ of the method of attack from the beginning,

* So called, because the frigate *Kennington* was stationed off this point of the coast.

† This is the formation given in the *London Gazette* of August 19, 1758, but is at variance with that given in other works.

‡ Our attempt to land where we did was rash and injudicious, and our success unexpected (by me) and undeserved.—Letters to Rickson quoted by Wright.

the attempt seemed hopeless, and he had given the signal to sheer off.* The honour of the landing, and perhaps the success of the whole expedition, therefore falls to three young officers,† Lieuts. Hopkins and Brown, and Ensign Grant, who, with 100 men of the light infantry, made directly for the shore and succeeded in effecting a lodgment, followed immediately by Major Scott, who scrambled on shore though his boat was stove in on the rocks. Wolfe was quick to support his subalterns, and though many boats were destroyed, the division succeeded in effecting its purpose.

Murray, with his Grenadiers, landed with, or immediately after, the light infantry, the centre attack meantime landing their first detachments. Although the disembarkation of the troops was necessarily a slow and gradual process, giving the enemy every possible chance to repel the invaders, yet the French made no stand at all, and that such should be the case is almost inexplicable. That over a thousand men behind breastworks, and aided by artillery, permitted a few boatloads to disembark on a difficult shore, speaks little for their *morale*, and it is only possible to attribute their failure to the contagious example of the French officials, who thought more of luxury and peculation than of duty. Montcalm's astonishment at the success of the landing has already been quoted ; he, at least, understood the fatal nature of the blow. The defenders, having left their trenches, fled precipitately to the town—they were unsupported, possibly Drucour had no other troops available.

The British loss was trifling. Capt. Bailie, Lieut. Cuthbert of Fraser's Highlanders, and Lieut. Nicholson of the 15th, and 43 men killed, out of which no fewer than 21 were of Murray's composite battalion of Grenadiers. A large part of this latter loss was due to the upsetting of

---

* *Parkman,* vol. ii. p. 62.

† As far as I can ascertain, Lieut. Hopkins was an officer of the 48th Foot. Lieut. John Grant of the 58th. There were three Browns, one of 22nd, one of 28th, and one of 35th. I regret I cannot distinguish which was the gallant officer in question.

a boat, by which thirteen Grenadiers of the 15th were drowned. On the enemy's side only one officer and " several men " were reported as killed ! Yet with this small loss was decided an operation which was of paramount importance to the fate of Canada. The troops once landed, the fate of the town, cut off from relief by sea by Boscawen's powerful squadron, was but a matter of time.

It is unnecessary to follow in detail the land operations which followed the landing. There were some instances of gallant resistance on the part of the enemy, and the brave commander, de Vauquelin, of the French frigate *Aréthuse*,* especially distinguished himself, but with few exceptions the defence was not worthy of France, and it is an open question if it was conducted without treachery on the part of some of the leaders. On July 27 the French governor, Drucour, sent out an officer to capitulate.

Thus fell the " Dunkirk of America." 5637 prisoners † fell into our hands, and the French squadron of eleven ships was destroyed or captured, the loss on our side being 168 officers and men killed and 352 wounded. A prayer of thanksgiving for the taking of Louisburg was used in the churches and chapels throughout the kingdom, and there were great rejoicings in the cities and in most places in the country.‡ The affair was in fact brilliant, and if it depended in some measure on good fortune, and few victories do not, it nevertheless owed the greater part of the success to the dogged pertinacity of Amherst and Boscawen, and the officers and men under them.

Of Murray's personal part in this affair the private correspondence gives practically no insight. We obtain, however, a glimpse of his activity from Wolfe's correspondence with Lord George Sackville.

" Murray, my old antagonist, has acted with infinite spirit. The public is much indebted to him for great

---

* On July 15 the *Aréthuse*, taking advantage of a dark night, succeeded in eluding the fleet and escaped to France.

† Being the regiments of Artois, Bourgogne, Cambise, Volontaires Etrangers, and about 700 Canadians.

‡ *London Magazine.*

service in advancing by every method in his power the affairs of the siege. Amherst, no doubt, will do all manner of justice, and your lordship will get him a regiment or the rank of colonel."

This is Wolfe's characteristic generosity, and as evidencing his broad principle of giving praise to those to whom it was due, he adds : " The Highlanders have behaved with great distinction, and their company of Grenadiers has suffered three officers killed and the fourth dangerously wounded."

Unfortunately Murray's legitimate aspirations to obtain the coveted position of command of a regiment were not at the time fulfilled. He had already had the mortification of seeing himself passed over by Robert Monckton, who, junior to him in age, and below him on the list of lieut.-colonels, had been posted as colonel of the 4th battalion 60th Foot in the previous December, but a still more bitter blow was the promotion of Lieut.-Col. Thomas Gage to the rank of colonel in May, 1758. The rumour of this impending appointment had evidently reached Murray before leaving England, but the fact did not come to his hearing until after the siege of Louisburg, when, no doubt, the consciousness of having deserved more consideration made it doubly repugnant. In January of 1758 Murray had written to the Duke of Newcastle :

" I take the liberty to leave in writing, what perhaps I did not so fully explain in the conversation your Grace was pleased to honour me with, I mean the pretensions * I have to preferment, which I can venture to assure myself, from your Grace's known goodness and justice, will prevent any attempts to put a junior officer over my head. I have served His Majesty twenty years and paid three thousand pounds for my several commissions. Last war I was three years in the West Indies, in Flanders, and present in all the variety of service on which the regiment was ordered, and was severely wounded. I have had the honour to command the fifteenth regiment for some years, and have

* Claims.

F

constantly had the thanks of the generals who reviewed it. In 1755, when it was ordered from Ireland, it consisted of no more than one hundred old soldiers; as it is confess'd now to be inferior to no regiment in the service, it is distinguished by the choice made of it on this occasion for the intended enterprise, which I flatter myself is a proof of the diligence of its officers. As I conceive America to be the scene of action, I have for two years past solicited to go there in the room of lieut.-colonels returned unfit for that service when their regiments were ordered for it. I am at this time the oldest * lieut.-colonel belonging to the troops to be employed in America. There is a battalion vacant there by the resignation of Colonel Prevost. If a junior officer is preferred to it, the mortification to me will be insupportable, and I can venture to affirm, the example, as it will be the first of its kind that ever happened, must prejudice the king's service, unless it can be made evident that I am unworthy of rank and preferment in my turn in actual service. It is this only, my lord, that I ask, and as the generals that know me are now at the head of the army, and join with the Secretary at War in assuring me that nothing in their power shall be wanting to procure it for me, it is impossible to suppose that your Grace, who has hitherto been my patron, will oppose them on this occasion without at least securing to me the rank of colonel in the army by brevet or otherwise as may be thought convenient. If this is done I cheerfully resign all pretensions to the battalion in favour of Mr. Gage, who, I daresay, is a man of too much honesty to desire to come over my head. Without declaring myself destitute of the spirit which should characterise a soldier, I cannot stoop to be commanded by a junior officer who has not superior military pretensions.

"As the regiment I am in was not destined for service when Colonel Monckton was put over my head, I joyfully heard the news of his promotion, because he is connected with your Grace's family, and, as I was then situated, it was no disgrace to me; but should I now be laid aside on Mr. Gage's account, I never can hold up my head, must be totally undone and deservedly despised if capable of submitting to it.

"In confidence that no injury will be done me, I go

* Senior.

with the utmost alacrity to serve my country; if I am preferred I hope I shall give satisfaction to those who recommend me to the king; if I am laid aside, I flatter myself the generals who command the enterprise will be able to make reports of my service which will give the authors of my misfortune some concern, and then I can retire to Sussex, and, as contentedly as I can, reflect upon the sums and constitution I have squandered in His Majesty's service."

This spirited remonstrance met with some response, for Murray's name appeared in the *Gazette* of January 24, 1758, as receiving the rank of colonel " in America." The same *Gazette* included the name of Thomas Gage to similar local rank. The *Gazette* of May 9 following, however, included Gage to be colonel of a regiment of Rangers, which gave him substantive rank, and he was at the same time appointed a brigadier in America, and thus superseded Murray. I think there can be no question that Murray had good reason for complaint. It must be remembered that at this time political influence counted for much, and it was common for officers to be dismissed, or to be passed over, if their vote or opinions was known to be unfavourable to the Ministry. It is only necessary to quote the case of William Pitt himself, who was deprived of his commission when, as a young man, he spoke in Parliament against the measures introduced by Walpole (1735).

In Murray's case the political action of his brother Alexander, which I have already noticed, and the known opinion of Lord Elibank, were too recent and well known to make it likely that a Ministry in which Newcastle was a power would do much to help him, and it is the strongest testimony to his worth that he succeeded in making headway at all against such serious disabilities. In the meantime, however, he was undoubtedly discontented with his prospects, and actually went the length of resigning his commission, as we are told in a letter from Amherst to Lord George Sackville. This was in January, 1759. I am not certain as to the reply made by the Commander-in-Chief to this letter of resignation, but probably Lord Ligonier, who knew Murray's worth well, mollified him with the promise of a brigade in the approaching operations against Quebec. His promotion to substantive colonel, however, did not take place until October of 1759.

The siege of Louisburg successfully accomplished, Wolfe, all impetuosity, was for an immediate advance on Quebec, and expressed his views both to Amherst and others with no little assurance. Apart, however, from the general situation, the proposal was obviously impossible. To re-fit and re-victual the fleet and the transports would alone have taken time. The re-embarkation of the troops and artillery, and completion of the stores, would have still further delayed a departure. The St. Lawrence could not, in any circumstance, be reached before the beginning of September, much too late to commence operations. The admirals condemned, and quite rightly, the proposal out of hand. Besides, Amherst was not in a position to decide; he was still subordinate to Abercrombie, and that general, after his severe defeat at Ticonderoga in July, had no desire to embark a large force on a new expedition. He ordered Amherst to join him as soon as possible with reinforcements.

Much had to be done before Amherst could leave. Troops under Monckton and Rollo were sent to take over the outposts of the surrendered territory, and the despatch to France of the civil population of Louisburg and the prisoners was itself a considerable task. At the end of August Amherst left for Boston, via Halifax, to join Abercrombie. Wolfe had asked permission to take the reinforcements, but Amherst, as the senior in America next to Abercrombie, had considered it proper to proceed himself, and his judgment was correct, for Abercrombie was withdrawn and Amherst himself appointed to the chief command, and thus found himself on the spot. In order to employ Wolfe as well as to make a demonstration at the mouth of the St. Lawrence, a strong detachment, consisting of the 15th, 28th, and 58th were sent under convoy of a fleet which left Louisburg on August 28 under Sir Charles Hardy, to Gaspé, with orders to ascend the St. Lawrence and lay waste the bordering villages. Murray accompanied the force, and, after visiting Gaspé with Wolfe, was detached with 800 men to Miramichi Bay, where the settlements were destroyed, and from whence he returned to Louisburg on September 24.

The whole of this proceeding can hardly be called one of importance or even of military necessity, for the only destruction effected was that of fishing villages; and having in view the greater operations pending, it was neither necessary nor even desirable to attack a region so far removed from the true objective, though a mere reconnaissance might be justified.* Information of importance as to the conditions in Quebec was obtained. In a letter from Wolfe, dated September 30, he says :

" All the prisoners paint the distress of Canada—the inhabitants and even the troops are reduced to horseflesh. Bread is now 1s. a pound at Quebec, and everything else in proportion. If our squadron gets up to the Isle Bic in good time, the destruction of Canada, I should think, is inevitable."

The instructions from England to the new Commander-in-Chief at the end of 1758 were :

" To build forts at Lake George and the Oneida Carrying Place " (at the head of the Mohawk river, on the Oswego route).
" To invade Canada, by Crown Point or La Gallette, or both, and invade and attack Montreal or Quebec, or both, by the forces in one body, or by dividing them. To give due attention to Lake Ontario. To attack Niagara. To rebuild Fort Duquesne." (Chatham MSS., Bundle 98 in P.R.O.)

From which it will be seen that it was Pitt's desire that

---

* Quite possibly this was the intention, though it is not stated. Montcalm considered Gaspé a more important port than Louisburg. " C'est la porte du Canada ; sa position est infiniment préférable à celle de Louisburg."

the new advance should proceed cautiously, and this should be remembered when considering Amherst's movements in the following years.

The king's instructions were conveyed to Amherst by Pitt under date December 29, 1758.

" His Majesty having nothing so much at heart as to improve the great and important advantages gained in the last campaign (capture of Louisburg), as well as to repair the disappointments at Ticonderoga . . . *and to avert all future dangers to His Majesty's subjects in North America* * . . . the King has come to the resolution to allow an adequate proportion of His Majesty's forces in America, amounting to 12,005 men, to make an attack on Quebec by the river St. Lawrence, against which place they are to proceed from Louisburg as early in the year as on or about May 7, if the season shall permit, under Brig.-Gen. Wolfe, who will have the rank of major-general for that expedition only . . . and to take especial care that . . . the total forces do amount to the full number. . . . I now come to that part of the operations for the ensuing campaign in North America which are to be under your own immediate directions, and which from their importance, difficulty, and extent, as well as from the correspondence and intercourse with the several governors . . . must require the presence of the Commander-in-Chief. . . . Nothing can contribute so much to the success of the operations, and particularly the attempt at Quebec, as putting the forces early in motion on the frontiers of Canada and obliging (the enemy) to divide their strength."

To admiral Durrell, commanding the naval force at Halifax, Pitt sent orders, dated December 29, 1758, to proceed early to the St. Lawrence and ascend as far as the Isle de Bic and prevent succours from reaching the enemy, and then await further orders from Admiral Saunders. Most unfortunately these orders were not obeyed, as we shall see.

The above orders constituted the base work for the campaign of 1759, which we now proceed to consider; but

---

* My italics—a policy which had its danger, as will be seen later.

it is especially desirable to note the orders issued as to the number of men intended for Quebec, and also the particular instructions given to Admiral Durrell, for as neither was complied with, much difficulty subsequently arose.

Murray passed the winter of 1758 in command of the troops at Halifax, under Governor Lawrence.

CHAPTER V

NEW FRANCE

In these dull days all the maps are coloured, and those white blanks marked " unexplored " have vanished ! Palace steamers carry the traveller from place to place with the regularity of the clock, and the issue of daily newspapers giving details of the happenings at home and abroad is possible in mid-ocean. How can we imagine or picture to ourselves the daily routine on the adventurous *Caravel*, with its crowd of brave men and braver women, on their voyages of unknown duration ; six weeks if they had luck, two months often, even four months, to cross the Atlantic ? Think of these little vessels, no bigger than our coasting schooners, ill-equipped according to our ideas, with few of the scientific methods of navigation known to us, and with accommodation that would make our most hardened shellback shudder ; but think, too, of the glorious excitement of landing on new continents, of raising the national standard and proclaiming in the Sovereign's name, New France, New Spain, New Netherlands, New England, New Scotland ! New in every sense, unknown, and full of possibilities, which the sanguine founders painted in glowing colours, too often finding their hopes unrealised, but seldom deterred thereby from fresh enterprise, or left without hardy imitators, who sought to improve on the efforts of those who preceded them.

It does not come within the scope of this work to refer to the fascinating story of the creation of New France, to Jacques Cartier, Samuel de Champlain, Frontenac, and a host of others ; martyrs in the cause of religion, victims of climate or of war, successful adventurers, many of them. Their endurance succeeded in founding that great Dominion, which, now the ornament of another crown, retains with pride the ineffaceable stamp of the great nation from which it sprang. To those who have not hitherto read the stirring story of New France, let me recommend the works of Parkman, Kingsford, Doughty, Wrong, wherein the student or the general reader will find a wealth of intimate knowledge woven into stories of absorbing interest.

For me it must suffice to give a brief sketch of Canada, leading up to the period when James Murray, whose destiny it was to take a remarkable part in her history, made his first acquaintance with the country which he loved, and for which he expended his utmost efforts—efforts which I venture to believe bore fruit in much that has remained to this day, giving evidence of the broad statesmanlike view which he brought to the difficult task allotted to him. Unfortunately my task necessitates that I should dwell on the period of decadence that preceded the campaign of 1759, and on the men whose want of every quality that connotes patriotism were the causes of the fall. It had been a pleasanter task to deal with the heroes who were the leaders of New France in the golden age of Louis Quatorze.

The decade which saw the final transference of Canada to the English Crown was the fifteenth since the first arrival of Champlain at Tadussac, to recommence, and finally to succeed, in the effort of founding a French colony in New France. During that 150 years the standard of France had proclaimed successively the sovereignty of Louis XIII., XIV., and XV. If it is not too much to say that the first of these monarchs failed to realise the value and importance of the great heritage which the valour of his subjects had bestowed on him, on the other hand the " Grand Monarque " sought to make amends for the negligence of his predecessor, and dreamt of an empire beyond the seas. Reversing the policy which treated Canada as a purely trading base, in which colonisation was rather discouraged than assisted ; sending out troops for the protection of the colonists and royal officials to look after their interests, exhibiting a close concern in their well-being, which even extended to estimating the probable birth rate from the batches of *demoiselles bien choisis* (and otherwise), which were sent out as wives for the settlers ! It was in 1663, exactly 100 years preceding the final cession of Canada, that the chartered company of New France ceased to exist, and the country became a royal province. Up to this period the French had made little impression, being masters of scarcely more than a few trading posts on the St. Lawrence ; but from now onwards pioneers and explorers proceeded to build up constant territorial additions, encouraged and aided by Richelieu and Colbert, both men of imperial ideas, extending gradually inland up to the great lakes, and thence trending southwards by the Ohio and Mississippi valleys, to form that nebulous state then known as Louisiana, enclosing the provinces of New England by a chain of posts, and claiming right to bar their extension westwards, a claim constantly disputed and frequently leading to frays between the disputants.

To strengthen the seaward position and form a base for the protection of the Gulf of the St. Lawrence the fortress of Louisburg was built on Cape Breton Island after the treaty of Utrecht in 1713. The *mot d'ordre* was expansion, and a gradual strengthening of the position, which, if continued on the lines planned by Louis XIV., might have resulted in the creation of an enduring empire. Fate, however, willed it otherwise, and the accession of Louis XV., '' Bien aimé,'' produced a change in the situation.

The Peace of Utrecht, in 1713, concluding a long series of wars, had undoubtedly left the French naval power in a weakened state and the finances of the country in chaos. The maintenance of great land armies over a lengthened period had drained the treasury, and the navy had suffered in consequence. England, on the contrary, had profited enormously by the very causes which militated against

France. With little responsibility on the continent, her statesmen had seen that the way to empire lay upon the ocean. At the end of the war she became the mistress of the seas, her power disputable only by the combined fleets of France and Spain. Had France utilised the period of peace which followed to rehabilitate her navy, the world's history might have been changed; but neither while under the guidance of Fleuri, still less under the corrupt and licentious influence which governed him during his later years, did Louis XV. make any serious attempt to regain the lost power. Moreover, the corruption which gradually spread from the Court to the administration in France was reflected, as was inevitable, in the colonies, and New France, which under the Grand Monarque had been governed by honest and conscientious officials, became a source of illegitimate profit to a host of fortune-seekers, high and low.

" The small salaries given by the French government to civil officers led to extortion and peculation, and there are many instances of clerks and men in petty places on six or eight hundred livres making fortunes of three or four hundred thousand in three or four years." *

The French colonial policy, too, differed essentially from that which had been inculcated in New England. The latter aimed at, or at least achieved, the settlement of an independent people,† taught from the beginning to look to themselves and to be independent of support as well as to extend their commerce, to occupy the new lands in the fullest sense and populate it with a hardy, enduring race of agriculturists and seafarers. In New France, on the contrary, the government was centralised and paternal, dictated from the mother country and, as I have said, in later times, corrupt to so great an extent that the colonists

---

* Murray report on " State of the Government of Quebec."

† I should say rather " Independent peoples," as each state or province had its separate assembly, controlling the finance and military. This was, however, in itself no source of strength, but rather the reverse, from the endless jealousies which existed between the separate settlements.

took little interest in agriculture or commerce, the profits of which would be filched from them.

Even the troops were dependent, to a considerable extent, on food supplies from France. The people were, moreover, trained in arms,* which formed further grounds for neglecting their duty as settlers and rendered the inducements to immigrants less attractive. In 1750 the population of New England outnumbered them by fifteen to one.

Thus it came about when in 1756 the war, which had been in active operation in America and on the sea for at least two years, was officially declared in London and Versailles, the French possessions were in grave peril both from within and without. In the debateable hinterland they had, it is true, successes, due rather to the incapacity of the English commanders than to inherent strength on their part.

General Braddock had been disastrously defeated at Fort Duquesne, and in 1756 Montcalm, newly arrived from France, had taken Oswego. In 1757 Loudon's expedition against Louisburg had ended in nothing, while during his absence Montcalm had taken Fort William Henry. But these successes, even when added to the disastrous defeat of the brave but incompetent Abercrombie, when with a force much superior to the enemy he advanced against Ticonderoga in July, 1758, were but flashes of the expiring fire. Pitt had assumed the direction of affairs, and to him it was clear that the strength of the English strategical position rendered the final result inevitable. To recall the feeble commanders, to establish a firm base for the fleet, and then to crush the French resistance between the upper millstone of a slow but certain movement on the west, and the nether stone of an unassailable fleet shutting off all hope of succour by the sea, was the plan which he undertook, and of which the final success could hardly be in question.

* Every male between the ages of fifteen and sixty was liable to service, and the constant demand on the small population interfered seriously with settled industries.

On November 1, 1758, Abercrombie's letters of recall reached him, and Amherst * succeeded him as Commander-in-Chief in North America. His reputation was that of a man silent, purposeful, and cautious ; one who, having decided on a certain course, would not turn back until it was accomplished. This was the man Pitt wanted. The command of the sea, a powerful asset in the minister's hand, gave him time to pursue a plan of campaign which did not involve forced marches or premature assaults, and Amherst was better suited to such a mode than to one requiring rapidity and the taking of risks.

Murray's letter of farewell, when Amherst relinquished command after six years of strenuous action, shows the esteem and respect in which he held his commander. " Every thinking man," he writes, " who wishes well to the service and welfare of this country, must lament the loss of you at any time, but especially at this juncture. I cannot, I dare not, say all I think." It is, unfortunately, too true that Amherst's successor was a man far less fitted to take charge in a crisis, and the forebodings which were clearly in Murray's mind were realised in the event.

The military position, involving as it did the assembly of important enemy forces, was not the danger which most nearly threatened the French rule in North America. Against military attack a resolute government in old France, governing a vigorous colony through loyal and clean-handed officers, could have opposed a strength which, at the least, would have caused a prolonged struggle, and certainly added seriously to the difficulties to be faced. Unfortunately for France resolution in the government was conspicuously absent ; loyalty and probity amongst the officials did not exist, or if here and there we can discern an attempt on the part of an individual to arrest

* Sir Jeffrey Amherst, afterwards Lord Amherst, was born in 1717. Entering the service young, he was present at most of the great battles of the war of the Austrian Succession. In 1756, as colonel of the 15th, he became the friend of James Murray, then lieut.-colonel of that battalion, and in 1757, while serving under Prince Ferdinand in Germany, he was selected by Pitt to command in America, with the local rank of major-general.

the decay which had eaten far into the body, it was ineffectual against the great mass of corruption.

The Court of Versailles was governed by the Pompadour, and she had little knowledge and less interest in the well-being or fate of the colonies. Whether in the east, in India, or the west, in America, the same masterly inactivity was exhibited by this government, swayed by a courtesan who thought more of secret negotiations with the Courts of Maria Theresa or of the King of Prussia, both of whom held her in contempt, than any responsible attempt to strengthen the outlying parts of the kingdom against attack that was inevitable.

The French Court and the French administration was honeycombed with intrigue ; none could prosper who were not the *protégés* of the king's mistress, and it is needless to describe the qualifications which found favour in the eyes of a vain and frivolous woman.

In such circumstances the danger from within cannot be considered less important than that from without. One by one the men who might have saved France were removed to give place to the puppets of the Pompadour— Machault from the navy, Argenson from the ministry of war, d'Estrées from command of the armies.

" We have no administration . . . the men in office are unfit for their work, and the public has no confidence in them. Madame de Pompadour controls the government with the caprices of an infant, while the king looks blandly on undisturbed by our inquietudes and indifferent to public embarrassments."

Thus wrote the Abbé Bernis, who, as minister of foreign affairs, had reason to know.

It is not to be wondered at that the administration of the French colonies in North America was no less corrupt than that of the mother country, and that the Court of the Governor-General should be modelled on that of the king, his master. Licence, extravagance, and roguery flourished under the rule of the Marquis de Vaudreuil. To what extent he was himself a knave is perhaps indeterminate, but that he was led blindly to sanction malversations is at least certain, and the most charitable assumption is that he was too incompetent to be aware of what was going on. But whatever judgment may be passed on his actual complicity with the frauds which undoubtedly were the prime cause of the loss to France of its North American colonies, there can be no question of his weak duplicity. It is only necessary to read his correspondence to be quite certain that in character he was quite capable of being an accomplice in any form of villainy that might be in question.

Take, for instance, his letters concerning the mission on which de Bougainville was sent to France in September, 1758, to obtain by verbal representations much-needed supplies. To the minister (presumably Bernis, then Minister of Foreign Affairs, who was succeeded by the Duc de Choiseul in December, 1758) the first letter is dated September 4, 1758 :

" . . . J'ai choisi d'accordance M. le Marquis de Montcalm, M. de Bougainville . . . Il est á tous égards plus en état que personne de remplir cet objet. Trois campaignes en Canada, de l'application, du discernment l'ont mis au fait de ce pays. Je lui ai donné mes instructions, et vous pouvez, monsieur, ajouter touts créances à ce qu'il vous dira."

The second letter, dated September 3, was in a different vein :

" . . . J'ai accordé à M. Bougainville des lettres de créances mais je dois avoir l'honneur de vous observer, monsieur, que ces messieurs ne connaissent point assez parfaitement la colonie et ses vrais interêts pour pouvoir l'honneur de vous en parler positivement."

A month after the death of Montcalm, he wrote :

" Depuis le moment de l'arrivée de M. de Montcalm, en cette colonie, puisque celui de sa mort, il n'a cessé de tout sacrifier à son ambition démensurée il semait la zizanie dans les troupes, tolerait les propos les plus indécens contre le gouvernement, s'attachait les plus mauvais sujets, faisait en *sorte de corrompre les plus vertueux, en devenait l'ennemi cruel lorsqu'il n'y pouvait réussir . . . diffamait les honnêtes gens, soutenait l'insubordination, fermait les yeux au pillage du soldat, le tolerait même au point de leur voir vendre les denrées et bestiaux qu'ils avaient volés, à l'habitant." **

Nothing can justify an attack such as this on the honour of one who could no longer defend himself, and that Vaudreuil was capable of making such statements, and many others which could be quoted, is sufficient proof that if he himself was not actually participator in the frauds he was quite capable of being such. He appears to have been obsessed with a jealousy of Montcalm which almost amounted to insanity. He was constantly at pains to explain that Montcalm's successes were due to *his* advice and the help of the Canadians, or that the successes might have been more decisive if his advice had been fully followed. The troops of Old France were to Vaudreuil the object of hatred, and when in 1759 he received orders to conform to the military opinions of Montcalm, his cup of bitterness fairly ran over. He loved Canada, and I cannot bring myself to believe that he had any hand in selling it ; but to ruin Montcalm he would go to almost any length, and probably the astute Bigot, and the still more astute Cadet, made use of his blind desire for revenge.

There is a French proverb, " *qui s'excuse s'accuse*," and Vaudreuil should have remembered it when he wrote to the minister on November 9, 1759, complaining that Montcalm had handed to one Robaud, a Jesuit missionary, two packets for transmission to Mme. la Marquise de Pompadour. These packets were said to contain various notes made by Montcalm on the business methods of the officers in charge of the French trading posts.

" *Entre autres un qui disait que j'envoyais tous les ans 200 équipements à la mission de St. François pour les sauvages et qu'en lieu de leur distribuer ces presents, le S. Gamelin qui en etait chargé les leur vendait à son profit, avec mon approbation, pour les pelleteries.*"

* Letters of Vaudreuil in the Archives at Ottawa.

Much the same opinion is expressed in many places in Montcalm's Journal, and he at all events was under no illusion as to the honesty of his compatriots.

"*Depuis dix ans, le pays a changé de face. Avant ce temps on y était heureux parceque avec peu on avait toutes les choses nécessaires à la vie en abondance. . . . Verrès * arrive ; en construisant l'edifice d'une fortune immense, il associe à ses rapines quelques gens nécessaires à ses vices ou a ses plaisirs. . . .*"

The honour of Montcalm was above suspicion. He had done everything possible to apprise the Ministry of the state of affairs, but it is not unlikely that those who should have taken cognisance were themselves interested, and disinclined to take urgent action ; nevertheless, it was almost certainly due to Montcalm that investigations were ultimately ordered. For the rest, it is sufficient to say Montcalm died in debt, though surrounded by men whose fortunes knew no limits. His entry in his Journal, dated December 10, 1758, may be quoted as indicative of his state of mind.

"*O Roi digne d'être mieux servi ; chère patrie écrasée d'impôts pour enricher des fripons et des avides et que tout y concourt ! Garderai-je mon innocence comme j'ai fait jusqu'à présent au milieu de la corruption ? J'aurai défendu la colonie, je devrai dix mille écus, et je verrai s'être enrichi un Ralig, un Coban, un Cécile, un tas d'hommes sans foi, des va-nu-pieds interessés dans l'entreprise des vivres, gagnant dans un an des quatre ou cinq cent mille livres, qui font des dépenses insultantes. . . .*"

The two culprits, regarding whose guilt one need not hesitate to pronounce an opinion, were François Bigot, intendant of New France, and Joseph Cadet, munitionaire-général, and these had a host of minor satellites, who pillaged the government and the people indiscriminately and in so barefaced a fashion that it is only astonishing that their success endured so long ; nor, indeed, is it

---

* Montcalm evidently designates the intendant Bigot by this name of the Roman governor of Sicily, who was notorious for his extortions.

possible to suppose that their success could have continued had not the administration at home winked at, if it did not connive at, the frauds in Canada.

In the hands of the intendant was almost unlimited power. He was chief in all civil affairs, and superintended justice, police, and finance. He issued ordinances fixing a price upon all kinds of provisions at his will and pleasure. His record was bad, and in no other government than the one which now misgoverned France could he have retained his position for long. He was apparently of respectable birth, and had some powerful connections, and due to these he was appointed a Commissaire de la Marine, a department which included among its activities the control of the colonies. Than the marine there was no department of the French government more entirely suited to a man of Bigot's proclivities, it was * "A chaos of abuse; there was no system of accounting; there was no order; the principles of administration were erroneous, and honesty was almost unknown." Bigot had been intendant or civil administrator at Louisburg for some years when that town first fell into English hands in 1745. He was shrewdly suspected of having had a good deal to do with the surrender. At the second capture of Louisburg one Prévost occupied the post formerly held by Bigot, and worthily sustained the traditions of his predecessor. The *modus operandi* is described by Montcalm in his Journal :

" *Les magasins du Roi sont derrière un des points d'attaque ; on en transporte donc presque tous les effets dane les magasins des particuliers ; on rend la place plus tôt afin d'obtenir par la capitulation, que les habitants conservent leurs effets et puissent, ou les faire passer en France, ou les vendre aux assiégeants. . . . Ainsi fit M. B(igot) en 1745. . . . M. Prévost élève de M. Bigot marche à grands pas sur les traces de son maitre.*"

In other words, the king's stores, which alone fell to the victors by the terms of surrender, were emptied before capitulation, and the contents removed to private charge,

* Bernis to Choiseul, quoted by Perkins (*France under Louis XV.*).

from whence the king's officials sold them for their private benefit.*

It is said that on his return to France, in 1745, Bigot was received with favour by the Pompadour, then in the early days of her concubinage, and that at her instance proceedings against him on account of Louisburg were quashed. The story is quite probable. In 1748 he was sent as intendant to Quebec, and the ten years referred to by Montcalm in the quotation made at p. 83 commenced. During this period every species of villainy was perpetrated, and Bigot, surrounded by a crowd of imitators, of whom the principal was Joseph Cadet, created at his instance munitionaire-général, carried on a policy of fraud which has probably never been paralleled.

He created the so-called Grande Société, locally and openly known as La Friponne, which, being a combination of merchants in Bordeaux and functionaries in Quebec, were able to operate at both ends of the line of supply.† The cargoes were taken into the intendant's stores and sold at his will at immense profit. The troops were defrauded of their dues, and the inhabitants driven to despair. The means of defence did not exist, and the money provided for the purpose was fraudulently withheld. Montcalm wrote :

" *La concussion lève la masque ; elle ne connait plus de bornes ; les entreprises augmentent, se multiplient ; une Société seule absorbe tout le commerce intérieur, extérieur, toute la substance d'un pays qu'elle dévore. . . . L'agriculture languit, la population diminue, la guerre survient, et c'est la Grande Société qui . . . fournit aux vues ambitieuses des Anglois le prétexte d'en allumer le flambeau.*"

* A provision was inserted in the Articles of Capitulation at Montreal in 1760, that all goods in the stores of the munitionaire should be preserved to his use. But this was not accepted by Amherst, and Murray seems later to have had much comfort in hunting out the property of Cadet, whom he knew to be a robber.
† In fairness to the Grand Society, it should be said that they frequently supplied the means of existence to the colony when the French government failed in its duties. If the members had thought less of profit, one could have regarded them rather as saviours than as destroyers.

Bigot aped the king his master, and like the king he took to himself a mistress, Madame de Péan, wife of a civil functionary. Madame played the Pompadour with grace and effect. Her relatives and her favourites monopolised all posts wherein perquisites could be obtained or extortion practised. Her balls and receptions kept society moving, and even if the good bishop was scandalised when the masquers appeared as bishops and nuns, still the misery outside must be forgotten as well as the enemy at the gates. Thackeray's description of another society would have applied very well to this one : " There were no Pharisees, they professed no hypocrisy of virtue, they flung no stones at discovered sinners ; they smiled, shrugged their shoulders and passed on." Thus they fiddled whilst Rome burned. Quebec and Montreal were never more gay than in the last winter.

The visit of Bougainville to France in the autumn of 1758 may have been the lever which operated to open the king's mind to the true state of affairs. In his capacity of first aide-de-camp to Montcalm he undoubtedly knew his chief's mind, and he was, moreover, known to and favourably regarded by Madame de Pompadour.* At all events, the year 1759 brought about a change in the aspect of affairs which was ominous to Bigot and his associates, and indicated to them pretty clearly that they had exceeded the limits of robbery permissible even in the lax government of Louis XV.

One of the first signs of the storm was a letter from the Minister of Marine, de Berryer, to Bigot, concerning the sale of the cargo of an English vessel, the *Mary*, which had been captured.

" *Peut-on imaginer*," he writes, " *une operation plus contraire au bien de la colonie et plus ruineuse pour le Roy*.† He refers to the confusion, " *Sans bornes qui régne dans cette colonie*," and adds, " *C'est à vous à prendre les moyens les*

---

* Montcalm's Journal, under date March 15, 1756.

† Montcalm writes : " On fait acheter par un quidam une prise angloise, sept cent mille livres, huit jours après le Roi l'a racheté, deux millions cent mille livres." De Berryer was not too severe.

plus promptes pour l'arrêter. Et je vous prie de faire en sorte que pendant mon Ministère j'aie à rendre compte au Roy de meilleurs comptes du detail de votre administration qui ne pourrait que devenir suspectes par la fortune de ceux qui ont été employeés sous vos ordres." *

Another step was taken which must also have been a sign of trouble to come. A certain M. Querdisien de Tremain, *premier écrivain du departement de la Marine*, was sent to Canada. His mission was euphemistically described as "*pour aider M. Bigot dans sa comptabilité et qui connaissait mieux que personne le désarroi qui y régnait.*"† It was probably on the report of this official that the drastic step was taken to cease acceptance of the bills of exchange. These bills were drawn by the intendant, and represented the moneys due to the merchants for goods purchased or services performed, and they had increased to such an enormous extent that the exhausted French treasury was literally unable to meet them.

"*Je prévoyais alors la fâcheuse situation où nous nous trouverions pour faire face à tant de dépenses, et la cruelle necessité d'en cesser tout à coup les payements. Ce n'est qu'après avoir épuisé toutes les ressources que le Roi s'est déterminé à suspendre l'acquitement des lettres de change.*"

A definite order was issued that under no pretext whatever should bills be drawn exceeding 2,400,000 livres. This serious blow struck at once both the credit of Bigot as representing the civil administration, and the profits of the swarm of holders of the bills.

On his return to Canada in May, 1759, de Bougainville had apparently made no secret of the king's displeasure at the administration of the colony. Bigot, unwisely, considered himself aggrieved, and made complaint to the Ministry. Matters had, however, gone too far, and he no longer received support. He received in reply the following crushing rejoinder, dated February 22, 1760 :

"*J'ay reçue, monsieur, la ettre que vous m'aves ecrite*

* Paris, *Archives de la Marines* (B. 4 Campagnes, 1759, p. 65).
† *Ibid.*

*pour nous plaindre de l'indiscretion qu'a eu le S. de Bougain-
ville de repandre dans la Colonie les reproches que je vous ai
faites par mes lettres sur les dépenses énormes du Canada,
et sur les fortunes qui sont y faites . . . les plaintes étaient
trop generales et trop fondées sur l'immensité des lettres de
change que vous avez tirées pour ne pas faire connaître les
intentions du Roi sur un pareil dérangement.*

*" A l'égard des raisons que vous donnés pour justifier
l'augmentation de votre fortune, par le commerce heureux et
suivi que vous aves fait, et qui vous a donné plus de 600 mille
livres de profit dans le seule année 1759, elles me paraissent
aussi singulières que l'assurance avec laquelle vous regardés
ces profits legitimes, surtout de la part du'un intendant, et
je ne puis que remettre à une autrefois de vous répondre sur
cet article qui exige de ma part la plus grande attention et
l'examen le plus sérieux pour en rendre compte particulier
à sa Majesté." *

It is said that Montcalm wrote to Belleisle, the Minister
of War, in April, 1759 : " It seems as if they were all
hastening to make their fortunes before the loss of the
colony ; *which many of them desire as a veil to their conduct."*
Montcalm was certainly convinced that Bigot had not
stopped short of selling his country at Louisburg. He
suspected Bigot's successor of the same thing at a later
period. He knew that Duchambon de Vergor, who was
a creature of Bigot's, had done the same thing at Beauséjour. Surely he was fully justified in suspecting treachery
at Quebec.

Enough has been said to depict the state of affairs when
in 1759 the English forces approached Quebec. The
colony was bankrupt, the administration in utter confusion,
the troops discontented and ill-equipped, the inhabitants,
who should ordinarily have been the main defence, were
ruined and in despair. It is to their credit that they
remained as loyal as they did, and only the fear assiduously
spread by Vaudreuil that their lot under English rule
would be still worse, kept them for a time ready to take up
arms. The mother country saw in the colony only a

* Paris, *Archives de Colonie*, Serie B, vol. iii. (Depeches Armée,
1760).

source of expense, and was indifferent to its fate ; moreover, the extravagance of the Court * and administration, and the prosecution of the war against Russia, had exhausted the treasury. Well might Berryer reply to Bougainville's appeal for help, " *Quand le feu est à la maison on ne s'occupe pas des écuries.*" †

If the combination which Pitt formed for the conquest of Canada was strong, it can hardly be gainsaid that the defence was weakened, almost destroyed, by the disease of corruption that prevented unity and mutual confidence among the defenders.

In a subsequent chapter I have referred to the grave reasons there are for suspecting that the surrender of Quebec was not free from treachery. I think what is written above indicates that there is at least *primâ facie* evidence that the condition of affairs and the actors in the drama justify the suspicion.

* Madame de Pompadour is said to have received in the nineteen years she remained in favour 37 millions of livres.

† To which Bougainville is said to have answered, " *On ne dira pas du moins, monsieur, que vous parlez comme un cheval !* "

CHAPTER VI

QUEBEC

WE are only concerned with the steps taken to carry out the eastern or Quebec section of the general scheme for the conquest of Canada. Pitt had discussed the details with Wolfe during his stay in England in the winter of 1758–59, and had agreed, as we have seen, to place a force of 12,000 men at his disposal. In the actual result no more than three-fourths of that number were obtained, and there is no doubt that operations were severely handicapped by the smallness of the force, not so much because the French garrison, on paper, at all events, considerably outnumbered this army, but because the necessities of the Quebec campaign required the holding of several points at distances widely separated, and not in easy communication. This fact must be remembered when criticising Wolfe's failure to achieve an early or a decisive success.

The actual causes of this serious diminution of the force intended for the Quebec campaign are not easy to determine. The wastage in the battalions since the Louisburg campaign had been considerable, and, in those which ultimately proceeded to Quebec, amounted to 1550 men; there were besides 275 other men absent from various causes. Against this some 500 men had been recruited, presumably in North America, making the total shortage in Wolfe's battalions alone over 1300 men. Apparently this had been overlooked by Pitt.* Moreover, on arrival

* On May 19 (1759) Wolfe wrote to Whitmore, " Several regiments are much weaker than thought in England."—P.R.O., C.O. 5/51.

at Louisburg, Wolfe had written to the Governor, General Whitmore, explaining that reinforcements expected from the West Indies * had not come in, and, though not mentioned in the official instructions, he understood that several companies of light infantry were to be added to his force from that under Whitmore. Whitmore was, however, little inclined to assist the rather too forward young general ; he had probably heard, for there are always kind friends to convey such tit-bits, that Wolfe had stigmatised him as " a poor sleepy old man," and his reply to Wolfe's application was curt. His orders, he said, were from Major-General Amherst, or the Commander-in-Chief in America, and none had been received as to further loan of troops.

It is certainly remarkable that while some 15,000 men had been told off for the reduction of Louisburg, no more than 12,000 were considered to be sufficient for the much larger operation against Quebec, and even this number was not available.

The command of the force was given to James Wolfe, who for this purpose had the local rank in America of major-general (dated January 12, 1759). He was, however, clearly subordinate to Amherst as Commander-in-Chief in America. The three brigadiers were Robert Monckton, colonel of the 2nd Battalion Royal Americans ; George Townshend, colonel of the 64th Foot ; and James Murray, not yet appointed as substantive colonel, though he held the rank " in America "—" all men of great spirit," wrote Wolfe. Monckton was the senior, and had several years of active service in Nova Scotia, where he had derived useful experience in Indian warfare, which should have

---

* The intention had been that part of the force under General Hopson at Martinique and Guadeloupe should join Wolfe ; but General Hopson was dead, and his successor, Barrington, had made slow progress and incurred many difficulties from sickness and the too usual jealousies between the Army and Navy, and was unable to complete the operations until May of 1759.

Horace Walpole, in his vein of sarcastic levity, describes the situation : " The laurels we began to plant at Guadaloupe do not thrive. We have taken half the island and despair of the other half. . . . It seems all climates are not equally good for conquest. Alexander or Cæsar would have looked wretchedly after a yellow fever ! "

been a benefit to the major-general commanding. In point of age he was youngest of the three brigadiers, and only six months older than Wolfe himself—and, like him, his promotion had been phenomenally rapid. George Townshend was two years older, and, through his family, possessed much influence. Grandson of a great Whig minister and brother of a then rising politician, who afterwards became famous, nephew of the Duke of Newcastle, and intimate with William Pitt, and himself a politician who was not unknown, he was perhaps inclined to assume an air of superiority which at the period was less remarkable and less repugnant to good taste than we should consider it now.

Some time about 1755 Townshend had incurred the resentment of the Duke of Cumberland, and in 1757 he resigned his commission, but so favoured a personage had little difficulty in obtaining further employment as soon as Cumberland had withdrawn from his post as Commander-in-Chief, and in May, 1758, Pitt offered him a commission as colonel, which Townshend accepted. In December came his appointment as brigadier under Wolfe.

Campaigning in America was not fashionable, and it was not quite what Townshend was hoping for, nor, indeed, is it likely that he appreciated his appointment under Wolfe. It is said that his quarrel with the Duke had been due to his singular capacity for caricaturing—a faculty which has got many people into trouble—and it is not surprising that Wolfe's odd appearance and mannerisms attracted Townshend's peculiar form of humour. There was certainly a state of tension between the two which came to the surface more than once during the campaign ; but apart from this, Townshend was certainly a brave and capable commander, and a more tactful chief would probably have found him an important asset, both on account of his abilities and his influence at home. Tact was not, unfortunately, one of Wolfe's many good qualities.

Except Monckton, none of the superior officers had any experience of American warfare, and that term included a vast range of conditions which required a long apprentice-ship and an adaptability, which the rigid formations and formulæ derived from experience in the continental wars gave little hope of attaining. The Louisburg operations and the subsequent foray in the Gulf of St. Lawrence in the previous year added little to Wolfe's knowledge. Murray, it is true, had had the West Indian experience of 1740–42, which, at least, covered much that was useful in conducting operations from a sea base. For the rest their knowledge was almost entirely based on Dettingen, Fonte-noy, Lauffeldt, and a series of sieges, advances, and retreats, executed according to an etiquette more complicated and not less exact than that which the age prescribed for social observances.

Nor in the composition of Wolfe's army do we find any leaders of note among the colonial troops, on whose advice Wolfe might have relied if he had been so minded ; but in any case, it is to be feared that " advice " was the last thing the young commander wanted. Besides, Wolfe despised the colonial troops, both in his own camp and that of the enemy—" the worst soldiers in the Universe," is his pithy description ; and, no doubt, to a commander accustomed to issue precise orders on questions relating to movements, clothing, and discipline they appeared such.

The enemy, on the other hand, possessed among the superior officers men who had been brought up from their youth with the colonial militia, and who thoroughly under-stood their peculiarities and their value. Montcalm, it is true, as a king's officer, *pur sang*, held much the same views as Wolfe, but Vaudreuil, who possessed most of the faults a commander could have, was at least in touch with the Canadian and Indian auxiliaries, and there were other capable men with similar qualifications, as De Ramezay, Contrecœur, Repentigny.

Of the remainder of the staff of Wolfe's army two names stand out prominently. Carleton, with the appoint-ment of Deputy Quartermaster-General, with the rank of " Colonel in America," and Barré, the " Deputy-Adjutant."

The former had long been a close friend of Wolfe. Barré, on the other hand, had been previously unknown to Wolfe,* but his strong personality and faithfulness evidently rendered him a trusted subordinate at a time when strained relations with his other officers made things difficult for a man of Wolfe's temperament.

There is one other name, seldom referred to in works on the subject, which deserves a more ample consideration— that of Colonel Williamson, who commanded the artillery. This arm of the service had not long been included as part of the regular army, and Williamson, by scientific study of the possibility of his weapons, had done much to increase its efficiency. At Quebec the great value of Williamson's branch of the service was fully demonstrated. Apart from the bombardment of the town itself, and the almost complete destruction of the public buildings, a matter on the utility of which different opinions may easily be held, there was the decisive result that under the cover of the guns the mastery of the river, above and below the town, was secured. The fleet alone could not have accomplished this, for their guns could not be trained on the heights, and to Williamson's heavy artillery belongs a share of the success which, I think, has met with scant recognition.

The assembly of the Quebec army at Louisburg in the spring of 1759 took place during the latter end of May.

Ten battalions only were detailed by Amherst for the service.† A battalion of Grenadiers was formed, consisting of 313 men under Lieut.-Col. Alexander Murray ‡ of the 45th Foot. These were drawn from the three battalions remaining at Louisburg (22nd, 40th, 45th), and there were

---

* So it is stated in a letter quoted in Wright's *Life of Wolfe*, but I believe Barré served in the Rochefort expedition.

† From Halifax: 15th, 58th, 2/60th, 3/60th. From New York, Boston, and the continent: 47th, 48th, 78th. From Louisburg: 28th. From Bay of Fundy: 35th, 43rd.

‡ Alexander Murray, son of Sir William Murray, of Blackbarony, and great-grandfather of the late General Sir James Wolfe-Murray. He was an intimate friend of Wolfe's, who was godfather to his son. He was also, of course, a distant cousin of James Murray of this memoir.

also six companies of Rangers, recruited in New England, each of 80 to 100 men, commanded by Major Scott of the 40th Foot. A corps of light infantry was formed from the battalions of the army, under command of Major Dalling of the 28th Regiment.

The embarkation return signed by Wolfe on board the *Neptune* on June 5 shows the strength of the force as under :

Regiment.	Colonel.	Officers.	N.C.Os. and men.	Arrived at Louisburg.	
15th	Amherst	31	560	May 30	*Staff.*
28th	Bragg	26	565	—	D.Q.M.G. :
35th	Otway	36	863	May 31	Col. Carleton.
43rd	Kennedy	29	686	May 24	
47th	Lascelles	36	643	May 22	Dep.-Adjutant :
48th	Webb	36	816	May 24	Major Barré.
58th	Anstruther	27	589	May 31	
2/60th	Monckton	27	554	,,	Majors of Brigade :
3/60th	Lawrence	29	578	,,	Capt. Spital,
78th	Fraser	50	1219	May 17	Capt. Gwillam,
Special Units.					Capt. Maitland,
Grenadiers of Louisburg	Alex. Murray	13	313	—	Lt. Dobson.
					Aide-de-camps :
					Capt. Smyth,
Companies of Rangers	Goreham	7	88	—	Capt. Bell.
					A.Q.M.Gs. :
,,	Stark	3	92	May 26	Capt. Leslie,
,,	Brewer	3	82	May 31	Capt. Coldwell
,,	Hazzan	3	86	,,	
,,	Rogers	4	108	,,	
,,	Danks	(not arrived at date of return)			
Royal Artillery	Williamson	21	309		
	Total	387	8241*		

The nett result was that Wolfe's force started woefully short of its proper complement, and except for a small force of about 100 men, nothing was added to his effective strength during the campaign.

* Including 3 officers and 90 men of Dank's company of Rangers. In addition Wolfe had assistance from the navy, both marines and sailors, for guard duties and gunners, but these took no part in offensive movements.

Admiral Holmes, with a small squadron and a convoy of 59 transport and ordnance ships, sailed from St. Helen's on February 14, a part of the convoy being for New York. Saunders, with the rest of the squadron, followed, Wolfe, Townshend, and Carleton being with him. The winter had been unusually severe, and Louisburg harbour was ice-bound, a rare occurrence. Saunders was therefore obliged to carry on to Halifax, arriving on April 30, where he found Admiral Durrel with fourteen sail ready to start for the St. Lawrence. Durrel's squadron had wintered at Halifax. It formed the fleet of observation, and its object was to prevent any enemy ships from ascending that river. Whether on this occasion he considered it necessary to await the arrival of his chief is not clear, but it is certain that the delay in appearing at his post had serious consequences, and Wolfe expressed himself freely on the dilatoriness of the admiral, though I cannot find that the naval Commander-in-Chief expressed the same views.* Durrel's squadron left Halifax on May 2, with transports carrying 650 of the troops under Carleton, which were to form an advanced guard (of these 400 were required for supplementing the crews), and arrived in the river on the 14th, to find that a French fleet of eighteen transports, commanded by Jacques Kanon, convoyed by three frigates,† had stolen a march on them, and had arrived at Quebec four days previously, carrying some 340 recruits and 1500 sailors, as well as a much-needed supply of stores, though much less than had been asked for, and also de Bougain-

---

* On March 10 (1759) Admiral Saunders wrote to Pitt that he had sent orders to Durrel, " to enforce the absolute necessity there is for him to be very early in the river St. Lawrence; " but writing on May 1 from Halifax he merely mentions that he finds Durrel ready to sail, but makes no comment on the delay. (See P.R.O., c/o. 5/51.)

† Saunders' despatch, May 5, 1759, in P.R.O. c/o 5/51. The three king's ships were *La Pomone, L'Atalante,* and *La Pie.* The two former being frigates, the latter a smaller type known as a " flute." This expedition, fitted out by the energy of the famous French Armateurs of Bordeaux, impelled, I think, by the genius of de Bougainville, was a remarkable feat. A very interesting brochure by Jean de Maupassant, entitled, *Les deux Expéditions de Pierre Desclaux au Canada,* gives full details of it.

ville, returning from his almost fruitless embassy to try and induce the French Government to send reinforcements to the colony. No better evidence of the demoralised state of the French Government can be given than the letter written by Belleisle, then Minister of War, to Montcalm in reference to this embassy of Bougainville's :

" Besides increasing the dearth of provisions, it is to be feared that reinforcements, if despatched, would fall into the hands of the English. The king is unable to send succours proportioned to the force the English can place in the field to oppose you. You must confine yourself to the defensive, and concentrate all your force within as narrow limits as possible." *

Every difficulty seems to have been put in the way of the expedition—it was even refused to provide the recruits with arms ! Durrel only succeeded in capturing three or four of the laggards of the convoy, and through want of enterprise he lost the great opportunity of striking a blow which would have crippled the enemy to such an extent that it is doubtful if Quebec could have been held at all. Bougainville acknowledged afterwards that the colony was literally starving when this convoy arrived.

" The severity of the winter has greatly retarded our sailing from Louisburg, and has by much exceeded any that can be remembered by the oldest inhabitant in this part of the world. . . . I am now off the Island of Scatari, and standing for the Gulf of St. Lawrence with the wind at west, the whole number of transports not having been able to get out to me till this morning."

Thus wrote Saunders to the minister on June 6, and Wolfe, notwithstanding his natural impatience to be gone, wrote on the same date that the fogs and climate were so unfavourable to military operations " that if we had been collected a week sooner I doubt if it would have been

* These orders exhibit clearly the want of appreciation of the conditions in Canada. The narrowest possible limits of defence was the line of the St. Lawrence from Montreal to Quebec, 180 miles apart, with several intermediate vulnerable points.

possible to sail before we did." Yet the French convoy had managed to reach the St. Lawrence nearly a month previously !

The progress of this great armada, consisting of more than 200 vessels, great and small, up the river, took some thirteen days from the entry into the estuary in sight of the island of Anticosti—the distance traversed was about 380 miles. The wind was often contrary, and one can imagine the difficulties in tacking and reaching of a crowd of vessels in a waterway subject to strong tidal currents, and growing constantly narrower as the fleet ascended higher towards its goal. Often the ships were obliged to anchor and wait for the flood tide before progress could be made. Townshend, in his diary, gives some insight into the navigation dangers which must have occurred not once but many times :

" Five of the men-of-war upon a tack were nearly running on board each other ; the current being very strong, few would answer their helm at first. The *Royal William* of 90 tons, and the *Orford* a 70-gun ship, nearly ran down our ship, the *Diana* frigate. In this critical situation the breeze sprang up, and seconding the ability of the respective commanders of those ships saved us from that shock which a few moments before seemed inevitable." *

It is, perhaps, not difficult to visualise the scene as the great fleet made its slow irresistible passage. The trim war ships, the rows of open gun-ports, from each of which peeped the muzzles of the 32 or 18-pounder guns, the high poops of the larger ships and the great stern galleries, carrying the usual three lanterns, the two outermost supported by massive figures gaily decorated, the forest of tall spars and the maze of rigging, which added so much to the fascination of the old wooden walls of England. At dawn two hundred capstans clanked, and ten thousand feet raised a mighty tramp as the great hemp cables groaned

---

* Townshend Diary, quoted by Col. C. V. F. Townshend, D.S.O., in his Life of his Ancestor, p. 156 (now Sir Charles Townshend, the gallant defender of Kut-el-Amara).

through the hawse-holes, and the fife and drum on the war-ships, and the fiddles of the transports,* lent rhythm to the deep-throated chorus of the sailors singing the popular sea tunes of the day :

> " Then why should we quarrel for riches
>   Or any such glittering toys ?
> A light heart and a thin pair of breeches
>   Goes thro' the world, brave boys." †

The boatswains' whistles sounded up and down the river, blocks creaked as willing crews and equally willing soldiers hoisted the fore and aft sails to aid the ships in their constant tacking, the water crowded with boats taking soundings, marking channels or shoals, occasionally making a raid on shore.

The convoy was in three divisions, each with its accompaniment of ships of the line, and each ship carrying a distinguishing flag. Thus the first division, Monckton's, led by the *Lowestoft*, was marked by a white flag, and the several regiments had their respective variations, the transports of the 43rd a white flag with one red ball, the 78th white with two blue balls. The second division, led by the *Diana*, was red with similar variations, while Murray's troops in the third division, led by the *Trent*, carried blue, plain for the 35th regiment, with one white ball for the 48th, and three for the 3rd battalion Royal Americans (60th). The Grenadiers, the light infantry, the Rangers, the artillery, all had their distinguishing flags ; and besides this gay equipment, let us picture a constant succession of signal flags, displayed and answered. The white, blue, or red ensigns, which in those days distinguished the rank of the admiral commanding, and the Union flags, which then only contained the Crosses of St. Andrew and St. George, fluttering on the quaintly massive bowsprits with their strange rigging of sprit topmast and sprit yards,

---

* Knox tells us of some of these, which included such homely names as " Charming Polly," " Good Intent," " Prosperity."

† This was Lieut. Bowling's song in *Roderick Random*, but Dibden and the real " Tom Bowling " were yet to come. " Hearts of Oak " was not written until late in 1759, and originated from Hawke's famous victory in Quiberon Bay.

H

a style even then going out of fashion, and indicative that the fleet now moving on the St. Lawrence was not of the most modern build.

The transports were, no doubt, a motley crowd of all sizes and rigs. Most of them had crossed the Atlantic, and bore marks of the rough handling they had had in the stormy passage of February, March, April; many others were New York or Boston built, distinguishable by their lower free-board; but if they lacked something of the gallant appearance of the war-ships, the crowd of red-coated soldiers, who lined their bulwarks, and discussed the novelties of the stirring scene before them, gave them a distinct value of their own in the animated picture. It was these transports which in ordinary times carried on the commerce of England, and their crews formed the most skilful sailors in the world. The French had hoped much from the difficulties of navigating a large fleet in the hazardous waters of the great river, and their amazement was great to see the vessels, large and small, guided in safety through the most difficult channels with apparent ease; and that, too, without the usual pilot marks, which they had been careful to remove. What quaint old salts were the masters of these battered craft; accustomed to daily and hourly danger, ready to tackle a privateer and lay her " aboard luff for luff," as the phrase went, if there was a chance of success, or to out-sail her by sheer seamanship, if the worst came to the worst; nothing was possible of wind or weather that could daunt them, so long as they had a good offing and no land under the lee.

What were the reflections of Wolfe and his generals as they passed onwards to the scene of their great endeavour? People were great diarists in those days, but, unfortunately, little has remained to give us the thoughts of Wolfe or of Murray or Monckton. Townshend's diary is preserved by his descendants, and is partly quoted by Col. C. V. Townshend in his work. It is to be hoped that some day more may be given to the public. He found leisure to jot down many interesting details, and noted the wild uncultivated character of the shores, " save where a few straggly French settlements appear." Murray, who kept a careful diary of the operations in the following year, probably kept one at this time, and if he did, we may be sure it recorded an intelligent appreciation of the possibilities of developing to advantage the new country into which they were penetrating, which not one of them doubted would fall before their attack. It was a peculiarity of Murray's character that, intensely military though he was, and capable and ready to discuss the chances of the campaign, and the measures required to meet the ever-changing conditions, he never for a moment lost sight of the practical problems of deriving the utmost benefit from the results of the military action.

At Tadoussac the fleet had anchored for a brief period to collect stragglers and make arrangements for the progress up the rapidly narrowing estuary, and here, no doubt, Murray and his comrades recalled the story of Champlain's first coming a century and a half before ; of Kirk and his fleet of raiders, which made here their first *rendezvous ;* of the terrible sufferings of the fur traders, who essayed to pass the winter here, and of whom few survived to tell the tale. Could Murray have foreseen the future he would have known that within half a year his own experiences would resemble theirs. Beyond Tadoussac some twenty miles brought them to the first of the islands in the narrow river, and following the northern bank no instinct can have told Murray that the little river, known to the French as *Noire*, would form the eastern boundary of the seigneury to be called after him, Mount Murray, or that eighteen miles higher up the two bold headlands, the easternmost of which forms Cap à l'Aigle, and the western, Pointe au Pic, enclosed the beautiful bay that was to be known as Murray Bay. Even then the French settlers had discovered the beauties of a place which in these later years forms a fashionable summer resort, and a village nestled on the shore of the bay, sheltered from the north by the rising hills. Fire and sword were soon to leave little of this peaceful hamlet, but a little later here arose the comfortable manor house around which is woven Professor Wrong's fascinating story, *A Canadian Manor and its Seigneurs.* Besides Murray, there were two others to whom the gift of second sight would have disclosed a close connection with the St. Lawrence shore about Murray Bay. On one of the vessels, distinguished by the white flag with two blue balls, indicating Fraser's Highlanders,* were two young officers, John Nairne and Malcolm Fraser, who were destined to spend their lives here, as owners respectively of the two seigneuries of Murray Bay and Mount Murray, both of them scions of old Scots families, and both poor. It is not unlikely in their case that dreams of settling in the new land may have occurred to them.

It is perhaps uncertain if either of these two officers was personally known to Murray at the time, though Nairne had served in the Scots Brigade in Holland, as he had done himself, but at a later date ; he was soon, however, to know them well, nor only from their gallant bearing, but from the personal recommendation of his brother George, dated October 23, 1759, " I have no occasion to apologise for recommending the bearer,† honest John Nairne's son, our relation. They are folks we greatly respect." I cannot ascertain in what way the families were " related," probably by intermarriage ; but the circumstance accounts for the interest which Murray showed in his *protégé,* and the pecuniary assistance he gave him not only to purchase a company in the 78th, but also in aiding his settlement in the Murray Bay seigneury, which the grateful recipients acknowledged by begging to

* This battalion, one of the first Highland regiments, was raised by Simon Fraser, son of Lord Lovat. The *Army List* of 1758, in which it appears as the 63rd or 2nd Highland Regiment, shows that among the officers were seventeen Frasers, of whom six were Simons ! In 1759 it became the 78th Foot, and in 1764 the regiment was broken up.

† The word " bearer " would appear to indicate that Nairne was not present with the regiment at the Siege of Quebec. He was gazetted lieutenant in " Fraser's " on July 16, 1757, and there is nothing to show that he was not present. The letter may have been sent to Nairne by George Murray, to deliver to his brother.

be allowed " to give the lands to be granted such name as will perpetuate their sense of his great kindness to them."

Beyond Murray Bay the fleet came to Île aux Coudres on June 23, and found here Admiral Durrel's squadron. Wolfe had already received the news of the admiral's failure to intercept the French fleet of supply transports, and his chagrin was but natural. The remarks in Wolfe's Journal and that of his aide-de-camp, Captain Bell, show pretty clearly what was in the minds of the writers. " The succours from France anchored *at Bic, the 9th of May*." " There had been no ice in the river these two months." * " All in general are agreed that they (the French) must have starved if the succours from France had not arrived." Probably Wolfe did not exaggerate the importance of the " succours," and it is beyond doubt that they afforded much-needed assistance and had an important bearing on the campaign, not only that of 1759, but also of 1760, for quite apart from the men and supplies, it gave the French an important addition of ships for transport purposes, without which their attack on Quebec, in the spring of 1760, would hardly have been possible.

By June 25 the fleet had arrived at the Traverse, a narrow difficult passage between the island of Orleans and the frowning headland of Cap Tourmente, " a remarkably high, black-looking promontory," says Knox. Here the channel turned and twisted in a most puzzling fashion, yet to the great astonishment of the French the whole fleet passed it with apparent ease. It was here on the slopes of Cap Tourmente, commanding the navigable channel which ran close in shore, that Montcalm had urged the erection of batteries to oppose the English fleet; but in the confusion of divided counsels, which he refers to with great bitterness in his Journal, nothing was done, and beyond the natural difficulties of the navigation the fleet suffered no hindrance.

---

* In Montcalm's Journal it is recorded that the ice broke up earlier than usual at Montreal, on April 5, and that it would be seven or eight days longer in the lower part of the river.

The voyagers were now almost within sight of their goal. From the 24th to 26th (June, 1759) a crowd of vessels continually arrived in the south channel beyond the island of Orleans. Here they were " entertained with a most agreeable prospect of a delightful country on every side—windmills, water-mills, churches, chapels, and compact farm-houses, all built with stone, and covered, some with wood and others with straw."

Quebec itself was not yet in view, but the opening of the " bason " could just be seen, and a glimpse is to be had of the Falls of Montmorency, which many of the voyagers were soon to have a disastrous acquaintance with.

On June 26, Wolfe, from his headquarters on the *Richmond* frigate, issued his orders for landing on the Isle of Orleans. The honour of the first landing belongs to Lieutenant Meech of the Rangers, who landed at night on the 26th with forty Rangers, and had some little skirmishing but no real opposition. He maintained his position all night, and in the morning the army commenced the disembarkation. No opposition * was encountered, the inhabitants had abandoned their houses. Even the parish priest of St. Lawrence had thought it wiser to leave the ground clear for these invaders, whose character he had been taught to estimate as of the lowest order. Yet he must have had some doubts on the subject, for before leaving he affixed to the doors of the church a letter, " To the worthy officers of the British Army," praying for their protection of his church and its sacred furniture. He added a little touch, that shows him something of a humourist ; had the landing occurred a little earlier, he said, the worthy officers might have enjoyed the benefit of the vegetables his garden produced, but these " are now gone to seed."

Wolfe, all eagerness to view Quebec, took an escort of

---

* According to Montcalm, a detachment of 500 Canadians, under M. de Courtemanche, had proceeded to Orleans to oppose a landing. On June 28, he says, " Le singulier est que notre gros détachement à l'île d'Orléans a vu sans s'y opposer les Anglais y débarquer en désordre." It seems certain, at least, that if Courtemanche had been alert he could have captured Meech's weak detachment, and certainly harassed the landing next day.

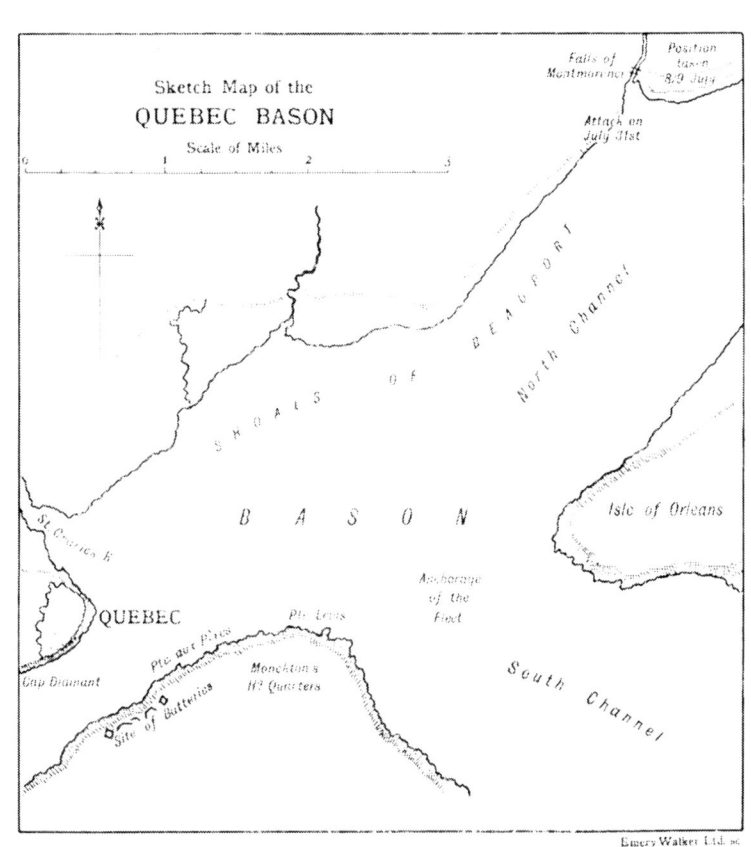

Sketch Map of the
QUEBEC BASON

Scale of Miles

0   1   2   3

Falls of
Montmorenci

Position
taken
8.9 July

Attack on
July 31st

S H O A L S   o f   B E A U P O R T

North Channel

B A S O N

St Charles R.

Isle of Orleans

Anchorage
of the
Fleet

QUEBEC

Pte Levis

Cap Diamant

Pte aux Péres

Monckton's
H? Quarters

South Channel

Site of Batteries

Emery Walker Ltd. sc.

light infantry, and, accompanied by Major McKellar, the chief engineer, proceeded to the west end of the island, whence an uninterrupted view across the bason of Quebec was obtainable. What Wolfe saw on that June day, while it cannot but have quickened his ambition to be master of Quebec, must also have given him a warning that the task before him was one of extraordinary difficulty. In front of him the four miles' expanse of the " bason," the steep, almost precipitous coast-line culminating at Cape Diamond, on which was built the citadel ; the walls and batteries of the town crowning the heights and sloping gently towards the estuary of the St. Charles River, on the hither side of which, along the less elevated but still formidable shore-line, as far as the opening of the Montmorency River, it was easy to see the French lines and the encampments which continued almost without intermission for some six miles. It was not difficult to judge that a numerous force was assembled, and that almost the whole strength of France had been concentrated here to dispute his passage.

On the left hand the prospect was scarcely less magnificent, nor was it more inviting so far as attack was concerned. Immediately across the southern channel rose the steep shore of Beaumont, rising gradually to the Point of Levis, and extending beyond in heights scarcely less forbidding than that of the citadel itself. The narrow channel between the citadel and the heights of Levis could not be fully seen, as the coast-line bends at that part of the Levis position, known as Pointe des Pères ; but here the river narrows to about a thousand yards, fully commanded by the batteries of the town, and adding seriously to the problem of getting ships or even boats up the river.

It will be convenient here to recall the plan of campaign which Wolfe had formed before leaving Louisburg. It is contained in a letter written to his uncle, under date May 19, 1759 : *

---

* It should be noted, however, that General Amherst, writing to Pitt on January 18, 1759 (P.R.O., A.W. 1, vol. 89), had prepared a

" To invest the place *and cut off all communication with the colony,* it will be necessary to encamp with our right on the river St. Lawrence and our left to the river St. Charles. From the St. Charles to Beauport the communication must be kept open by strong entrenched posts and redoubts."

Obviously Wolfe pictured himself surrounding the city and enclosing the garrison within the walls. The question of the French field army, which would presumably remain within the " colony," appears hardly to have entered his calculations. The lines he prepared to hold from the St. Lawrence to the St. Charles on the shortest measurement would be not less than 2200 yards, while the line of posts and redoubts would be at least 2000 yards more. For such a scheme his force of 8000 men would be quite insufficient, even without allowing an independent reserve to repel the attack of a relieving force, which certainly should be reckoned on. The letter continues :

" It is the business of the naval force to be masters of the river both above and below the town. . . . I reckon we shall have a smart action at the passage of the St. Charles, *unless we can steal a detachment up the river St. Lawrence and land there three, four, or five miles or more above the town,* and get time to entrench so strongly that they won't care to attack."

The passage which I have put in italics is important ; but the main idea, clearly, was to land if possible at Beauport, pass the St. Charles, invest the town, and besiege it in due form ; yet the alternative of going up the river to a *distance* above the town was certainly then in Wolfe's mind. At the time he wrote this letter he knew the force which would be at his disposal, and this alone should have given him cause to modify his views ; but when he surveyed the scene from the west point of Orleans, two things at

plan similar in many respects, viz. " The best place for landing troops seems to be below the Charles River on the north shore, where there is a plain three miles in length, and by what Colonel Schuyler tells me, the Charles River is everywhere fordable and good passing when the tide is out. The town to the land side is weak, and the approaches are cover'd by hills, which are near the town and high " least should have been obvious—that the French army was a much larger one than would in all probability suffer itself to be shut up in the city, and that a landing at Beauport, in face of such a force, was impracticable. Yet throughout all the subsequent proceedings this idea never wholly left Wolfe's mind.

As an initial conception, before ever seeing the ground or being in a position to judge, by observation, the defences, or the degree of concentration of the enemy, the letter shows a bold and vigorous idea; but when actual facts presented themselves, it seems apparent that the whole plan should have been immediately and radically modified, the more so that Wolfe himself referred to the necessity of cutting off communication with the colony (by which he meant the upper river and Montreal), and of landing at some distance above the town.

A commander of genius could hardly fail to have grasped the fact that command of the waterway placed most of the trump cards in his hand. The French concentration below Quebec was in itself in his favour, and it was in his power to dictate the place of attack anywhere within twenty or thirty miles above the town. The instant the English naval force passed Cape Diamond, Montcalm, with the true instincts of a soldier, recorded in his diary : " Si l'ennemi prend la parte de remonter la fleuve et peut descendre dans un point quelconque, il intercepte toute communications avec nos vivres et nos munitions de guerre."

I would, however, make it clear that the first steps taken by Wolfe in the attack were unquestionably most proper, and, indeed, might lead to the supposition that he *did* modify his initial plans as a result of his reconnaissance on June 27; unfortunately he did not steadfastly maintain the line of strategy which was apparently laid down in the beginning.

Much has been said regarding the failure of Amherst to attract to himself the larger part of the French force. But it does not appear that this is justifiable. Wolfe knew that for the western armies to make themselves felt at

Montreal would take time, though he certainly put the total of the enemy forces that would oppose him at too low a figure. He estimated the enemy's force as six battalions of regulars, some companies of marine troops, with four or five thousand Canadians, and some Indians. In all he reckoned about the same number as he had himself, that is, some 8500 men. From all the sources of information, and they are none of them very reliable, I think the total French force assembled at Quebec was approximately 12,000 men, composed as under :

French Regulars of five battalions	..	2,100	men
,, Marine troops	.. ..	800	,,
Quebec Government Militia *	..	3,000	,,
Three Rivers Government Militia *	..	700	,,
Montreal Government Militia *	..	2,000	,,
Montreal Town Volunteers	.. ..	1,000	,,
Cavalry and sundry volunteers	..	800	,,
Quebec Garrison, including 1000 sailors		1,650	,,
Total (excluding Indians)	..	12,050	,,

Even if we discount this formidable total on account of the indifferent quality of a large part of the force, and on account of the internal conditions already described, it is still apparent how serious a problem presented itself to the British commander, and how little likely direct frontal attack, on a naturally difficult position held by a numerically superior force, was to succeed.

On June 29 Wolfe records in his Journal : " The Admiral expressed his desire that we should get possession

* Amherst, in his letter to Pitt, dated October 4, 1760 (P.R.O. c/o. 5/59), estimated the militias of the three governments as :

Montreal	..	..	..	..	..	7331
Three Rivers	..	..	..	..	..	1105
Quebec	..	..	..	..	..	7976

but probably these were the paper figures of all men and youths of age to bear arms, from which large deductions are necessary. Besides, we know that nearly 1200 of the Montreal and Three Rivers Militia were at the Île aux Noix, and a considerable number at other places. It must also be remembered that a number of parishes in the Quebec province were dominated by Wolfe's army. I think the above figures are maxima, very unlikely to have been exceeded.

of Point Levy, and sent Captain Wheelock to signify it to me." No doubt the admiral found the narrow waters south of the island a very uncomfortable anchorage, and a sudden hurricane on the 27th, to say nothing of an unsuccessful attempt to destroy the fleet by sending down fireships, quickened his desire to get out into the open waters of the bason. It is, however, pretty certain that occupation of Point Levis jumped with Wolfe's own ideas, and orders to carry out this first important step in the campaign were given at once. Monckton's brigade was detailed for the duty, and one battalion and some light infantry crossed that night and took possession of the church and village of Beaumont with slight opposition, the remaining battalions crossed the next day (June 30). On this day the light infantry, having had a successful skirmish with some French marine troops, went forward to survey the country. "There was no regular road up the hill, only a serpentine path with trees and undergrowth on every side of us; " * by ten o'clock the whole brigade moved up the hill and marched to Point Levis, where they found an enemy force in possession of the church and houses of St. Joseph near the Point. Knox estimates their number at 1000, including 600 colony troops. The resistance was not formidable, and this commanding position was soon in Monckton's possession.

The occupation of the Levis heights was a move of the greatest importance, and it is astonishing that the French permitted it with hardly any show of resistance. I think Knox is certainly inaccurate in saying that 600 colony troops were present. In Montcalm's Journal a certain M. de Lery (an officer of marine troops) is mentioned as being there with some Indians, and it is stated that Montcalm had endeavoured without effect to persuade Vaudreuil to send a large detachment to hold the position. It was undoubtedly, for Monckton, a very fortunate error of judgment on Vaudreuil's part. Possession of Point Levis

* Knox's Journal. He was present on this occasion with his regiment, the 43rd, which was part of Monckton's brigade.

gave Wolfe the first step towards mastery of the river, both above and below the town.

The next important step taken is also recorded in Wolfe's diary, under the date July 3 : *

" Consultation with the admiral about landing, our notions agreeing to get ashore, *if possible above the town*, we determined to attempt it—troops and ships prepared accordingly. The admiral of opinion that *none of the ships would be of use in an attempt on the Beauport side. Resolution to begin with a warm bombardment from Point aux Pères.*"

This entry certainly involves that modification of Wolfe's first conception as contained in his letter to his uncle, which I have already alluded to—the abandonment of direct attack on the Beauport front and commencement of activity *above* the town. Unfortunately two things speedily became manifest. The first, that Wolfe could not bring himself really to give up the Beauport scheme, and the second, that landing above the town meant, in his mind, a landing close to the town—in fact, to accomplish the original plea of investing the town, by landing immediately above it instead of below.

The measures taken after consulting with the admiral were, however, in accordance with the agreement arrived at. Townshend's brigade was ordered to land on the north shore below Montmorency, in order " to draw the enemy's attention that way and *favour the projected attempt (above the town).*"

Had Wolfe's force been adequate this move would have been sound strategy. A force, even a small one, entrenched on the French left, would undoubtedly pin a large body to their lines, and the position on the left bank of the Montmorency River was not easily attacked, and had open communication by water in rear. At this place, after a steep rise from the water, the land rose gradually in an open grass-covered slope. The falls of the Montmorency

---

* From other evidence it appears probable that this consultation took place on the 1st or 2nd, though entered in the diary as the 3rd.

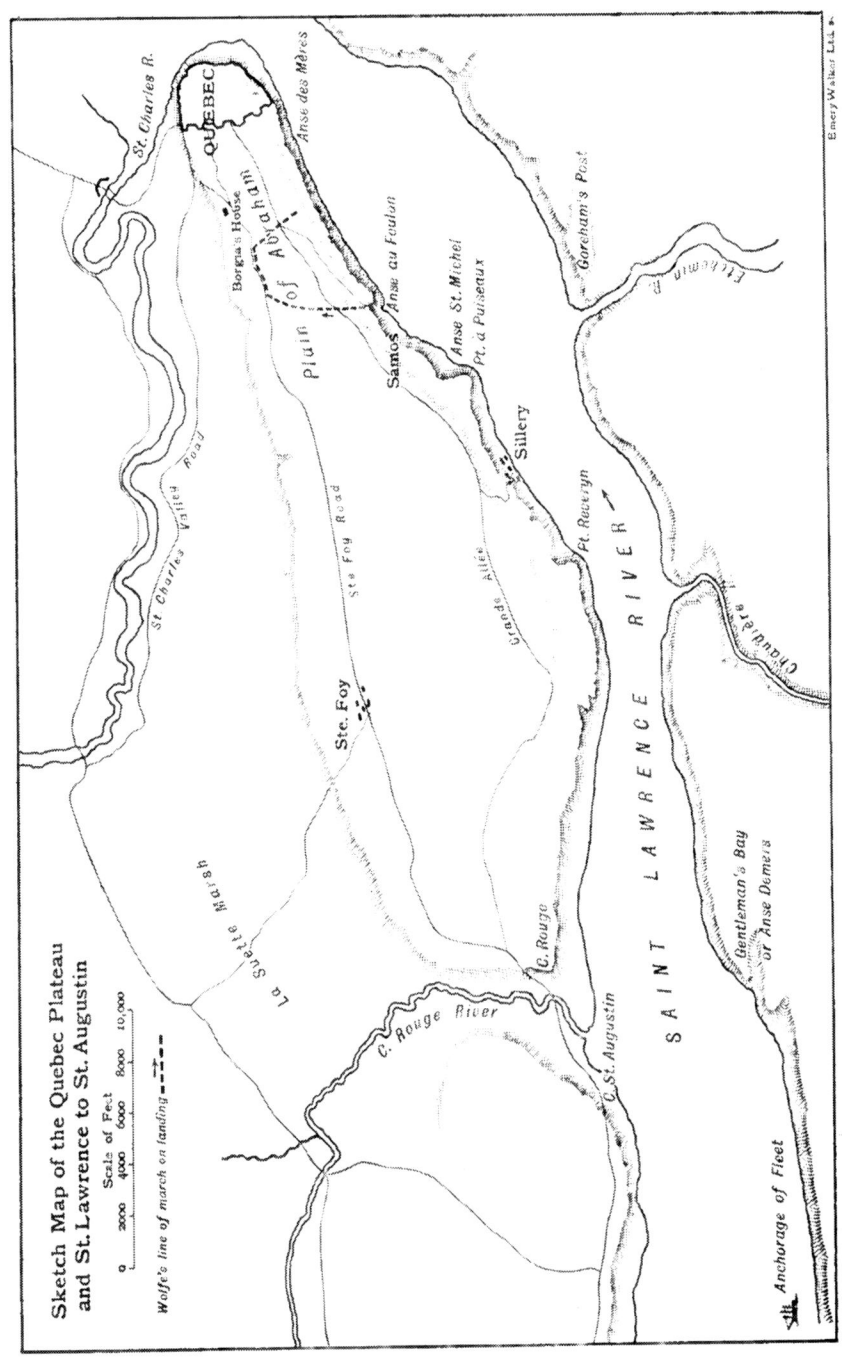

Sketch Map of the Quebec Plateau and St. Lawrence to St. Augustin

Scale of Feet
0 2000 4000 6000 8000 10,000

Wolfe's line of march on landing ---→

St. Charles R.

QUEBEC

St. Charles R.

Borgia's House

Anse des Mères

Plain of Abraham

Anse au Foulon

St. Charles Valley Road

Anse St. Michel

Samos

Pt. à Puiseaux

Ste Foy Road

Sillery

Grande Allée

Pt. Rocervn

Ste. Foy

La Suette Marsh

C. Rouge

C. Rouge River

C. St. Augustin

SAINT LAWRENCE RIVER

Etchemin R.

Goreham's Post

Chaudière

Gentleman's Bay or Anse Demers

Anchorage of Fleet

Emery Walker Ltd. sc.

River on the left—on the right some distance away a considerable hill, which commanded to a great extent the camping ground. In front thick wood bordering the side of the Montmorency River. In the circumstances in which he was actually placed, to detach so large a proportion of his troops to a position far removed from the main theatre, where they were unable to do more than demonstrate, certainly cannot be commended. The brigade was useless for attack, for it was separated from the French by the deep chasm of the Montmorency, nor was it strong enough to venture higher up the river where the crossing was possible, nor numerically sufficient to be a serious menace to the French.

At the same time General Murray received instructions to " reconnoitre la Chaudière, St. Michel, and Anse des Mères." I quote from an entry in Wolfe's Journal, dated July 4, but there is little doubt that Murray proceeded on this duty on the 2nd or possibly 3rd, under the escort of a body of Rangers commanded by Major Scott. The duty was obviously in furtherance of the plan of campaign of attacking the enemy *above* Quebec. For the proper understanding of much that followed later a careful consideration of this order is necessary, the more so that it has been neglected by writers on the subject. The last of the places mentioned is almost certainly a mistake for Anse Demers. To instruct Murray to make a reconnaissance to the Chaudière River, some eight or nine miles above the camp at Levis, and at the same time to include Anse des Mères, is obviously unlikely, for this lay almost opposite the position at Pointe aux Pères (on the north side of the river), which Wolfe had selected on July 2 as a site for the batteries to bombard Quebec, and whatever could be learnt by viewing the Anse des Mères from the south shore was already known to him.

On the other hand, Anse Demers is a little cove some two miles or so beyond the Chaudière River and almost directly opposite Cap Rouge, and its inclusion in Murray's orders would be quite probable. This place is the same as

that which Murray refers to later as " Gentleman's Bay "
(*see* p. 124), and here again we have a curious misrendering
of the name. On the great map of the St. Lawrence,
now in the British Museum, executed under Murray's
orders, the place is carefully drawn in and named " Ance
de Messieurs." The use of " de " seems to indicate that
" Messieurs " was not the original name.

I visited this little bay in September, 1915, in company
of Dr. Doughty and Colonel Wood, and we found by
inquiring from a local inhabitant, that though the bay
itself appeared not to have any special name, the land
surrounding it was known by the name of an early proprietor as Demers, and I do not doubt that both Wolfe's
and Murray's rendering was due to a misconception of
the real name.

But a further curious point arises. Whence came the
knowledge of this little-known cove, which induced Wolfe
within a few days of his arrival to seek further information ?
The answer to this question seems to point clearly to
Major Stobo, who had made his remarkable escape from
Quebec after five years' captivity, during the early part
of which he had a great deal of liberty and opportunity
to make himself acquainted with the country about Quebec.
Stobo left Louisburg on June 11 on board the *Seahorse*
frigate, and arrived off the island of Bic in the St. Lawrence
on June 22, whence he proceeded in haste to join Wolfe,
and would have reached headquarters by June 27 or 28.
He was, therefore, in plenty of time to give Wolfe any
information of which he was possessed. " C'est lui, dit
on, conduit tout," wrote Montcalm in his Journal, " et il
est en état de rendre bon compte de la situation de notre
colonie à tous égards."

He was the bearer of a letter from Lord Rollo, then at
Louisburg, addressed to Colonel Alexander Murray (which,
strangely enough, is now among the papers left by General
Murray). The letter says :

" The bearer, Captain Stobo, will, I hope, bring you agreeable accounts of the condition of the place and disposition

of the French troops, and is able to point out the avenues of the place, which will greatly forward your approaches. . . ."

In that strange document, *The Memoirs of Major Robert Stobo*, by an unknown author, it is stated, " He pointed out the place to land, where afterwards they did, and were successful. . . ." It appears then circumstantially probable that Stobo, in close touch with Wolfe during the first days of considering the plan of campaign, was the source whence the general drew his information, and it appears also that from him two distinct plans were derived. The one, an embarkation at Anse Demers and a landing on the north shore somewhere in the neighbourhood of Cap Rouge or even higher up the river; the other, a landing at St. Michel. As to the first, the Anse was peculiarly suited for the purpose, for a ridge of high ground screened the foreshore of the cove from any view of the enemy, and a large number of men could be assembled there in secrecy. It was this notion that attracted General Murray, as we shall see. As to St. Michel, this place remained for the rest of the campaign a lure to General Wolfe ; but, unfortunately, he did not steadfastly maintain his first intention.

This long digression must be completed by a word regarding St. Michel.* The village of Sillery stood then, as it stands to-day, just above the promontory correctly called Pointe à Puiseaux, but more generally known to Wolfe's army as Sillery Point. The fief of St. Michel,

* The story of St. Michel is full of interest from an historical point of view. A delightful volume, *Une Paroisse Historique de la Nouvelle France*, has been published by the Abbe H. A. Scott, Curé of S. Foy (Quebec, 1902). It was from here that (1642) Paul de Chomédy started for Montreal to found the religious community of Ville Marie. When it was attempted to dissuade him from his project, he returned the noble answer, " Je ne suis pas venue pour délibérer, mais bien pour exécuter, et tous les arbres de l'Île de Montreal serroient-ils changés en autant d'Iroquois, il est de mon devoir et de mon honneur d'aller y établir une colonie." The names of several of the brave Jesuit martyrs are connected with this chapel of St. Michel, and here too many thrilling incidents occurred in those early days when the marauding Indians took frequent toll of the lives of the priests who ventured with admirable courage among them.

which included the Point, was as far back as 1687 in possession of a M. de Puiseaux ; a chapel dedicated to St.
Michel had been built on the foreshore above the Point,
but a house occupied afterwards by Madame de Puiseaux
had been built on the foreshore just below the Point, and
the little bay before this house had been named Anse St.
Michel ; it was to this place General Wolfe referred in his
instructions to Murray. It should be mentioned that all
these little bays, created by the irregularities of the river
bank, were rather nebulous in their confines, and this may
be the explanation why the memoirs of Major Stobo refer
to the actual landing by Wolfe as having taken place at
the spot indicated by him, though, in fact, Wolfe's cove,
properly called Anse au Foulon, is some 1200 yards lower
down the river than Anse St. Michel. General Murray
also, as we shall see, combined the two places as one. For
the rest, the Anse St. Michel, like the Anse au Foulon, was
approached by a path leading from the main road on the
plateau, and was thus a place which offered certain facilities
to a landing force. It was, however, more under the protection of Sillery Point when the French had a post and
a battery.

To return to General Murray. It does not appear that
General Wolfe pinned much faith on the Anse Demers
project, at all events he did not persist in the matter of
the reconnaissance there, when, as happened, Major Scott's
force, which was a small one, returned without reaching
the limit prescribed. Apparently it got no further than
somewhere near the Étchemin River, and Murray was
only able to examine St. Michel, and his report on this
is entered in Wolfe's Journal under date July 4 : " Brigadier
Murray's report—he is satisfied of the practicability of
the attempt at St. Michel's." Whether Murray returned
on July 4 or sent this report by hand, returning with
Major Scott on July 7, is not clear ; but by the latter date
Wolfe's intention had undergone a complete change, the
up-river scheme was dead for the moment, and Murray
received orders to join Townshend at Montmorency with

two battalions of his brigade. Townshend's force had been further augmented by a large body of light infantry and Grenadiers; and what was originally to have been a mere demonstration was now converted into a concentration of more than half the total available force. This fatal error appears to have occasioned remonstrance on the part of the brigadiers, and there was much friction. Admiral Holmes, writing later (September 18), described the situation :

" It (the attack on St. Michel) had been proposed to him (Wolfe) a month before, when the first ships passed the town, and when it (St. Michel) was entirely defenceless and unguarded; but Montmorency was then his favourite scheme, and he rejected it." *

Townshend's brigade, with the greater part of the Grenadiers of the army and the light infantry, took possession of the position east of the falls on the night of the 8th–9th without opposition, and on the 10th (July) Murray followed with two additional battalions, so that on this date the army was divided into three divisions— at Montmorency, at Levis, and on Orleans—and there was, in fact, no force left available for executing a movement above the town, certainly not a movement of any importance.

It is not easy to enter into the state of Wolfe's mind at this period. He records, in his diary on July 7, a dispute with an " inferior officer," probably Townshend, and the latter's diary tells us of considerable friction at Montmorency. He was not getting on very well with the admiral either, and seemed to criticise the action or want of action of the fleet. He thought that passage above the

---

* This statement as regards time is not literally correct. For one month we should read two, and it was *before* the ships passed the town that the proposal was made. The statement, however, represents the opinions current of Wolfe's change of mind. It is to be noted that the admiral regarded Anse Michel and Anse au Foulon as much the same area, and this was no doubt the general view in the force.

town might have been taken sooner. Yet, if this delay was the cause of his new decision, he had opportunity to revert to the scheme concerted with Admiral Saunders, for on the night of July 18 the admiral was able to make the projected ascent of the river. The *Sutherland* (Captain Rous, 50 guns), the *Squirrel* (sloop, 20 guns, Captain Hamilton), three transports, and two provision vessels, passed the narrows without damage accompanied by a number of flat-bottom boats. The frigate *Diana* (36 guns, Captain Schomberg), however, ran aground. It is surprising that the French frigates did not seize the opportunity of attacking this weak force. It is said that there was intention of doing so, but that the crews having been removed from the vessels the idea was given up. An opportunity lost! With this small squadron was Colonel Carleton with three companies of Grenadiers and the 3rd battalion of the 60th— in all about 600 men, which was all the force that could be spared.

On the 19th and 20th important progress was made, and the post, known afterwards as Goreham's, was established in " a large house," which was on an eminence near the embouchure of the Étchemin River. This place, immediately opposite Sillery Point (Pointe à Puiseaux), became one of much importance later, as the connecting station on the south shore between the fleet above Quebec and the headquarters below. Taking advantage of the escort which this movement furnished, Wolfe " reconnoitred the country immediately above Quebec," and he adds, dated July 19, " And found if we had ventured the stroke that was first intended we should probably * have succeeded."

This entry in Wolfe's Journal certainly seems to imply that while he was fully prepared for the " venture," which refers to the " stroke " at St. Michels, there were causes beyond his control which prevented it. Blame is apparently imputed to the navy, in that the passage of the ships

---

* In the original the word " infallibly " was first written, and altered to " probably."

had not yet taken place. But a reference to his consultation with Admiral Saunders shows that the commencement of the bombardment was one preliminary, and this did not open until the 12th, and a favourable condition of wind and tide was necessary, which did not occur until the 16th, when Wolfe has an entry: "Conference with the admiral concerning projected descent—a squadron of men-of-war were to have gone by the town and post themselves above. The wind fair, tide favourable, but yet Captain Rous did not go there." This comment is not justifiable, for the log of the *Squirrel* contains the entry for this date: " 9.30 hove short and hoisted the topsails ready to run above the town; also falling little wind the *Sutherland's* boat came on board with orders to lay fast." The 17th night was also without breeze. On the 18th the passage was made.

Had Wolfe been whole-hearted in the affair the morning of the 19th would have found him at St. Michel, or better still, if Carleton's raid on Pointe-aux-Trembles on the night of the 21st had been a serious and supported landing, a different story would be told. Montcalm's fears would have been realised, his forces cut off from their supplies, and in all probability a decisive victory for the English army would have ensued. But Wolfe's heart and energies were then centred at Montmorency.

However, the best reply to this entry in Wolfe's Journal is to quote his own opinion, written to Pitt on September 2:

" This (*i.e.* the passage of the ships) inabled me to reconnoitre the country above, where I found the same attention on the enemy's side, and great difficulties on ours, arising from the nature of the ground, and the obstacles to our communication with the fleet. But what I feared most was, that, if we should *land between the town and the River Cap Rouge, the body first landed could not be reinforced before they were attacked by the enemy's whole army* (my italics). Notwithstanding these difficulties, I thought once of attempting it at St. Michaels about three miles above the town ; but perceiving that the enemy, jealous of the design, were preparing against it, and had actually brought artillery and a mortar,* which being so near Quebec they could increase as they please, to play upon the shipping; and as it must have been many hours before we could attack them, even supposing a favourable night for the boats to pass the town unhurt, it seemed so hazardous that I thought it best to desist."

It does not appear to have occurred to Wolfe that had he got athwart the enemy's communications there would have been no question of his attacking *them*. The French could not have existed a week without having to attack *him*.

On the 20th (July) the *Sutherland* dropped up the river with the tide, accompanied by the troops, and anchored at 3 p.m. about twelve miles above the town, that is to say, they passed beyond Cap Rouge and were somewhere off the parish of S. Augustin. At midnight on the 20th–21st Carleton's troops dropped further up the river in boats, and made a raid on Pointe-aux-Trembles; but there was no military value in the affair, and as Carleton was back at the *Sutherland* by 4 a.m. (21st), it is not likely that he had much opportunity of examining the shore as he passed. It is clear that nothing more than a raid was intended, for there were no supporting troops. Yet Carleton had no difficulty in landing, and here was the opportunity referred to above.

The completion of this expedition seems to have banished for the moment any further intentions on the part of the General to attack above the town, whether at St. Michel or elsewhere, and he now devoted all his energy to the Montmorency venture. On the 26th (July) at one o'clock in the morning Murray proceeded to make a reconnaissance up the Montmorency River, the General accompanied him, but a flank march of this nature in

---

* These were sent up on July 19 (Montcalm's Journal) and opened fire on the 21st (Knox), and, I think, placed on Sillery Point (where a battery exists at this day) and not at Samos, as supposed by Dr. Doughty. The Samos battery would have been useless to play on ships off Sillery.

difficult country, especially at night, was a dangerous operation and nearly ended in disaster. The object was to find a ford which was reported to exist some eight or nine miles up the river; but it is hardly possible to suppose that a watchful enemy, with free movement on the opposite bank, could allow themselves to be surprised. In the result Murray's force was heavily attacked, and the 35th (Otway's) regiment was put in some confusion and lost a number of men and officers. Murray evidently behaved with great gallantry, rallied the men, and making a desperate counter attack, drove the Canadians and Indians into the river,* and succeeded in bringing the detachment back to the camp.

There had been a consultation of the leaders on board the admiral's ship on July 23, but beyond the fact that the method of attacking the French army was debated, nothing is known of the proceedings. It is clear that there was want of unanimity. Wolfe's diary is sufficient to show this, and from general evidence it is probable that at the consultation he proposed his two alternatives—to cross the Montmorency some miles up and fall on the French left wing, or to make a frontal attack of the Beauport position. It is certain that the brigadiers did not approve of either. Murray's reconnaissance of the 26th was the result of the first-named proposition. Wolfe's disastrous attack on July 31 was the outcome of the second.

It is unnecessary here to detail the latter event. Unquestionably Wolfe's plans were carefully thought out, and he did everything that was possible to make his movement a success; but looking at the matter from the standpoint that we can now assume, having the evidence of the French preparedness before us, it is impossible to think, even if some of the ill-luck which delayed his time table had not occurred, that the attack, made by a numerically inferior force on a difficult position in broad daylight, could have succeeded. A more cogent argument is, that had it succeeded it would certainly have resulted in

* Townshend's Diary, quoted by Colonel Townshend.

driving the French army intact or nearly so behind the
St. Charles River and towards their supplies, and as a
decisive military operation it could hardly have been
successful, whatever degree of good luck had attended
it. Murray's brigade was very slightly engaged in the
affair.

CHAPTER VII

QUEBEC (*continued*)

THE month of August passed without any sign of decisive action on the part of the General. His situation was one which commands sympathy ; he was worn out by exertion, and the almost tropic heat of a Canadian summer prostrated his energy. He seemed dazed by the failure at Montmorency, and to a man of his sensitive temperament the knowledge that his chief subordinates disapproved of his dispositions, be it said with good reason, must have added to his discomfort. Even Carleton had apparently expressed himself against the Montmorency venture.*

Several expeditions were despatched to chastise the villages on both banks of the river so far as his control extended, and the bombardment of the town by the batteries at Pointe aux Pères was continued ruthlessly. The former was a military measure that added seriously to the difficulties of the French commanders. Not only were their supplies from the surrounding villages cut off, but the inhabitants themselves were driven to seek shelter in the upper part of the colony, and consumed food that would otherwise have been available. The latter measure —that is, the bombardment—was not useful as affecting the military situation. The range was too great for accuracy with the poor artillery of the period, and the French batteries suffered less than the town, a great part of which was laid in ruins, and valuable stores of cord wood were burnt, a result which recoiled almost disastrously on

* Bell's Diary.

the victors when at last they became masters of the place.

The only movement bearing directly on the campaign was a reconnaissance in force up the river under the command of Murray, the naval force being under Admiral Holmes. The flotilla of flat-bottomed boats available above the town had been considerably augmented, but several failures to add to the war-ships in the upper river had occurred, and Holmes' squadron was dangerously weak. The main object of the expedition was to seek the French frigates * which had retired up to the River Richelieu, and now mounted higher still, as the French seem to have been well informed of what was afoot. Wolfe's instructions to Murray seem to indicate no settled plan. He was merely to seek every opportunity of fighting the enemy.

The force detailed was a considerable one of 1260 men,† and it attracted a good deal of attention from the enemy, who had also been informed by a deserter of the movement. De Bougainville, with a strong detachment, was sent up the river immediately, to take command of all the troops above Quebec, and from that time the defence of the river above the town was greatly strengthened. I cannot but think that at the consultations, when the question of how best to attack the enemy was raised, the brigadiers must have suggested, as they afterwards reiterated, an attack on the north shore at a distance above the town. If this were the case, it was a mistake to draw the enemy's attention that way, by despatching a large body on a mere reconnaissance, the more so that a certain amount of information already existed. It appears probable that Murray's real object was to gain information to

---

* There were at this time four armed vessels—the *Atalante*, *Pomone*, *Machault*, and *Senneterre*—besides one or two smaller ships. Their united strength was certainly at least equal to that of Admiral Holmes' vessels, viz. the *Sutherland* and *Squirrel*, the latter a very small vessel. Only the discord existing between the French commanders prevented an attack.

† The 15th Foot with 300 men of the 3rd 60th, with a company of Highlanders, 200 light infantry, and 200 marines.

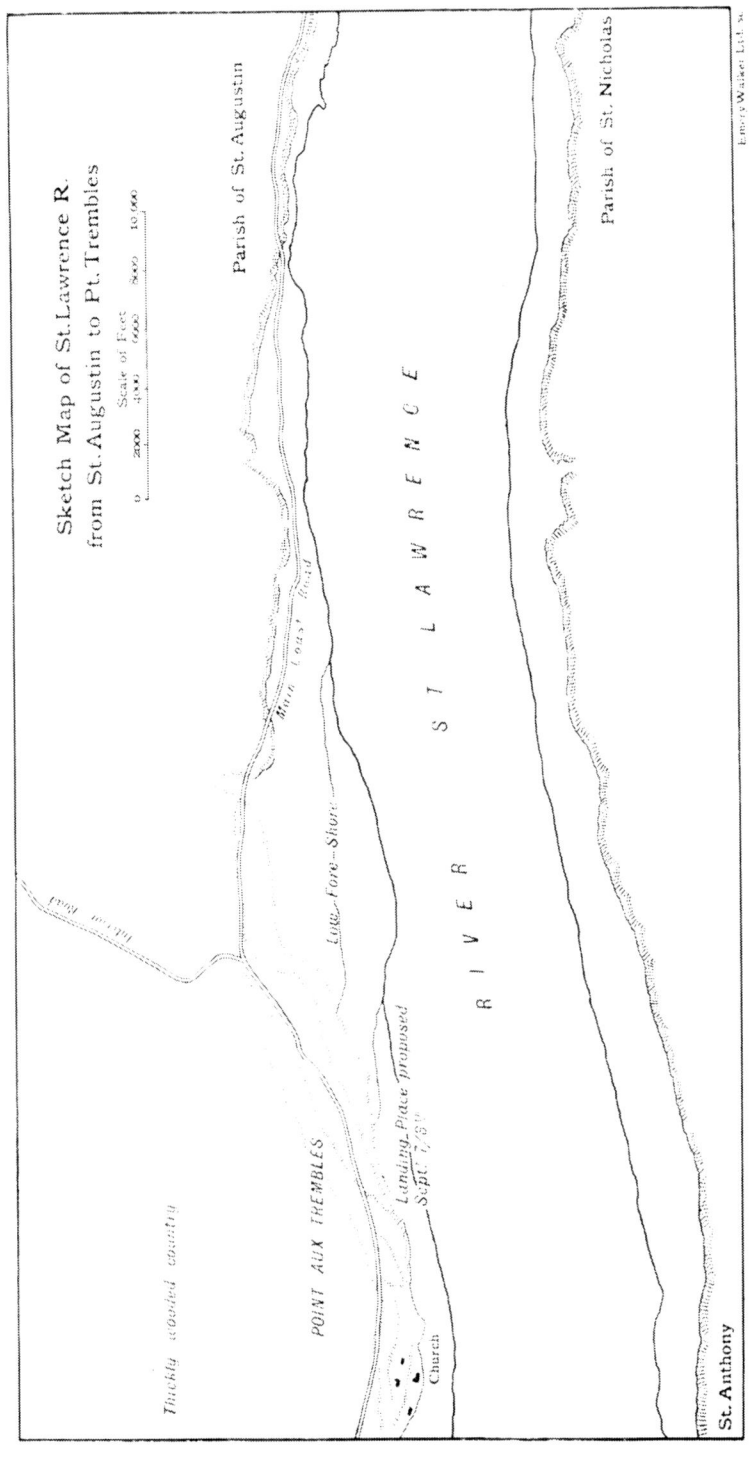

Sketch Map of St. Lawrence R.
from St. Augustin to Pt. Trembles

Scale of Feet
0   2000   4000   6000   8000   10000

Parish of St. Augustin

Parish of St. Nicholas

Thickly wooded country

POINT AUX TREMBLES

Landing Place proposed
Sept. 7, 8th

Church

Main Coast Road

Low Fore-Shore

ST. LAWRENCE RIVER

St. Anthony

Emery Walker Ltd. sc.

enable him to report on the means of making such an attack.

In company with Admiral Holmes, Murray joined the ships on August 6, having marched at night probably to avoid discovery by the enemy. An interesting point occurs in his first report to Wolfe : " On my way I made a feint to land at St. Michel, where they are entrenched and sufficiently on their guard." In the draft of this report, which is before me, come the words : " I did this with a view to," but these were erased. We are left in doubt what the intention was, but it seems very probable that the sentence might be completed by the words, " ascertain if an attack at this place was now possible."

On the 8th (August) he had arrived off Pointe-aux-Trembles, and here he made an attack which was unsuccessful. He gives an interesting description of the action, which, however, I need not quote ; but it may be noted that the attempt was made close to the church on the Point, and considerably higher up than the plaçe which will be referred to again later.

On the 9th (August) Murray established himself at St. Anthony on the south bank, and sent a note to Wolfe, which is rather characteristic :

" I have attacked them three times with various success. Hitherto they may sing *Te Deum*, but the tune will certainly be mine in a few days . . . the ship scheme (no doubt the capture of the French frigates) won't do. I fear we want water to carry us much higher."

On the 11th (August) he is still at St. Anthony, awaiting a suitable tide to enable him to carry out the attack on Deschambeau,* some fourteen and a half miles further upstream, which formed one of the objects of the expedition. The tide was not suitable until the 18th, and Murray brought his troops up at night † and succeeded in outwitting the

* Properly, D'Eschambault, a family of that name, of which Madame de Vaudreuil was a member.

† This night movement of Murray's fourteen miles up a hitherto unreconnoitred part of the river was a remarkable feat, and shows that pilots, or people acquainted with the locality, were available.

enemy and destroying the stores, which were of considerable importance.   After this experience Murray made a significant report to Wolfe, which included the following :

" Tides are more *aporté* (suitable) to attempt anything you may think proper against the north shore, from Cap Rouge to Jacques Cartier * . . . a landing from Gentleman's Bay † may be stole at any time but it must be by night and at high water.   The impossibility of doing it under the cover of your ships and the nature of the shore makes that necessary.   The night of September 2 the soonest the tide will answer."

On the night of September 2 the tide turned to flood at about 10.10 p.m.   There would be no moon.   Murray's advice clearly was to approach " Gentleman's Bay " by land, embark in flat-bottomed boats after dark, and effect a landing on the north shore above Cap Rouge.   *He was opposed to using the ships, as their movements could not be concealed.*

The report quoted is dated August 25, and at nightfall on this date Murray returned and rejoined at Point Levis. He found that Wolfe had been very ill during his absence, and was scarcely yet convalescent.   There was some tendency on Wolfe's part to blame Murray for a too prolonged stay in the upper river ; but it is hardly possible that he could have completed the object in view at Deschambeau before the 19th, or have returned before the 21st, so that I do not think there is much real ground for complaint ; besides, it appears that Murray awaited Wolfe's decision whether further operations were to be conducted.‡

Immediately after Murray's return there were important councils of the General and his principal officers, together with Admiral Saunders.   Wolfe's illness had caused him to view the situation despondently ;   he recognised the

* Jacques Cartier is about midway between Pointe-aux-Trembles and Deschambeau, and not far from a place referred to later as the Height of St. John.

† *See* p. 112.

‡ Wolfe's report to Pitt, dated September 2.

mistakes that had been made,* and being himself too unwell to continue to direct, he instructed the brigadiers to consult together as to the best steps to take. The admiral had intimated that there was little time to lose, as the fleet could not, in his opinion, safely remain in the river much longer. The document which Wolfe caused to be addressed to the brigadiers on this occasion was remarkable. Although not dated, I think from other evidence that it issued from the headquarters at Montmorency on August 27, and was addressed in the first place to General Monckton at Point Levis. Townshend and Murray were both at Montmorency, and no doubt the intention to call a council at Point Levis was communicated to them.

The letter ran as follows :

" That the public service may not suffer by the General's indisposition, he begs the brigadiers will be so good to meet and consult together for the public utility and advantage, and consider the best method to attack the enemy.

" If the French army is attacked and defeated, the General concludes, the town would immediately surrender, because he does not find they have any provisions in the place.

" The General is of opinion that the army should be attacked in preference to the place, because of the difficulties of penetrating from the lower to the upper town, in which attempt neither the guns of the shipping or of our own batteries could be of much use.

" There appears to be three methods of attacking the army. ' First : In dry weather a large detachment may march in a day and a night so as to arrive at Beauport (fording the Montmorency eight or nine miles up) before day in the morning. It is likely they would be discovered upon this march on both sides of the river. If such a detachment penetrates to the intrenchments, and the rest of the troops are ready, the consequences are plain.'

" 'Second : If the troops encamped here (*i.e.* Montmorency Camp) pass the ford with the falling water, and in the night march on directly towards the Point of

* Letter to Saunders of August 30.

Beauport, the light infantry have a good chance to get up the Woody Hill, trying different places and moving quick to the right would soon discover a proper place for the rest. The upper redoubt must be attacked and kept by a company of Grenadiers. Brigadier Monckton must be ready off the Point of Beauport to land when our people get up the hill, for which signals must be appointed.'

" ' Third : All the chosen troops of the army may attack at Beauport at low water. A diversion must be made across the ford an hour before the second attack.' "

It is very difficult to believe that Wolfe was the author of this document He was asking for the consideration of the best procedure, and yet defines three schemes—or perhaps I should say two, for the two last are almost identical, *which had already been tried* and been unsuccessful ; moreover, he must have known that the brigadiers were opposed to them. I can only suppose that he was still too unwell to attend to the matter, but following the urgent solicitations of Murray, had given instructions to call a council, and had left the wording to a subordinate.

At all events, there is a complete absence of any mention of the original conception of an attack at St. Michel or of any movement above the town, and the only reference to it at this period is contained in a letter to Admiral Saunders, written on August 30 : " My ill state of health hinders me from executing my own plan ; it is of too desperate a nature to order others to execute." It is, however, not easy to see how an attack on St. Michel, or any other place, should be more desperate than any of the three schemes referred to above.

The " reply " of the brigadiers was delivered on August 30 (it was dated August 29), and in it they definitely decided against Wolfe's suggestions, and recommended the abandonment of Montmorency and a descent on the north shore above the town, where " we are (shall be) between him (The French commander) and his provisions, and between him and the army opposing General Amherst." The " reply " was accompained by a " plan " for carrying out the advice, and this plan makes it perfectly clear that in proposing a landing on the north shore above the town the brigadiers had no thought of any place in the neighbourhood of Quebec, such as St. Michel. The army was to proceed by land and encamp on the other (west) side of the Étchemin, and the landing was to take place between the Cap Rouge River and the Height of St. John.

There is some misconception regarding this reply of the brigadiers. The copy hitherto quoted as representing their views is similar to, or taken from, the one contained in the British Museum (Newcastle Papers, Addl. MS. 32895, f. 90). This is obviously not an original, for it is unsigned, and written on the same sheet and in the same handwriting as the copy of Wolfe's letter, to which it is a reply. A copy signed by the three brigadiers exists in the Public Record Office (Chatham Papers, vol. 50), which has been unaccountably overlooked. This differs from the " Newcastle " copy in several details, and is no doubt the genuine document submitted to Wolfe. In his *Life* of his Ancestor, Col. C. V. Townshend gives the paper taken from " originals " among the Raynham Papers ; but I presume this is unsigned, at all events it is similar to the " Newcastle " copy. The " Newcastle " letter seems to have been a rough draft, subsequently altered, and, especially as to the last paragraph, indicates that the council had some difficulty in wording their answer.

The signed paper in the Chatham correspondence commences with a paragraph which is omitted in the " Newcastle " copy.

" Having met this day, in consequence of General Wolfe's desire, to consult together for the public utility and advantage, and to consider of the best methods of attacking the enemy, we read His Majesty's private instructions, which the General was pleased to communicate to us, and considered some propositions of his with respect to our future operations, and think it our duty to offer our opinion as follows."

Then follows the body of the report, which is the same in both copies, but the last paragraph in the rough draft is quite dissimilar to the signed original. I have put the two below side by side.

Newcastle MS. Rough Draft.

" With respect to the expediency of making an immediate attack or the postponing it, to be able the more effectually to prevent the harvest and destroy the colony, or with a view of facilitating the operations of our armies now advancing into the heart of the country, we cannot take upon us to advise, altho' we cannot but be convinced that a decisive affair to our disadvantage must enable the enemy to make head against the army under the command of General Amherst already far advanced by the diversion this army has made on this side."

Public Record Office Signed Original.

"With respect to the expediency of making an immediate attack or the postponing it, more effectually to prevent the harvest and otherwise distroy the colony, or with a view to facilitate the operations of General Amherst's armys now advancing into the heart of the country, we cannot presume to advise, although we are fully convinced that the progress of his troops hath, and must still depend upon the detention of, the greatest part of the enemy's force on this side, for the defence of their capital.

"We cannot conclude without assuring the General that whatever he determines to do, he will find us most hearty and zealous in the execution of his orders."

Following the copy in the Newcastle Papers, Mr. Edward Salmon makes some very caustic remarks : " The brigadiers proposed a plan but with the same dip of ink cast doubts on the expediency of carrying it out. If they had been men of less grit and less worthy soldiers one might be forced to unpleasant conclusions." *

The correct version in the Chatham Papers is, however, not open to the same comment. It is apparent from the

* *Makers of National History: Wolfe,* by Edward Salmon.

FACSIMILE OF THE LAST PARAGRAPH OF THE REPLY TO GENERAL WOLFE.

From the original in the Chatham Papers, Public Record Office.

words, " With respect to the expediency," etc., that a question, not included in the original references, that is, whether the attack should be made immediately, or whether the raiding of the parishes, which had already had an immense effect on the Canadians, should continue, had been conveyed, perhaps by a verbal message, to the brigadiers. Without knowing something of the genesis of the question and the form in which it was put, it is difficult to form a just opinion of the reply. We know, however, that at the very time that the question was put Wolfe had already taken the step of detaching a strong force, which numbered not less than one-fourth of the available strength, on a raiding expedition *down* the river,* and it is more than probable that the brigadiers could not acquiesce in this serious weakening of the army. To what extent they had expressed themselves on this subject there is nothing on record to show. But it may well be that the wording of the paragraph, which was apparently the subject of discussion and alteration, was not unconnected with the despatch of this contingent.

They stated a decided opinion on the direct propositions put before them, and a decided opinion on the question asked as to the best method of attacking the enemy ; they gave their reasons and the plan they suggested for carrying it out, but they did not feel it their duty to assume responsibility for the general conduct of the campaign, the more so that, while asking for their views, the Commander-in-Chief had already taken action in a way they could not approve of.

So far as contemporary evidence is concerned, there is nothing to show that the action of the brigadiers in this matter caused any difficulty to the commander. Wolfe, in his letters to Pitt and to Lord Holderness, on

---

* John Knox, under date July 30 and 31, states that the force consisted of 170 volunteers of the 43rd Regiment with a detachment from the two brigades at Montmorency and a " large corps " of Rangers, the whole commanded by Major Scott. They proceeded down river as far as there are any settlements. The whole detachment numbered 1600 men (Doughty), and returned on September 20, *after the fall of Quebec,*

September 2 and 9 respectively, merely refers to the unanimity of the brigadiers as to the method of attack. Mante, in his *History*, written in 1772, quotes the letter without the last paragraph; and perhaps a still better argument against any supposition that the signed document contained anything which could be construed in a sense derogatory to the brigadiers, is the fact that it escaped the mordant wit of the author of *A Letter to an Honourable Brigadier-General*. This letter, written in 1760, was obviously inspired, if not written, by some one in close contact with the events of the campaign—probably a member of the headquarter staff. It is a bitter attack on Townshend, and it is unbelievable, if an adverse construction could have been put on it, that an opportunity for criticism of this paragraph would have been neglected.

Wolfe accepted the advice of the brigadiers, and at once proceeded to put it into execution. The retirement from Montmorency was effected very skilfully and without loss, and by September 6 the army had been transferred to the ships and boats lying off the Étchemin River. The two war-ships in the upper river had been reinforced by the *Lowestoft* (frigate, 28 guns), the *Hunter* (sloop, 10 guns), and the *Seahorse* * (sloop, 20 guns). Thus the naval force was now ample, but the addition only just arrived in time, for a movement was afoot to make an attack on the *Sutherland*, and 490 sailors had been despatched from Quebec to bring down the French frigates for that purpose.† It is surprising that this rather obvious action had been so long deferred. The idea was, however, abandoned when the above-named vessels joined the English force (Bougainville correspondence).

The movements of the troops from Montmorency and of the ships up the river were closely watched, and well

---

* The *Lowestoft* and *Hunter*, after several attempts, made the passage past the town on the night of August 28. The *Seahorse*, together with two transports and two victualling vessels, got past the town on the night of August 31. Some accounts state that the first two got up at an earlier date, but this is incorrect.

† Montcalm's Journal.

known to the French. Assuredly the new scheme contained nothing in the nature of a surprise; thus, on September 5 Montcalm's Journal records : " *Une Colonne ennemie de quelque deux mille hommes est montée par terre jusqu'à la rivière d'Étchemin à la côte du Sud.*" On September 6 he records : " *On a vu marcher des troupes du camp de la pointe de Levis et remonter de la même manière que la veille.*" In the Bougainville correspondence we find the report of Remigny, an officer of the Regiment de la Sarre, who commanded the post at Sillery : " *La Colonne des ennemis m'a paru estre de 4 mil cinq cents h'mes, y compris les troupes legères qui formoient l'avant garde.*" Remigny, it may be noted, was an accurate and careful observer and very little escaped him.

To meet this new danger the French had considerably strengthened the corps under the command of de Bougainville, who was in charge of the defences above Quebec. On September 6 Vaudreuil wrote a letter, which detailed the force at his (de Bougainville's) disposal. From this we learn that :

At Anse des Mères et du Foulon were	100	men
The Samos Battery ..	30	,,
At St. Michel (the Anse is certainly intended)..	50	,,
At Sillery	100	,,
At Cap Rouge	250	,,
Flying Column available to support any of these posts	965	,, plus 130 cavalry
At St. Augustin	180	,,
At Pointe-aux-Trembles	190	,,
At Jacques Cartier ..	200	,,

This gives a total of 2195 men and the cavalry, and they included about 500 regular troops besides a picked body of the Montreal Volunteers, who were regarded as the best troops after the regulars. Two pieces of field artillery had also been sent.

K

So far as the evidence goes, and it is somewhat meagre, de Bougainville was satisfied that this force would suffice to enable him to repel any probable attack. We are informed that the remainder of the regiment of Guyenne, probably 300 men (the Grenadiers (50 men), and a picquet (50 men) of this regiment already formed part of the force) had been offered to him as an additional reinforcement, and one must conclude from the letters * that he did not desire it. The movements of this regiment became important and somewhat mysterious, and I shall refer to them again ; here it need only be mentioned that the addition of the regiment to de Bougainville's force was a different question to the one that arose afterwards of placing this corps in reserve near Sillery—or between that place and Quebec.

The army which Wolfe was able to collect at the Étchemin River numbered approximately 3700 men. One strong battalion (Webb's, 48th Foot) was left behind at Point Levis, and the Rangers did not accompany the troops, the greater part of them were absent, as already mentioned. There were also garrisons at Orleans and with the batteries at Pointe-aux-Pères and Levis.† It is not at all clear what artillery accompanied the force, and

---

* Bougainville correspondence.

† I do not know of any accurate statement of the number of troops that embarked at Goreham's post. In Wolfe's orders the distribution of the troops in boats and ships is given, but the figures are obviously round numbers, and total to 3660. In Knox's Journal the number of men present at the battle of September 13, in the corresponding units, was 3924.

The 7386 N.C.Os. and men included in Wolfe's embarkation return in the previous June (*i.e.* not including artillery and Rangers) may be accounted for as under :

Expedition above Quebec	3700
Webb's Regiment under Burton at Pointe-aux-Pères	650
Monckton's battalion at Orleans *	400 * *See* Bell's
Guard on sick, etc., at Levis *	300 Journal.
Sundry detachments with Scott in his expedition in Lower River	700
Killed, wounded, and missing during the operations to September 2	797
Sick, and sundry details	839
	7386

the point is of some importance when we remember that the ostensible object in view was to land and entrench a position. There were floating batteries and plenty of naval ordnance, and it may well have been the intention to land some of the guns thus available. A detachment of artillery, however, did accompany the force. Thus the total number of troops available was certainly small, and it is difficult to explain why a large body of Rangers, with some regulars, the whole amounting to about 1600 men, should have been detached on August 31 to raid the parishes bordering the lower reaches of the river. It would appear that having in hand the important operations now pending, as large a force as possible should have been retained. This detachment did not return until after Quebec had surrendered.*

Before returning to the movements of the army, it will be convenient to trace the movements of the fleet in the upper river and the corresponding action of the French. During the period of evacuating Montmorency, it is clear that Admiral Holmes had orders to distract the enemy's attention ; but as there were no English troops in the upper river, or at all events very few, it is rather surprising that Bougainville should have concerned himself. Thus on August 29 the *Sutherland* and the *Squirrel* were off St. Augustin. On the 31st they had ascended to Pointe-aux-Trembles, and Bougainville followed with his corps. On September 1 the squadron dropped down again to the neighbourhood of Cap Rouge—Bougainville still in attendance. On the 2nd the squadron dropped down river still further to near Goreham's Point, and Bougainville followed to Sillery. After this there was no particular change on either side from the 3rd to the 6th (September). On the 7th the squadron, with all the transports and troops, was off Cap Rouge, and Bougainville shifted his headquarters to this place, which was only a short march away from Sillery. From September 7 to 12 the squadron remained in the neighbourhood of Cap Rouge, and only a few isolated

* *Vide* Knox's Journal, vol. ii. pp. 54, 55, 136.

movements took place.   Thus the *Hunter* dropped up twice
to Pointe-aux-Trembles and then to Goreham's Point, and
the *Seahorse* was at Goreham's Point until relieved by the
Hunter; but these movements did not apparently call for
any on Bougainville's part.   He remained at Cap Rouge.
A good deal was said in the Bougainville correspondence
about the amount of marching and countermarching which
had to be undertaken by the flying column, but there
seems to have been rather exaggerated ideas on the subject.
On the English side the plan seems to have been to deceive
the enemy with movements of the ships and then to
descend on the shore secretly in boats.   This, at all events,
was the plan outlined by Murray both to Admiral Holmes
and to General Wolfe.   To the former he had written :
" What I attempt against them must be by surprise.
I never can surprise them by moving with the fleet."   To
the latter : " The impossibility of doing it (*i.e.* making a
surprise attack) under cover of your ships . . . makes
that necessary (*i.e.* a night attack)."

There seems little doubt, and the date of the movements confirms this view, that the movement of the ships
up and down the river was a part of the plan discussed at
the meeting of the generals and the admiral on August 29
and 30.   At these meetings Wolfe was not present, though
it is quite likely and probable that Murray discussed the
point with him when at Montmorency on August 26–27,
and no doubt received his orders.

It is now time to return again to Wolfe's army assembled
on the ships lying above Goreham's Point on September 6.

In what follows I have collected in detail the sequence
of events.   Perhaps this may be wearisome to the general
reader, but as the result of a good deal of research it will
be useful to correct the inaccurate opinions that have been
formed on the subject.   The object I have in view is to
show that General Wolfe did in fact intend to act upon
the advice given by the brigadiers, and attack the French
communications rather than the French *army ;* that he
suddenly, as the result of information received, altered his

intentions, and made the hazardous move on the Plains of Abraham, which resulted in the capture of Quebec; that the action he fought, which a great many writers represent as a decisive battle, was very far from being so; and that, in fact, it was Murray's operations of the winter and spring, aided in a most important degree by a squadron of the fleet under command of Commodore Swanton, which really brought about the decisive result of the conquest of Canada.

At dawn on the 7th the fleet and transports dropped up with the tide and anchored a little above Cap Rouge, a short mile above the place named by Murray, Gentleman's Bay, and in the morning Wolfe issued his battle orders for the approaching attack.* The army was divided into three brigades, that under Murray to contain Otway's (35th), Anstruther's (58th), and the Louisburg Grenadiers, under his kinsman, Alexander Murray. The order concludes thus :

"When the coast has been examined and the best landing places pitched upon the troops will be ordered to disembark, *perhaps this night's tide.* . . . The corps ordered for embarkation are to carry with them two days' provisions, which they are to receive immediately."

There was a little skirmishing with the enemy floating batteries at Cap Rouge, and the French showed themselves in force, making it quite clear where Bougainville's headquarters were. At 3.30 p.m. the troops entered the flat-bottom boats and made some movements, but obviously nothing was intended immediately, for at 4 o'clock the general,† accompanied by three brigadiers, left the fleet and ascended the river on board the sloop *Hunter ;* no

* In Townshend's diary it is stated that Wolfe and the three brigadiers met in the forenoon on board the *Sutherland,* so that presumably the scheme was discussed. No details of the discussion have been published.

† Townshend, in his diary, says that the three brigadiers went on board the *Hunter,* but that General Wolfe went up in his barge. It may be that he did so, but the logs of both *Sutherland* and *Hunter* show that he was on board the latter vessel with the brigadiers during some part of the reconnaissance.

doubt Wolfe intended to examine for himself the landing places between Cap Rouge and the Pointe-aux-Trembles.

A TIDE TABLE AT QUEBEC IN SEPTEMBER, 1759.

The undergiven information on the tides at Quebec on the important days of September, 1759, was kindly prepared by Mr. W. Bell Dawson, Superintendent of the Tidal Survey of Canada. In italics I have added the time of flood and ebb in the neighbourhood of Cap Rouge by adding fifty minutes to the Quebec time, which is near enough for the purpose of the calculations in this volume.

Full moon occurred at Quebec on September 7, 1759, at 0 h. 28 m.

	At Quebec.			At Cap Rouge.	
1759.	Time of high water.	Flood stream begins.	Ebb stream begins.	Flood stream begins.	Ebb stream begins.
	h. m.	h. m.	h. m.	h. m.	h. m.
Sept. 6	5.51	———	6.55	———	*7.45*
	18.19	13.50	19.25	*14.40*	*20.15*
,, 7	6.46	2.20	7.50 Full moon	*3.10*	*8.40*
	19.13	14.55	20.15	*15.54*	*21.05*
,, 8	7.40	3.20	8.45	*4.10*	*9.53*
	20.06	15.55	21.10	*16.45*	*22.00*
,, 9	8.33	4.20	9.35	*5.10*	*10.25*
	21.00	16.55	22.05	*17.54*	*22.55*
,, 10	9.26	5.20	10.30	*6.10*	*11.20*
	21.53	17.55	23.00	*18.45*	*23.50*
,, 11	10.20	6.20	11.25	*7.10*	*12.15*
	22.47	18.55	23.50	*19.45*	———
,, 12	11.15	7.20	12.20	*8.10*	*13.10*
	23.42	19.50	———	*20.40*	———
,, 13	12.10	8.20	0.45	*9.10*	*1.35*
	———	20.50	13.15	*21.40*	*14.05*
,, 14	0.38	9.15	1.40 Last quarter	*10.05*	*2.30*
	13.07	21.45	14.10	*22.35*	*15.00*

NOTE.—In the region of Pointe-aux-Trembles the tide movements would occur about 1 hour 20 minutes later than at Quebec.

The morning flood commenced at a little after 4 a.m., and it may have been this tide that Wolfe referred to in the order above quoted, " Perhaps this night's tide." The night of September 7 was full moon, and this would be all against getting the boats up secretly. Nevertheless, the position of the ships one and a half miles above Cap Rouge, where the bulk of the enemy force was, gave them a good start, and they would probably make at least a mile before discovery and almost certainly arrive at the rendezvous a full hour, probably more, before de Bougainville could overtake them. An alternative plan, possibly the one originally intended, would be to start at dusk at about 6.45 p.m. on the tail of the flood, which would carry the boats almost, if not entirely, the whole distance. What gives colour to this is that a demonstration, evidently concerted, took place by the boats of the fleet below the town at Point Levis. At 8.30 p.m. all the boats, manned with sailors and marines, put off and rowed towards the Beauport shore, making apparently as much noise as possible, for Montcalm records : "*Il sortoit un grand bruit de ces berges et des cris de hourra ! qui si leur dessein étoit d'attaquer annoncoient du moins qu'elles ne vouloient pas nous surprendre.*" The log of the *Pembroke* records that this demonstration was : "*To make a feint at Beauport, in order to favour the proceedings of General Wolfe above the town.*" These boats returned on shipboard at midnight.

The troops in the boats at Cap Rouge returned on shipboard at 6.30 p.m. We are not told why ; it is quite possible that Wolfe made a signal from the *Hunter* (which would be in view of the fleet during the passage to Pointe-aux-Trembles) by rocket or otherwise, that the attack was postponed. During the night the weather, which had been fine and warm, changed, a fresh north-easterly wind sprang up accompanied by rain. The *Hunter* returned with the night tide, rejoining the fleet at 2 a.m. on the 8th (September). The general and the brigadiers returned by barge.* Whatever the reason may have been, Wolfe decided to make no attack on the night of the 7th–8th (September). It does not seem that either the moon or the weather had anything to do with the decision ; it can only be supposed that, as a result of the reconnaissance, he considered that more precise orders were necessary, and the late hour of return prevented this being done at once. Another reason may have been that the night tide of the

---

* Knox makes this statement. Townshend, on the other hand, says, "The generals were obliged to lay on board the *Hunter* till two in the morning, when the tide carried them down to the Fleet." Possibly Wolfe returned alone in his barge.

following night (8th–9th September) would be more
suitable, as the flood began at Cap Rouge an hour later,
but subsequent events do not confirm this.

During the daytime of the 8th (September) no movement took place, but in the afternoon Wolfe issued fresh
orders, and from them one can understand to a great
extent the views that had been in his mind on the previous
day. These orders read as follows :

" At anchor at Cap Rouge, September 8. The *Laurel*
transport with ye Royal American battalion on board,
and the *Eden and Mary* with ye Light Infantry are to
proceed with the next tide under the convoy of ye *Hunter*
sloop opposite to ye Pointe-aux-Trembles and come to
anchor there."

This part of the order was actually carried out, and
without waiting for the tide and favoured by the wind the
Hunter and her convoy left at 5 p.m. and arrived off
Pointe-aux-Trembles at 8 p.m. This movement was
noted and remarked upon by the French (Bougainville
Letters), as of course would be the case, as the vessels
started during daylight. Wolfe's orders continue :

" The five battalions are to embark in the flat-bottomed
boats, so as to be in readiness to put off with the first of
the *morning's flood* (my italics). Captain Shads will be so good
as to conduct them, so as to arrive at the landing place
about an hour and a half before high water. If ye two
floating batteries cannot keep up, Captain Shads * will order
some of ye best rowing boats to take them in tow."

From this we learn that Wolfe had discarded Murray's
advice to make a surprise night landing. The " first of
the morning's flood " would be about 5.15 a.m. Starting
at this hour it would be daylight, and the arrival at the
landing place would be about 8 o'clock in the morning.†

---

* Captain Chadds of the *Vesuvius* sloop, who was in charge of
several landing operations, and evidently was much relied on as a
capable officer.
† Townshend's diary says, " The troops was ordered to land to-
morrow morning at 4 o'clock "—but this seems certainly wrong.
Possibly with the assistance of the N.E. wind they might have
started before the tide turned, but I do not think they could get
up by 4 a.m. in any case.

The passage of the ships the evening before had already alarmed Bougainville, so that obviously all precautions to oppose a landing would have been taken. The orders continue :

" When Colonel Young perceives that Brigadier Monekton's corps is landed, he will fall down opposite to ye place, and endeavour that his people and the light infantry may be put on shore at low water, if it can be done."

From this we learn that Colonel Young was in command of the troops that proceeded up the previous evening, and that the place of landing was below Pointe-aux-Trembles, but the reference to low water is not easy to follow. It would not be " low water " until late in the afternoon, and there may be some error in the instructions. The orders continue :

" The *Ann Elizabeth* with Bragg's regiment on board, and the *Ward* with Lascelles', are to fall up after ye flatbottom'd boats and anchor opposite to ye landing place, so that ye flat-bottom'd boats may endeavour to land them the same time, or if it cannot be done at low water."

From this we see that the last shred of " surprise " is removed by sending up ships with the boats in the morning, which could not fail to be observed. Here again the reference to low water is obscure, and apparently due to misapprehension. The remainder of these orders * is not of immediate interest.

The troops were to be in the boats at 2 a.m. (9th morning) ready for the movement (Knox), but an order was issued evidently late in the afternoon (8th) : " Seeing that the weather sets in bad, a signal will be made at one o'clock (a.m. on 9th, I presume) to lie fast in case it does not clear up." Presumably this signal was made, for no movement took place. In the morning of the 9th (September) the whole intention was definitely abandoned, " As the weather is so bad that no military operations can take place."

* The text of the orders is printed in *Literary and Historical Society of Quebec, Historical Documents*, Fourth Series.

Arrangements were made to put half the troops ashore under the command of Monckton and Murray, in order to refresh the men and relieve the crowded transports. In the evening of the 9th the weather cleared.*

A review of these operations leads to certain conclusions which have an important bearing on our subject. The first is that Wolfe certainly did intend to follow the advice of the brigadiers and effect a landing on the north shore near, but below, Pointe-aux-Trembles. It is not possible to accept any other explanation of his acquiescence in the brigadiers' proposals and the elaborate movements undertaken to put them into execution. The second is that had Wolfe made his descent on the night of the 7th–8th (September) he would have succeeded in placing his force astride the enemy's communications and brought about a decisive action. The third is that the dispositions for the attack proposed for the night of the 8th–9th (September) were faulty, by reason of their neglecting the element of surprise, and thus making no use of Murray's experience. The fourth conclusion is that the bad weather of the 8th (September) was in reality an advantage which the commander would have been wise to seize, for whereas the rain could have had little effect on the operations by water, it was an almost complete bar to movement by land, and probably Bougainville would not have been able to defend Pointe-aux-Trembles at all.

The question of what caused this sudden abandonment of the proposal put before him by the brigadiers is an interesting one which I will more fully discuss later; I will here merely emphasise that from September 9 the plan of a descent on the north shore near Pointe-aux-Trembles was definitely abandoned. On the morning of that day Major Barré arrived at headquarters from Goreham's Post. Barré was deputy-adjutant and Wolfe's confidant. Whether he brought some information is only

* On this date Colonel Young's detachment returned from Pointe-aux-Trembles. *See* letter dated 9th from Vaudreuil to de Levis, " Une frégate et quelques berges qui s'en étoient détachées ont rétrogradé de la Pointe-aux-Trembles."

conjecture ; at all events, it was shortly after his arrival that the orders were issued for the troops to land on the south shore, and it became clear that no further action was in contemplation for the time being. It was on this date that Wolfe wrote his last despatch, addressed to Lord Holderness. It is in very general terms, and makes no mention of the operations of the two previous days, although it contains an interesting résumé of the campaign. Regarding the business immediately in hand, it merely states, " We are now here (in the upper river) with about 3600 men waiting an opportunity to attack them when and wherever they can be best got at."

On September 10 a resolution was taken, which abruptly changed the whole character of the plan. At about 1.30 p.m. Wolfe, together with Monckton, Townshend, and McKellar (the chief engineer), and Colonel Carleton * and a small escort, left the fleet and proceeded in three boats direct to Goreham's Post (Admiral Holmes and Captain Chadds also appear to have been present), where they arrived at 3 o'clock in the afternoon (Bougainville Letters).† Arrived here, Wolfe announced, evidently to the great astonishment of his subordinates, that he intended to attack Quebec by landing at Anse au Foulon, a small bay situated some 1200 yards from the Anse St. Michel, and nearer to the town. This cove was used by the French as a landing-place, a small stream descended through a narrow wooded gorge to the river, and the banks on either side of the gorge were very steep and abrupt and to a great extent covered with trees or undergrowth. The foreshore of the bay is to-day a considerable area of almost level land—probably in 1759 there was less ; ‡ on the east, or

---

* Knox states that Carleton was present, but in a letter to Colonel Burton Wolfe refers to Carleton as being at Orleans. It is quite possible that he went to Orleans from Goreham's Post, in order verbally to communicate the intentions to Colonel Burton at Point Levis, and to the commander at the Isle of Orleans.

† Remigny, the acute French observer at Sillery Point, reported the arrival in great detail to Bougainville under date September 11.

‡ The railway which now runs along the foreshore has reclaimed a considerable amount of land.

Quebec, side of the gorge the land is at present little wooded—probably in those days there was only brushwood upon it. A road ran down to the landing-place partly along the eastern side of the gorge, and this was visible to the observers at Goreham's Post. The tents of the guard and some abattis or defences could also be distinguished.

So far as can be ascertained this dramatic change of intention was first announced when Wolfe called his principal subordinates together at Goreham's Post and pointed out, without apparently any hesitation, the place of attack ; it is certain that his decision had been arrived at before he left the fleet. The only indication, so far as I am aware, that this sudden change of plan was based upon personal examination on the part of Wolfe is contained in a remark in Townshend's diary under date September 8, when he says, " General Wolfe went a reconnoitring down the river." This incident is not mentioned by Knox, who followed the movements pretty carefully. An examination of all the circumstances makes it very improbable that Wolfe could have reconnoitred the Anse au Foulon on the 8th. We know that on that date he was busy with preparation and issuing orders for the proposed assault at Pointe-aux-Trembles on the following morning. We know, too, that at this time there was no war-ship between the fleet and Goreham's Point, and with numerous enemy canoes about it would have been hazardous for the General to venture in this direction * without an escort. It was a wet, blustery day, and to see anything of Anse au Foulon it would be necessary to row some fourteen miles there and back, the tide would not serve for the return journey until past 4 o'clock p.m., and the General could hardly have been back before late afternoon, when, judging from the orders given, he was on board the *Sutherland*. Finally,

---

* Knox tells us that on the morning of the 9th the *Seahorse* frigate was ordered down " to preserve the communication between Admiral Holmes' fleet and Goreham's Post." This was ordered in consequence of the adjutant-general's being chased by some canoes as he came up in a boat this morning.

there is no mention of the General's absence in the *Sutherland* log. I conclude that whatever reconnoitring Wolfe did on the 8th he certainly could not have gone so far as Anse au Foulon or anywhere near it.

We are thus driven to suppose that Wolfe's decision to abandon the plan proposed by the brigadiers and substitute one which unquestionably was his and his alone, was based upon some information he had very recently received, or, to put it another way, was based on the confirmation of some information which may have been before him for some time. Townshend's diary, already quoted, gives some indication ; he says, under date September 10, " By some intelligence the General has had he has changed his mind as to the place he intended to land." Clearly Townshend, at all events, attributed the change to " intelligence," and not to the result of any reconnoitring on September 8.*

That the new move came as a surprise to the brigadiers is shown by a letter from Murray to Townshend, which will be referred to again, but of which an extract will be useful here :

" I have no copy of the paper I sent by you to General Wolfe concerning his scheme of landing between Pointe-aux-Trembles and St. Augustin, but the public orders are a sufficient proof of his intention to do it, *and likewise of the suddenness of the thought of landing when we did* " (my italics).

From which we learn that, as might be anticipated, Murray had been called upon to report on the question of landing near Pointe-aux-Trembles, on which, of course, he had a full experience, and that the change of plan was " sudden." Moreover, it is clear that the brigadiers did not share the " intelligence " upon which Wolfe based his intention, for they evidently had little enthusiasm for the project, which indeed to all appearance was a desperate venture.

It is necessary to pause for a moment to consider what

* I have emphasised this, because it has a bearing on the subject of the next chapter, in which I examine the cause which led to Wolfe's abandonment of the brigadiers' plan.

happened at the meeting of the general officers at Goreham's Post in the afternoon of September 10. Murray was
not there, having been left behind at St. Nicholas to command the troops on shore. All the other chief actors were,
however, present. From Remigny's reports * we know
that the party landed at three o'clock, "*devant la poste de
la petite Maison*," and that all the officers, " *Monterent
jusqu'à la plus haute des Maisons qui sont sur le grand
Chemin*." It is not quite clear which house Remigny
referred to ; possibly the one known as Dalling's House,
but the point is not of much importance. It is at least
certain that the distance of the observers from the place
known as Anse au Foulon was not less than 2900 yards,
and it lay, not immediately across the water, but rather
to right of the observers. Across the water, facing the
observers, lay Anse de St. Michel, distant about 2200 yards.
We know that this latter place had for a long time been in
Wolfe's mind. What was the secret of his casting off this
old love and choosing a new and more distant place,
which, to all outward appearance, was no more favourably
situated, and which certainly could not be so well reconnoitred from Goreham's Post ? The " spy-glasses " of
our generals must have been unusually good, for we are
told they observed " an encampment of twelve or thirteen
tents and an abattis below it," also a " breastwork " ; a
" naked rock " was also noted, which was to form the landmark for the boats when approaching. The reconnoitring
party took to their boats on the return journey at 6 o'clock
(Remigny). The tide being at commencement of flood
they would reach the fleet by about 7.30 p.m.

The following day (September 11) orders were issued
for the troops on shore to hold themselves in readiness to
embark on shipboard early in the morning of September 12.
The distribution of the men in the boats to form the landing
party was detailed, but apparently in round numbers, and
from this we learn that the first landing party would consist
of thirty flat-bottom boats, plus five ships' boats, containing :

* Bougainville Correspondence.

Howe's Light Infantry..   ..   ..   400 men
(28th) Bragg's battalion   300   ,,
(43rd) Kennedy's battalion   200   ,,
    (A part of this battalion was with
       Scott's expedition below Quebec.
       The *Seahorse* log gives the number
       as 248 including officers.)
(58th) Anstruther's battalion   300   ,,
(47th) Lascelle's battalion   250   ,,
(2/60th) Monckton's battalion   ..   50   ,,
(78th) Fraser's Highlanders   200   ,,

Total of the first landing party   ..   1700   ,,

Following the boats the *Lowestoft*, *Squirrel*, *Seahorse*, and *Hunter*, three armed vessels, two transports, and some ordnance vessels (number not given) were to carry:

(15th) Amherst's battalion   ..   ..   300 men
(78th) Fraser's Highlanders   370   ,,
Louisburg Grenadiers   240   ,,
(2/60th) Monckton's battalion   ..   400   ,,
(35th) Otway's battalion   400   ,,
    With Artillery not detailed.   —
    Total of force in ships   1710   ,,

The third contingent to be ferried across from the Point Levis side is not referred to in Wolfe's orders, and the actual number stands in some doubt. The full available strength would be about:

(48th) Webb's battalion, about   ..   652* men
(3/60th) Lawrence's battalion, about   516*   ,,

Total of Colonel Burton's force   ..   1168   ,,

This makes a grand total of 4578 men and N.C.O.s (excluding officers), which agrees very nearly with Knox's statement of the numbers present at the battle of September 13. The evening of this date (September 11) the *Seahorse* dropped up river from Goreham's Point and joined the

* These are Knox's figures.

fleet above Cap Rouge, in order to take her place in the forthcoming operations. The *Hunter* came down to relieve her at the station. These were the only movements of the fleet, and the intention expressed by Wolfe in a letter to Colonel Barton, dated September 11, of sailing " up the river a little higher, as if intending to land on the north shore," *was not carried out.*

It is a point for remark that Wolfe, having decided on the 10th the place of attack, did not at once proceed to put the plan into action. The troops could equally have re-embarked on the 11th as on the 12th. The tide was equally suitable, rather more so. On the face of it, so far as can be seen, there was no special reason for the delay. The impression is given that the commander was waiting for something. The day of the 11th passed in quiet. On the Beauport side, the sailors of the fleet took some buoys out and anchored them towards the north shore, a proceeding intended to give the French the idea that an attack in this quarter was pending. A manœuvre which succeeded well enough, and the extraordinary tenacity with which Vaudreuil retained a large part of his army east of Quebec, though well aware that the bulk of his enemy had gone west, is one of the strangest facts of the campaign.

On the 12th (September) the troops commenced to re-embark from St. Nicholas, where, Townshend tells us, the salutary fear that Murray had instilled on his previous visit kept the inhabitants from making any attempts against them. In the afternoon (4 p.m.) Murray and Townshend went on board the *Sutherland*. Probably Monckton was already there. Neither Knox nor Townshend mention this in their diaries, but the fact is recorded in the log of the *Squirrel*. This visit is of some importance with reference to a correspondence * which it must be presumed had taken place earlier in the day, or possibly late at night on the previous day, for the dates seem doubtful. The first letter is dated on board the *Lowestoft*

* British Museum, Addl. MSS., No. 35893, vol. 50, ff. 232–237.

September 12, and is signed by Monckton, Townshend, and Murray. It runs :

" Sir, as we do not think ourselves sufficiently informed of the several parts which fall to our share in the execution of the descent which you intend to-morrow, we must beg leave to request from you as distinct orders as the nature of the thing will admit of, particularly *the place or places* we are to attack. This circumstance (perhaps very decisive) we cannot learn from the public orders, neither may it be in the power of the naval officer who leads the troops to instruct us.

" As we should be sorry, no less for the public service than ourselves, to commit any mistakes, we are persuaded you will see the necessity of this application, which can proceed from nothing but a desire to execute your orders with the utmost punctuality."

It is certainly the case that such of the " Public Orders " as have come to light give no detail whatever, such as had been given on previous occasions of the brigading of the troops, or the order in which they were to take post after landing, and apparently the brigadiers, having waited almost to the eleventh hour for these details, felt, and I think with reason, that they should be informed. The incident indicates that this change in the plan was opposed to the sense of the brigadiers, and indeed, Admiral Holmes, who was in close touch with the whole affair, says as much in a despatch written by him a few days later.

Wolfe's reply is addressed to Monckton, and is dated September 12 :

" Sir, my reason for desiring the honour of your company with me at Goreham's Post yesterday * was to show you, as well as the distance would permit, the situation of the enemy and the place where I meant they should be attacked. As you are charged with that duty, I should be

---

* " Yesterday " would mean September 11, but the visit to Goreham's Post was on the 10th. Possibly both this letter and the one to which it is a reply should have been dated 11th and not 12th. It is curious that the captain's log of the *Sutherland* records the visit as having taken place on the 11th, but it is certain that 10th is the correct date.

glad to give you all further light and assistance in my power.

" The place is *called* Foulon, distant about two to two and a half miles above Quebec, where you remarked an encampment of twelve or thirteen tents and an abattis below it."

At this point let us note that Wolfe's terms of reference to this place, Anse au Foulon, are a little remarkable. It is not a name which had appeared previously in any of the various records of the campaign, and it was clearly not known to the brigadiers. Its distance was about one and a half miles above the town and not two and a half miles, which appears to indicate that Wolfe himself was somewhat new in his acquaintance with it. The letter continued:

" You mentioned *to-day* that you had perceived a breastwork there, which made me imagine you as well acquainted with the place as the nature of the thing would admit."

This indicates that Wolfe and Monckton had been in consultation on the subject either on the 11th or 12th (September), and adds to the mystery of why the General had not given his general officers a fuller knowledge. Clearly they had been informed that the place of the abattis and breastwork was the point of attack, but apparently the detail of the movement and the name of the place had not been given them. The letter continues:

" I took Captain Shads with me also and desired the admiral's attendance (Holmes), that as the former is charged by Mr. Saunders with conducting the boats he might make himself as much master of his part as possible, and as several of the ships of war are to fall down with the troops, Mr. Holmes will be able to station them properly after he had seen the place. I have desired Mr. Holmes to send the boats down half an hour before day, *as you desired,* to avoid the disaster of a night attack, and I shall be present myself to give you all the assistance in my power."

This passage makes it clear that Wolfe had discussed the matter with Monckton verbally, and had apparently at first designed an attack at an earlier hour, but had yielded to Monckton's aversion from a night landing. In this Monckton evidently was not at one with Murray, who had already successfully carried out a night attack at Deschambeau, and was in favour of this method. The rest of the letter need not be quoted, but the tone of the whole correspondence is eloquent enough of the astonishment and aversion of the brigadiers to the new plan of operations. It is probable, almost certain, that at the meeting on the *Sutherland* in the afternoon of the 12th (September), already referred to, Wolfe entered into more details, for the brigadiers fell into their places during the actual landing without confusion. We know now that Monckton was in command of the first landing from the boats, with Murray as his second, and that Townshend commanded the landing of the troops that remained on the ships. The whole story makes it absolutely certain that neither Murray, Townshend, nor Monckton had anything to do with the choice of Anse au Foulon as the place of attack.

In the night of the 12th (September) at 11 p.m.* two deserters came on board the *Hunter*, then stationed off Sillery Point, bringing information that a French convoy of provisions was expected down the river from Cap Rouge that night. Having in view the strict orders that existed that deserters were to be sent immediately to headquarters without any person putting any questions,† it may be taken as certain that these men were sent forward at once to Wolfe, and the several fantastic stories that have grown round this incident may be dismissed. There is no reasonable doubt that Wolfe was in possession of the information brought by the deserters before the troops started for the attack, and furthermore, that he received it, so far at all events as these deserters were concerned, a very short time before the boats started. There is also no doubt that

---

* *Hunter* log.
† Order of August 4, quoted by Knox: " The officer . . . is not to permit him to be examined or any questions asked him by any person whatsoever until he is presented to the General."

the stories told, partly in connection with these deserters, that the captain of the *Hunter* was about to fire on the troops, mistaking them for the convoy, and not being aware of the proposed attack, have no foundation. The *Hunter* was, in fact, sent down on September 11 by the admiral for the express purpose of aiding the movement, and I have not the least doubt that Captain Adams had received confidential instructions.

On September 12 Wolfe issued his last orders to his army. He referred to the progress of the commander-in-chief, Amherst, and the division of the enemy, the discontent of the Canadians, and the scarcity of provisions in the enemy's camp ; and concluded with a phrase which should be better known, and which surely deserves as wide a recognition as Nelson's famous signal :

" *The officers and men will remember what their country expects from them*, and what a determined body of soldiers, inured to war, is capable of doing against five weak French battalions mingled with a disorderly peasantry."

Whatever opinions may be formed concerning Wolfe's strategy, or of the wisdom or unwisdom of the proceedings to which he was now committed, we must all agree to give tribute to his indomitable spirit. To me, after closely following his movements during all the days that followed Murray's return from the upper river up to this day of days which marked the last milestone in the rough road of his life, nothing can better indicate the truly heroic soul which controlled his frail body. Let us remember that during all this period he was barely recovered from a serious illness, and yet faced with ceaseless energy the physical exertion required by the activity which began by the abandonment of Montmorency ; and the not less fatiguing mental strain imposed by the important decisions which the commander of an army in the field has to take. Let us remember, too, that the consciousness of failure which he lays bare in his letter to Lord Holderness must have reacted on his sensitive mind, and rendered it more than ever difficult to adopt an independent line which, rightly or wrongly, he felt was the path of duty. Remembering this, let us revere the memory of a very gallant Englishman.

At 9 p.m. the troops of the first landing embarked in the boats under shelter of the ships. The tide did not serve until 1.30 in the morning, and we can better imagine than describe the long hours of suppressed excitement. The men knew that a big movement was afoot, and the most stolid and phlegmatic among them must have felt a thrill of anticipation. At 2 a.m. the flotilla cast off; the night, we are told, was clear; the moon was in its last quarter, and would give a fair light over the great river and render visible the precipitous wooded banks which arose on both sides. During the first three miles or so it would have been possible for the boats to keep at a distance from the north shore, which may conceivably have prevented observation from the enemy posts, but after arrival in the region of the Chaudière the river narrows, and the boats could hardly avoid discovery. We are told * that the intention had been to pass as close as possible under the banks of the south shore, but that on the representation of the naval officer in charge it had been found desirable to make the north shore, at least during the last stages of the journey; besides, it must be remembered that a genuine convoy, which the boats were to pretend to be, would in any case hug the north shore. However this may have been decided, it is certain that the passage of more than thirty heavy boats could not have been accomplished so silently or at such a distance as would prevent detection, and, apart from observers on shore, it was the practice of the French to have patrols on the water,† all of which points to the fact that the passage

---

* Townshend's rough notes. Townshend, however, could not have been present, as he was with the troops on shipboard, and not with the boats.

† *Relation du Siège de Québec* says, referring to the landing, " *Sans qu'on en eut de connoiscance, quoi qu'il y eut des canots d'observation sur cette côte.*" See also Montcalm's Journal, under date September 7–8, 1759, " *Nos rondes sur l'eau ont aperçu grand nombre de berges. . . .*"

of the boats must have been observed and presumably reported. We can only conclude therefore that very careful instructions indeed must have been given to all sentries and patrols to allow the alleged convoy of provisions to pass. It is also noteworthy that on the occasion of a previous genuine convoy it had been arranged that an escort should accompany the flotilla along the shore, and that passwords should be instituted to ensure that friendly boats should not be fired on (*see* Vaudreuil to Bougainville, August 23, 1759). Such an escort cannot have been provided on this occasion.

After passing Reveryns Point, opposite the Chaudière, which would be at a little after 3 o'clock in the morning, we may assume that a light would be in sight from the *Hunter* stationed off Sillery Point, and no doubt posted there as a mark for the officer in charge to make sure of his position. The log of the *Hunter* records the passing of the boats with several sloops at 3 a.m., but I think this hour must be only an approximation, for the boats could hardly get so far in one hour from the start, remembering that in the first stage of the journey the tide would not have acquired its maximum velocity of about four and a half knots an hour. The logs are, in fact, not always reliable as to exact hours, and appear to record the nearest hour and occasionally the half-hour, but seldom any smaller division of time.

The order in which the boats proceeded may be gathered from the instructions issued on the 11th. The light infantry,* under Colonel Howe, led. According to the author of the *Particular Transactions*, the foremost

* There were two distinct bodies of light infantry, that commanded by Major Dalling and that by Colonel Howe. The latter had as second in command Major Hussey and at least two captains, viz. Wiliam Delaune of the 67th, and Cardin. The last named is probably the same as referred to by Wolfe writing to Lord G. Sackville, " Cardin the American has a great deal of merit. Hotham has a letter from Murray recommending him in the strongest way upon former acquaintance in war " (Hist. MSS., 9th Report, Pt. iii.). I believe that Captain Donald McDonald of Frasers was also a captain under Colonel Howe. Captain Fraser, also probably of the Highlanders, was also in the corps, which was, I suppose, of four companies.

boat contained twenty-four volunteers under Captain Delaune, a bold enterprising officer, and a great favourite of General Wolfe's. This party was to make the first ascent of the bank. The corps was in eight boats, no doubt two boats to each company; probably a small interval separated this leading detachment from the six boats following conveying Bragg's (28th Foot), and behind them came in order the 43rd, 47th, 58th, and a detachment of Highlanders and American Grenadiers (2nd/60th) bringing up the rear. There is no mention at all of any Rangers accompanying the force, and presumably the whole of them were with Major Scott in the expedition down the river already mentioned.

At about the time that the boats, with the armed sloops following, reached the *Hunter*, all the war-ships and at least two transports at Cap Rouge (the *Sutherland* only remained at anchor) weighed and dropped down stream, that is, at 3 to 3.30 a.m. This movement was, of course, plainly visible from the north shore from Cap Rouge to Sillery. We remember that the second body of some 1700 men were on board, and that about an hour separated the two detachments as regards time. The wind, however, was favourable and the ships would rapidly overtake the boats, the two detachments being intended to arrive simultaneously at the rendezvous. The precise happenings when the leading boats passed Sillery Point and arrived near to the point of debarkation are somewhat obscure; no very clear account is forthcoming. From Sillery Point to the Foulon is approximately 2000 yards, and this would take about twenty minutes to cover. Several accounts tell us that the leading boats went past the appointed landing-place. What seems most probable is that the first two boats containing Delaune's company, with Colonel Howe, passed the Foulon and landed a little distance below; but it is not possible to believe that they could have been carried so far as Anse des Mères (as has been stated), which is some 2000 yards further on, and would take them twenty minutes to cover, and at least that

length of time to return on land after they had ascended
the cliffs there.* The other three companies of light
infantry, with Captains McDonald, Fraser, and, I suppose,
Cardin (though he is not mentioned), appear to have landed
at the proper place. It was this force which ascended at
De Vergor's post, and after a slight scuffle took possession
of it. Colonel Howe and Delaune, with the first body,
having ascended, made their way to the left, and joined
the rest, having run some risk of being mistaken for the
enemy as they made their way along the bank towards
the post. The advanced party having taken possession, the
remaining troops commenced and continued their landing.

The extent to which the landing was interfered with is
not very accurately known. Knox, whose statements can
generally be relied on when his information was first hand,
was not present at the first landing; he refers only to
sentries posted on the summit of the cliffs. The description
of Major Moncrief, confirmed by other sources, indicates
that the first party got up before any firing commenced,
and I think it is almost certain that De Vergor's post offered
no resistance until the light infantry was among them.
There was then some firing—De Vergor is said to have been
wounded (in the heel !) and taken prisoner. That there
were sentries on the beach is probable. The author of
Particular Transactions, who was probably present, says
that two sentries were passed without challenge, and the
third was apparently easily satisfied. The story, however,
is not reliable, though often repeated, for we are told that
when the sentry inquired what regiment was in the boats,
he was told " De la Reine," though, as a matter of fact,

---

* It is, however, to be noted that Anse des Mères seems to have
been a name somewhat loosely applied and covering any part of
the coast between Sillery Point and Cape Diamond. Thus, Chevalier
Johnston, in the *Dialogue in Hades*, says, " Nothing is more incomprehensible to me in all the conduct in Canada than your landing at
Ance des Mères on the 13th September at the foot of a steep hill,
when a few men with sticks and stones only must have easily beaten
you, and where we had three posts of 100 men each, one commanded
by Douglas, Captain of Languedoc, another by Rimini (Remigny)
Captain of La Sarre, and the third by De Vergor, Captain in the colony
troops, at whose post you made your descent."

this corps was not with Bougainville or in the neighbourhood of Quebec at all. If there is any truth in the story,
the words " De la Reine " may have been the password
already referred to.

The logs of several of the ships stationed off Point
Levis record that the sound of firing of cannon and small
arms was heard. On the *Stirling Castle* the entry was at
4.30 a.m., on the *Captain* and the *Centurion* the hour was
4 a.m. Piecing the various narratives together, it seems
no firing occurred until after the first landing of the light
infantry and their attack on the post, and that then the
battery at Samos, situated about 300 yards higher up the
river, opened fire on the boats * lying below and waiting
orders to land. This was no doubt the cannon heard by
the fleet, and the hour would be near 4.30 a.m. It is worthy
of notice that the ships which recorded this firing were at
anchor over five miles away from the Samos battery, and
Cap Rouge was approximately the same distance away
in the opposite direction.†

I have thus far followed in detail the events up to the
point of landing at the Anse au Foulon, partly because
these have not, I believe, hitherto been studied so closely,
but chiefly because it is necessary that an event of such
importance in the career of James Murray should be
carefully examined. In the next chapter I shall endeavour
to arrive at the reasons which led the General in command
to take this step, and to give grounds for the opinion that
it was fraught with serious consequences which would in
all probability have been avoided had the views of the
brigadiers, embodied in their " advice," been adopted.
From this point onwards to the capture of the town I
shall enter less into detail. The monumental work of

---

* It was this firing which Knox describes as having done some
damage.
It should be noted that the log of the *Seahorse* records that one
shot was fired over her from Quebec. If this is correct, it would
indicate that the town was aware of the movement a little after
5 o'clock a.m.
† The wind was south-west and was not strong, and the sound
of firing should have been heard at Cap Rouge as easily as at Point
Levis.

Dr. Doughty, *The Siege of Quebec*, and the careful research of Colonel William Wood in his book, *The Fight for Canada*, give all the information that is available on the events of the five days up to the capitulation, and it is unnecessary to repeat it, except in some phases of the affair.

While the army was assembling on the slopes above the landing-place the nature of the terrain imposed on Wolfe the necessity of advancing to higher and more open ground. It may be inferred from Knox's statement that the first troops to move off were the Louisburg Grenadiers,* 28th, 43rd, and 47th Regiments. The distance traversed was, to the Ste. Foy road, nearly a mile, and then about half a mile along this road toward Quebec. Knox says that about 6 o'clock the first detachment of the enemy was seen on the heights, and that then Wolfe wheeled to the right and commenced to form his line of battle. I should judge the time would be rather later, for it would take fully forty-five minutes to cover the distance in strange country and imperfect light. Knox does not refer to the advanced party which pushed forward another half-mile along the road and occupied the house or mill known as Borgias, which was situated close to the main road and near a junction with a road leading to the suburb of St. Roch. The troops at this point would be in full view of the General Hospital situated in the plain below on the banks of the St. Charles River, and we know from other sources that information was sent from the hospital between 6 and 7 o'clock of the approach of the English. The information, however, cannot have been the first to be received in the French camp, and the messenger must have met the French advanced detachments already filing up towards the heights.

According to Knox the 15th and 35th Regiments came up with the advanced guard after an interval, and they were followed by the 48th, 58th, the two battalions of the

* As the Louisburg Grenadiers were not part of the first landing, it is clear that this detachment did not move for some time after the troops had made good the ascent of the bank. It would hardly be daylight before 5.30, and this would probably be the approximate time of starting.

60th, and the 78th. Except the 58th these troops formed the second landing, which no doubt accounts for the delay, and the 58th had been detached to silence the Samos battery immediately after the first landing.

The remarkable feature of this operation is the confidence which Wolfe displayed regarding his rear. For a time, at all events, his force was divided and his communications with the shore scarcely protected, while he himself penetrated with a comparatively weak detachment towards an enemy numerically superior and in possession of a sufficient artillery,* and by all the rules of war he would also have to reckon with a force of 2000 men under Bougainville † operating on his flank and threatening his rear. What would have happened if De Levis had commanded above Quebec instead of Bougainville is a question the answer to which can scarcely be in doubt.

On the Quebec side extraordinary confusion reigned, and all the evil due to ill-defined responsibility on the part of the commanders. I do not propose to venture an opinion on the proportion of blame to be borne by Vaudreuil or Montcalm. The former, by his writings, lays himself open to the greater suspicion ; but it may be that Montcalm's attitude brought about some of the troubles which might have been avoided by a greater display of tact. One thing seems clear, that some evil genius was at work which did not hesitate to play on the weaknesses of both and bring them into conflict for personal ends. The journals and diaries of the events in Quebec on September 12 and 13 are too obviously coloured by the partisanship of the writers to be entirely reliable. De Levis' Journal, which as a rule gives a moderate and impartial view, is in this case of little use for reference, for he was not present, and what he has written is almost word for word, with some

---

* That the enemy would not bring the artillery force at his disposal into action was a factor on which Wolfe could hardly count.

† Bougainville was thirty years of age at the time, and his reputation was rather that of a scholar than a soldier. He was author of a treatise on the Integral Calculus at twenty-three, and a Member of the Royal Society of London, where he had been stationed in the Embassy.

minor amplifications, similar to the account of the Chevalier
de la Pause, who, since he also was not present, must
obviously have received it from a third person not named.

The Chevalier Johnston, as friend and also aide-de-
camp of Montcalm, has left an account of personal contact
with Montcalm which certainly carries the impress of truth
on the writer's part, so far at least as he could be acquainted
with the facts, but no doubt Johnston was at no pains to
view the events in any light unfavourable to his friend and
commander. At all events, he was certainly an eye-witness,
as was also the writer of the last part of Montcalm's
Journal, and both accounts agree in many details. Johnston
tells us that no intimation of any attack above Quebec
was conveyed to Montcalm, and that between 6 and 7 in
the morning Montcalm, accompanied by Johnston, set
out for Vaudreuil's headquarters, and learnt, to their
surprise, that the English army was on the Heights of
Abraham. Johnston was at once sent to order Poularies
(Colonel of the Royal Roussillon Regiment) to keep
200 men at the Beauport ravine and send all the
rest of the left of the army to the Heights of Abraham.
What followed is certainly very circumstantial. Johnston
found Brig.-General de Sennezergue, and M. de
Lotbinière, an aide-de-camp of Vaudreuil, with Poularies,
who showed Johnston a written order signed Montreuil,
that not a man was to stir from the left.* Johnston
declared on his honour that his message was word for word
Montcalm's order, and entreated them to have no regard
for the orders signed "Montreuil," "as the want of 2000
men which formed the left must be of great consequence."
There are other details, but Johnston left De Sennezergue
irresolute and doubtful how to act, and spurred to rejoin
Montcalm on the heights. This would be near 8 o'clock
a.m.

---

* Compare the statement made by the author of *Memoirs sur
le Canada:* " *M. Vaudreuil donna au contraire ordre au Canadiens
de rester et leur defendit de passer la rivière ne voulant pas risquer une
bataille, par la persuasion de Cadet et quelques autres qui y avoient
un intérêt particulier.*"

According to Johnston, the choice of the battle-ground was not Montcalm's. He says that the picquets and part of the troops were already marched up to the heights before Montcalm arrived or even knew of the landing, and all the right of the army was marching in the same direction when he came on the scene. We know from other sources that some troops had arrived not much after 6 o'clock, which makes it pretty certain that some part of the force had taken post before Montcalm was on the scene. The same authority gives Montcalm's view of the proper course, viz. to march by Lorette to Ste. Foy, and having joined hands with Bougainville to fall upon the English army.* We are also told that De Ramezay, the governor of the town, refused to send artillery when demanded by Montcalm.

The other eye-witnesses' account, albeit likewise not innocent of bias, tells us that a little before daybreak (that would be about 4.30 a.m.) shots were heard above Quebec. A signal was made from the town, " qu'il avoit passé quel qu'chose." This seems to confirm in some degree the statement made in the footnote to p. 155, and fixed the time at which the alarm was first given, viz. about 5 o'clock a.m., and incidentally confirms, to some extent, Johnston's statement that no intimation was given to Montcalm. At daylight all appeared quiet, says the narrative, when a fugitive from the post at Foulon gave the alarm. But even this does not appear to have greatly disconcerted the writer, whose statement, however, is by no means clear. Some time certainly elapsed before he (the writer) thought it necessary to proceed to the heights, where he found Montcalm ranging the troops, as they arrived, in battle order. This was between 7 and 8 o'clock. The writer refers to seeing Wolfe's army stretching from the Ste. Foy road towards the river, and mentions his (Wolfe's) holding the fortified advanced post (Borgias House), which, however, was shortly afterwards set on fire. He relates a short conversation with Montcalm, who

* There can be no doubt that this course would have been the proper one to pursue. *See also* the remarks on p. 165.

said, " We cannot avoid an action.   The enemy is entrenching—he has already two field pieces.   If we give him time to establish himself we shall never be able to attack with our small numbers."   And the Marquis added, " *Avec une espèce de saisissement, Est il possible que Bougainville n'entends pas cela?* " *   This account also indicates that Montreuil was responsible for the first dispositions of the troops before the arrival of Montcalm, and this is confirmed by the author of the statement copied by De Levis and De la Pause, already referred to, " *Le Major-Général (Montreuil) en fut instruit le premier par un fuyard . . . Il étoit non loin du pont prés duquel étoit rangé le régiment de Guienne, au quel il donna l'ordre à Marcher,*" etc. Assuming for the moment that this " fuyard " conveyed the first intimation, it can be safely deduced that it would take approximately an hour from the time of the first attack on Vergor's post before he could find and report to Montreuil, that is, about 5.15 a.m.

It is noteworthy that none of these accounts indicates the presence of Vaudreuil, who seems to have remained in rear ; but we have two letters, the one dated September 13 at 4.30 p.m., written to De Levis, in which he describes his action :

" *M. Le Marquis de Montcalm est arrivé avec le premier détachment* (this is almost certainly untrue). *Je faisois l'arrière —garde et faisois hâter le pas aux troupes de Milice qui étoient sur ma route . . . J'avois fait prévenir M. de Bougainville, qui dans l'instant s'est mis en marche du Cap Rouge avec les cinq compagnies de Grenadiers, deux pièces de canon, la cavalerie et ce qu'il avoit de meilleurs . . . il ne nous fallait qu'attendre le moment de l'arrivé de M. de Bougainville, parceque, tandis que nous l'attaquerions avec toutes nos forces, il serroit pris par les derriers, mais la malheur nous en a voulu, au point, que l'affaire s'est engagée avec trop de vivacité.*"

All this is hardly a frank statement.   Bougainville did not appear on the scene until after 11 o'clock.   In the

---

* Probably referring to the fire of the field pieces on either side.

position in which he was placed it is certain that Montcalm could not have avoided contact for so long a period.

The other letter, written on November 9 to the Minister Berryer or the Marquis de Belleisle, is even less creditable :

"*Toute la campagne, Monseigneur, a été caracterisée par des traits d'insubordination* (on the part of Montcalm !) *parfaite jusqu'au 13 Septr. ou il voulut absolument donner des preuves d'une autorité indépendante, sans s'enquiéter s'il perdroit ou sauveroit la colonie. Je lui écrivais de ne point prématurer l'affaire je me rendis avec mes aides-de-camp pour prendre commandement et attendre la réunion de nos forces j'eus la douleur de voir notre défaite au moment que je me promettais de battre l'ennemi.*"

The letter which Vaudreuil claims in this last quoted document to have sent was said to have been delivered by a mounted orderly after the army was assembled on the Heights. All the circumstances seem to indicate that the letter was a concoction of a subsequent date intended to throw the blame of the defeat on Montcalm. The facts appear to be that Vaudreuil, or at all events, Montreuil,* who was probably with him, heard of the attack some time near 5 o'clock, and without acquainting Montcalm set about bringing up the troops—in the first place the Guienne Regiment from the bridge-head, and the militia holding the right of the French line on the Canardière. It is only on this assumption that the Guyenne Regiment could have arrived on the scene by shortly after 6 o'clock, for they had fully one and a half miles to march. So that when Montcalm was made aware of the attack he found the disposition of the troops already decided. This is a point which it is important to emphasise, because, if the deductions are correct, they show that Montcalm was in no way responsible for giving battle in a disadvantageous position with a portion only of his force.

* Montreuil was an officer of the regular troops, and as such might be supposed likely to support Montcalm ; but he had been in the colony before Montcalm's arrival, and appears to have been attached to the Vaudreuil faction.

As regards the numbers available to oppose the English army, no very reliable record exists. We can give an estimate of the maximum number that could have been present, but it is very difficult to say to what extent this maximum may have been reduced. Thus, from the original 12,000 men probably available, we have:

Detached with De Levis	800	
Detached with Bougain-ville	2320	
Remaining on the French left	1500	(some accounts say 1900)
Remaining on the French right, say ..	500	
In garrison of Quebec, say	500	
Deserted, sick, killed, and wounded, about	1000	(very likely more)
Total ..	6620	

which would leave a maximum of about 5400 men for assembly on the plain, of which perhaps 2000 at the outside were regulars. The *Journal Tenu à l'Armée* gives the number at 4500, but these and all French accounts are likely to be on the low side.

It was at about 7.30 a.m. that Wolfe completed the deployment of his troops. Monckton's brigade occupied the right, Murray's the left, Townshend's the left rear. By 8.30 a.m. the preliminary French movements were completed, and Montcalm had assembled his available force on or close behind the ridge known as Buttes-à-Neveu,* and now decided on advancing towards the enemy. In doing so it is interesting to note he took precisely the same action which Murray took in the following spring, as we shall see; that is, he descended the gently

---

* It must be remembered that a large part of the force had marched between three and four miles from the French camps—an operation which, including warning and assembling the men, would have taken not less than two and a half hours to three hours, which tends to confirm that the first news was received near about 5 o'clock,

sloping terrain towards the plain. There was, however, this difference, that the distance to be traversed was much less in the present case, and contact between the two forces occurred after an advance of some 700 yards. It appears from various accounts that Montcalm's troops executed the first part of the advance in three columns, but after covering some 300 to 400 yards he formed in line, and the English at the same time advanced a short distance, bringing their left forward to meet the French line more squarely. The detail of the actual fight need not detain us long; indeed, it only lasted a few minutes.

The French line advanced rapidly over the remaining interval of some 400 yards, and commenced a desultory fire at about 130 yards, where it was probably almost ineffective, continuing to advance up to 40 yards, the English troops reserving their fire until at close range they poured in deadly and effective volleys. The French troops gave way at once and fled precipitately; but it must be said, for the credit of the troops of Old France, which had been victors in many actions during the war, that they were in this instance co-mingled with ill-disciplined militia, quite unaccustomed to steady movements or fighting in the open. They were, besides, hurriedly drawn together, and for many months had been subject to scarcity of food and munitions. Murray's brigade of the 47th, 58th, and 78th, forming the left of the line, pursued vigorously, with a view of cutting off the retreating enemy from the bridge of boats. It was at this juncture that General Townshend took command, both Wolfe and Monckton being out of action. Townshend's position during the battle had been one of importance in protecting the left flank from attack of Indians and Canadians, who sought, under cover of the brushwood, to steal round the flank; but he now found the line in confusion, owing to the pursuit, and prudently, as I think, determined to re-order his units, so that the event of Bougainville's approach could be met with closed ranks. Exactly why it was apparently anticipated and calculated that Bougainville would not arrive on the scene until after 11 o'clock there is nothing on the surface to show ; but that officer was, or was supposed to be, no more than five and a half miles away, and one would imagine, unless some exceedingly good reason to the contrary existed, that he would be calculated as on the move from at least the moment of the first firing at Samos, which would have brought him on the scene certainly before 8 o'clock. Yet at that hour, and apparently until a good deal later, there was no rear guard * at the Anse au Foulon, other than sailors and marines engaged in landing guns and stores. De Bougainville tells us that he knew nothing until 9 o'clock —an inexplicable statement that I will refer to again— but in any case it shows that he was able to cover the distance in from two to two and a half hours. Why, then, was such confidence shown that he would not put in an appearance until well towards 11 o'clock, when Townshend prepared to meet him ?

I will pause here for a moment to examine the actual results of the battle which has just been briefly described. We must remember that the plateau, or at least the elevated ground on one end of which stood the city of Quebec, formed, in a sense, an island, surrounded on the south side by the St. Lawrence, and on the others by the valleys of the Cap Rouge River and the St. Charles—at its broadest, perhaps two and a quarter miles in width, narrowing at the eastern end to a mile or thereabouts—on all sides approached by more or less precipitous banks. On the north side, in the broad flat valley land of the St. Charles, good roads on both sides of the river communicated with the French encampments on the Beauport side of Quebec and led westward via Old Lorette to Pointe-aux-Trembles, Three Rivers, and ultimately Montreal. We have seen that the whole force at Wolfe's disposal was only sufficient to cover a part of the elevated land at the narrow end of the Quebec " island." There was nothing, and could be nothing, which would enter into any prudent

---

* A battalion of Royal Americans was detached during the action to cover the landing-place, but this was not until about 10 a.m.

calculation, to prevent the French army from taking either the course of retiring by the St. Charles valley roads—as was, in fact, intended by Montcalm (p. 159)—well away from possible attack of so small a force as Wolfe had, or of retreating * by this route (as actually happened) in the event of defeat, and either of these alternatives was undoubtedly facilitated by the presence of a strong undefeated force, such as that of De Bougainville, which would prevent the invaders from acting at any considerable distance from their base.

It is this consideration which leads me to conclude that strategically it was a false move to attack the elevated " island " of Quebec at all, if, as seems reasonably certain, the plan proposed by the brigadiers had good chances of success, for that plan cut the retreat by the only possible route, and, moreover, *contained* all the opposing forces, not only preventing their access to their depôts of supply, but also rendering any further assistance, on their part, in the defence of the colony impossible. In his *History of the British Army*, Fortescue has put the case in a sentence : " The consequence was that the work was but *half done*, and as shall soon be seen only narrowly escaped undoing." It is because the work was only half done that in this story it becomes of particular importance to deal with the causes which influenced the decision, for on James Murray fell the onus of meeting conditions and repelling attacks which this error in strategy created or rendered possible.

For the moment, however, the victory was complete, much more complete than the victors knew or could have imagined. Bougainville, on arrival in the neighbourhood of Ste. Foy, and learning of the disaster which had overtaken the French arms, retired at once, and, on the opposite side of the St. Charles River, where the fugitives had gathered in a helpless mob, there can be small doubt that an attack

* The only possible chance of rendering the victory decisive was to cut off the fugitives from the bridge of boats, and Murray's advance attempted this, but actually only succeeded in driving the enemy before him, while the action of the Indians and Canadians and the fear of Bougainville prevented the pursuit being driven home.

would have resulted in a complete destruction of the French military strength east of Quebec.* Townshend, in his new position of commander of the British forces, has been blamed unfairly, I believe, for not showing greater enterprise ; but we must consider at least three things : the first, that his troops were probably physically incapable of further exertion, for they had not only a night in which little or no rest had been possible, but a day of tremendous activity, and, indeed, one might add, a considerable amount of activity and want of rest for several days previously ; the second, that it was impossible to know the extraordinary state of demoralisation of the enemy ; the third, that Bougainville's fresh troops still hovered, to an unknown extent, on their rear. To this we may add that the garrison of the town and its capability for offence was an unknown quantity. In these circumstances I do not think any impartial reader will disagree with the opinion that he was wise to content himself with holding what had been won.

To Murray the day had been a glorious one, and in the flush of victory he probably had little thought of the morrow. The brigade he led of the 47th, 58th, and 78th had taken the most active and prominent part in the victory, and perhaps it was a source of some particular satisfaction to their General when the Highlanders, drawing their broadswords, repeated the famous rush that won the game at Prestonpans and Falkirk, in which actions it is quite possible some of them may have taken part. The 47th, too, greatly distinguished itself, and it is said † might have entered the town on the heels of the fugitives, had they not been recalled.

Of the proceedings on the French side after the battle little need be said. They ended in a disgraceful, disorderly flight along the St. Charles valley roads the same night.

* I must again emphasise how decisively important the American Rangers, whom Wolfe had detached, would have been, could they have been let loose on the retreating French army at this juncture.

† I doubt if there is much in this, for the fugitives did not in fact enter the town, but passed it by the St. Charles bridge-head.

The evidence seems to show that Vaudreuil was greatly influenced by his evil genius, Bigot, aided, and perhaps even exceeded, by Cadet. Everything was abandoned in the camp, including the artillery. A wild panic had seized the men. With the exception of the Royal Roussillon Regiment, which, under its colonel, Poularies, appears to have maintained some discipline, not thirty men were together of any regiment—the whole resolved itself into a mob of fugitives, running as hard as they could. The Chevalier Johnston, who describes the retreat in language of indignation, adds: "In fact it would appear by this strange conduct that a class of men there, from interested views, were furiously bent on giving up the colony to the English as soon as they could have a plausible pretext to colour their designs."

Vaudreuil did at least one wise thing. He sent an express to De Levis requesting his immediate presence, and on the 17th the remnants of the army were reassembled at Jacques Cartier, and some semblance of discipline was at once imparted by this energetic commander. Action was taken to direct De Ramezay, the Governor of Quebec, to hold out until assistance came ; but this was too late, for without ever a shot being fired against the town De Ramezay capitulated on the 18th. For this action Vaudreuil attempted to inculpate his subordinate, but the latter was able to prove that his orders were from Vaudreuil himself, and that he had been left by the ignominious flight of his superior without means of sustaining an assault or even of withstanding a siege of short duration.

There are many incidents connected with the operations ending with the capitulation of Quebec that appear mysterious, and of these none is more so than the extraordinary number of casualties among the leaders. On the English side Townshend and Murray were the only two of the principal staff officers who escaped. Wolfe died gloriously, Monckton, Carleton, Barré, were all wounded. Montcalm, and both his brigadiers, De Sennezergue and St. Ours, were killed. One can almost suppose that the same evil genius, which rumour held was rushing the colony to ruin, had taken precautions that the men who knew too much should not survive. However this may be, it is singular that from sources widely different there emanated the idea that both Wolfe and Montcalm met their deaths from circumstances not connected with legitimate warfare.*

In the next chapter I propose to deal with what appears to be the *mystery* of Wolfe's landing at the Anse au Foulon, and at the same time to clear up, as far as possible, the point that has been much in dispute, viz. to whom the genesis of this plan was due. As regards the first, I think there is little doubt that secret information was conveyed to the Commander-in-Chief, leading him suddenly to abandon the plans put before him by the brigadiers ; as regards the second, it appears to me that many writers have confused the recommendation of the brigadiers to act above the town, that is, at a point above Cap Rouge, with Wolfe's decision to act above the town, but at a point close to it. The latter plan, as I have said, was Wolfe's alone. The former, had it been carried out, would certainly have been one for which the credit could not be given to Wolfe.

That Wolfe was a gallant leader and an able organiser is so obvious that it is almost impertinent to state the fact, but one salient point forces itself on our attention, when studying the operations of 1759, and that is that to " fight " the enemy, to " get at " them when and where he could was the limit of his strategical range of thought. The wider movements by which he could place his opponent at a disadvantage and force him to the attack scarcely seem to have occurred to him.

---

* The story was current on the authority of Sir William Musgrave (Addl. MSS., Brit. Mus. 5723), that Wolfe was shot by a deserter serving in the French ranks. It is said Wolfe was hit three times, which seems to give some confirmation that he was marked out for attack. As for Montcalm, the Chevalier Johnston says, " It was reported in Canada that the ball which killed that great, good, and honest man was not fired by an English musket." He adds, " But I never credited this."

The views of his subordinate generals, on the other hand, at all events in the later stages of the campaign, were certainly based on a truer military estimate of the situation. Whether this estimate was due to one of them more than another it is difficult to say, without more complete evidence than is at present available. The only thing that can be said with any certainty is that the change of strategy made itself apparent from the moment of Murray's return from his reconnaissance, and that his reports expressed his belief in the possibility of effecting a landing at the true strategic point. Moreover, the plan of operations submitted to the commander was in his handwriting, though this in itself is no proof that it was his idea. One other point may be mentioned, though it is an anticipation of subsequent events, and that is that in his movements of the following year, from Quebec to Montreal, Murray showed a real strategic grasp of the situation, declining to turn aside from his main objective by any temptation, or to fritter away his strength on minor actions which in themselves could not be decisive.

CHAPTER VIII

THE MYSTERY OF THE ANSE AU FOULON *

IN the last chapter I have detailed the circumstances leading up to the landing on the north shore at the Anse au Foulon, and the broad outlines of this review of the steps taken indicate that some information, not made public, guided the commander in his choice of the place for attack.

Very briefly summarised, the facts were that Wolfe, preparing to follow the advice given at a council of war, was making his dispositions to land near Pointe-aux-Trembles, when, apparently without antecedent cause, he changed his mind and landed with a force, not exceeding 4500 men, in the heart of the enemy's position, the place chosen being one, not only of extraordinary difficulty in itself but giving access to a terrain which his force could not cover, thereby allowing the enemy important strategic and tactical advantages. There must have been some strong determining cause for such a decision.

Let us remember that the projected landing near Pointe-aux-Trembles, where all the roads leading westward from Quebec to the interior of the colony merged into one, was a scheme essentially different from a landing at the place chosen, which left unguarded several roads for the movement of the enemy. In the first case, to get astride the single line of communication effectually cut the whole enemy force from its supplies. In the second, there was nothing to prevent the enemy from moving towards its

* An article under this title, by the present writer, appeared in *Blackwood's Magazine* of March, 1917, being a resume of matter contained in this and the preceding chapter. Messrs. Blackwood have given their kind permission for its use.

centre, to continue the defence of the colony. The one contained all the elements of decisive action, the other could not be decisive.

Inland at Pointe-aux-Trembles the broken, marshy, or densely wooded country prevented any movement of the troops. An entrenched position across the only road inevitably involved the surrender of the French forces, for they had no provisions to enable them to hold out, and an attack by them on the entrenched position would have been unlikely to succeed. This scheme was that which the advice of the brigadier-generals suggested, in which Wolfe acquiesced, and which he suddenly abandoned. It has been suggested by some writers that Wolfe never intended to follow the advice of his brigadiers, and only pretended to do so as a blind to his real intentions ; but the examination of the action taken, given in the preceding chapter, shows, I think, conclusively, that this argument cannot be maintained. What then was the reason that influenced him ?

It has become so much a habit of writers on the subject to represent Wolfe as constantly struggling against the views of his subordinates, that I think it advisable to emphasise that the advice of the brigadiers' council was tendered at Wolfe's request. There is much to indicate that this plan had been in their minds before the army had been committed to the fatal frontal attack on the French left, and that it was pressed on the General, both before and after that event, and finally took the form of recommending a reconnaissance of the upper river. On his return, Murray, to whom the duty had been entrusted, evidently strongly favoured the proposal. General Monckton, the second in command, supported his view,* and together with Townshend submitted it to the commander-in-chief. The plan of operations proposed

* *See* a letter quoted by Colonel Townshend in his book, p. 187, but which, I think, the author has wrongly attributed to an earlier period. This letter, which is undated, refers, I think, to the end of August, and General Monckton says, " I think our motion this way must be attended with a decisive success."

was so clear and so advantageous that Wolfe probably had no thought at any time but to accept the recommendation.

We know that during September 8 Wolfe was busily engaged in preparing for attack near Pointe-aux-Trembles. On the 9th the attack was definitely abandoned. It may be merely a coincidence that Major Barré, Wolfe's confidant, had just arrived from the lower river (Point Levis or Isle of Orleans) when the decision was arrived at.

On September 9 the log of the *Porcupine*, stationed off the Beauport shore, records that a deserter came on board in the forenoon. This man would have left the Beauport lines, where, let us remember, the French headquarters were situated, early in the morning. He was transferred to the *Stirling Castle* the same afternoon. At 4 a.m. the next morning (10th) we learn from the log of the *Seahorse*, which had been specially sent to lie off Goreham's Post to preserve the communications, that a signal was made from the shore to send a boat for letters. Finally, after some delay, owing to enemy canoes, " a packet " was brought off and despatched to General Wolfe. Now, it is clear that the " packet " must have been of a very urgent nature to merit being dispatched through the night to Goreham's Post, necessitating an escort and considerable arrangements between Point Levis camp and the Post. This " packet " would have been delivered to General Wolfe in the forenoon of September 10. On this date Townshend made the entry in his diary :

" By some intelligence the General has had, he has changed his mind as to the place he intended to land ; heard we had some deserters from the enemy's camp at Beauport."

This is a very significant statement, and it seems impossible to dissociate the deserters, the urgent " packet," and the action that followed. Within two or three hours after receiving this packet General Wolfe was on his way to view the Anse au Foulon, as already recorded (p. 141), which he pointed out evidently for the first time, and apparently with some want of familiarity with the place, to his staff.

Wolfe, having decided on the 10th to attack at the Foulon, for some reason unexplained did not proceed to action at once. On the face of it there appears to be no particular reason why the attack should not have taken place on the same night, or at all events on the 11th, but on the night of the 12th, the date selected, just before starting, news of the alleged convoy * was brought to him by a deserter, who apparently came from the very place about to be attacked—a very remarkable fact.

The passage of the boats conveying the troops down the river is generally alluded to as having been carried out silently on the tide, without knowledge of the enemy, but I have pointed out how impossible it would be to escape observation. I have alluded to Remigny, the acute observer at Sillery. His reports to his chief (De Bougainville) are models of what a good intelligence officer would record. Take this one for instance, written September 6 :

" *Depuis que la lune est devoillée j'ay été avertis que six berges chargées étoient descendues du costé de la rivie d'Eschemains peut estre qu'il y en aurait d'autres qui auraient descendues avant qu'elle se fut* (i.e. *la lune devoillée*). *J'ay mandé à M. Duglas* (who was stationed at Anse St. Michel) *d'y faire grande attention . . . il pourait se faire que n'ayant pas passeé cette rivière elles seroient allée pour prendre les troupes qui sont arrivées ce soir ou en déposer d'autres parcequ'elles ont parues bien chargées sans qu'on pu distinguer si'l y avoit des home ou autres choses . . . Il font à peut près la même bruit que hier soir, c'est à dire au prorata de ce qu'ils avoient et de ce qu'ils ont aujourd'huy. Cependant je crois que les troupes qui sont venues ce soir s'en sont retournées sur leurs pas parceque les berges n'ont point fait de va-t-et-viens, pour onze à douze cents hommes comme ils nous ont parus. La mer besse et la lune nous favorise.*"

Let us remember that this observation from Sillery, across the river to the south shore near the Étchemin River, was made at a distance of at least 1000 yards. How

* *See* p. 149.

much easier would observation be of *ships* and boats passing down river at a much smaller distance. Yet there is nothing on record to show what part Remigny took on the all-important night of the 12th–13th. If he made reports, as one must believe he did, they have been destroyed and, rather strangely, all mention of Remigny ceases.* Yet Remigny's station was not more than four miles from Bougainville's headquarters at Cap Rouge, and the boats would have passed him about 3.30 a.m. and the ships a very little later !

The extraordinary care evidently taken, that the alleged convoy of provisions should pass down without molestation, has been alluded to. Let us examine for a moment what is known of the methods adopted by the French in reference to these provision convoys. The Bougainville correspondence, printed in extenso in Dr. Doughty's work, gives reliable and illuminating information. Immense care and preparation marked the despatch of a convoy which Cadet was sent to organise on August 10 at Batiscan. Fifteen days' provisions were to be brought down, and a long series of orders and arrangements, including escorts to follow on land the progress of the boats, so as to protect them if attacked, orders for the *future* use of passwords † to enable the boats to be recognised, were also issued. This convoy finally reached Quebec in two sections, on August 24 and 29, showing that the undertaking was no mean adventure, and at this time the English naval force, which must be passed, was by no means so great as it afterwards became.

---

* A little circumstance mentioned in his letter of September 11 (the date is remarkable) may have a bearing on the case: " Il *m'a été volé avant hier au soir un de mes chevaux . . . les deux autres qui sont ici sont boitteux.*" He also complains that a mounted orderly, who was to have been sent for his use, had not arrived, from which it would appear that precautions to prevent his having means of rapid communication had been taken.

† " *M. Beaubassin m'a écrit que les sauvages qui faisoient la patrouille auroient tirés sur ces batteaux s'ils n'avoient été prévenus de leurs passage. Comme il importe de prévoir à tout inconvenient, je vous prie de vouloir bien à l'avenir donner un signal, ou un mot de reconnoisance et d'en avertir les commandants des postes* " (Vaudreuil à Bougainville).

Regarding the alleged convoy of the night of the 12th several remarkable facts force themselves on our attention. On September 12 (note the date) Cadet wrote to Bougainville :

"*J'ai reçu la lettre que vous m'avés fait l'honneur de m'écrire ce jour . . . je vous prie, monsieur, de vouloir bien passer les batteaux cette nuit si'l y a de la possibilité, sans quoi je serai obligé de faire passer demain des charettes pour aller chercher ces vivres parceque j'en ai absolument besoin, mais s'ils venoient par eau, cela nous épargnerait bien de la peine.*"

This letter, at first sight, reads innocently enough, but it accords badly with the extensive preparations made on previous occasions, and the sudden request to send off the convoy " this night " seems to carry something unconvincing with it. The more so, that a strong English force was at the moment stationed off Cap Rouge. The boats certainly could not start until the tide ebbed, and, as already mentioned, the night was moonlit.

There is no record of what Bougainville did on receipt of this letter, if he received it on the 12th at all,* but it is quite certain *that he did not despatch the convoy.* If he had done so it would have started at approximately the same time as the troops left the *Sutherland*, and the two flotillas would have met, which they certainly did not.

If Bougainville did not send the convoy, who warned the posts on the river bank, and especially that at the Foulon, and undoubtedly they had been warned that a convoy was coming ? There appears to have been no escort to follow the boats, as had been definitely ordered, and if the story as to the use of a password by the English officers is true, it adds to the strangeness of the affair.

It was obviously Bougainville's business to send out the orders to the posts, and unless we suppose that he intended to send the convoy and then changed his mind,

* It appears to me very improbable that Bougainville received the letter on the 12th, or, for that matter, that he was intended to receive it.

it cannot be that he did so, and judging from the care taken to warn the posts it is apparent that some one else took up this business. Let us summarise this series of incidents. An attack is planned on the 10th to take place on the night of the 12th ; on the morning of that very day Cadet asks for a convoy " this night." Information of the same is conveyed by a deserter to Wolfe in the evening ; the posts are warned to expect a convoy, but no convoy actually starts, nor does De Bougainville say a word about it in any subsequent letter.

If all these incidents were merely fortuitous they surely constitute a strange vagary of fortune. It seems almost proven that the reason Wolfe suddenly abandoned the " advice " given by the brigadiers and ordered the landing at the Anse au Foulon, was that he had received definite information from some one, probably Cadet, that the landing would be unopposed ; and let it be said here that, with every suspicion that treachery was at work in Quebec, it seems impossible to believe that Vaudreuil was a party to it. Rather it appears that, whatever his faults, he was heart and soul in the defence, but was guided by some sinister influence which seems to have, in a sense, hypnotised him and caused him to act as it were against his will. The presence of Cadet at his hand shows clearly in several of the letters ; for example : " *M. Cadet qui est présent,*" or " *Dans le temps que je vous écris M. Cadet entra* " (Letters 114 and 126, Doughty, vol. iv.). To what extent the Intendant Bigot shared the secret may well be left to the imagination—very probably he was a full co-partner, but Cadet was the more adept scoundrel and the bolder spirit.

There are other links in this chain of circumstances which confirm suspicion. Montcalm and Vaudreuil, but especially the former, had repeatedly drawn De Bougainville's attention to the movements of the English and the necessity of guarding against surprise. So late as September 5, Montcalm wrote :

" *Le mouvement des ennemis, mon cher Bougainville, est*

si considerable que je crains qu'il ne passe la rivière des Ecchemins et qu'il ne cherche à nous dérober une marche pour nous couper la communication."

On the same date Vaudreuil :

" Je n'ay pas besoin de vous dire, monsieur, que la salut de la colonie est en vos mains que certainement le projet des ennemis est de nous couper la communication en faisant des débarquements au Nord."

Yet the next day (September 5) Vaudreuil informed Bougainville that after conferring with Montcalm he had appointed M. de Vergor to take charge of the post at Anse au Foulon.

Foligné, in his diary, says, under date September 13, *"poste (i.e. Anse au Foulon) ou M. Vergor étoit placé depuis trois ou quatre jours."* The author of the last part of Montcalm's journal says, " *M. de Vergor à qui on avoit bien mal à propos confié celui (la poste) de l' Anse au Foulon."* Another French writer (*Memoires sur le Canada*) says, regarding this selection : " *On ne pouvoit mieux seconder les intentions du général Anglois."*

The opinions entertained of De Vergor are obviously unfavourable. His record was bad. He was an intimate of the intendants, and the " memoires " record that " *cette amitié ne faisoit honneur ni à l'un ni à l'autre."* To him, according to the same authority, Bigot had written (August 20, 1754) : " *Profitez, mon cher Vergor, de votre place ; Taillez, rognez, vous avez tout pouvoir afin que vous puissiez bientôt venir me joindre en France et acheter un bien à portée de moi."* * He was strongly suspected of surrendering Beauséjour to Monckton four years previously without much effort at defending it, and had been tried by court-martial at Quebec in the previous year.

It is difficult to imagine a worse selection, and the fact that such a man was sent to replace M. de St. Martin, a brave and trustworthy officer, *at the very time when* Wolfe's

---

* It is difficult to believe that so incriminating a letter could have been written. I quote it merely to show the sentiment which existed *vis-a-vis* Bigot and Vergor.

sudden intention to land at this place became manifest, is very remarkable.

That the Anse au Foulon was regarded as an important post there is no doubt. It was frequently used as a landing-place, and a fair road led through the narrow gorge.

Writing on the 6th De Remigny, who from his post at Sillery * had full view of the Foulon, gave a clear warning :

" De la manœuvre des ennemis il n'y a pas à douter qu'ils ne veulleut tenter une descente, peut estre esce entre la poste de vos voluntaires et le mien, l'ance et belle pour cet effet, je crois qu'il conviendroit que vous y envoyés du monde parce que celuy que j'ay ne peut fournir si considerablement."

It is not quite clear whether the " Ance " referred to by Remigny was Anse au Foulon or Anse St. Michel, probably the latter, but the two places were not far apart, and the warning would be applicable to either and equally effective had it been attended to.

And this brings us to another link in the chain of evidence, namely, the movement of the Regiment of Guienne. This regiment had for a long time been retained as a reserve and encamped at the bridge-head on the St. Charles River. On September 5 Montreuil, who exercised the functions of major-general or, as we should say now, of adjutant-general, wrote to Bougainville :

" M. le Marquis de Montcalm (who it should be remembered commanded directly the troupes de terre, that is, the regular regiments from Old France) *m'a chargé de marquer à M. de Bougainville que le régiment de Guyenne seroit en réserve sur le grand chemin derrière l'Anse St. Michel ou Sillery pour être à portée de secourir la gauche et la droite."*

This arrangement did not meet with Vaudreuil's approval. He wrote at 11 o'clock the next day (6th) : *" . . . Si vous vous croyés assez fort avec ces dispositions comme cela vous parait, nous retirerons le régiment de Guyenne*

* Remigny was in command of the Sillery post, but it is pretty certain that for purposes of observation he would be at Point à Puiseau, which overlooks Sillery Bay.

pour la faire rentrer dans son Champ," and at the end of the letter, as a kind of afterthought, he added, " *À l'égard de laisser Guyenne à l'ance des mères cela ne se peut parce qu'il n'y a pas de bois.*"

This is a curious letter. The Anse des Meres was not anywhere near the original place (*see,* however, note to p. 154) ordered by Montcalm, and the reason given that there was " no wood there " (*i.e.* at Anse des Mères) is too flimsy to be taken seriously. The place was only a few hundred yards distant from the town, and there surely could have been no difficulty in supplying wood. One cannot avoid suspecting the Cadet influence here, and the touch regarding supplies adds confirmation. Suspicion of this kind was evidently in the mind of the author of the " Memoires," when he wrote respecting Vaudreuil's hesitation to support Montcalm on the morning of the 13th, " *par la persuasion de Cadet et quelques autres qui y avoient un interêt particulier.*"

However, the result of Vaudreuil's interference was the formal intimation from Montreuil : " *J'ai eu l'ordre de faire rentrer le régt. de Guyenne dans son Camp.*"

It appears that a few days later Montcalm made a further attempt to put some regular troops in a position to defend the heights. The Abbé Recher, in his Journal, records, under date " *12th Mercredi—Ordre donné par M. de Montcalm et ensuite révoqué par M. de Vaudreuil, disant 'nous verrons cela demain', au bataillon de Guyenne d'aller camper au foulon.*" In this work is a note as follows :

" *C'est là une accusation des plus graves contre M. de Vaudreuil et qui ne s'accorde pas beaucoup avec ce qu'il a écrit lui même, je fis, dit il, rester l'armée en bivouac la nuit du 12 ou 13. Je comptais beaucoup sur le bataillon de Guyenne, je le croyais toujours sur le hauteur de Québec ; mais M. de Montcalm l'avoit rappelé le même jour à l'entrée de la nuit sans m'en prévenir.*"

It is impossible to believe this statement of Vaudreuil, and it is not too much to say that his statements made

N

after the death of Montcalm, regarding the preceding event, are entirely unworthy of credence.

We have, besides, the explicit statement of the Chevalier Johnston, who, in his *Dialogue in Hades*, puts the following words into Montcalm's mouth :

" I remained at M. Vaudreuil's until 1 o'clock in the morning (*i.e.* September 11), when I left him in order that I might return to my lodging, having with me M. Montreuil, major-general of the Army, and M. Johnston.   On my sending away M. de Montreuil, after giving him my order, I related immediately to M. Johnston all the measures I had concerted with M. de Vaudreuil. . . .   He answered me that your (*i.e.* Wolfe's) army, being now assembled at Point Levi, and part of it gone above Quebec on the south side of the River St. Lawrence, it appeared very doubtful where you (Wolfe) might attempt a descent—whether above the town or below it towards the Canardière ; he added that he believed a body of troops might be advantageously placed upon the Heights of Abraham, where they would, with certainty, confront you wherever you landed. I approved greatly of his idea.   I called back Montreuil, who was as yet not far from us, and I ordered him to send the Regiment of Guienne, which was encamped near the horn-work at the River St. Charles, to pass the night on the Heights of Abraham.   Next morning (12th ?) I wrote to Montreuil, ordering him to make the regiment encamp upon the Heights of Abraham and remain there until further orders.   Thus, in consequence of my repeated orders, I had all reason possible to believe that this regiment constituted a permanent post there ; so that the declaration of the deserters * from the three posts (*i.e.* Foulon, Michel, Sillery) might have led you (Wolfe) into a dangerous snare.

" Why this regiment continued the 12th in their camp at the horn-work, in spite of my express orders to encamp on the Heights, I know not. . . .   It is nevertheless evident that if you had found the Regiment of Guienne on the top of the hill, where it ought to have been, had my

---

* This refers to the deserter or deserters of the night of September 12, who came from the very place marked out for attack *three days previously !*

orders been obeyed, you would have been repulsed shame-fully."

The author of the last part of Montcalm's Journal, who was certainly not Johnston, and was evidently an officer of position near Montcalm, gives the same idea: "*Le Régiment de Guyenne qu'on avoit résolu de faire camper sur les hauters au dessus de Québec, étoit il encore dans notre camp ?*"

Reviewing the whole story, it is impossible to avoid the conclusion that the removal of the regiment from the scene of action was intentional and very suspicious; one can hardly avoid connecting it with the plot in which Vaudreuil may have been only a tool. It seems that De Bougainville was acquainted with the first withdrawal; whether he was told of the second movement we are not told.

There remains now to be considered another mysterious circumstance. Where was Bougainville on the night of September 12–13 ? He commanded a picked corps, comprising a flying column of 1100 men, which included 130 cavalry. He had, besides, 500 men in the posts from Cap Rouge to the Foulon on which he could count, without withdrawing the garrisons, which included another 570 men, above Cap Rouge.

Yet Wolfe's movements on landing clearly indicated that he anticipated no attack from this formidable body. He marched his force directly inland, as already related, as far as the Ste. Foy road, leaving his rear and communications weakly guarded.

Where was Bougainville ? We know that he was supposed to be at Cap Rouge. Montreuil addressed a letter to him there as late as 5 o'clock on the evening of the 11th. Cadet wrote the letter already quoted about the convoy on the 12th (September), addressing the letter to Cap Rouge, and in the absence of any military reason for his being elsewhere we must suppose that nominally, at all events, he was at Cap Rouge. Yet Bougainville, in his Memoire (*see* Doughty, vol. iv.) concerning the events, says : " *Je n'en fus averti qu'à neuf heures du matin,*" * that is, he did not hear of the landing until 9 o'clock. Incredible ! Leaving Samos and the Foulon out of the question, there was the garrison at Sillery, with that acute observer De Remigny, in full view and hearing of the attack made at 4 a.m. on the Foulon, and not more than four miles from Bougainville's headquarters. If Bougainville had been at Cap Rouge it is not possible to suppose that it would take five hours for the news to reach him.

Moreover, it is beyond belief that the movement of the boats *and ships* was unknown to the French outposts long before the Foulon was reached, and in any case the sound of the firing at Samos, which took place some time between 4 and 4.30 o'clock, was audible to the ships lying in the bason off Point Levis (as recorded in the logs), and must have attracted attention at Cap Rouge, which is about the same distance away. It may well be true, as recorded in the " Journal," that Montcalm exclaimed, " Est ce possible que Bougainville n'entende pas cela " (p. 613).

There can only be one explanation—that Bougainville was not at Cap Rouge, and apparently with the queer notions of military discipline which existed, in some respects so much slacker than ours, in others much more bound by etiquette, no movement could be made in his absence. Dr. Doughty, for whose opinion I have the greatest respect, explains the matter by referring to Wolfe's letter to Colonel Burton, in which it is stated that after the troops had embarked " the fleet sails up the river a little higher, as if intending to land above," † and the doctor adds : " This plan was undoubtedly carried out, and while Bougainville was on his way to St. Augustin

---

* In a letter to Bourlamaque, dated September 18, Bougainville mentions 8 o'clock as the hour ; but 9 o'clock seems more likely to be correct. *See* M. de Kerallain's work, *La Jeunesse de Bougainville*, p. 151.

† The same idea is given in Townshend's despatch to Pitt. Probably this had been the intention, but the state of the wind and tide prevented its being carried out.

and Pointe-aux-Trembles the boats dropped down the river." I am afraid so simple an explanation will not bear examination. There is nothing in the ships' logs to indicate that they made any movement up river after taking the troops on board, as I think would certainly have been the case had they done so. But apart from this, if the ships had made such a movement on the flood tide they could not have got back until the ebb, and finally if we suppose that with the wind they could make way against the flood and arrive back in time for the boats to start, it would appear that Bougainville would have been fully aware of the movement and have followed it. Bougainville himself makes no reference to such a reason, nor does De Levis nor Vaudreuil, but I think they certainly would have done so had it been the case.*

The Bougainville correspondence, already referred to, seems to contain a possible clue and incidentally to bring out another circumstance.

A certain Sieur de Vienne, it is stated, had a house which Vaudreuil occupied during the operations—presumably this was the house on the Canardière which was Vaudreuil's headquarters ; at all events it was in that neighbourhood.† De Vienne was an officer of the intendant's department, which does not argue much to his credit, and he was afterwards arrested in Paris for complicity in the frauds in Canada. Madame de Vienne was evidently a lady of notoriety and charm. Was she the lure that called Bougainville from his duty ?

* It is true that of the seven transports or " Catts," as they were often called, which accompanied the fleet in the upper river, only two were used to carry troops of the attacking force on the night of the 12th–13th. Of the remaining five, it would appear that one was a hospital ship and at least one other was a provision ship ; but there is no indication whatever that any of them made a movement up river to threaten the French communications. Nor does it appear that any armed vessels except the *Sutherland* remained to protect them. All the armed sloops accompanied the attacking army. Had any body of sailors or marines proceeded up river in boats or otherwise the fact would have been recorded in the *Sutherland's* log."

† The redan de Vienne, a post of the French lines, was nearly opposite this place.

On September 11 the Sieur de Blau, who commanded at Jacques Cartier, wrote to Bougainville at Cap Rouge :

" *Les dames n'ont point besoin de recommendations auprez de moi et Madame de Vienne moins qu'une autre. J'aurois esté charmé qu'elle m'eut mis à même de la mettre à couvert de la peur et des inquiétudes pour le transport de ces effets mais elle m'a brulé* (passed me by without stopping) *et à l'arrivée de votre lettre j'ay fais courir aprez elle, moins dans l'espoir de réussir à luy estre bon à quelque chose que pour luy marquer, et a vous mon cher colonel, ma bonne volonté et mon zèle pour le service des dames et surtout de Mme. de Vienne dont le mari vient de couvrir le centre de mon individu et le mettre à l'abri du froid ; j'aurais bien voulu mettre cette dame à l'abri de la peur des Anglois et des angoisses pour les voitures ; cela aurait esté pour moi une espèce de revanche heureuse dont elle m'a méchamment privé.*"

Whether Bougainville's message had any effect on arresting the journey of the lady, whether he went on the following day (12th) to see to her comforts himself, is only conjecture, but it may be said with some certainty that he was not to be found at his post at the critical moment on the night of that September 12–13.

Incidentally this other question arises, why did Madame de Vienne, starting from the house which contained the headquarter staff, undertake this hurried flight on September 11, with much anxiety as to the safety of her goods ?   She had apparently found it convenient to reside there during the anxieties of the preceding period.   She must have travelled by the inland route, avoiding Cap Rouge, else one would assume Bougainville would have been able to afford her any necessary assistance without writing to De Blau at Jacques Cartier.   The mere fact that " voitures " * were placed at her disposal at a time when carriage was a question of extreme importance, indicates that she was travelling under the ægis of some one in

---

* One is reminded of Montcalm's remark in the Journal : " *Les voitures manquent pour les fortifications mais non pour voiturer les matériaux nécessaires pous faire une casemate chez Mme. Péan.*"

authority. Was she in possession of some hint of impending misfortune, which rendered it desirable to put her " effects " in a place of safety ? It certainly looks like it.

Let us put the most charitable construction possible on the affair, and suppose that madame was the unconscious tool of Bigot or Cadet, who had arranged a route for her which would keep her well out of De Bougainville's way until she had got far up river to or beyond Jacques Cartier. Bougainville was young, probably impulsive. An appeal from the lady to come to her assistance, on whatever ground it may have been, would probably find him ready to obey. It is remarkable that Bougainville was connected with Madame de Vienne in some distant relationship ; it was at her house that the young officer, freshly arrived from Europe in 1756, had his first welcome and made his *début* in the Canadian world ; it is probable that madame and he were close friends. Thus in selecting her as the instrument of his scheme the astute Cadet had in all probability laid his plans securely, knowing that Bougainville would find an appeal from the lady impossible to resist.

Let us pass over the strange backwardness of Vaudreuil in meeting the critical situation that developed on the morning of the 13th—the disgraceful flight of the commander-in-chief without even communicating his intentions to his subordinates ; all this is mentioned by contemporary writers, giving colour to the remark of Chevalier Johnston :

" In fact it would appear by this strange conduct that a class of men there, from interested views, were furiously bent on giving up the colony to the English, so soon as they could have a plausible pretext to colour their designs."

Let us pass over also the suppression or destruction of papers or reports which would throw light on the occurrences. We know that Vaudreuil's first action on reaching Montreal was to examine Montcalm's papers, and we know that in 1763 the Marquise de Montcalm wrote :

" *Il étoit l'homme du monde qui les gardoit le plus soigneusement. . . . Par quelle fatalité la famille d'un commandant universellement regretté se trouve-t-elle privée de la consolation de posséder ses lettres. . . . Et comment cette privation peut aller au point qu'il n'existe aucune trace de ses papiers ?* "

Wolfe himself destroyed his journal of the days in September. Barré, who probably knew the whole story, has left no record. Carleton's private papers were destroyed after his death by his wife, presumably at his request.

Enough, however, remains to make the reason for Wolfe's sudden change of mind at least a matter of great probability. Whether, with the information before him of the tempting conditions for attack at the Foulon, he should still have adhered to the plan of landing at Pointe-aux-Trembles is a question on which different opinions may be held. Had the unfortunate delay on the occasion of the reconnaissance of September 7 not taken place, and had the landing been effected as intended then, there is no moral doubt that the General would have reaped the greater laurels of a decisive defeat of the enemy and the surrender of the colony. As it was the work was but " half done," and Murray's sickly battalions, after a winter of incredible suffering, had to face the French army again, little impaired as regards personnel.

Let it not be supposed that I would detract from the brilliant achievement of September 13. If Wolfe acted on secret information, as I believe to be the case, he was most thoroughly justified in doing so; and whatever information had been given him, and at the most he could only have guarantee of an unopposed landing, and perhaps some degree of freedom from attack by Bougainville, he could not be certain of the course of events. In any case, it was a bold move to seek battle against superior numbers in a situation where his support by the fleet was ineffective by reason of the high banks. He was certainly justified in using any means at his disposal; but the question is, was he wise in using this particular one ? I think not.

Perhaps one of the most inexplicable things about the affair is the complete absence of any question as to Bougainville's failure to defend the position. *Before* the event we have frequent references to the necessity for keeping careful watch, to the reliance placed in him, to his great activity ; *after* the event, there is not one allusion to the delay, or the strange circumstance that he knew nothing of a movement which commenced under his nose, until after a lapse of seven hours ! De Levis makes no remark inferring any blame, but it is noteworthy that he did not employ Bougainville on his Quebec campaign of the following spring, though it is true that he was sent to the important post of Île-aux-Noix. Vaudreuil, though quite ready to lay blame on any one, so long as he diverted it from himself, makes no suggestion of dissatisfaction with Bougainville. Yet it seems quite impossible to relieve that officer of grave responsibility, though I would add that there is not an iota of evidence to impute any suggestion that Bougainville was a party to the treachery in which he became an actor. However blameworthy his action appears to have been, it was far removed from the category in which I think the conduct of Cadet and Bigot must be placed.

CHAPTER IX

WHEN on September 18 Lieut.-Colonel Alexander Murray, with his three companies of Louisburg Grenadiers, took possession of the gates of the upper town of Quebec, and Captain Hugh Palliser of the Royal Navy, with a body of seamen, similarly took formal possession of the lower town, an important event was marked in the history of the British Empire. It was certainly not possible at the time to appreciate to its full the far-reaching character of this laying of the foundation-stone of a Dominion, now the heritage of a people proud to be the greatest and not the least loyal of the numerous offsprings of the Mother Country. A Dominion taking its full share in that great defence * which has proved to the world that those crabbed doubters, who accused the old mother of decadence and slumber, have under-estimated her power to rise to a great occasion.

Events moved rapidly after the hoisting of the Union flag on the citadel of Cape Diamond. Free from immediate anxiety that Vaudreuil would attempt any important operations to regain possession of the town, Townshend despatched Major Eliot with 500 men to take possession of the enemy's lines on the Beauport side, and to make good the occupation of the country surrounding the city. The camp was found deserted, and much of the provisions and equipment left behind by Vaudreuil, in his hurried retreat on the night of the 13th, was found to have been

* 1914–1918.

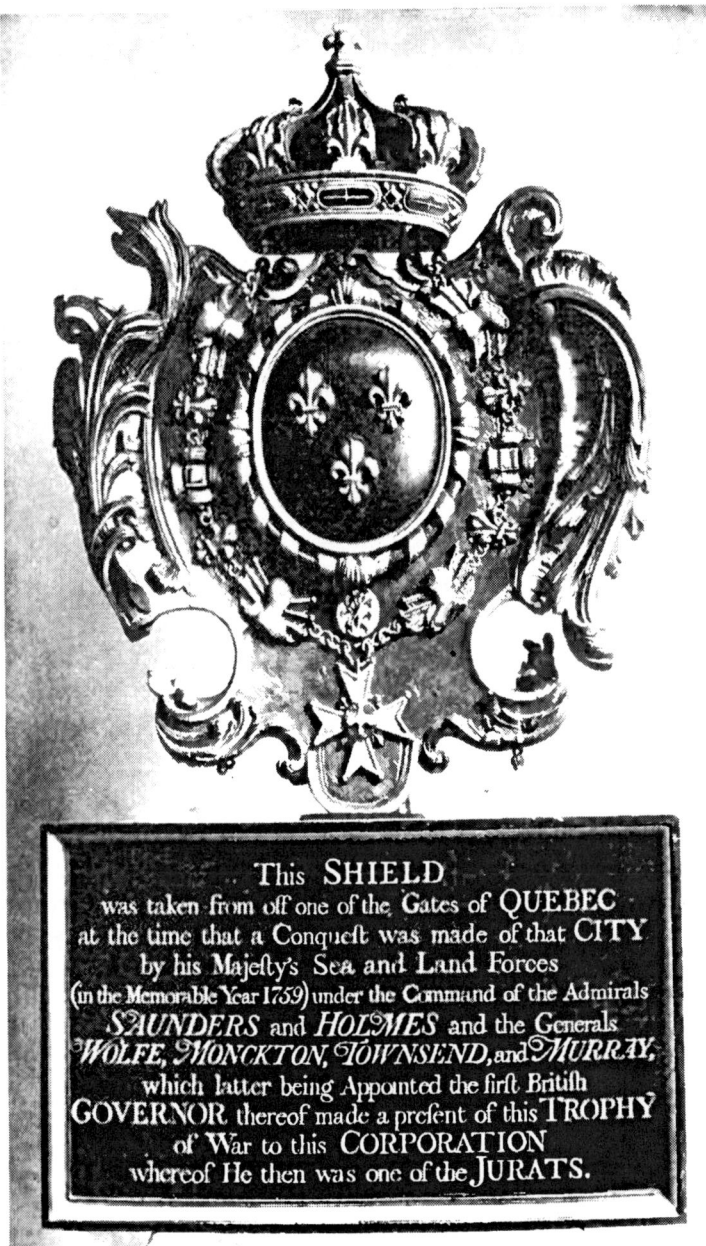

SHIELD IN THE TOWN HALL, HASTINGS.

taken or destroyed by the Indians and Canadians. Some writers have blamed Townshend for not acting more promptly. The question is open to argument; but it must be remembered that it was impossible for the General in command to know the complete state of demoralisation of the French army, nor to be certain that a fresh attack by the superior numbers which they still possessed would not force him to defend his rear, and especially his line of communication, with the fleet at the Anse au Foulon. His force was none too large to assume the double duty of attacking the town still held by De Ramezay, and of defending himself from further attack from the west, and not a man could be spared. His decision to confine his efforts to the main purpose appears to be justified, and as soon as his communication with the river, by the more convenient passage of the lower town, was established, he took the necessary action to complete the zone of military occupation.

There has, moreover, been a disposition to attack Townshend for having assumed a position to which he was not entitled during the negotiations for the capitulation and subsequently. To whatever source the origin of such statements may be traceable, there is no doubt but that the prosecution of them in England was purely the outcome of political animosity, which then frequently found voice in anonymous pamphlets. The letter " To an Honourable Brigadier-General " (already referred to), in which Townshend was roundly accused of assuming Monckton's place, is an instance. The facts, however, indicate that there was no justification for the attack. Monckton was wounded and in the doctor's hands, and technically he was not in military command; moreover, the letters which passed between them at the time do not give colour to the accusation. Nor in the despatch sent by Townshend to Pitt on September 20 is there any indication of self-laudation; on the contrary, the prominent position as commander of the first disembarkation and the front line of battle is given to Monckton and Murray, and he refers to himself as being in the second.   His own services as commanding the covering force on the left rear, an important and honourable post, especially having in view the danger of attack from Bougainville's force approaching from Cap Rouge, he refers to but slightly, and adds, " the action on our left and rear was not so severe." *   On September 20 it is true that Townshend wrote to Pitt a despatch reporting the action and relating the signing of the capitulation by " Us " (meaning himself and Saunders), but there had been correspondence with General Monckton on the 16th and 18th.   In the former Monckton says : " I have wrote a short letter to Mr. Pitt, referring him to yours for the particulars of that day," and in the latter :

" You are one of the last men in the world that could give me offence, and I do most sincerely assure you that I have never said anything, either pro or con (that is that Townshend had presumed too much), except that I did suppose I should see the capitulation before it was signed, and *that* to Admiral Saunders and Colonel Carleton, the latter of whom was of that opinion."

This letter was written on the same date as the signing, which took place at 8 o'clock in the morning.   Monckton was on board the *Medway,* and Townshend was rightly anxious to get the matter settled, and events proved him to be very wise—a delay in sending to Monckton might have had important consequences.

On the 26th Townshend wrote to Amherst : " Having General Monckton's *commands* to write to you a relation of the action."   In this letter he attributes the victory to the " admirable and determined firmness of every British soldier in the field."   In all this I confess I see no reason for attributing to Townshend any intention of self-laudation. Nor, indeed, would it be necessary for me to refer to the matter at all were it not that the same malicious tongues which commenced the intrigue against Townshend also

* Writing to Lady Ferrars (his wife) he said : " I was not in the warmest part of the action."

involved Murray, though Townshend's political prominence attracted to him the greater part of the attack.*

On September 19 Murray records in his diary : " This day I marched into the town, or more properly the ruins of it, with the battalions of Amherst, Bragg, and Otway " (the 15th, 28th, and 35th Foot). The ruin had indeed been complete. More than one-third of the houses were entirely destroyed, and those that remained were so shattered as to be for the most part uninhabitable ; many were unsafe and had to be pulled down, while the streets were badly blocked by the fallen beams and masonry. In the lower town the destruction had been even greater than in the upper, and that famous monument that connoted the idea of victory to the French colonists, " Nôtre Dame des Victoires," was now as completely destroyed as were the hopes of the French themselves.

Townshend had never altered his intention of returning to Europe at the end of the campaign—the prospect of a winter in the frozen north, and of passing it in the ruined city, did not appeal to him. Monckton, in the doctor's hands, seriously wounded in the right lung, was advised that he must go south at the earliest opportunity. There remained Murray, and to him the military governorship of Quebec was deputed.

The entry in the diary under date September 21 records : " This night it was resolved in a council of war, consisting of the admiral and generals, that we should keep posses- sion of Quebec, and that I should remain in command." There is nothing on record to show whether this appoint- ment was one which attracted Murray at the time or not. To him, as to Townshend, the glamour of war service in Europe was, no doubt, preferable to service in America. He had, however, the sturdy soldierly spirit which led him to accept, without question, whatever service fell in his way, without attempting to pick or choose a path which appeared

* The source of these attacks is a matter of interest. *See* an article in *Blackwood's Magazine* for January, 1917, by the present writer.

at the moment more to his inclination.   At a later period he wrote concerning the long-deferred confirmation of his Governorship :

"I have heard nothing about the government of Canada.   If any propositions are made to me relative to it, I shall know how to answer them ; in the meantime, I desire that my friends may be assured that I never made an application (so far from proposition) for the government of Canada.   I am always ready to do what the King pleases, provided I am not ordered to serve under such a . . . as . . . which is all I ever wrote to my friends in the matter." *

But apart from his adherence to the sound principle of accepting without demur any service that offered, Murray was singularly gifted with the power of taking the "long view" of the existing situation.   Everything goes to prove that he recognised, and in no way under-estimated, the difficulties of the situation—a ruined city to defend, surrounded by a still powerful enemy, whose resources, though seriously diminished, were yet formidable, and who still commanded the allegiance of the European population of the colony and a numerous body of Indian auxiliaries, of whose prowess, in their particular form of warfare, he had already had sufficient experience. Cut off by the long winter months from all succour by sea, and without command of the river communication from the moment the fleet should sail ; separated by an immense distance from Amherst, whose slow and methodical advance could not possibly relieve the stress which an active enemy might exert against him, at earliest until the following summer ; and more than all, faced by the unknown quantity of a Canadian winter, which we may be sure was not painted to him by the inhabitants in colours less vivid than the reality.   Yet there remained in the background the military position ; the defender of an important outpost,

---

* At the same time one gathers that he was not sorry to be quit of the disputes and cabals which had been somewhat frequent during the late campaign.   Writing to Amherst, he says, " Everybody is cheerful and happy in having Quebec. . . . All those that did not like it are, thank God, gone to places they like better ! "

the command of a considerable body of troops, the hope of victory, if attacked, which might bring with it the glory of completing the conquest of Canada before the commander-in-chief could reach Montreal; and besides all this, we may easily suppose that Murray's administrative instincts were aroused by the magnificent prospect of bringing into solidarity with his country a province of whose future he could see, if only dimly, the immense and splendid possibilities.

At thirty-nine James Murray was still full of ardour; ambition in him may perhaps have been tempered by experience which had had little of military success. The horrors of the Cartagena campaign, followed by participation in the inglorious campaigns of the Netherlands, and the unfortunate descents on the French coast, cannot but have had a steadying effect on as clear a brain as his. It is of interest to read the following character-sketch by an enemy, with whom Murray had been in contact at this period :

" *L'homme est jeune, bouillant, fier de ses forces, decidée dans ses idées, avide de figurer. Bon par caractère, méchant ou à craindre par opposition, prompt à s'allumer et dans ces moments prêt à tout faire ; et un moment après, cherchant à faire du bien mille fois plus qu'il n'a fait de mal. Devant lui chacun des siens craint que le pied ne lui glisse. J'avais prévu de longue mains quel il tenait, et j'agis en conséquence.*"

Thus wrote the commissary Bernier, who remained with Murray during part of the winter in Quebec,* and if the opinions expressed are not altogether complimentary, at least we can accept that Murray was a man of character, who would not be lightly influenced by anticipated difficulties.

Whatever views he may have held at this time on the question of civil government, there were many months to pass before any possibility of putting them into practice could occur, and the first labours of the governor must unquestionably be devoted to strengthening the military

* La Jeunesse de Bougainville.

position, which was very far from satisfactory. To this problem Murray applied himself at once with characteristic energy ; disarming the militia which had formed part of the garrison, administering the oath of allegiance to the colonists of the conquered districts, and embarking the French troops to be sent to Europe under the terms of the capitulation, were the first duties. The inhabitants of the town, rendered houseless by the bombardment, were allowed to withdraw with their effects, but nothing likely to be of use to the garrison was permitted to be taken away. From the very commencement he endeavoured to anticipate the requirements of the army and of the towns-people who elected to remain, and on September 26 he records :

" As a prodigious quantity of wood would be wanted in so cold a country for the fuel of this garrison, a field officer with 150 regulars and 350 irregulars was ordered for Isle Madame to cut trees, provided with proper tools . . . now we had the occasion to regret the quantity of fine cord wood we had burned, and to consider, though too late, we had been a little too hasty in so doing."

It is to be feared that the newly-made governor had cause to regret many things which had been done during the operations preceding the capitulation. The fuel supply became one of enormous importance and great difficulty, as we shall see, and, indeed, may be said to have exercised an effect on the garrison which was largely responsible for the troubles which followed. The very promiscuous bombardment which lasted for sixty-three days had much to answer for in creating a situation which almost led to disaster, and besides causing the destruction of the available supplies, had rendered the housing of the troops almost impossible.

On September 29 the remaining troops and the field train were brought into the town. " What made this necessary was the ruinous condition of the several quarters allotted to them, which, considering the quick approaches of a severe winter, called for a speedy repair." The men were thus brought nearer to their work, and also to that of landing and lodging the provisions—a work of immense labour, as the whole had to be dragged to the upper town. At the same time the repair of the batteries was put in hand, and continued "without ceasing in such a way that not a man but was constantly employed." On Sunday, October 4, a " solemn thanksgiving for the success of His Majesty's arms " * was celebrated ; the troops were excused all duties of labour and fatigue, and about 11 o'clock " the several regiments " marched to the church of the Ursulines, preceded by our general officers, where they heard an excellent sermon suitable to the occasion. The sermon was preached by the Rev. Eli Dawson, Chaplain of H.M.S. *Stirling Castle*, the text being, " Give thanks unto Thee, O Lord, among the Gentiles." No doubt the Rev. Eli felt that an opportunity of exhorting his hearers in the very precincts of those whom he regarded as being far from a chosen people was one not lightly to be missed ! On this date the effective strength of the garrison is recorded as officers, 340 ; other ranks, 6973.

In these early days, rapidly shortening, of the Indian summer, let us pause for a moment and survey the scene which lay before Murray and his comrades. The least emotional man among them could scarce avoid a feeling of personal pride in the magnificent spectacle, and Murray himself, born and bred in the rugged and unlovely surround-ings of his Scottish home, could not but be affected by the almost indescribable beauty of the panorama.

From the high pinnacle of Cape Diamond the spectator is at once awed and charmed by the wide stretches of the river lying more than 300 feet below. In its spacious distance it resembles rather a great lake. Beyond the city to the eastward the north shore of the St. Lawrence fades away in indistinct outlines, terminated by the frowning headland of Cap Tourmente ; every detail is familiar— beyond the St. Charles River lies the Beauport shore, which from this height and distance seems comparatively flat and

* Knox.

low lying; the entrenched lines lately occupied by the French army are still intact. A little further on, the scar which indicates the chasm through which the Montmorency River tumbles is visible; this side of the chasm is the fatal redoubt which cost so many lives on July 31. Across the water lies the Island of Orleans, the high land at its nearer end decreasing gently in the distance, until the further extremity, some twenty-five miles away, seems to blend into the slopes of Cap Tourmente, and this arm of the waters almost appears landlocked.

On the other side of the island the southern branch of the river can only be seen as another bay, land-barred by the Beaumont shore and the Point of Levis.

Levis itself and the bluff headland of Pointe-aux-Pères frame the view across the river, and there can be easily discerned the batteries which wrought such havoc in the city. On the right the narrow water (from which the city is said to take its name) expands into the broad bay, which seems enclosed by the upland of Sillery, with its church and spire standing then, as now, a landmark for mariners. This side of the promontory is the place of the adventurous landing of September 13. Away across this bay is Goreham's Post, with many memories of difficulties overcome, the Étchemin River, and in the distance the embouchure of the Chaudière.

Northward and westward the prospect must be viewed from the high ground outside the citadel. In the middle distance lies the broad valley through which the St. Charles River winds its way. Beyond is the rising country on which stand the villages of Lorette and Ste. Foy, with its church standing delightfully situated on the higher slopes, commanding an extensive prospect over cultivated lands and wooded areas. Below Ste. Foy are the marshes of the Suette, wherein that devious streamlet finds its way to the St. Charles. Beyond, and closing the picture as far as the eye can reach, the Laurentian Mountains rise tier on tier, forming a fitting background to a landscape which can scarcely be excelled by any in the world.

Lying in the bason between Orleans and Levis, far below the spectator, is the great fleet. Even the *Neptune* of 90 guns looks dwarfed, and the trim and saucy frigates seem miniature and little formidable. The sound of preparation for departure comes from the ships—10,000 busy hands are getting ready for the rough voyage which has still to be faced ; some, indeed, did they know it, are bound for fresh laurels.*

And below, on the sloping ground, lies the city itself—not as now closely packed with houses and streets innumerable, but generously spaced with gardens and open ground. The shining roofs of the Basilica with its quaint tower—the slender spirette of the Ursulines surrounded by trees and gardens. The Seminary, the Jesuits' College, the Hôtel Dieu, and the Château with its gardens, stand out from the clustering houses. Low down on the shore is a glimpse of one end of the Basse Ville, and conspicuous is the Church of Our Lady of Victory, dear to the citizens as commemorative of deliverance from the enemy which had twice sought a footing at its altars.† Now unroofed and partly in ruins the charm is broken, and the conqueror of to-day, soon to be the friend and protector, stands within the walls.

Over all this beautiful scene Nature is casting her most lavish colours. No Venetian of them all could have transferred to his canvas a blend of colour at once so harmonious, so varied, or so vivid. The wooded banks of Orleans, of Beauport, of Levis, all the shore up and down the river, is an endless succession of arresting beauty spots. The dark blue-green of the firs and spruces are thrown into sharp relief by the gold and yellow of the beeches and elms, the greens of willows, and poplars blend with the russet brown of the oaks, while the dead white

* A part of Saunders' squadron joined Sir Edward Hawke and assisted in the victory over Conflans, on November 3.
† Built originally in 1683 as Nôtre Dame de la Victoire, to commemorate the failure of Sir William Phipps, it became in 1711 Nôtre Dame des Victoires, when Sir Hovenden Walker's expedition ended in nothing.

stems of the birches begin to stand out like silver threads among the lessening foliage.

But green and gold, russet and brown, are but the background which the great artist has designed to bring out the tone which really dominates the colour scheme. Reds, crimsons, scarlet, ruby, rose, pink, every variety and gradation of the queen of colours. Nature is preparing for the winter, but before succumbing to the long months of ice and snow she has donned her finest finery. On the precipitous rock at one's feet are great splashes of red-leafed undergrowth, liberally decorating the grey bare stone. The maples show every shade of scarlet and crimson, and far in the distance the hills themselves, fading in ethereal blue, have nevertheless a rose-pink under-colour due to the autumnal foliage which clothes them.

Down in the low country about Ste. Foy it is the same; wide stretches of blueberry are reddening in the sunlight; even the grass itself asserts a rosy hue from the tinted undergrowth showing from below.

Over all the clear blue sky of the Indian summer, as they call it, the bright sunlight still comforting, and the exhilarating breeze, which yet has a touch of the coming winter.

Perhaps I am too enthusiastic on the subject of this prospect, but I have stood on this spot and watched the changing light on the scene below and tried to picture to myself the feelings of my ancestor as he, too, surveyed the scene. If any reader thinks I exaggerate, let me recommend him to see Quebec for himself on a clear day in autumn— I will guarantee that he is not disappointed!

On October 12 Murray wrote his first reports to Pitt and the Duke of Newcastle, and though the latter was too thoroughly Whig in principles to do much for a brother of so pronounced a Jacobite as Lord Elibank, he was, nevertheless, on terms of friendship with him, and, through his Collier connections, Murray could always count, or at least always counted, on his good will, which was a considerable asset to those fortunate enough to possess it.

"My Lord," he wrote to Newcastle, " General Monckton, having honoured me with the command of His Majesty's troops left here, I take the first opportunity of assuring your Grace that, unequal as I feel myself to the task, I shall, with great zeal and assiduity, exert the utmost of my abilities to preserve to His Majesty this important conquest. Your Grace will be informed, no doubt, by the General how weak the fortifications here are, the rampart not being complete, that it can be called at best a strong cantonment, and that its safety must chiefly depend upon the vigilance and bravery of those who guard it, and I think I can venture to say, this little army has given sufficient proofs there will be no failure on their part. . . . There is one unlucky circumstance which I much fear will in some measure obstruct the service—the small sum of money left me to subsist the troops, provide fuel, procure intelligence, and every other possible contingency ; to remedy the scarcity I propose establishing a paper currency, and endeavour to give it all the credit I can. . . ."

To Amherst he wrote a few days later :

" We have little cash, much labour, no prospects of fresh provisions, a great scarcity of fuel, and ill-housed ; but everybody is cheerful and happy in having Quebec. All those that did not like it are, thank God, gone to places they like better."

There is another passage in the same letter worth quoting, which appears to show that Murray had views on the subject of the American colonies, which were justified by later events.

" Everybody will inform you how powerful and flourishing this colony was, and how formidable it might be under any other governor than Monsieur Vaudreuil, *en bonne politique ;* it should be perhaps destroyed, *but there may be reasons why it should remain, as it is a guarantee for the good behaviour of* its neighbouring colonies." *

* It is a curious circumstance that Montcalm had written in much the same style to De Molé (President of the French Parliament) on August 24, 1759 : " But in this I console myself that the loss of this colony will one day be of more service to my country than a victory, and that the conqueror in aggrandizing himself will find a tomb even in that " (Dartmouth Papers).

To his brother George he wrote :

" The news of the battle of Quebec will have reached you long before this can come to your hands. I had too great a share in it to condescend to particulars, because I hold it odious to speak of oneself. I have the honour to be appointed Governor of Quebec and the conquered country, which is a noble one, indeed infinitely beyond what any in Britain imagined it to be, whether for fertility of its soil or number of its inhabitants. . . .

" I have now served two campaigns under three officers who were put over my head, and I don't find I have got a regiment yet, though I have had the strongest assurances from the ministers. I think I cannot miss it now, and I believe my enemies will agree that I have earned it.

" Pray, my dear George, let me hear from you in the spring, and write sometimes to my dear wife, who has been too much neglected by all my family, except yourself. I am making provision for snow shoes for a winter expedition, and will not allow Chevalier de Levis to be quiet in his cantonment. I have an eye on his magazines. I have 6000 as brave troops as ever existed. Business may, and shall, be done with them, and those who have hitherto deprived me of my preferment may repine of it.

" Your old acquaintance, Saunders, is much my friend. He is a worthy brave fellow, and if it lies in your way I wish you would wait on him and let him know how much I think myself obliged to him. Make my compliments to all relatives about you."

On October 18 the sound of guns was heard again in the war-worn town, but this time without the accompanying shriek of projectiles or the sound of falling masonry. The citadel was firing its farewell salute to the fleet whose co-operation had done so much to procure success, and giving the honour due to an admiral whose faithful interpretation of his duty had contributed, to an extent which has hardly been recognised, to the founding of the British Dominion of Canada. In the many combined land and sea campaigns of the past there were not wanting unfortunate instances, of which none knew the disastrous results better than Murray, when the want of cordial relations between the navy and army had caused disaster; but no General had ever more loyal and thorough support than that given by Saunders and his second in command, Holmes, and we may be sure that the salute which echoed over the St. Lawrence on this day, when Admiral Saunders and the main part of his squadron sailed past the Isle of Orleans and were lost to sight on their homeward voyage, meant more than the mere compliment which his rank entitled him to. With the admiral sailed Townshend, and a week later Monckton, almost recovered from his wounds, sailed in the *Fowey en route* for New York in company with the *Medway* and *Orford*, the last of the squadron. The sole representatives of the naval might of Britain left behind were the *Porcupine* and *Racehorse*, sloops of war, besides three small schooners.

This departure of the fleet was, no doubt, considered necessary to avoid hazarding the ships during the winter, and yet the situation in which the loss of command of the river left Murray was one which might well have condoned the risk of leaving a small squadron in the St. Lawrence. The omission to do so was described at the time by the chronicler of the *Annual Register* * as a " misfortune." Had this " misfortune " been avoided it cannot be in doubt that the subsequent advance of De Levis would have been rendered far more difficult if not impossible. It must not be forgotten that the French squadron still lay intact in the upper river, and placed at the disposal of Vaudreuil a naval force much superior to the sloops left behind by Saunders. Under the able and enterprising command of the French commodore, De Vauquelin, the French seamen were not likely to remain passive.

When the last echoes of the salutes had reverberated from the height of Point Levis, Quebec and its garrison passed from knowledge of the outside world, and the people of England, occupied by constant fresh adventures, ceased to think further of the commander and the gallant

* *Ann. Reg.* 1760.

troops holding this outpost on the frontier of the Empire. " Who the deuce was thinking of Quebec ? " exclaimed Horace Walpole a few months later. " America was like a book one has read and done with, or at least if one looked at the book one just recollected that there was a supplement promised, to contain a chapter on Montreal, the starving or surrender of it," and Walpole's attitude of mind may be accepted as typical of the mind of the country ; probably not one man in England estimated the situation at its true value, and when Murray was called upon to face the inevitable result of mistaken strategy, for which he was not only without responsibility, but had done his utmost to rectify, the result in England was a feeling of irritation that an affair which the public regarded as closed should again be thrust on its notice, and that too in a fashion which at first seemed to threaten disaster.

Left to his own resources, Murray's first care was to reduce by every means the number of inhabitants within the walls, in order to economise his provisions and fuel. The Jesuit priests were ordered out of the town, partly, no doubt, to save their subsistence, but also and principally because they were strongly suspected of giving information to the enemy, who lurked in the neighbourhood and raided up to the walls of the town, often aided by the Canadians of the adjoining districts. It was these frequent attacks, as well as the necessity to hold an area within comparatively easy reach of the town for the purpose of obtaining fuel, that decided Murray to extend the zone of his authority, and at the same time advance his outposts, serving the double purpose of keeping the enemy at a distance and observing their movements.

By this time the necessity of housing the troops, distributing the stores, and preparing for the winter had been got into a forward state, and the Governor felt at liberty to undertake a more active policy. In order to leave no doubt as to his intentions, he issued a manifesto to the Canadians, in which, with a fine *fanfare*, he describes himself as " The Honourable James Murray, Brigadier-

General, Commander-in-Chief of His Britannic Majesty's Troops in the River St. Lawrence (*dans la Rivière de St. Laurent*), Governor-General of Quebec and of the conquered country, etc., etc." How many additional titles the et cetera included is left to the imagination, but Murray's proclamation could leave no doubt in the minds of those to whom it was addressed exactly what his view of the situation was, and what he intended to do to confirm it.

" In consequence of a most severe and painful campaign, we thought of nothing else but to repose our troops and to let the people breathe in tranquility after the misfortunes they have suffered in the course of this year, marked with so many grand and decisive events ; but, notwithstanding such, our humane intentions, I see myself, through that fidelity which I owe to my king, and for the protection of the people submitted to his arms, again called into the field. By what authority can M. Vaudreuil issue his commands to the people whom he has abandoned to their distresses ? What reason can he assign for the unjust and cruel orders he has given to the savages to fall upon and destroy the Canadians thus deserted, and thus, after a series of injustice and insolence, to put the finishing stroke to their misfortunes ? As the generals of the enemy have thought proper to raise contributions on the parishes that are submitted to us, the laws of war and of justice oblige me to make reprisals on those of the upper country—in such cases in future their conduct shall always regulate mine. . . . All communications with the ocean stopped up, without hope, without resource, with an army of experienced veterans in the heart of your country, another at its gates, almost all your frontier barriers snatched from you or abandoned ! We ardently ask you to have recourse to a free people, wise, generous, ready to embrace you, to free you from a severe despotism, and to make you partake of the blessings of a moderate and upright government.

" But if you will not profit by this advice, you must expect the most rigorous treatment consistent with the laws of war. . . . Seeing therefore that the Canadians have no further excuse, if ever they shall presume to have recourse to arms, they must expect all the horrors that

can be inflicted by a victorious and justly enraged army ;
the blame will then revert upon themselves ; human
nature will warrant such a procedure, and the laws of
nations and of war will sufficiently justify it.   Given at
Quebec and sealed with the seal of our arms.   By His
Excellency's command,

" CRAMAHÉ." *

At the same time, while thoroughly prepared to treat
military action with the utmost rigour, he took every
precaution that the susceptibilities of the *habitant* should
not be wounded ; thus he ordered due respect to be paid
to the religious processions which frequently appeared in
the streets of Quebec.

" Officers are to pay them the compliment of the hat,
because it is a civility due to the people who have chosen
to live under the protection of our laws.   Should this piece
of ceremony be repugnant to the conscience of any one
they (*sic*) must retire when the procession approaches."

On November 12 the diary records :

" I thought it proper to march a strong detachment
out, which, after reconnoitring the country myself, I took
post in the churches of St. Foix and Lorette to command
all the avenues to Quebec, so that no considerable body
could march to it without first forcing these two posts,
and for this purpose I fortified them in such manner as to
resist any attack without cannon to support it . . . also
established a civil jurisdiction for the inhabitants, and
appointed Colonel Young chief judge, taking into the other
offices some of the men of best character I could find in
the place."

The winter was setting in, and Knox, who gossiped on
every subject, and seemed to have been a forerunner of
that most chatty of war correspondents known to us in
the early days of the Great War as " Eye Witness," tells
us that the wet and stormy weather was giving way to
hard frosts with cold nights, which tried the troops a good

* Hector Theophilus Cramahé, captain in the 15th Foot from
March 3, 1754.

deal. The post at Ste. Foy, which was about five miles from Quebec, proved most useful, and enabled the wood-cutting parties to work, not only in comparative safety, but to accomplish the arduous work of carrying the cut timber to the town with considerably less labour. " We are secured of an excellent vein of wood in the forest of St. Foy," is the quaint entry in Knox's record. The occupation of Ste. Foy and Lorette was undoubtedly a strong and useful measure, which secured to a much greater extent than heretofore the safety of the garrison, which in the early days could scarce venture, except in well-armed parties, beyond the gates.

To add to many other troubles, Murray was faced with considerable want of discipline in the garrison. " The plundering kind of war which had been carried on this last campaign had so debauched the soldiers that there was no putting a stop to these without severe punishment." Desertion and drunkenness were common offences, and the inhabitants, and especially the Jesuits, gave connivance to these offences, in the one case supplying liquor, and in the other aiding the soldiers to hide until they could be conveyed up country. The Governor was not a man to be trifled with, and he records very briefly : " I recalled all licenses, and ordered for the future every man who was found drunk to receive twenty lashes every morning till he acknowledged where he got the liquor, and to forfeit his allowance of rum for six weeks." On November 16 a man was hanged for plundering, on the 18th a Frenchman received the same fate for inducing men to desert, one soldier received 1000 lashes for exciting to mutiny, and another 300 for being out of quarters at undue time, a third to 1000 for intent to desert, and another the death sentence for desertion. These stern measures show the extent of the evil, and happily had the desired effect, though it took some time to bring the men to a sense of the danger induced by their actions.

On November 15 Murray made his first considerable military movement. He had received intelligence that the enemy had but a small force between Cap Rouge and Jacques Cartier, and ordered out Colonel Hunt-Walsh with 700 men to make a night march to surprise Pointe-aux-Trembles, to raise contributions in that parish and that of Ecureuils beyond it, to publish the manifestoes, and to burn the habitations of such as were with the enemy. This scheme, through a mistake or misapprehension of orders, was effected only in part, and the colonel, having advanced to within a mile of Pointe-aux-Trembles, retired to the place whence he departed, after burning a few of the habitations.

The failure of this expedition was unfortunate, for it brought a large body of French troops " this side of Jacques Cartier," and the diary records : " I had now reason to consider how unlucky it was my scheme had not been thoroughly executed, as in that case the enemy could not have subsisted any body of troops." On November 22 activity of the French ships was reported, ten of them " came to an anchor in sight of the town (from the upper river), but the wind falling and fearing a bombardment, they removed again out of sight." This movement ended in a double disaster, for on the following day " we found five of the ten ships wrecked by the bungling management of the French," and

" Captain Miller of the *Racehorse* went up with the boats manned, without my knowledge, and boarded one of the vessels. Having lighted a fire, he unfortunately blew himself up, his lieutenant, and several men ; the rest were taken, as was a schooner which had been stationed above the town to watch the enemy's motions and to make signals."

In this accident Murray lost the ships' carpenters, on whom he principally relied for building his floating batteries in the spring.*

* This was a matter of very great importance, for it was the floating batteries that Murray intended should counter the French frigates.

About this date Gossip Knox records an order which reads humorously. Apparently there had been complaints as to the quantity of the rations issued, and Murray, after explaining that these were in excess of any that " ever was allowed in any of the King's provisions before," added :

" Every officer, sergeant, corporal, and *faithful* soldier is enjoined to discover any man who shall presume to complain of the said allowance, *that the offender may be brought to trial for sedition and receive the punishment so notorious a crime deserves ;* on the other hand, if the soldiers find any deficiency, they will be redressed on representing it to their commanding officer, and the defrauder will not escape the Governor's resentment, be he who he will."

Certainly Murray had " long hands," and it was not good to incur his displeasure. For the taming of men grown insubordinate as the result of too much licence no better commander could have been found. But a little incident that follows shows that the men had confidence in him. Finding himself in great difficulty for money to carry on the government, he issued a

" Kind of proclamation to encourage the friends and well-wishers of His Majesty to lend what they could afford, for which Colonel Burton (the officer next in command to me) and I gave our bills, to be repaid in six months, with interest at 5 per cent. This in a short time produced so considerable a sum as £8000 . . . and be it remembered to the honour of the Highland or 63rd Regiment,* commanded by Colonel Fraser,† that the non-commissioned officers and private men of that single regiment contributed of that sum £2000."

Gossip Knox tells us this was due to the " remarkable frugality and sobriety " of the Highlanders !

The weather was growing every day more inclement, and the men were obliged to undergo incredible fatigues ; it became necessary to relieve the sentries every hour.

* Formerly 63rd, but at this period properly 78th.
† Simon Fraser, son of the Lord Lovat who was executed after the rising of 1745–46.

Murray decided on building a chain of block-houses to protect the weak fortifications, which had no outworks, from a *coup de main*, and this work, together with the everlasting one of dragging timber from Ste. Foy through what was now deep snow, told heavily on the garrison. On November 30 Knox records the first hint of the coming misfortunes :

" Our brave fellows growing sickly, their disorders are chiefly scorbutic, with fever and dysentery ; this is far from surprising when we consider the fatigues and hardships they have hitherto undergone, which from indifferent clothing, uncomfortable barracks, worse bedding, and their being entirely confined to salt diet, are sufficient to reduce or emaciate the most robust constitution."

On December 14 Murray records : " No less than fifty men this day frost bitten on the wooding and sleying (*sic*) parties." On the next day sixty-five men were incapacitated from the same cause. Yet it was impossible to reduce the effort to obtain fuel for which the garrison was now in great straits. On December 24 the diary tells us :

" From December 17–24 153 have been frost bit ; this happens always on the sleying parties ; nor is there any possibility to avoid this, as, notwithstanding every measure taken, and the diligence of the officers, whose particular province it is, the Canadian horses do not bring in a sufficient quantity to provide for the present or against the spring."

On the 25th Captain Leslie, who had been sent on an expedition to the south shore to subdue the parishes about Point Levis, returned.

" Every officer and soldier of the party has been frost bit more or less, but none dangerously, except two. He had not been able to proceed quite as far as I intended, by reason that the lower parishes were entirely burned and there was no lodging for the troops."

About this time Knox records :

" The weather is now become inconceivably severe, and our soldiers grow numerous in the hospitals ; some who died within these few days are laid in the snow until the spring, the ground being at this time impenetrably bound up with frost."

The men were demoralised by their suffering, and discipline was affected, and severe sentences are again recorded. " For quitting post and robbing, two were to suffer death and two to receive 1000 lashes each, another for trying to impose on the French inhabitants 800 lashes." This last was reduced to 200 lashes in consideration of the " extreme severity of the weather." Of the two death sentences a curious record exists.

" The two men condemned to die for robbery have thrown dice for life, the Governor having been generously pleased to pardon one of them ; eleven was the lucky number which fell to the lot of a soldier of the 43rd Regiment, who, it was remarked, did not discover the least satisfaction upon the occasion by his complexion or otherwise."

Nothing could better indicate the abject misery of the men than this sidelight. The sentences of the courts-martial, of course, appear to us to be brutal, but all this occurred 150 years ago, when hanging was a sentence inflicted for misdemeanours which are now considered of small account. Murray had, indeed, nothing to do with the sentences, and in confirming them he frequently made remissions, for there is no doubt that his natural inclination was towards leniency ; but at the same time the circumstances of the time necessitated making examples if he would keep his men, whose condition of living drove them almost to despair, in that state of control which alone could save them from destruction.

On December 27 Lieut. Butler and four others of the New England Rangers started with despatches for Sir Jeffrey Amherst, a difficult and very dangerous embassy, both in respect of the climatic conditions and the number of hostile Indians through whose haunts the party must pass. The despatch, dated December 24, is of interest, as showing Murray's views and information at the time, and is here inserted, though some parts of it have already been referred to :

" Quebec, 24th December, 1759.

" DEAR SIR,

" I send you the bearer, Lieut. Butler, that you may know how well we are here.* We have had some difficulties, but they are now removed, and we wish for nothing more than the visit Monsieur de Levis has threatened to pay us. If he really intends it, I suppose he will think proper to put it off till the spring, which does not begin till the month of April. I am told he may then bring all the force in Canada against us, as it will be impossible for your army to advance upon them till July, for you must know they look upon the Isle aux Noix as impregnable, and the approaches to Montreal in any other way impracticable till the sun has had its influence. At present their regular troops are in cantonments in the government of Montreal,† and 1200 of the Troupes de Colonie are at Jacques Cartier, ten leagues from here. They have made a fort there, have some Canadians, and are daily bringing more. In the course of the winter, when the rivers are all froze over, there may be a possibility of surprising it, but if I attempt it, I will be sure of my blow ; a little patience, and the game is sure. This post is of no consequence in the operations of next campaign—it will be out of the question ; be master of the river St. Lawrence, and the passage is open to Montreal. I am sorry to tell you I can do little to make you so. By an unhappy imprudence we have lost all our ship carpenters—of the twelve French ships which attempted to pass us the 18th ultimo, five run ashore ; Captain Miller, of the *Seahorse*, with a lieutenant, all the carpenters, and almost all the petty officers of the navy left with us, without my knowledge, eager for plunder, I suppose, went on board one of the wrecks, lighted a fire in her cabin, which by carelessness communicated to some powder, and blew her and themselves to atoms ; two out of six and forty are only saved. You must not therefore depend on me for the craft I formerly promised to provide. My boats are in very bad order, but I flatter myself I shall be able to fit out as many as

---

* It is clear that this optimism was intended to deceive the enemy should the despatch fall into their hands.
† The letter is torn at this place and words omitted.

will embark 1800 or 2000 men. I have only five floating batteries of one gun each. They shall be in order, but further I cannot promise. For this reason, chiefly, I send Mr. Butler that you may have time enough to provide what craft may be necessary for the river next summer. Monsieur Vaudreuil has kept four frigates in Canada. They winter in the River Sorel, and, as I am informed, are to be placed advantageously in the spring to obstruct our passage from this to Montreal. Everybody will have informed you that last summer we never could call ourselves masters of the St. Lawrence, on which river our frigates have little command of the shore ; besides, their progress in it is very uncertain. Flat-bottomed vessels are the things, and a number of them will make all very easy. Butler will tell you of the villainy of our English merchants, and of the methods I have taken to prevent the effects of it. He will inform you of the sobriety and good behaviour of the troops, who will wait patiently till cash arrives from England. . . ."

It has been hinted, and sometimes definitely stated, by various writers that Murray was a headstrong officer, acting without due consideration, and not always taking proper precautions to ascertain the movements of his opponents. I shall have occasion to examine these opinions more fully, but in the meantime there is nothing in the letter other than the considered views of a commander who, while well informed of the intentions of the French, was by no means disposed to underrate their power, and his anxiety to assist and co-operate with the commander-in-chief is obvious. He made it clear elsewhere in this letter that his intention was to entrench and defend a position outside the town ;—this should be remembered in connection with the subsequent course of events. In further confirmation of this we have the record made early in January : " This day Major McKellar gave me his opinion in writing, that the best method to defend the place was to fortify the Heights of Abraham, there to await our reinforcements."

Unfortunately the despatch above quoted never reached Amherst. Lieut. Butler and his party found it impossible

P

to push through the country, and, finding numerous recent trails of Indians, he decided to return to Quebec.

On the last day of the year Murray recorded in his diary a brief statement of the events of the preceding three months :

" Quebec had not only capitulated for itself ; but now the Province from Cap Rouge on the northern, and from the Chaudière on the southern, shore, had submitted ; the inhabitants had taken an oath of fidelity, and surrendered their arms ; my orders were obeyed everywhere within this extent, and the parishes within reach of the garrison assisted to carry in our wood. . . .

" Mr. Wolfe, after warning the Canadians, chastised them for not returning to their houses and quitting their arms. Mr. Monckton rightly considered that the conquest of the land, if bereaved of its inhabitants and stock, would be of little value, gave them the strongest assurances of safety, and even encouragement, if they submitted. They confided in his promises. The country was as yet but partially conquered, and it would have been as impolitic to have crushed the inhabitants at this time as it was necessary to oblige them to give a reasonable assistance to His Majesty's forces. After all, with skill and tender management twenty years will hardly restore this province to the state it was in the beginning of this year."

The first week of the new year opened badly for the garrison, and Knox records :

" The weather is so severe, with frequent showers of freezing rain, that notwithstanding our distress for fuel the sleighing parties could not go out. The men grow more and more unhealthy. Scarce a day passes without two or three funerals."

Nevertheless, the men remained cheerful, and submitted to the necessity of the times. " Exerting all the *man* and the good soldier upon every occasion." A century and a half was to pass before the campaigning cry, " Are we downhearted ? No ! " became the assurance that British soldiers in the winter of 1914–15 were worthy descendants of the old fighting stock ; but let us remember with pride the heroism of these soldiers of the winter in 1759–60, badly clothed, badly fed, and without a grateful motherland providing to the utmost possible extent comforts to relieve their sufferings.

On January 26 another officer, Lieut. Montressor, with twelve New England Rangers, was sent to endeavour to open up communication with Amherst. Presumably the same despatch brought up-to-date was sent, but I have no copy of it. This attempt was successful, and after an adventurous journey the lieutenant delivered his message to Amherst at New York.

Early in February the river was frozen over; a party of the enemy came down and established themselves near Point Levis, and Murray determined to attack them. Experiment showed that the ice would bear the passage of troops, and on the 13th a party under Major Dalling, with two field pieces, marched directly over the ice to the church at Point Levis, while a detachment of light infantry crossed above the town to cut off the retreat. There was some difficulty, as the landings were bad on account of the rise and fall of the tide, but the expedition was successful, with trifling loss, an officer and eleven men were taken prisoners, while seven dead were found in one house. A post was established, and 200 men left to defend it, with orders to hold it to the last extremity, unless attacked by artillery, in which case a retreat over the river to the town was ordered.

On the 22nd intelligence was received of further activity on the part of the enemy, and that 700 men, including some regulars, had passed the river above the town with the intention of attacking the outpost at Point Levis. A further detachment of a captain and 80 light infantry was sent over to hold a suitable landing-place to facilitate the despatch of any further body of troops found necessary to support the post. On the 24th the intelligence indicated that about 1000 or 1200 men were marching on Point Levis, and Murray, having detached the 28th and 63rd (properly 78th) Highlanders to cover his right on the northern shore, marched across the ice with light infantry, the 15th Foot, 300 Highlanders, and four guns; but the enemy gave way at once, and although Colonel Fraser with the Highlanders endeavoured to cut them off by marching up the river on the ice, he was only able to come on their rear, and took some fifteen or twenty prisoners. In punishment of the inhabitants for their aid given in this attack, the village of St. Michel on the west side of the Étchemin River was burned by Major Eliot, who crossed the river with 300 men for that purpose.

In the beginning of March the health of the garrison grew worse, the hospitals were crowded, and the garrison was reduced to 4800 effectives. It is remarkable that the fevers, dysentery, and scurvy which decimated the men did not seem to affect the women at all. These latter were heroines, too, and took all kinds of work, nursing the sick, and even at a later stage assisting at the batteries. Knox records in his diary that a return of the females being called for he found them to total 569 :

" And it is remarkable that we have not lost one of them in the whole course of this severe winter, nor have they even been sickly. The sergeant who brought me this return reported them all well, able to eat their allowance, and fit for duty both by day and by night."

It seemed that the severe fatigue the men were obliged to undergo, and the great amount of guard duties to be performed, were the causes of their bad condition, and orders were issued to reduce all regimental guard mounting and only to retain those necessary on the defences. Murray was evidently an optimist, for at this time he issued an order which reads strangely, though perhaps its intention is obvious, the order included the words : " Perhaps there is not a garrison that has been for so long a time so healthy as this, the sobriety of the soldier and the vigilance of the officer have greatly contributed to it." Knox remarks with dry humour :

" With respect to this salutary order it was thought to

be the effects of good policy; it was said that perhaps His Excellency's superior experience, particularly in the beginning of the late war at Porto Bello and Carthagena, when he had the opportunity of seeing both officers and men buried not by dozens or scores, but by hundreds, might influence him to think less of the daily decease of our most able duty men . . . at the same time it has manifestly appeared that that excellent ingredient in the composition of an able and observant General, the preservation of the health of the soldiery, has been particularly prevalent in the Governor."

Which latter quaint remark we may suspect was intended for his Excellency's eye!

On March 20 Captain Donald McDonald,* of the Highlanders, who frequently figures in the diary, and whom Murray elsewhere describes as a " brave, experienced, and enterprising officer," carried out a surprise at Calvaire, and Captain Archibald at another village called Brulé, " with so good success that the former made seventy prisoners, and the latter seventeen. Our loss was one man killed and six wounded, but many were frost bit from the coldness of the night."

Towards the end of March the activities on both sides increased. Murray prepared a survey of the Heights of Abraham with a view to preparing an entrenched position as soon as the state of the ground would permit it, and began to collect fascines for the purpose. De Levis began to strengthen his advanced guards, and sent the whole regiment of Languedoc to Pointe-aux-Trembles and St. Augustin, while at the same time he called for pilots to help in navigating the frigates lying in the Sorel River.

Early in April the news from the upper river was disquieting; the French had armed several vessels, and with the frigates now possessed six, together with two galleys and a number of flat-bottomed boats. This squadron was overwhelmingly superior to anything which Murray could bring to oppose it, and the intelligence indicated they only

* This officer is frequently mentioned. He was, unfortunately, killed at the battle of April 28.

awaited the breaking up of the ice to transport their troops to Cap Rouge. The plan of campaign was obvious, possessing interior lines, and aware that Amherst could not threaten Montreal in an important degree before the summer, and having as an additional and decisive factor the command of the water approach, De Levis intended to bring all the force at his command against Quebec, weakly defended by a worn-out garrison, and having conquered there, to return in good time to meet Amherst at Île aux Noix and Niagara.

To counter this, Murray decided to occupy Cap Rouge, and thus to hinder the enemy from using the water transport for their artillery, and force them to utilise the bad roads available. He recognised from the first that the game would fall to the combatant whose fleet first ascended the St. Lawrence on the opening of the river, and that to delay a decision until that event was the first consideration. A schooner was fitted out and despatched on April 21 to Lord Colville, commanding the naval force at Louisburg, informing him of the intelligence received and urging despatch in sending relief. The letter runs :

" MY LORD,
        " I have despatched the bearer to inform you of the good state of this garrison. He will at the same time give you an account of the misfortune which happened to our frigates last November, from which accident, and the sickness of their crews in the course of the winter, they are at present almost unable to act. From this circumstance and until the arrival of your squadron, the enemy must remain master of the river, as their naval force consists of four frigates and two row galleys. This may enable them to put in execution the design of bombarding the town. We have certain intelligence that they have assembled 12,000 men and made all necessary preparation for this or some other attempt, which, however chimerical, will still appear more so the instant any part of your squadron appears in the basin, etc."

The inhabitants of the town, excepting the religious orders, were apprised by proclamation of the prospects of an early siege, and were ordered to quit. Three days' notice was given, but even with this indulgence the misery of the people thus necessarily turned adrift was very great. The men, it appears, restrained their sentiments, but the women were loud in their denunciation of Murray for what they held to be a breach of the terms of the capitulation.

On April 23 the ice gave way everywhere, and the river was open once more.

" In consequence, I ordered the 15th Regiment, 28th, 47th, and 58th, and 2nd Royal Americans, together with the Grenadier companies of the whole (about 1600 men), to hold themselves in readiness to encamp on the shortest notice. My design," continued the diary, " was, if the weather had permitted, to have encamped with this body at St. Foy, to be at hand to strengthen any of my advanced posts and to prevent the enemy's landing, but it froze so hard every night that I could not venture on this measure yet, considering the sickly state of the men."

On the 25th the record states that 200 men had fallen sick during the week. The ground was still so hard that the weak working parties could scarce make impression on it, and the impossibility of sending out a force of sufficient strength to support the outposts forced Murray, in view of the imminence of the French advance, to withdraw his outposts from Lorette to Ste. Foy, after breaking all the bridges over the Cap Rouge River. On April 26 Major McKellar marked out the ground for the entrenchment on the Heights of Abraham, but the ground was still too hard to permit a commencement.

On the 27th at 3 o'clock in the mornig the news was brought to Murray that the enemy had landed during the night at St. Augustin,* and were marching on Lorette. With them to cover the landing seven armed vessels laden with

* In his diary Murray says, " landed at Pointe-aux-Trembles," but this is evidently a slip. The enemy had already a large force at Pointe-aux-Trembles, as Murray knew and mentions elsewhere. What occurred was apparently that the frigates and boats conveyed the artillery stores and provisions and some part of the troops to St. Augustin, the remainder marching overland from Pointe-aux-Trembles.

artillery and provisions. The dramatic story has often been told of how this information was conveyed by an unfortunate French sergeant, who, having fallen overboard during the landing, succeeded in clinging to a block of ice and thus carried down the river, was rescued by the crew of the *Racehorse* when almost at the last gasp. The story has been used in some quarters to point to the complete surprise which the French succeeded in giving Murray, but I think readers of the foregoing pages will agree that Murray was very fully informed of the enemy's approach, and had taken such steps as his circumstances admitted to counter the danger. The landing at St. Augustin was possibly made known to him by this strange method, but in all probability he would have had it in any case the following morning, and it was certainly an event he was hourly expecting. The Journal of the Chevalier Johnston goes so far as to say that De Levis " reached Cap Rouge without the enemy (the English) having any information of his having left Montreal ! " Vaudreuil, writing to De Levis on May 2, says :

" It is a pity that the terrible storm of the 26th and 27th (April) was the cause of upsetting your plans. If you had, as you had good reason for hoping, surprised the enemy, you would have decided in a single day, by your foresight, the fortunes of the colony."

CHAPTER X

THE SECOND BATTLE OF THE PLAINS OF ABRAHAM * AND
THE SIEGE OF QUEBEC

In the last chapter we have carried the story to the commencement of De Levis' long-threatened advance ; once again hostile armies were moving on the Plains of Abraham.

Let us consider the state of the garrison before reviewing the steps taken by Murray to meet this new danger. We know that at an early date after the capture of Quebec the garrison, excluding officers, sergeants, and drummers, consisted of 4873 men fit for duty, besides 1376 who were sick or wounded. In successive months these figures varied as follows :

Nov. 24,	4857	men fit, and	1317	in hospital.	Total		6174
Dec. 24,	4680	,,	,,	1407	,,	,,	6087
Jan. 24,	4807	,,	,,	1167	,,	,,	5974
Feb. 24,	4551	,,	,,	1307	,,	,,	5858
Mar. 24,	3860	,,	,,	1856	,,	,,	5716
Apr. 24,	3266	,,	,,	2299	,,	,,	5565
May 21,†	2372	,,	,,	2846	,,	,,	5218

Figures which are eloquent enough of the constant drain on the available fighting force. In March 166 men had died from disease, in April the number was 149. The total number of deaths from disease up to the end of April was over 700. There were, besides men discharged as unfit, desertions, and losses from action, nearly 100 more (excluding the battle of April 28).

Of the total effective strength Knox states that 3140 only were available for action outside the town. Murray,

* This has been called the battle of Ste. Foy, but Ste. Foy was not actually the scene of the struggle.
† That is at the end of De Levis' investment.

in his despatch to the minister, gives the strength in round figures as 3000 ; but he details the actual marching-out strength on April 28 as follows, and, to show the great reductions, I have inserted the figures of the embarkation returns when the force started for Quebec in the previous year :

		On April 28, 1760.		*On June* 6, 1759.	
15th Foot	..	362	N.C.O.s and men	560	N.C.O.s and men.
28th	,,	.. 303	,,	565	,,
35th	,,	.. 317	,,	863	,,
43rd	,,	.. 191	,,	686	,,
47th	,,	.. 294	,,	643	,,
48th	,,	.. 350	,,	816	,,
58th	,,	.. 309	,,	589	,,
2/60th	,,	.. 213	,,	554	,,
3/60th	,,	.. 261	,,	578	,,
78th	,,	.. 414	,,	1219	,,
Hazzen's Rangers		82	,,	86	,,
Light Infantry	..	377	,,	—	included in regts.
Total	..	3476 *		7159	
Royal Artillery	..	116		209	

Thus the battalions were less than half their original strength. The Highlanders hardly one-third, for they had suffered severely both in action and from sickness, the latter probably due to their unsuitable clothing. The 43rd, too, were almost non-existent—" the unhealthiest corps in the garrison," Knox describes them ; nor can it be doubted that many men, though classed as " fit," were in reality only convalescent, and were not in a condition to undergo the fatigues of an exhausting march over country in the worst possible condition.

It will be convenient here to review the forces that De Levis was able to bring into the field. All the eight battalions of French regular troops—that is, the whole available force in the colony—had been assembled (the Regiment La Reine, and the two battalions of the Regiment de Berry, had been added to the five which had formed Montcalm's force in the preceding year). The two battalions of marine troops were also present, and all ten

* This includes 258 sergeants, 107 drummers, and 3111 rank and file.

battalions had been strengthened by the inclusion of detachments of militia, which brought them up to the strength below (Journal de Levis) :

		Regular troops.	Militia.	Total.
Brigade La Reine	La Reine ..	370	223	593
	Languedoc ..	280	285	565
Brigade La Sarre	La Sarre ..	339	230	569
	Béarn	371	221	592
Brigade R. Roussillon	Royal Roussillon	305	279	581
	Guyenne ..	320	261	581
Brigade de Berry	De Berry (2 batts.)	727	519	1246
Brigade la Marine	La Marine (2 batts.)	898	216	1144
		3610 *		
Special troops	Militia of Montreal		287	287
	Cavalry ..		200	200
	Savages ..		270	270
			Total	6631

This figure, excluding the cavalry and savages, contained 2551 men of the militia, and as De Levis had detailed the militia of all the available parishes to the number of 3086 (Journal), it may be assumed that the lower figure is somewhat below the mark, probably, too, the number of savages is too small; but it does not appear that De Levis' active force would have exceeded 7000 men. The men of Quebec and its neighbouring parishes had been disarmed by Murray, and De Levis had no means of re-arming them. No doubt, however, they assisted him in other ways and relieved the soldiers of non-military duties. He also counted on them as pioneers (Journal). Murray, in

---

* The number of prisoners of war sent to France after the rendition of Canada was as follows, which is tolerably in agreement with the above figures :

Brigade La Reine	La Reine..	..	..	117
	Languedoc	..	..	382
Brigade La Sarre	La Sarre ..	..	..	276
	Béarn ..	..	..	408
Brigade R. Roussillon	Royal Roussillon		..	329
	Guyenne	..	..	297
Brigade de Berry	De Berry	..	..	772
Brigade La Marine	La Marine	..	..	1013
	Total	..	..	3894

a letter dated May 19 to Amherst, estimated the number of the enemy at 10,000. Knox gives a still larger figure, but admits that he thinks the return on which he relied was exaggerated (Knox's Journal). Taking into consideration the figures tolerably well known of the strengths of the French regular battalions at the time of the siege of Quebec, I think Murray over-estimated,* and that De Levis' statement is trustworthy.

As I said before, statements have been made that Murray was hot-headed and impetuous, inclined to underrate the offensive power of his opponents. In his Journal, and in the measures he took, there is surely nothing to give colour to such an opinion. On the contrary, with the action taken by both sides now clearly before us, it is impossible to come to any other conclusion than that the preliminary measures which were taken were wise and soldierlike ; and far from underrating his enemy, he makes it clear that his object in the various steps he took was to delay a progress which, from the known strength of the French and his own equally well-known weakness, he saw was inevitable, particularly as the French had the command of the water-way. His object in occupying Cap Rouge, for instance, was " to hinder the enemy from landing their cannon in the river, and (to) oblige them to bring it round by land, which, considering the badness of the road, would in that case delay the operations a considerable time " (Murray's Journal, April 17). At the same time, he had taken every possible step to expedite the appearance of Lord Colville's squadron in the river, recognising that while they remained masters of the river the French had an advantage of the most momentous importance.

It is proper to repeat here that the removal of practically the whole of the English fleet was a mistake of the gravest nature. If the French ships could winter in the Sorel River, and if the *Racehorse* (8 guns) and *Porcupine* (14 guns) sloops, besides three smaller sloops, could winter

---

* It is quite likely that De Levis had over 10,000 men, but a number of these were for the " services " of the army.

at Quebec, there seems no possible reason why a force sufficiently large to counter the French frigates should not have remained also.   Had this been the case this battle of the plains would most probably never have been fought.

Murray recognised most clearly that De Levis would bring his force down to St. Augustin by water, that in face of opposition there, and with the bridges broken down, he would be obliged to pass inland and cross the Cap Rouge River higher up, debouching at Lorette and attacking at Ste. Foy, hence the post of Ste. Foy was held in force.

As an aid to a second line of defence he saw the advantage of a redoubt some 1500 yards from the walls of the town commanding the almost level ground of the Plains of Abraham.   This redoubt was about 160 yards to the east of the present racecourse, and 100 yards south of the Sillery road, and was of great assistance during the subsequent battle, as will be seen.

His third and principal defence was to be a fortified line covering the ridge of high ground known as the Buttes-à-Neveu, about 800 yards outside the walls, the axis of which is roughly parallel to the trace, and formed an exceedingly important position dominating the town defences by its considerable height, commanding also the ground over which a hostile force must approach.

A fourth line, intended to remedy the defective trace of the fortification, was a line of six blockhouses built outside the walls at distances varying from 50 to 250 yards.

It was on April 17 that Murray records in his Journal:

" The best intelligence was now procured that the French had armed six ships which had remained in the river last autumn, with two gallies which they had built ; that they designed to bring down this squadron with a number of boats to transport the troops to Cap Rouge."

De Levis records in his Journal that on this same date he sent M. de la Pause, " Aide Maréchal-Général des Logis," to prepare Jacques Cartier for the disembarkation.   On the 20th the whole army moved, and pushing forward in spite of great difficulties from floating ice, arrived at Pointe-aux-Trembles on the 25th and 26th (April).

Murray continued work on his post at Cap Rouge and on his advanced redoubt, but he found the utmost difficulty on account of the state of the men. " As the garrison was so sickly," he says, " I was obliged to use them with the utmost tenderness." At this time he ordered all the people out of the town, " that I might not be obliged to watch within as well as without." Two pieces of cannon were drawn " with infinite labour and trouble to St. Foix." Knox tells us that the roads being impassable for horses by reason of the dissolving snow, these guns were dragged by the men.

The advantage of Murray's dispositions were summed up very clearly by De Levis in his Journal :

" *Il (l'ennemi) comptoit défendre tous les passages depuis le Cap Rouge jusqu'à Québec dont l'espèce est de trois lieues ; il ne parut pas possible de tenter de passer au bas de la dite rivière suivant le grand chemin de Montréal à Québec, ni de tenter de faire un débarquement depuis le Cap Rouge jusqu'à Québec ; il fut résolu qu'on chercheroit à se rendre maître des hauteurs en passant dans l'intérieur des terres, traversant la Rivière de Cap Rouge à deux lieues au dessus de son embouchure, passant par la vieille Lorette et traversant les Marais de la rivière de la Suette pour s'emparer des hauteurs de Sainte Foi et gagner le susdit grand chemin.*"

Thus necessitating a big detour over a very bad road and making a frontal attack over marshy, low-lying country, over which the troops could only advance on a narrow front against the said " hauteurs de Sainte Foi." The nature of the land below the present village of Sainte Foi has vastly changed from what it was at the time with which we are dealing. Drainage and cultivation have converted it into fields and grazing grounds, and almost extinguished the little river Suette, which, indeed, is hardly known to the inhabitants of to-day, but in those days it was described thus :

" *La rivière Suete . . . tombe dans la plaine qui sépare*

Lorette de Sainte Foy à environ deux milles à l'ouest de l'église de l'ancienne Lorette, y fait mille et mille de tours, traverse le chemin de la Suete, puis gagne l'est directement jusqu'à son arrivée dans la petite rivière Saint Charles à deux milles environ au Sud-est de l'église (de Sainte Foy)" (Bulletin des Recherches Historiques).

On the 26th De Levis and his army embarked at Pointe-aux-Trembles and came by water to St. Augustin, opposite to Cap Rouge on the other side of the river of that name. On this date De Bourlamaque, who had been sent forward at once to reconnoitre and to construct bridges at the selected point over the Cap Rouge, sent back word to De Levis at two o'clock that a passage was possible. The army advanced at once and before nightfall a brigade had occupied Lorette. The night passed by the French army is thus described by De Levis:

"*Il fit une nuit des plus affreuses, un orage et un froid terribles, ce qui fit beaucoup suffrir l'armée qui ne put finir de passer que bien avant dans la nuit. Les ponts s'étant rompus les soldats passoient dans l'eau. Les ouvriers avoient peine à les réparer dans l'obscurité, et, sans les éclairs on eut été forcé de s'arreter.*"

Three pieces of artillery only could be landed, and these could not be carried across the river until the next day.

As mentioned at the end of the last chapter, a good deal has been made of this to show that Murray had been caught napping. I do not think this is justified; had he known every detail of De Levis' movements he could hardly have acted otherwise than he did, and we know of his desire to encamp his force at Ste. Foy had the state of the men permitted it. Two hundred men had been put on the sick list during the week, and he dared not risk it. The great storm of the 26th–27th would probably have been fatal *had* he risked it. In his Journal De Levis tells us that De Bourlamaque, with the advanced guard, had been sent forward across the Suete Marsh, and had taken post in some houses below Ste. Foy. It would seem probable, therefore, that the outpost knew of the presence of the enemy, though Murray does not mention the fact. Knox, however, records on the 21st, that " the French begin to appear numerous in the vicinity of Cap Rouge and Lorette," and it is certainly the case that the whole garrison was on the alert.

There can be no doubt that De Levis had performed a military operation which deserves the highest encomium. Not only had every detail of the disposition of the troops and of the incorporation of the militia in the cadres of the regular units been thoroughly thought out and embodied in clear and precise orders, which are quoted in his Journal,* but, starting on the 20th of the month, he had in seven days, partly by land and partly by water, conveyed a large force through bitter weather and incredible difficulties a distance of quite 150 miles. It is true that some part of the force were cantoned at Jacques Cartier, and it is true that the men had spent a winter in surroundings to which they were accustomed, and were probably fit to face hardships ; but, having all the circumstances in consideration, and the difficulty experienced in obtaining military supplies, of which the French were very short, this march of De Levis should be remembered as an example of what a brave and resolute commander can accomplish.

Immediately on receiving the news that De Levis was at Lorette, Murray marched out with the Grenadiers, picquets, and Amhersts, and two field pieces—perhaps 500 men in all. Three other regiments, commanded by Colonel Walsh (probably 28th, 47th, and 58th, about 700 men), were to march out to support this advanced body (Knox refers to ten field pieces as having been taken— possibly the remainder were with the supporting body). The 35th Regiment, under Major Morris, was sent forward to Sillery to support the outpost at Cap Rouge.

---

* Of these I will quote part of one only : " *La force d'infanterie consiste dans la discipline et l'ordre. Messieurs les commandants des corps et officiers en général doivent donner leurs attentions et applications pour mettre en vigueur ces deux points, malheureusement trop négligés dans nos troupes.*"

It was ten o'clock before De Levis was able to move. He had been obliged to defer any attack, on account of the plight of his troops, following on the hardships of the preceding night. This gave Murray ample time to bring up his reinforcements to Ste. Foy, and, as De Levis tells us, they opened a lively fire on any of his (De Levis') troops that showed themselves outside the woods that patched the low ground in several places. De Levis describes the situation very succinctly:

"*Ayant vu les ennemis se renforcer, ne pouvant juger de leur nombre et en paroissant occuper les endroits accessibles et la colline où ils étoient . . . comme d'ailleurs, l'église de Sainte-Foi qui étoit fortifiée avec du canon étant en face du chemin ou nous étions, il falloit les forcer dans cette église et dans les maisons voisines, qui se flanquoient, et que nous ne pouvions mener l'artillerie que par le chemin qui n'étoit pas practicable, ni déboucher qu'à travers des bois marécageux et nous former après les avoir passés que sous le feu de leur artillerie at mousqueterie, tout cela fit prendre la résolution à M. le Chevalier de Lévis, vu le mauvais état où avoit été l'armée depuis trente heures, d'attendre à l'entrée de la nuit à se mettre en marche pour aller les tourner sur leur gauche.*"

Murray records that he found the enemy

"in possession of all the woods from Lorette to St. Foix and just entering the plain. However, they declined to attack me in the advantageous position I had taken; but, finding their numbers increasing, and endeavouring to get round me by the woods, the weather very bad, and having received intelligence while I was out of a report that two French ships were at the Traverse (*i.e.* the east end of the Isle of Orleans), I thought it proper to retreat to the town."

The church at Ste. Foy was blown up,* as there was no means of removing the ammunition, etc., stored there. De Levis records that this took place at about one o'clock, and that

---

* An interesting little side-light on Murray's character was told me by the Abbé Scott, curé of the parish of Ste. Foy, that after the withdrawal of De Levis, Murray sent £25 as a contribution to restoring the church. This incident is recorded in the church records.

on seeing Sainte Foy abandoned he ordered his cavalry and advanced guard to occupy the ground.

Thus ended the first phase of the battle, which was indeed merely a reconnaissance. Murray certainly relinquished a strong position, and it seems barely possible that De Levis would have succeeded in making a night march with his weary troops over marshy stream-intersected ground, so as to make an attack between Ste. Foy and Cap Rouge. Almost certainly he could not have conveyed his artillery. The retirement gave his men a much-needed rest and a sense of victory, almost equally important. In normal circumstances it can hardly be disputed that Murray should have held on to Ste. Foy and brought up his reserves to cover the two miles of distance between his left and Cap Rouge. But the circumstances were not normal. The number of men he could dispose of was a maximum of 3000—he estimated the enemy at 10,000. We believe this estimate was excessive, but, at least, he was outnumbered by more than two to one. But probably the deciding factor was the condition of his troops. The march of some five miles in the snow-wreathed roads, the several hours of facing the enemy, had exhausted many of his sickly soldiers. The day was cold and wet ; another night such as the one just passed would have the worst possible effect. A defeat at or near Ste. Foy would almost certainly result in complete disaster. He thought it " proper " to retire ; he was probably right.

In the night we may suppose there were anxious councils. As for the troops, Knox draws a brief picture, which is eloquent enough :

" The army, being extremely harassed and wet with constant soaking rain, were allowed an extraordinary gill of rum per man ; and some old houses at St. Rocque were pulled down to provide them with firewood in order to dry their clothes."

The result of the war council may be given in Murray's words :

" The enemy was greatly superior in numbers it is true ; but when I considered that our little army was in the habit of beating the enemy, and had a very fine train of artillery, that shutting up ourselves at once within the walls was putting all upon the single chance of holding out for a considerable time a wretched fortification—a chance which an action in the field could scarcely alter—at the same time that it gave an additional one, perhaps a better, I resolved to give them battle, and if the event was not prosperous, to hold out to the last extremity, and then to retreat to the Isle of Orleans or Coudres with what was left of the garrison to wait for reinforcements. This night the necessary orders were given."

At 7 o'clock in the morning of April 28 the British army was in motion—formed in two divisions, the right column, issuing from St. John's Gate under Colonel Burton, contained the 15th, 58th, 2nd/60th, and 48th; the left column from St. Louis Gate, was commanded by Colonel Fraser, and contained the 43rd, 47th, 78th, and 28th. Each column of approximately 1200 men.

A corps of reserve, under Colonel Young, included the 35th and 3rd/60th. Major Dalling, with the light infantry (about 370 men) covered the right, Hazzen's Rangers and McDonald's Volunteers (about 300 men in all) the left.

There was little of pomp and circumstance in the appearance of this little army. The rigid customs of the day, which made the men don their best for battle and inculcated extra care in the dressing of queue and pipeclaying of belts, could have little adherence after the winter experience of Quebec, for the clothing was patched and ragged and replaced in many cases by such homely garments as could be improvised by the men themselves. The service buckled shoes had long since been replaced by the *soulier* of the country; many of the men were maimed or disfigured by frost bite, but no doubt from sheer custom they turned out at their smartest, and the drummers at the head of each corps, who in those days occupied the place of both band and buglers, tapped out their bravest ruffles.

But if the marching battalions as they filed out of the city gates showed to little advantage, what can be said of the wan-visaged details left behind to guard the city ? The greater number of them were men who had willingly donned accoutrements to take their share, but who up to that day had been lying in the hospitals. Even men too ill to stand had their firelocks, bayonets, and ammunition near them, that as many as possible of those fit to march might go out.

Of the women no writer has left us any description. We know only that they had suffered little from the rigours of the winter, but one may hazard the opinion that on this morning in April, and during the preceding night when the weary soldiers had returned from their dispiriting recon-naissance, they were doing, and had done, heroine's work in tending the sick and cheering the down-hearted. They were accustomed to war and accustomed to hard living, but they were women for all that, and had women's hearts under the rough exterior, and women's pity for these harassed men marching through the snow-drifts to an encounter from which many did not return.

For the rest, the town was empty. Almost the entire population had been driven out, as has been said, " to prevent the necessity of guarding within as well as without," and Murray and his following had to pass no inquisition of curious citizens—critical, unfriendly, or indifferent.

Outside the walls the two columns would be in open country. Burton's column on the right, with a clear view of the St. Charles valley on the one side, the open cultivated land bordering the Ste. Foy road on which they marched, ahead of them ; Fraser's column on the Sillery road, as soon as they ascended the rise to the Buttes-à-Neveu would have an uninterrupted view over the country stretching gently away to the west, with the St. Lawrence and its rough precipitous banks on their left hand. Arrived abreast of the eminence the columns formed line and took up a position which it was Murray's intention to hold and

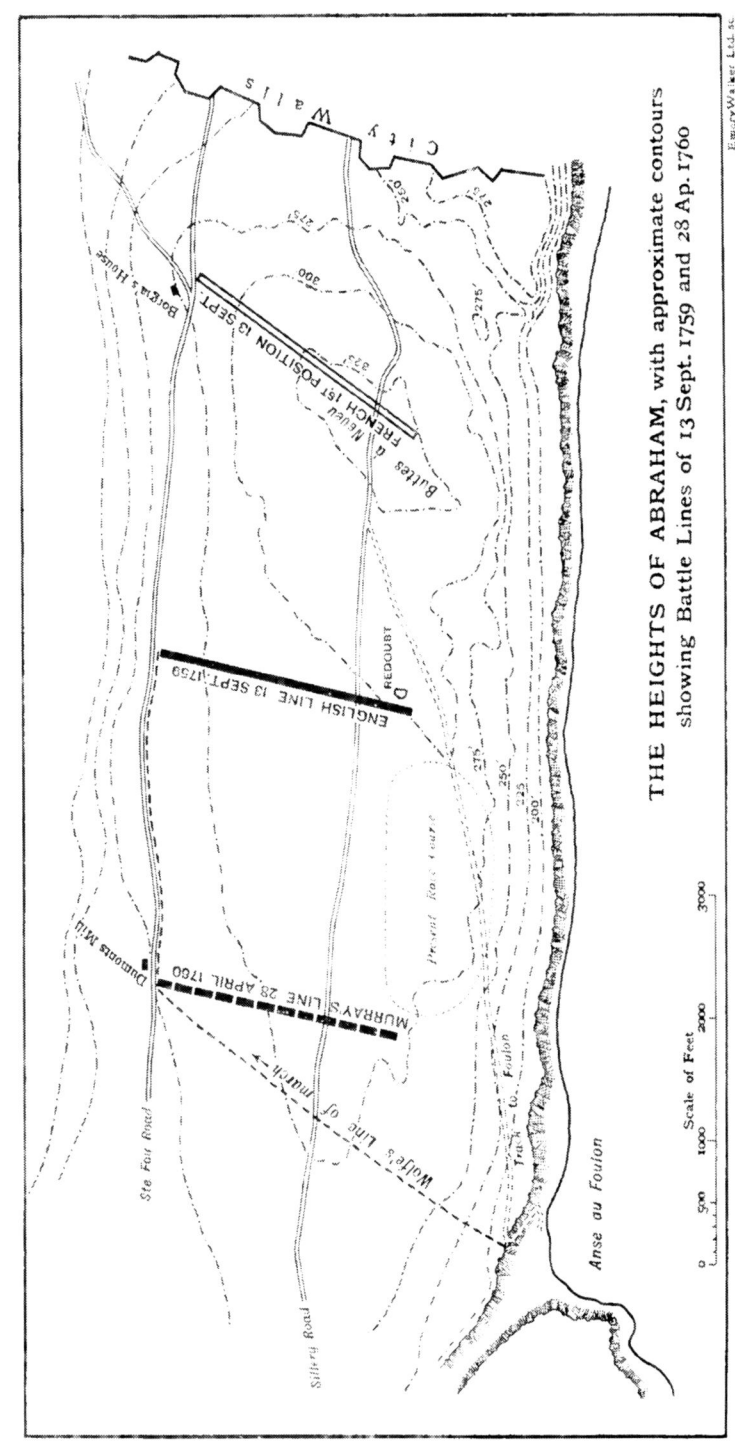

THE HEIGHTS OF ABRAHAM, with approximate contours
showing Battle Lines of 13 Sept. 1759 and 28 Ap. 1760

Emery Walker Ltd. sc.

City Walls

Borgia's House

Buttes à Neuve FRENCH 1st POSITION 13 SEPT.

300

325

275

260

300

275

ENGLISH LINE 13 SEPT. 1759

REDOUBT

Provost Rose Course

250

275

225

200

Dumont's Mill

MURRAY'S LINE 28 APRIL 1760

Wolfe's Line of march

Ste Foix Road

Track to Foulon

Sillery Road

Anse au Foulon

Scale of Feet

0   500   1000   2000   3000

fortify, and for this purpose he had burdened his men with entrenching tools.*

The line on the " buttes " could not have been formed before 8 o'clock, and while the battalions were taking up their positions Murray rode forward and reconnoitred the enemy.

His view extended over a stretch of open land, falling very gradually towards the west. On his left front, a mile away, the terrain was blocked by the woods which, commencing about the region of the Anse au Foulon, stretched for some distance towards the Cap Rouge ; all this open land, which in summer time was cultivated, was flecked with patches of half-melted snow which lay thick and slushy in the hollows. The ground surface was soft and muddy, but below this was still the hard bone of a frost that had extended several feet into the soil. Below, in the bottoms near the wood, the ground was marshy about the bases of the two little eminences, which were a feature of the landscape, one on each side of the Sillery road, where it entered and was lost to sight amongst the trees. On his right front was the Ste. Foy road, bordered at intervals by the houses of the *habitants ;* a short mile away Dumont's Mill was prominent, and beyond the road could be traced a considerable distance towards Ste. Foy. Along this road could be seen the marching columns of the French army. Some part of the enemy had already taken ground to their right and reached the outskirts of the wood. Another body was active about the mill ; more troops were continually arriving. Towards Dumont's Mill scattered groups of the British light infantry were already in action.

---

* We are told that twenty pieces of artillery were taken out, two by each battalion. Although not specifically stated, it may be assumed that these were man-handled—it would, in fact, have been impossible to use horses across country, having in view the partly dissolved snow which covered the ground ; and even assuming that each gun with its tumbril was unaccompanied by any other vehicle for reserve ammunition, not less than from four hundred to five hundred men would be necessary to drag them into position. This was naturally an immense added labour which seriously reduced the mobility of the troops, and the efficiency of their volume of fire.

On the French side, combining the statements of the Chevalier de Levis, M. de la Pause, and the account published in the *Gentleman's Magazine* of 1760 (being " The French Account of the Transactions of the Army in Canada "), we can follow the course of events pretty clearly. De Levis mounted early in the morning and reconnoitred, believing that the English had retired within the walls. He found, however, certain detachments of the enemy (this must be the detachment of light infantry mentioned by Knox : " Early this morning our light troops pushed out and without difficulty drove them to a greater distance "), and, being unsupported, he retired before them. Meanwhile, ten companies of Grenadiers, forming the van of the French army, occupied a position a little in advance of the knoll, which still can be seen just north of the Sillery road ; but De Levis gave orders that five of these should occupy Dumont's Mill on the Ste. Foy road, which he intended should cover the left of his line. The remaining companies of Grenadiers retired to the small eminence already mentioned. Orders for the five brigades, which in the meantime were marching down the Ste. Foy road, to deploy were given, and De la Pause was told off to direct them to their positions as they arrived.

It was at this period that Murray made his observation. It was, in his words, the " lucky moment." The order for an advance in line was given, the drums beating the " generale." He hoped to destroy the French force before it could fully deploy.

An advance in line over the rough open country, covered in many places by slushy snow-drifts, must have been slow, some 1300 yards were to be covered, and at least half an hour would elapse ; the English force was moreover descending the gently sloping ground and losing the advantage of its first position. The time was invaluable to the French ; the two first brigades had taken up their position on the left—they consisted of La Sarre and De Berry ; the third brigade of marine battalions was taking up its position in the centre. La Reine and Royal

Roussillon were still marching under cover of the woods to form the French right.

The first contact was at the mill known as Dumont's, which was now held by the French Grenadiers. The mill occupied the site, or very near it, of the present monument to De Levis and Murray, standing at the end of the "Avenue des Braves," which indicates the centre line of the conflict. Here Dalling's Light Infantry made a vigorous attack and drove out the Grenadiers. The Chevalier Johnston gives a spirited, if somewhat inaccurate, account of this, describing the " Highlanders " * (*sic*) and Grenadiers attacking each other with bayonet and dagger and taking and retaking the houses several times, until the Grenadiers were reduced to fourteen men. While this was going forward the English artillery had caused heavy casualties on the French left, and De Levis ordered a retirement within the shelter of the woods, that they might reform and await the attack of the brigades now forming on the right. This movement, while it saved the French left from being overthrown by the advancing English, also had the effect of leading Major Dalling's men into a too vigorous pursuit of the French Grenadiers, who were flying from Dumont's Mill. Dalling had unfortunately been wounded, and perhaps his men were out of hand ; at all events, they were severely handled by the French left brigades now retired within the wood ; they were forced back and almost annihilated (losing 218 men killed and wounded, almost two-thirds of their number), dispersing across the front and masking the fire of Colonel Burton's battalions. Seeing this confusion, Murray personally hurried up Otway's (35th Foot) battalion to cover his right.

While this partially successful action was going forward on the right, the left battalions of the English line had taken possession of the little eminence, south of the Sillery road, where now stands the Meréci Convent, on which stood two small redoubts partly ruined, remnants of

---

* There may have been a few Highlanders among the light infantry, but it is not very likely.

Townshend's entrenchments of the previous year. Unfortunately, success here was short-lived. The brigades forming the French right, La Reine and Royal Roussillon, which were now formed in the wood facing our left, and consisting of over 2000 men, easily outflanked the English battalions, and overpowering the Rangers and McDonald's Volunteers, who formed the only flank protection. Here the gallant McDonald * was killed, and many others. De Levis claims that this flank attack was carried out by the Roussillon brigade only, with some Canadians of the brigade La Reine, the regulars of the latter having moved off to the left through a mistake, and the truth of this is borne out by the light losses of the two battalions forming it. Even with this disadvantage, the numbers available were not less than 1700 men, opposed to two weak battalions of the British, and a small body of Rangers and Volunteers, which had become somewhat unsupported by the general inclination of the remaining battalions to the opposite flank.

The result was inevitable, and the whole British left crumpled up, after a gallant resistance, in which they lost half their strength. Murray did all that was now possible, and his second reserve battalions, the 3rd/60th, as well as the 43rd from the centre, were brought up to endeavour to stop the rout on the left, but without success, the battalions arrived too late.

On the English right also the inevitable outflanking by a superior force took effect. Brigadier de Bourlamaque, having rallied the brigade La Sarre, and taking advantage of the confusion caused by the overthrow of the light infantry, advanced the whole brigade, doubtless supported by that of De Berry, and surrounding the English left, finally recaptured the mill and broke the English resistance. The 15th and 48th bore the brunt of the fighting in this

---

* This officer had been foremost in all operations during the campaign. It was he who led the first party at the attack on the Anse au Foulon, in September, 1759, and his name constantly appears in Knox's and Murray's Journals. Murray particularly had a warm regard for him. and several times refers to his bravery, skill, and enterprise.

section. The English centre, meanwhile facing at short range the wood in which the French marine brigade was concealed, could do but little, and hardly contributed to the fortunes of the day.

A general retreat was enforced, and the disadvantage of having to retire up-hill became apparent. It was impossible to save the guns (it is stated that two only were saved); even some of the wounded must be left to the mercy of the enemy. The redoubt in rear of the English left, which, though but half complete, deceived the enemy, and held their advance for ten minutes (Mackellar's report), enabled the English to maintain some order in their retreat.

Whatever opinions may be formed on the battle tactics, there can be no argument as to the fighting bravery of the British troops. The battle lasted for three hours, we are told, *i.e.* presumably from the first contact at Dumont's Mill, that is to say, the retreat commenced about one o'clock. Out of a total of rather over 3000 men engaged, the loss in killed and missing, including prisoners, was 41 officers and 255 men, and of wounded, 89 officers and 724 men.* Thus at least thirty-three per cent. of the men were put out of action. On the French side De Levis gives a return of 933 † killed and wounded in the action alone, and it was believed that this statement was short of the facts. The details of the casualties in each regiment are given in De Levis' Journal, and these are of interest, whether accurate or not, as showing where the brunt of the fighting fell. Summarised these are :

		Killed and Wounded.	
French Left	Brigade la Sarre	27 officers	203 men
	Brigade de Berry ..	20 ,,	168 ,,
French Centre	Brigade de la Marine ..	18 ,,	97 ,,
French Right	Brigade Royal Roussillon	12 ,,	123 ,,
	Brigade La Reine ..	6 ,,	39 ,,

In addition, the Canadian Militia lost 12 officers and 203 men, which appears to indicate either that all the militia incorporated with the regular battalions are included in

---

* Murray's despatch to Amherst of April 30.
† De Levis' return puts the totals at 833, but the addition of the figures is wrong.

these figures, or else that many more were in the fighting line than De Levis admits.*

Thus upwards of 2000 casualties in the combined forces, estimated by me at about 10,000 men, testifies to the truth of Knox's remark, that " the action was immensely warm for near two hours." The figures above, moreover, confirm the claim that the action on the British right was within a measurable distance of success, but all the conditions were against probability of final victory.

It seems impossible to contend that Murray was justified in quitting the high ground and advancing to meet the enemy. The position on the Buttes-à-Neveu was not entrenched, it is true, although it certainly had been the intention to entrench it, and even at the eleventh hour, by taking entrenching tools, Murray had evident intention of advancing no further—he had prepared fascines, and with these a considerable cover could have been obtained without digging, or even driving in pickets, which the hard state of the ground prevented. The position was within easy reach of the town, and his flanks were tolerably well assured by the fire of the block-houses and from the walls. On the other hand, had this position been held De Levis would probably not have attacked—there was no special reason why he should. His position from Dumont's Mill to the Foulon gave him good communications, and his object in coming at all was less to make a regular siege than to be at hand should the expected French reinforcements enter the river.

If De Levis had chosen to play a waiting game Murray could scarcely have remained for any length of time on the " buttes " to await an attack ; his sickly troops would have melted away within a few days if exposed to the wet and cold of a bivouac or even an encampment, and he would probably have been obliged ultimately to retire

---

* In a letter to Bougainville, dated May 3, Bourlamaque writes : " *Nous perdrons l'élite des officiers, La Sarre, Berry, Béarn, et la Marine, surtout, sont écrasé, ainsi que les Grenadiers Mille hommes je crois tués ou blessés,*" and adds, " *Ne dites de cette lettre que ce que vous croirez convénable ; surtout diminuez notre perte.*"

within the walls. Perhaps it was this reflection which caused him to seize what he thought was the "lucky minute" and endeavour to overthrow the French army whilst it was still in column. It is difficult, perhaps impossible, for us to conjure up the circumstances in which Murray found himself, and the only criticisms that can, with any confidence, be offered, are that if an advance beyond the " buttes " was desirable, it should have been to a lesser distance, not bringing his line into the low ground ;   and that had he concentrated his artillery on the mill and the moving French columns at a range of, say, half a mile, he would probably have inflicted heavy loss on the enemy, while suffering very slightly himself, and then, if attacked, he could have regained his vantage point.

That his correct course was to remain passive within the walls, suffering De Levis to take up his position on the " buttes," cannot for a moment be admitted.   The Pyrrhic victory which De Levis had gained left his troops little desire for an assault, which under other conditions they might have undertaken with considerable chance of success.

A critic, writing in the *Annual Register* of 1760, in a judicial and not unfriendly strain, says :   " It is hard to understand how the chance of holding out a fortress should not be lessened after a defeat of the troops which compose the garrison," but he adds,   " These are matters not so easily comprehended by those who are at a distance from the scene of action."   To this criticism I will only reply in addition to what has been already said.   It would have been impossible to hold Quebec during the winter without the outposts at Cap Rouge and Ste. Foy, or to withdraw those outposts without advancing in force beyond the walls (hence a theory which relied on passive defence only, would have broken down in practice), though the argument still remains that having once withdrawn the outposts there was no necessity for risking further battle; but in this judgment I find it impossible to agree, for the reasons already given.

Once within the walls, Murray's chief object was to

restore the shaken morale of his troops. An order was at once issued which is worth quoting ; it concealed nothing, and appealed direct to the hearts of the men :

" The 28th of April has been unfortunate to the British arms, but affairs are not so desperate as to be irretrievable. The General often experienced the bravery of the troops he now commands, and is very sensible they will endeavour to regain what they have lost. The fleet may be hourly expected, reinforcements are at hand, and shall we lose in one moment the fruits of so much blood and treasure ? Both officers and men are exhorted patiently to undergo the fatigues they must suffer, and to expose themselves cheerfully to some dangers—a duty they owe to their KING, their COUNTRY, and THEMSELVES."

On April 30 Murray sent a despatch to General Amherst, in which he detailed his situation :

" The intelligence I had the honour to communicate to you by Lieut. Montressor of the enemy's designs proves true.

" The 17th of this month I was informed that they had everything in readiness to fall down the river, with eight frigates, the moment it was clear of ice, and it did not break up here sooner than the 23rd, consequently, as the country was covered with snow and the earth impenetrable, it was impossible to attempt intrenching myself on the Heights of Abraham, which I formerly told you was my plan of defence, before the 25th, and even then, as will no doubt appear by the Journal of the engineer-in-chief, it was hardly possible to drive in the first pickets, the thaw having reached no further than nine inches from the surface (here follow details already described).

" As we have been unfortunate I am sensible I may be blamed universally at home ; but I appeal to every officer in the field, if anything was wanting in the disposition or my endeavours to animate the men during the whole affair. The superiority which these troops had acquired over the enemy ever since the last campaign, together with the fine field train we were furnished with, might have tempted me with an action, supposing I had not been thoroughly convinced of the necessity of it.

" We lost in the battle about one-third of our army, and have certain intelligence that the enemy had no less than 10,000 men in the field. . . . *Had we been masters of the river, in which it is evident ships may safely winter, they would never have made the attempt* (my italics).

"I must do the justice to Colonel Burton in particular, and to the officers in general, that they have done everything that could be expected of them. . . ."

For a day or two the bonds of discipline were broken, and the men were inclined to panic and despair. "Immense irregularities were hourly committed," says Knox, and prompt stern measures were necessary. On the 30th a man was hanged without trial "for an example to the rest." All liquor "not belonging to the King" was spilled to prevent the men from getting it. Murray and his officers were everywhere encouraging the garrison and showing an intrepid activity. Within two days, while the French were entrenching on the "buttes" and busy landing their artillery and stores at the Foulon, guns had been dragged from the river front and mounted on the walls, platforms built for them, and embrasures cut in the weak parapet which formed the landward defences. Almost at the start another piece of ill-luck occurred in the destruction of the great block-house built outside the St. Louis gate. Knox describes this as accidental, but Murray seems to attribute it to the enemy's fire. He adds : "This was unlucky, as it was our most advanced work, roomy, strong, and *hors d'insulte*, having three pieces of cannon in it." Being considerably advanced towards the dominating position of the "buttes," this block-house was important as preventing the enemy from working on their batteries.

By May 2 the efforts of the governor and his officers had so far recovered the position that Knox was able to record :

"We no longer harbour a thought of visiting France or England, or of falling a sacrifice to a merciless scalping knife. We are roused from our lethargy ; we have recovered all our good humour, our sentiments for glory, and we seem, one and all, determined to defend our dearly-purchased garrison to the last extremity."

The activity of the garrison, in fact, knew no bounds. Guns there were in plenty, and fresh batteries were constantly being opened, which caused serious difficulties to the attackers. De Levis tells us :

" *Les ennemis, qui à tous moments démasquoient des pièces nous retardoient beaucoup par des précautions qu'il fallait prendre ; les boulets plongeant derrière les hauteurs, il y avoit peu d'endroits ou l'on fut à couvert, l'on fut même obligé d'éloigner le camp.*"

On May 1 the *Racehorse*, Captain MacCartney, was despatched to convey to Lord Colville the position of affairs, and to urge the early return of the fleet. As it turned out, it is unfortunate that this was done, for the *Racehorse* made Halifax in an exceptionally quick passage of ten days, and apparently passed Colville on the voyage. Governor Lawrence, however, thought it advisable to open the despatches (which were for Amherst), and wrote to Pitt by the *Richmond* on May 11, giving him a very pessimistic view of the situation. It was this news that arrived a few days before the intelligence of the final defeat of De Levis, and caused great consternation in England.* Murray's letter to Amherst has already been partly quoted on p. 238. It was a plain statement, and disguised nothing, but evidently the General felt that the support given him had been meagre, yet it gave his enemies a handle for much misrepresentation of which in after-years they made use.

The weather was improving, sorties were constantly made at night of small parties to harass the enemy. A detachment was maintained outside the walls at night to guard against surprise. A heavy fire on the enemy's works was kept up day and night ; up to the 3rd (May) no fewer than 4000 rounds had been fired. The convalescents and the women bore a hand making wadding for the guns, and filling sandbags—a hundred precautions were taken which are detailed in Murray's and Knox's

* The *Richmond* arrived in England on June 17. Ten days later Murray's despatch bringing news of the raising of the siege arrived.

Journals. Every one was busy and worked with a will. Discipline was severe. The Provost * " received orders to hang all stragglers and marauders."

On May 5 and 6 De Levis records, " *Les travaux n'avancerent pas beaucoup ; on perdoit toujours quelques hommes.*"

It was not until May 11 that the French batteries were able to open fire. The St. Louis and La Glacière bastions were chosen for attack, and three batteries of six, four, and three pieces were prepared. Fortunately for the garrison the pieces were old and of little power, and the powder was bad. Not more than twenty rounds per piece could be fired in the twenty-four hours, and even then some of the guns burst.

" *Le peu de poudre et le peu d'effet qu'on devoit attendre de cette artillerie qui étoit d'ailleurs trop éloignie obligerent M. le Chevalier de Levis, pour ne se trouver totalement dépourvu d'ordonner qu'il ne fut tiré que vingt coups par pièce dans les vingt quatre heures.*"

Murray's anxieties so far as artillery attack was concerned were greatly diminished, and, indeed, the machinery for killing in those days might be described as honestly clumsy, from the flint-lock muskets, ineffective beyond fifty yards, to the heavy siege 24-pounder, of which, by the way, De Levis says he possessed but one. Little could be done unless at close quarters, and the days were still distant when men were to set themselves to devise scientific methods of dealing death. " Singular Guillotin " was still a respectable practitioner, and cured the bodies that one day he would destroy. Zeppelin, inventor of murder machines for the destruction of women and children, was still in the womb of the future, and the unnamed scoundrel who devised poisonous gas as a means of attack was as yet undreamt of. Murder by these means would not have been tolerated at a period when gentlemen fought like gentlemen. Let us hope that the modern professors

* " Zachariah Flitner was appointed Provost-Marshal by General Murray. The official hangman was Benjamin Gable " (Doughty).

of the cult of indiscriminate slaughter will, to borrow a thought from the Sage of Chelsea, join the Ghost of Guillotin wandering through centuries on the wrong side of Styx and Lethe, hand in hand with William the Outcast! " There are crimes that obliterate the past and close the future." *

We must remember, however, that if the energy of the defence kept the enemy at a distance, still the walls were bad.   It was on the 12th that Murray noted :

" The chief acting-engineer reported to me, at four this afternoon, that, having observed the enemy direct their fire very briskly to the above-mentioned post (La Glacière Bastion) he had been out to observe the effect, and was surprised to find it so great, owing, as he supposed, to the rottenness and badness of the wall. . . . This was matter of astonishment, the enemy having fired but a short time, and at such a distance as rendered the effect very surprising."

But a danger greater than the effect of De Levis' weak artillery was the state of the sickly garrison, deprived of all means of obtaining the fresh food which was essential to remove the taint of scurvy, and when at 11 o'clock in the forenoon of May 9 our old friend the *Lowestoft* frigate worked up past the Isle of Orleans and saluted the garrison with twenty-one guns, we can imagine the joy and relief of the soldiers, once more in touch, after seven terribly trying months, with that long arm of England which reaches across all the seas.   " The gladness of the troops is not to be expressed ;   both officers and soldiers mounted the parapets in the face of the enemy and huzzaed with their hats in the air for almost an hour." The vessel was but the advanced guard, and on the 15th the *Vanguard* and *Diana* arrived, under command of Commodore Swanton.

* An expression of opinion, worth recalling, written in 1797 by John Almon, is the following : " Phlegm, sullenness, inhumanity, and a most inordinate love of power, are the characteristics of a German mind.   He only delights in riot and homicide, like his Thracian god Mars, to whom he sacrifices many human victims, and to whom he pours profuse libations."

The re-establishment in the St. Lawrence of sea-power, which should never have been relinquished, settled the question; De Levis recognised that the Court of France had abandoned hope in declining to enter the contest by sending relief.* He had done his possible, and done it well, with the small means at his disposal. He decided to raise the siege and retire to Montreal, leaving garrisons at Pointe-aux-Trembles, Jacques Cartier, and Deschambeau, as he retreated.

No time was lost in asserting the value of naval power. It appears that the French had a detachment on the Beauport side, who took Swanton's ships for Frenchmen, and reported accordingly to De Levis, " upon which it was concerted between Commodore Swanton and myself," wrote Murray in his Journal :

" that he should attack the (French) frigates with the first flood-tide in the morning (the *Vanguard* and *Diana* arrived in the evening, probably in the dusk), and, to persuade the enemy the ships that came up were not our friends, that I should beat to arms about one in the morning, as if much alarmed."

The ruse was quite successful,† and before dawn the French commander, the gallant Vauquelin,‡ though

---

* A store ship, laden with artillery munitions, which would have been of immense use to De Levis, arrived in the St. Lawrence in November, but, taking refuge in the Saguenay River, was ice-bound there, and the stores never reached their destination. A fleet of transports convoyed by the frigate *Machault*, which arrived in June, and took refuge in Gaspé Bay, was destroyed by Commodore Byron in July. They had been despatched on April 15, " *temps au quel ils devoient arriver*," as De Levis dryly remarks.

† De Levis states that though he was aware of the vessels being English, and had sent orders to his ships to retire, the officer conveying his instructions failed to deliver them owing to the bad weather.

‡ Vauquelin was commander of the French frigate *Aréthuse* at Louisburg in 1758, which, after causing great damage to the English attack by her fire, managed to escape and elude the English fleet. The Chevalier Johnston records after the action in the St. Lawrence that the English admiral was so " delighted at his bravery that he asked him how he could serve him, and at his request sent him back to France. . . . This noble and generous behaviour of the English did honour to their nation, far beyond what De Vauquelin met with from De Berryer, Secretary of the Navy, on his arrival in France."

R

surprised and hopelessly outclassed, fought his ship, the *Atalante*, to the last, and, refusing to lower his colours, was taken prisoner by a boarding party. The *Pomone* was driven ashore and burned, and all the transports destroyed excepting a small sloop of war, *La Marie*, which, by throwing her guns overboard, was enabled to escape up the river. This naval action had an effect on the final operations of the highest importance, for it deprived the French not only of the greater part of the stores that had been accumulated on the transports, but necessitated the abandonment of all the equipage that they had on shore, and, in their then circumstances, this was a decisive factor in preventing the French army again taking the field with any hope of success.

Thus ended the siege. The town had been invested for seventeen days only, but the energy and resource of Murray, who, with a ragged, sickly garrison (of 2000 effective men) had resolutely maintained his position with no hope of relief, except from the sea, compares to his credit with the conduct of De Ramezay in the previous September, when, with a garrison of at least equal numbers, he surrendered before a gun was fired against his walls after an investment of three days, while an army, which should have been capable of relieving him, was close at hand.

I have criticised General Murray's tactical movements in the foregoing—but what can be said in favour of De Levis ? His plans were bold and skilfully executed, but were they wise ? Should he have exposed the whole available naval strength of France and the greater part of his military resources to the hazard of action when by waiting he could at least have lost nothing. Had the expected French squadrons arrived first in the river Murray must have surrendered without the loss of a French soldier. Had De Levis awaited the event at St. Augustin beyond reach of Murray's army the arrival of the English squadron would have left him intact and in a position powerfully to dispute—practically, I think, to render impossible—Murray's subsequent ascent of the river to join Amherst at Montreal. Had matters fulfilled his best expectations and left him master of Quebec, his strength to oppose Amherst must have been greatly weakened. Had Montreal been held, the peace which even then was talked of would probably have left Canada to the French. French writers of the period called this the Folly of De Levis. I think they were right; at all events, Murray's defeat on April 28 was turned to victory, and De Levis, having staked everything, lost all. There was nothing left to hinder Murray joining Amherst; nothing of any great value to hinder Amherst or Haviland in the converging movement on Montreal. To Murray, for his strong resistance in desperate circumstances, and to Swanton, for his timely, effective co-operation, belong the laurels of the conquest of Canada.

Monsieur le Capitaine de Malartic of the regiment of Béarn was the officer left behind by De Levis to carry on negotiations with Murray regarding the prisoners of war, and, if we are to believe implicitly all that officer wrote to his chief, we obtain a certain insight into Murray's state of mind :

" *Il m'a aussi dit qu'il commande dans cette partie et M. Amherst dans la sienne, qu'il n'est pas tracassier, n'aime pas les difficultés et qu'il n'en auroit jamais vis-à-vis de vous, parcequ'il vous aime, vous estime, ayont vu que vous aimez à vous battre. . . . Il a voulu je crois me tirer le ver du nez ce matin en me demandant ce que vous vouliez faire, qu'il vous étoit impossible de conserver la colonie. . . . Il voudroit fort qu'on capitulât avec lui, à ce qu'il a dit à M. de Belle-combe qu'il feroit aux troupes le meilleures conditions qu'on pourroit exiger. M. de Bellecombe l'a assuré qu'il faudroit qu'il bataillât encore, s'il vouloit prendre le Canada. Il dit qu'il étoit bien assuré que vous saisiriez avec empressement toutes les occasions de combattre ; mais que l'armée ne peut pas subsister de l'air, et qu'on sera obligé de se rendre faute de pain.*"

Whether this little story is quite true or not one has no means of knowing. It is just possible that Murray's endeavour to "*tirer le ver du nez*" of M. Malartic may have had some foundation in fact. Amherst was a slow mover, though a sure one, and Murray may have had some not unnatural ambition to settle the fate of Canada before the invading armies could arrive at Montreal. Murray himself says nothing about it in his Journal, but hints at the same idea in his letter to Amherst, quoted at the end of this chapter. At a later date, indeed, writing to Pitt, he gives rather the reverse impression : " M. de Vaudreuil insinuated terms of surrender to me which I rejected, and sent information thereof to the commander-in-chief, who was then three days' march from Montreal." This was, however, in August, and the state of the case was then very different.

I will conclude this chapter with Murray's report to Amherst, written immediately after the retreat of the French army. In this letter he gives full credit to the far-reaching assistance of the navy.

"Quebec, May 19, 1760.

" DEAR SIR,
        " I have the honor to acquaint you that Monsieur de Levis last night raised the siege of Quebec, after three weeks' open trenches. He left behind him his camp standing, all his baggage, stores, ammunition, thirty-four pieces of cannon (four of which are brass 12-pounders), six mortars, four petards, a large provision of scaling ladders, and entrenching tools beyond number. Some of the field train we lost the day of the action we have again recovered. What the King's troops have done during this siege I dare not relate if I had time, it is so romantick, and our loss, considering, has been very inconsiderable. I had intended a strong sortie this morning, and for that purpose had the regiments of Amherst, Bragg, Lascelles, Anstruther, and Fraser's, with the Grenadiers and light infantry, under arms ; but was informed by Lieut. McAlpin, who I had sent out to make a small sally *selon les Reigles* (*sic*), that the trenches were abandoned. I instantly pushed out at the head of these corps, not doubting but I must penetrate their rear, and have ample revenge for April 28, but I was disappointed ; their rear had crossed

the River Caprouge before I could come up with them. However, we took several prisoners, stragglers, and much baggage which otherwise would have escaped. I cannot help taking this opportunity of mentioning Major Agnew in a distinguished light ; he commanded the corps of the light infantry, and old Addison, whose memorial I inclose, the Grenadiers.

" This enterprise has cost the enemy upwards of three thousand men, by their own confession. They are now at their old asilum at Jacques Cartier, and, for want of every necessary, must soon, I imagine, surrender at discretion. We are very low ; the scurvy makes terrible havock. For God's sake send us up melasses, and seeds which may produce vegetables. Whoever winters here again must be better provided with bedding and warm clothes than we were. Our medicines are entirely expended ; at present we get a very scanty supply from Lord Colvill's squadron, which arrived this day ; but Captain Swanton, in the *Vanguard*, with two frigates, came into the bason from England the night of the 17th, and next day destroyed and dispersed the enemy's squadron. *I have not words to express the alacrity and bravery of Swanton, Dean, and Schomberg—the honor they have acquired on this occasion should render their names immortal.** Our Louisburg friend, Monsieur Vauquelin, who commanded the French squadron, is taken prisoner, and his ship destroyed ; but poor Deane, after all, was over struck upon a rock, and I fear his ship will be lost. Lord Colvill agrees with me that as the news I sent you of April 28 may reach England and alarm the Ministry, it is necessary immediately to dispatch a frigate with advice to Mr. Pitt of the happy issue of Monsieur de Levis' enterprise. I send Major Maitland with my dispatches, and I hope he will reach London before the loss of the battle is known there. The Journal of the siege, and of all my proceedings since I had the honor to command here, are preparing for you, and shall be transmitted by the first opportunity. We have received the £20,000 sent in the *Hunter*—it is a poor sum for a garrison which has had no pay since August 24. I find His Majesty has appointed me colonel of the 2nd Batt. of R. Americans. I am very thankful to him for it. It

---

* My italics. How few people know the decisive nature of the service rendered by these naval officers in the conquest of Canada !

would have distressed me had Burton, as I hear was intended, purchased from Prevost over my head.   I could have raised money enough for that purchase, had I been consulted ; but it is better as it is, and I dare say you only recommended Mr. Burton's affairs in the event of my getting the rank before him.   I must think so until you tell me otherwise yourself,* for I have always flattered myself I had some share of your friendship, and am very confident I have done everything in my power to acquire it.

" This instant Lieut. Montresor is arrived, and has delivered to me your letter of April 15.   The orders in it shall be obeyed to the best of my ability.   Mr. Montresor tells me you would not credit the accounts I sent to you of the enemy's designs upon Quebec, but you will find they are not so prudent (pessimistic) as you imagined.   I flatter myself the check they have met with here will make everything very easy afterwards.   I do declare to you upon my salvation that they had an army of 15,000 men before Quebec, ten of which consisting of eight battalions of regulars, two of the troupes de colonie, and the Montrealists, were actually engaged in the battle of April 28 ; the other five thousand were the Canadians of the lower Canada, who joined them after the battle.†   The regulars are still at Jacques Cartier with a few Canadians who serve in those corps, and in all about five thousand men.   They have little powder left, and I am confident have as little provisions.   Deserters come in dayly.   If you make haste, for the honor of their colours, they may give you battle, but if you do not, for want of something to eat, they will surrender to me, for I have destroyed all the magazines they had prepared for the siege of Quebec.   You may depend upon my pressing them if I have but five hundred men.   It shall never be said with justice that anything has been wanting in me ; but if I know the country, and I believe I have a tolerable idea of it, I must beat their army before I can open your passage by the Isle-aux-Noix. The enemy are wiser than to divide their force, and, be assured, they have only two hundred of the troupes de colonie and four hundred Canadians at that post.   When

* In his reply to this letter Amherst stated he had no intention of superseding Murray by any promotion of Colonel Burton.
† That a large number of men from the lower parishes would join De Levis after the successful battle is very probable.

they know of your motions, I don't know what they may do. I shall watch theirs, and take every advantage of them in my power. I make no difficulties, the enemy have supplied us with boats or battoes, but God Almighty has reduced the large body of troops which were left at Quebec to an inconsiderable number, and had not the enemy's fleet in the river been destroyed, I apprehend without proper craft I could not have been master of it. . . . Montresor tells me you seemed surprised at the precautions I had taken in building block-houses in the winter, but you will not be so when you hear the designs which were formed and partly attempted against me in the winter and when you see the place—I believe very few of the gentlemen who left their posts to follow their pleasures on the continent gave themselves the trouble to examine the place and our situation. The fact is, we were surprised into a victory * which cost the conquered very little indeed, and it was very natural for these gentlemen to represent that there could possibly be no danger or difficulties here, since they had left their corps in garrison. . . ."

* The battle of September 13, 1759, is referred to. This view of the battle of Quebec is, no doubt, very correct; but I am afraid Murray's experiences of the winter 1759–60 had made him rather bitter in his memories of the plight in which he was left to defend the conquered city.

CHAPTER XI

MURRAY was essentially a man of action. Physically strong, enterprising, while yet caring for detail, and making his plans and forecasts with the cautiousness born of much experience, he was not likely to rest on his oars while work remained to be done. He had received Sir Jeffrey Amherst's instructions, dated April 15:

"I am now to acquaint you I have received His Majesty's commands for concerting the properest measures for pushing on the operations of this campaign with the utmost vigour, and as Montreal is evidently the great and essential object to compleat the glory of His Majesty's arms in North America, that I shall proceed to the vigorous attack of that place. . . . I therefore intend to advance on them (the enemy) in three places—from Quebec up the River St. Lawrence, from Crown Point by the Isle-aux-Noix, from Oswego down the River St. Lawrence. The first will depend entirely on you by pressing on the enemy with all the troops you can spare from the garrison of Quebec. . . ."

This letter of Amherst's was, of course, written before the events detailed in the last chapter, and the resistance that might be expected was estimated without knowledge of the serious blow to the French military power which resulted from the failure of De Levis' attempt on Quebec, a blow which, as we have seen, vastly reduced their offensive power both in men and munitions. It was not only the loss among the regular troops and the discouraging effect of further retreat, but the Canadians were becoming more and more convinced that the sceptre was passing, and were proportionately less inclined to sacrifice their future by complying with Vaudreuil's proclamations demanding their service—proclamations which, as Knox remarks, " discover great subtility of invention."

In his reply to Amherst, Murray could not refrain from letting his chief know that the French wave had expended itself, and that all the laurels were not for his gathering :

" I flatter myself the check they have met with here will make everything very easy afterwards. . . . If you make haste, for the honour of their colours, they may give you battle ; but if you do not, for want of something to eat, they will surrender to me."

" If you make haste " is good, but perhaps not quite diplomatic. Murray, like a good many others, was rather inclined to think the commander-in-chief a bit slow, though it is certainly doubtful if he was wise to say so ; but, as a matter of fact, Amherst found many difficulties in his way, and not the smallest of these was in dealing with the provincial assemblies and obtaining the necessary votes for supply of men and money ; a very great deal might be written in extenuation of Amherst's slow progress. The force intended to advance by way of Lake Champlain and thence by the Richelieu River to Montreal was under command of Brigadier-General William Haviland, and left Crown Point on August 11, while the main army,* under the immediate command of Amherst, left Albany *en route* for Oswego on June 21.

To prepare the Quebec force to concert with these movements required an immense amount of organisation. The whole army had to be re-equipped, clothed, and pro-visioned. Ships arrived " by every tide, with stores, liquor, and provisions of all kinds " (Knox). The *Hunter*

* Eight battalions of the line (1st and 2nd Royal Highlanders, 44th, 46th, 55th, 4/60th, 77th, 80th) with Grenadiers, light infantry, and a company of Rangers, in all 5299 N.C.O.s and men, with a force from the States of New York, New Jersey, Connecticut, of 4192 men. In all about 9491 men.

sloop had brought £20,000 in specie—" a poor sum for a garrison which has had no pay since August 24 " (Murray)— and more was expected early. So large a sum in the hands of the men—for one of Murray's first cares was to discharge the interest and principal of all borrowed moneys and pay the arrears due—was a sure attraction for a swarm of traders from the New England ports, who, it is to be feared, were far from being honest or scrupulous, either in their dealings with the men or the French inhabitants, and the Governor had from the start to take steps which did not suit their peculiar views, of which more will be heard later.

The convalescents and such of the sick as could be moved were conveyed to the Isle of Orleans, where, with warm weather, fresh food, and change of air, they made surprising recovery.

Urgent representations were made to Governor Whitmore at Louisburg to send reinforcements at the earliest possible date, without which " the losses we have suffered from the enemy and the sickness which has raged among us puts it out of my power (to support General Amherst) unless powerfully reinforced from you." It is interesting to note that Murray makes demand for a supply of coal, and grates to burn it in. This was probably the first demand for exporting coal from Cape Breton Island.*

On June 15 the state of the garrison was reported as 3275 N.C.O.s and men fit for duty, and 2463 sick and wounded, showing a considerable improvement. Detachments were sent out to swear in and disarm the inhabitants and to re-establish the post at Lorette. Murray was well aware of the importance of showing the flag, and his action in letting the inhabitants see the strength of his position

---

* The vessel sent for the coal was the *Good Intent*, William Hooper, master, and probably the pioneer of a trade which is now over five million tons a year, of which a large part is exported. It was during the building of [Louisburg fortress that coal came into general use, mined from the outcrops of what is now New Sydney, and it was no doubt at Louisburg that Murray became acquainted with its value.

no doubt reacted in his favour among those villages at a distance which could not be reached at the moment.

A flotilla was prepared comprising the *Porcupine* sloop and two other armed vessels, eight floating batteries, and twenty flat-bottomed boats, to be commanded by Captain Deane.* The troops were organised into two battalions of Grenadiers and five battalions of infantry, made up by equal quotas from the ten battalions in the garrison. The Grenadier battalions being of 300 men each, and each infantry battalion 294 men, a total of 2470 rank and file, with a detachment of 50 Rangers. This body was divided into two brigades, one to be commanded by Colonel Ralph Burton, the other by Colonel Howe.†

On July 5 the troops intended for the expedition moved out of the town. The General reviewed them on the 12th, and the embarkation took place on the 13th. The fleet ‡ sailed on the flood tide of the 14th. There was something that appeals to the imagination in this anabasis. Cut off from its base, dependent entirely on its own resources, the little force plunged into the midst of a hostile country, facing an enemy numerically, at least, far superior, and the dangerous navigation of a river whose channels were unknown, and from the banks of which, had material been available, an enterprising commander should have been able to inflict serious, if not disastrous, damage on the crowded boats. I cannot but think that this operation illustrates in a remarkable degree General Murray's genius for estimating with accuracy the military situation. He had informed Amherst that the French had little powder

---

* Captain Deane was commander of the *Lowestoft*, and an officer on whom Murray greatly relied. The ship was lost on the rocks during the operations above Quebec.

† The Hon. William Howe, Lieut.-Col. of the 58th Regt., commanded the light infantry at the attack on Quebec in September, 1759, but was not present during the winter campaign. He rejoined with the ships in May, 1760.

‡ The war vessels accompanying the flotilla were " the *Porcupine* sloop, the *Racehorse*, *Penzance*, *Diana*, *True Briton*, nine floating batteries, and many transports " (Doughty). There were besides twenty flat-bottomed boats, many of which had formed de Levis' equipment when he attacked Quebec.

and little provisions ; he believed them to be in a state of demoralisation, and he fully expected that the Canadians would no longer support their former masters.   In all this he relied solely on his judgment, but he had all the courage necessary to put his fate to the touch, and the event proved him right in every particular.   His intention was to make his way up the river, turning aside for nothing, and leaving the enemy to garrison any posts he chose, and the theory on which he acted was that the ill-equipped posts in his rear would matter little provided the junction with the commander-in-chief could be effected, and that the main French force was too immobile to do anything but await the concentration, which it could not resist, at Montreal.

Before starting he wrote a despatch to Mr. Pitt, which gives so clearly the calculations on which he based his opinion that I quote it *in extenso* :

"I have the honor to acquaint you that I shall set out to-morrow for Montreal at the head of two thousand two hundred chosen men.

"I was in expectation two regiments from Louisburg would have joined me before this time ; but as their arrival is very uncertain, and I cannot longer doubt of Mr. Amherst's being in motion, I think it necessary to proceed without them to do what I can to facilitate the entire reduction of Canada.   I am confident we are masters of the river ; in that case with this handfull of men I can safely nose the enemy at their capital, and if fortune favours us with an opportunity we may without risquing Quebec strike home.

"I have left seventeen hundred men fit for duty in Quebec, these with the sick and convalescents will make in all more than three thousand men in that garrison. Colonel Fraser, eager for the glory that may be acquired in the field, stays with great reluctance to command there ; but however desirous I may be of his assistance with me, I thought it absolutely necessary to leave an officer of distinguished address and abilitys with so important a command.

"I have left orders for the regiments from Louisburg

to proceed and join me without loss of time ; my corps will then consist of three thousand five hundred men.

"Though I have had no directions from General Amherst, I have ventur'd to press vessels for the conveyance of the troops, an expedient which will render all my operations safe and quick and powerful, and the expence is a meer trifle.

"The moment I arrive at Montreal I shall be probably master of the whole country. The Chevalier de Levis must assemble his army for the defence of that capital. If the Canadians do not join him, his force will not greatly exceed mine ; if they do, their country is abandoned to my mercy. My motions having the current of the river in my favour, must always be four times quicker than theirs, consequently it will be impossible for the Canadians to save their harvest this year if they assemble in arms, for the country is nowhere inhabited or cultivated above two miles from the river.

"I have the happiness to inform you, Sir, that since the weather has been warm our sick have recover'd surprisingly, and that all the transports except one are safely arriv'd from New York. They have brought cloathing for the garrison, and the recover'd men and officers which were sent from Quebec last autumn. I have no apprehensions that the missing ship is lost."

On the 15th Jacques Cartier * was passed in the morning. "The garrison fired several shots and threw some shells at our fleet, but the river being broad and the channel running close by the south shore, we were beyond their reach" (Knox).

In the evening they approached the Richelieu rapids off Deschambeau ; here the river was shallow and full of rocks and "the navigation difficult, by reason of the different turnings." De Levis had hoped for difficulties : "*On espérait qu'ils ne franchiroient pas aisement ce passage, quoique nous n'ayions pas à beaucoup près l'artillerie necessaire.*"

De Levis, writing to the Minister de Berryer, had

* The garrison left by De Levis at this place was three hundred men, under De Repentigny.

stated : " The point of greatest danger is the river. We are absolutely out of touch with it, and have no means of preventing the frigates and barges coming up as far as Montreal "—and in this he was undoubtedly right. It was not until the 26th (July) that the wind and tide being favourable the whole army was past this difficult place and concentrated some three and a half miles above Deschambeau. The intervening ten days had, however, been usefully spent in several very successful expeditions on the south shore, the principal object being to disarm and subdue the inhabitants of the neighbouring parishes of St. Croix, Lotbinière, and St. Antoine. To these Murray issued a proclamation urging submission, and Knox tells us " some of his Excellency's arguments," which were, no doubt, very convincing. " Who can carry on the war without ships, artillery, ammunition, or provisions ? At whose mercy are your habitations and that harvest which you expect to reap in the summer, together with all you are possessed of in this world ? " To the local priests he issued a more stringent warning, as " the source of all the mischiefs that have befallen the poor Canadians," and exhorted them to " preach the gospel, which alone is your province." The result was excellent, the inhabitants delivered up their arms with alacrity and brought in supplies of fresh provisions. They were, in fact, thoroughly tired of constant military disturbance, and openly expressed desire for the success of our force, so that they might remain in " peace and quietness."

By July 28 the army had arrived off Point Champlain. Here they were overtaken by a sloop from Quebec, bringing the welcome news of the arrival of two battalions from Louisburg (40th and 22nd). The flat-bottomed boats were returned at once * to take this reinforcement past the

---

* It is worth noting that Knox mentions that at this point in the river, in fact, at some distance below it, the tide had no longer any effect, whereas to-day the alterations of the river bed, due to clearing away rocks, has brought the tidal action considerably higher up, to the Lake of St. Peter, and there is now a range of nearly three feet at Point Champlain during spring tides.

shallows of Richelieu. On August 4 the fleet reached
Trois Rivières, where the enemy, as Knox records, were
busy throwing up retrenchments. Murray, however, took
no notice, and passed on, intent only on joining hands
with Amherst. De Levis remarks regretfully, referring
to Dumas, who commanded there, " *Il fut forcé de la
suivre.*"

On August 7 De Levis wrote a despatch to the Maréchal
de Belle-Isle, in which he voices the despair that had now
found its place in all hearts. I will quote some extracts
only. The whole letter is given in vol. ii. of the Champlain
Society's publication of John Knox's Journal :

" Their (the English) objective appears to be Montreal
or Sorel, in order to effect a junction with Mr. Amherst.
We have no means of stopping them . . . we are without
artillery and powder ; we are merely making a show of
defence in order to delay their advance. . . . The people
of the country are terrified at the fleet. They fear lest
their houses should be burnt. We are at the crisis of our
fate. . . . *The passage of the Quebec fleet up the river will
compel us to abandon all the frontiers.* The junction of
their three armies will then take place without opposition.
. . . You know the force at our disposal, and can judge
what the outcome must be. . . ."

De Levis had, in truth, very slender grounds for hope.
The ill-omened brood hatched by Bigot and Cadet, aided
by Vaudreuil and fostered by dissolute government at
home, were coming home to roost with a vengeance.
Shorn of every kind of military equipment, faced with the
open mutiny of the troops and the not less open refusal of
the Canadians to support him, one cannot blame De Levis
that he should recognise that the end had come and that
nothing short of a miracle could save the colony for France.
The millstones were coming together. Haviland was
embarking at Crown Point, Amherst at Oswego, Murray
at Trois Rivières—what hope could there be for a demoralised force thus pressed on all sides ?

Before evening (August 8) the fleet anchored at the

entrance of Lake St. Peter, and with some difficulty, on account of shallow water and uncertain channels, made slow progress up the lake during the next four days. During all this period Murray had maintained the cautious scheme that he had laid down for the guidance of his army, although frequent landings had taken place on the south shore, and the inhabitants of the various parishes disarmed and sworn to allegiance.* No serious contact with the enemy had been permitted, nor any landing on the north shore, the object of drawing all the French forces towards the centre was grimly adhered to. In his letter, dated July 30, Captain Cramahé, who had acted as Murray's secretary, refers to this plan, which I quote here as evidence of the caution of the General :

" If you persist in the wise and prudent resolution you have laid down not to hazard anything, all will go well. Why risk, when you may attain all your ends by patience ? Time, as you rightly say, fights for you, and the inhabitants, cut off from all succours, cannot lose their harvest. Pardon my freedom, it is well meant."

The reinforcements from Louisburg, which were now in progress up the river, were, however, ordered to effect the necessary disarmament in the north shore parishes, the French troops having left them to follow Murray's movements. Thus the country on both sides of the river—and it must be remembered that the populated area did not extend above two miles from the banks—was thoroughly pacified, a wise proceeding which did much to destroy any chances of Vaudreuil being able to assemble any considerable force at Montreal. During the passage of Lake St. Peter, a French force under De Bourlamaque was discovered at St. Francis, but the English force refused engagement, and De Bourlamaque was obliged to follow to Sorel, a small village at the mouth of the Richelieu River, where the fleet arrived on the 13th (August). At this point

* The men standing in a ring and holding up the right hand, each one repeating his own name and then the formula of the oath, Knox tells us, though possibly with mental reservations.

touch with the land armies began, and a message was sent to Brigadier Haviland to announce Murray's arrival. Murray's army maintained its position off Sorel until the 17th, when Lord Rollo (Lieut.-Colonel 22nd Foot), commanding the reinforcements, arrived, and the three brigades now numbered 3500 * non-commissioned officers and men— a very respectable force, with which the General felt himself more at liberty to take aggressive action.

In the meantime De Levis was in a dilemma. He describes his situation thus :

"*M. de Levis avait formé le projet, en se rapprochant de Montréal de rassembler ses forces et d'aller attaquer le corps des ennemis qui arriverait le premier ; mais il ne put exécuter ce projet, le Général* (Murray) *avançant toujours par eau sur Montréal, dont il serait aisement emparé, cette ville n'étant pas à l'abri d'un coup de main.*"

In short, the Quebec force was the deciding factor, and De Levis was unable to leave it in order to concentrate on either of the other two armies.

The regiments of La Reine and Royal Roussillon were sent to St. Johns (south of Sorel, on the Richelieu), together with the militia of Montreal, in the vain hope of arresting Haviland's progress, who was now formally attacking the Isle-aux-Noix. Amherst, on his side, had entered the River St. Lawrence from Lake Ontario, and was attacking Fort Levis, which was surrendered by M. Pauchot on the 25th (August). This was a severe blow, as the French had hoped that this fort, situated on an island blocking the passage of the river, would be able to delay the attack for a considerable time. Delay was, in fact, the only weapon left in De Levis' armoury, and his one faint chance, that the enemy might exhaust their supplies.

To return to the operations of the river army, which we left in position off Sorel. A night attack was planned

*	1st Brigade ..	..	..	..	..	..	1342
	2nd ,,	..	..	..	..	..	1227
	3rd ,,	..	..	..	..	..	1007
							3576

S

for August 21–22, when Lord Rollo's brigade landed a mile below the parish and succeeded in burning the greater part of the habitations. Knox tells us that this procedure " affected the General extremely, but the obstinate perseverance of the inhabitants in arms made it necessary." Murray was certainly averse from destruction, and his whole course of action had shown his desire to avoid it except when he found the inhabitants absent from their houses and bearing arms. Regarding this affair, he wrote to the Minister (Pitt) :

" I found the inhabitants of the parish of Sorel had deserted their habitations and were in arms. I was therefore under the cruel necessity of burning the greatest part of these poor unhappy people's houses. I pray God this example may suffice, for my nature revolts when this becomes a necessary part of my duty."

On the 23rd the fleet arrived at Contrecœur, twenty-seven miles from Montreal. Here they were detained three days, the wind being insufficient to work against the current. Knox notes that the enemy, being now confined within a narrow compass, are able to mass troops on both sides of the river, who accompanied " politely " every movement.

From Contrecœur Murray wrote to Pitt, acquainting him, *inter alia*, that M. de Vaudreuil had insinuated " terms of surrender to me which I rejected, and sent information thereof to the commander-in-chief, who was then three days' march from Montreal." No doubt Murray's action in this was strictly correct, though it must have gone sorely against the grain, for having borne the heat (or rather cold) and burden of the day he would naturally have liked to receive the swords of the conquered. Indeed, had he done so, though Amherst might have had objections from the point of view of etiquette, he would have been saved the dangerous passage of the rapids and the loss of many men.

On the 27th the Rangers and light infantry landed on the island of Térésa, which lies off the eastern end of the island of Montreal. He was now within sight of his goal. A few miles south-westward the Royal Mount stood out with its memories of more than two hundred years, consecrated to a royal master by the immortal Jacques Cartier. Below it, on the river bank, nestled the town, then surrounded by massive fortifications, and containing a population of four thousand souls. The Garden of Canada is the name given to this island of Montreal, formed by the encircling arms of the Ottawa River at its junction with the St. Lawrence. Knox is silent on the feelings of the army—we must imagine that pride of triumph was not wanting.

Meanwhile the steady progress of Haviland and Amherst was bringing about the final act of the drama. Isle-aux-Noix had been captured, and Haviland was resting at St. John, preparing to strike direct for Montreal via Chambly. Amherst, having completed the reduction of Fort Levis on Isle Royale, was continuing his cautious methods by repairing its fortifications and putting in a new garrison. He left nothing to chance, and was determined that no temporary repulse should place him in difficulties as to his rear. His army was also preparing for the dangerous passage of the Galop before entering Lake Francis. De Levis records that the Canadians were retiring wholesale to their parishes, and that there were many desertions among the troops.

On September 3 Murray's force, which had been marking time and awaiting progress of the land armies, but nevertheless had accomplished useful work in subjugating the parish of Varennes on the south shore, received information from Haviland that he expected to reach La Prairie, a village immediately opposite Montreal, in two or three days ; but during this period the Indian auxiliaries deserted the French *en bloc*, having, as they said, made peace with the English, and De Levis, hopeless with his depleted forces, decided to retire all the force opposing Haviland to the island of Montreal. His Journal describes again Murray's successful strategy :

"*Le Sieur Murray s'étendit le long de la côte du sud. Il est à observer qu'il n'avoit mis à terre dans la descente qu'il avait faite qu'un détachement que se tenoit toujours prêt à se rembarquer dans le moment qu'on aurait pu marcher à lui, ce fut cause que nous ne pûmes jamais le combattre.*"

Amherst was now well advanced in Lake Francis, having negotiated the Galop and Long Rapids with little loss, and he only had to pass the Cedar and Cascade Rapids to emerge in the bason of Montreal. These rapids formed indeed a formidable barrier : " The navigation was inconceivably dangerous, insomuch that the loss of the greatest part of the troops seemed inevitable." Amherst passed through first, regardless of his own safety, at the head of the Grenadiers, light infantry, and Rangers. " His Excellency most happily effected this passage with the loss only of forty-six batteaus, seventeen whale boats, and one row galley, whereby eighty-four men were drowned . . . if the enemy had been more attentive to this place, which was extremely natural to suppose they would," Knox opines, that much more serious loss would have ensued. The army, however, reached Isle Perrot without attack, and were now within striking distance of Montreal, twelve miles away.

On the same day (September 5) Murray proceeded to Longueuil, a short distance below Montreal, on the south bank, to clear the road for Haviland. It was apparently on this occasion that the French Indians (Hurons) came to Murray to make peace, and Knox draws an animated picture of the position of Murray and Colonel Burton, who seemed to be in the middle of a scrap that might have had unpleasant results. The Mohawks, who had been faithful to us, were apparently very anxious to set on the French Indians, comparing them with squaws, and hurling opprobrious epithets, and it was only the personal intervention of Murray and Burton that prevented a royal row ! Murray's treaty with the Hurons is preserved among the family papers, and he ordered that :

" Henceforth no English officer or party is to molest or interrupt them in returning to their settlement at Lorette, and they are to be received upon the same terms with the Canadians, being allowed free exercise of their religion, their customs and liberty of trading with the English garrisons, recommending it to the officers commanding the posts to treat them kindly."

On the 6th (September) Amherst's army passed from Isle Perrot to the island of Montreal; on the following day Murray's army made a like movement * from Isle Térésa, and landed on the lower end of the island and marched towards the town, the inhabitants everywhere coming out to meet the troops with refreshments. The enemy having broken down the bridges, the advance was slow, and by evening they stopped at the parish of Longue Pointe. Continuing the advance on the next day (September 8) Murray took up a position on the north-east side of the city under the shadow of Mount Royal. Amherst had taken post on the north-west side on the previous day. Haviland had arrived at Longueuil.

Thus the city was surrounded on all sides, and an operation was complete which from the mere time-table accuracy of its conception and fulfilment was perhaps as remarkable as any in the history of the British army. Three considerable armies had advanced on different lines widely separated through hostile country, two of them at least having exceptional difficulties to be surmounted, Amherst's force covering some three hundred miles from Oswego; Haviland and Murray covering each about one hundred and fifty miles from Crown Point and Quebec respectively. Each force for the time being cut off from its base, and relying solely on the supplies it carried, yet all three arrived at the rendezvous almost simultaneously—surely a fine military achievement.

If Amherst is entitled to the chief share of the credit, as far as the final concentration is concerned, his two subordinates are entitled to a high degree of praise, nor is

* The detailed orders issued are given in Knox's Journal.

it possible to consider any one of the three forces as other than complementary of the remaining two. But it is also the case that in a special degree Murray's force had worn down the enemy prior to the movement, and borne the brunt of the enemy's attacks, and it is also true that Commodore Swanton's bold and successful action in destroying the French power of movement by water had a most important, even decisive, effect on the result, and therefore both these officers are entitled to a special degree of merit ; but from the commencement of the concentration to its successful close the success of maintaining the advance according to schedule must be shared by the commanders of the land forces.

The rest of the story need not detain us long. It is simply told by the Chevalier de Levis in his Journal, under date September 6 :

" *Pendant la nuit, il fut tenu une assemblée chez M. le Marquis de Vaudreuil, composée des principaux officiers des troupes de tèrre et de la Marine. M. Bigot, Intendant, lut un mémoire sur la capitulation de la colonie et l'état actuel de ses affaires, et un projet de capitulation.*

" *Comme la désertion totale des Canadiens et celle d'un grand nombre de soldats avoit réduit les troupes au nombre d'environ deux mille quatre cents, tout au plus, que les sauvages domicilliés avoient fait leur paix avec les Anglois, et même leur avoient offert de prendre les armes pour achever de nous réduire, que la ville de Montréal étoit tout au plus à l'abri d'un coup de main . . . tout le monde pensa, comme le Marquis de Vaudreuil que l'interêt général de la colonie exigeoit que les choses ne fussent pas pousées à la dernière extremité, et qu'il convenait de préferer une capitulation avantageuse aux peuples et honorable aux troupes.*"

On the morning of the 7th De Bougainville was sent out to propose terms of capitulation, but Amherst refused in this case, and to several other embassies, to abate one jot of his demand for the unconditional surrender of the troops. This severe condition he imposed as a reprisal for the " infamous part the troops of France had acted in exciting the savages to perpetrate the most horrid and unheard of barbarities." It must be remembered that the sting of this condition lay in the fact that the whole of the French officers would be out of commission during the remainder of the war, a circumstance which bore particularly severely on men entirely dependent on their military service. Notwithstanding the pressure brought by De Levis to endeavour to persuade the governor-general to break off the negotiations,* the latter was firm for immediate capitulation on such terms as the English commander chose to impose. Indeed, it is scarcely to be doubted that, notwithstanding many bombastic letters in which he assured the Minister of his determination to fight to the last, Vaudreuil was not made of heroic stuff, and was not disinclined to end † the affair with as little inconvenience to himself as might be obtained. The Articles, fifty-five in number, were duly signed on September 8, 1760. La Nouvelle France had ceased to exist.

The Articles of Capitulation related for the most part to the surrender and transfer of the officials and military to France, the former being allowed to take their papers without examination. The hand of Cadet is visible in an attempt to secure for himself the provisions and stores in the magazines, which he claimed as private property ; but this was not admitted. The free exercise of the Catholic, Apostolic, and Roman religion was guaranteed to the inhabitants, and it was sought to obtain an obligation

* De Levis reported to the Marechal de Belleisle on arrival at Rochelle in November, 1760. . . . "The signing of the Capitulation made by the Marquis de Vaudreuil, wherein I had no other share save that of having protested against it in respect of the treatment meted out to the troops of the line, who should have deserved more attention on the part of M. de Vaudreuil, and more consideration from General Amherst."

† Vaudreuil received a stinging reproof dated December 5, 1760. "Though His Majesty was perfectly aware of the state of Canada, nevertheless after the assurances you had given to make the utmost efforts to sustain the honour of his arms, he did not expect to hear so soon of the surrender of Montreal and the whole colony. But granting that capitulation was necessary, His Majesty was not less surprised and ill-pleased at the conditions so little honourable to which you submitted, especially after the representations made to you by the Chevalier de Levis " (*Archives des Colonies*, quoted by Doughty in Champlain Society's edition of John Knox's Journal).

that tithes and taxes hitherto paid to the priests should be admitted ; this was refused pending the King's pleasure being known. It was also refused that the right of nominating the Bishop of the colony should remain a right of the French Crown. The Communities of Nuns were guaranteed, but a like privilege to the Jesuits and Récollets was refused pending the King's pleasure. In this one may trace Murray's hand, whose experience of the Jesuit priests had not been altogether happy. The terms allowed to the Roman Catholic religion were, however, extremely broadminded and statesmanlike, when one considers that laws of brutal stringency were still maintained against Catholics in Ireland. A proposal to exempt French or Canadians from taking arms against the French king on any future occasion was refused, with the pithy remark : " They become subjects of the King of England " ; as was an attempt to impose the laws of France for usage with all inhabitants.

The number of regular troops taken prisoner, comprising the whole strength of the ten regular battalions (*i.e.* eight of the line and two of the marine), is stated by Amherst (Co. 5/59) to have been 3544. Knox put the number at 4011, possibly correct at the time, for a number of men deserted and took up residence with the inhabitants. The militia was estimated by Knox to include 170 companies and 16,422 men, giving a total of available troops (according to Knox) of over 20,000 men—a force sufficient, had they not lacked equipment and given good government, to have held the colony against the troops brought against it.

A curious circumstance arose with regard to the colours of the French regiments ; these being demanded, answer was given that " these being of little use in this woody country we had destroyed them," and this answer being transmitted to General Amherst, he demanded that the Marquis de Vaudreuil and the Chevalier de Levis should affirm it on their *parole d'honneur*, which they instantly complied with (Knox). De Levis, however, records a different story in his Journal :

" M. le Chevalier de Lévis voyant avec douleur que rien ne pouvait faire changer la détermination de M. le Marquis Vaudreuil, voulant épargner aux troupes une partie de l'humiliation qu'elles alloient subir, leur ordonna de bruler leurs drapeaux pour se soustraire à la dure condition de les remettre aux ennemis."

Which seems to indicate that De Levis was not above a quibble, which should hardly be included in a *parole d'honneur !* *

The least possible time was spent in clearing out the French army. Within eight days (September 16) the last of the regular regiments embarked on the journey to Quebec, and Murray proceeded thither in haste to prepare for their despatch to France.

Let me conclude this chapter by quoting the views held by the Chevalier Johnston, who served with the French throughout the campaign :

" General Murray conducted himself as an officer of great understanding, knowledge, and capacity, and left nothing to do for General Amherst. He employed five weeks in coming from Quebec to Montreal, which is only sixty leagues, and did us during his march more harm by his policy than by his army. He stopped often in the villages ; spoke kindly to the inhabitants he found at home in their houses, whom hunger and famine had obliged to fly from our army at Montreal ; gave provisions to these unhappy creatures perishing from want of sustenance. He burned in some cases the houses of those who were absent from home and in the French army at Montreal, publishing everywhere amnesty and good treatment to all Canadians who should return to their habitations and live peaceably. In short, flattering some and frightening others, he succeeded so well that at last there was no possibility of keeping them at Montreal."

Johnston was, of course, a " brither Scot," but there is no special reason to suspect him of bias in favour of one who, according to his view, was fighting on the wrong side.

* One is reminded of a somewhat similar happening after the late war, but this time the colours were demanded by the French.

CHAPTER XII

PUBLIC OPINION AND HOME LETTERS

MURRAY returned to Quebec about September 20, 1760. It is more than probable that a good many things had occurred which brought to him a feeling that he had received something less than a just consideration of his efforts. Amherst's despatch on the Montreal operations, in its reference to the part taken by the subordinate officers, was certainly brevity itself, and it scarcely conformed to Murray's own habit of giving generous acknowledgment to the action of others: " I should not do justice to Governor Murray and Colonel Haviland if I did not assure you they have executed the orders I gave them to the utmost of my wishes " (Amherst Despatch to Pitt, dated September 8, 1760).

If Murray was too loyal and too proud to say anything on the subject, he could hardly avoid reflecting that his men and himself had met with less than their due share of mention.

But not less galling was the inevitable criticisms of the newswriters, which began to filter through in open comments and inuendoes. The armchair critic of to-day is a mild and comparatively harmless individual compared with the mud-slinger of those days of unbridled anonymous license, when any name could be dragged through the dirt, if only the initial letters and a few asterisks were used to form a disguise which every one could see through ; when a person who had failed in business was described as a " bxxkxxpt," to avoid any chance of libel !

The Grub Street fraternity were unlikely to lose a chance of sharpening their wits on the operations of the previous April, and men, whose nearest approach to active service was to bolt from an attachment bailiff, were quite prepared to criticise the action of those who had faced hardships and dangers of which they had no conception. But, quite apart from mere Grub Streeters, there were others, higher placed, who did not scruple to condemn what they did not understand; and it must be remembered that the Whigs were not likely to lose an opportunity of having a stab at Lord Elibank's brother. Horace Walpole wrote of " General Murray, who got into a mistake and a morass, attacked two bodies that were joined where he hopes to come up with one of them before the junction, was enclosed, embogged, and defeated." * But Walpole would no doubt have shone less as a leader than as a letter writer.

There was, besides, not a little evidence that there was a traitor from within the camp itself, who did not scruple to launch into anonymous attacks on superiors, as witness the scurrilous pamphlet which attempted to impute to Townshend much that he certainly was innocent of having done.

Even Townshend himself, who had left Quebec with the full intention of clearing up the dark places, had failed to come forward, and had probably found quite as much to do as he wanted in repelling attacks made on himself. He had, however, made in public some cryptic remarks † on Murray's siege, which did not tend to make the latter feel good-tempered.

There was also a considerable current of opinion in England, which had probably by now reached Murray, that belittled the importance of the conquest of Canada, and urged its restoration at the peace, which was even then

---

* Walpole to Sir Horace Mann, June 28, 1760.

† The *Daily Advertiser* of June 19, 1760, said : " A certain great officer who had a principal share in the reduction of Quebec has given it as his opinion that it is able to hold out a considerable siege." Townshend promptly declared that there was no foundation for the statement, and thus rather added to the general dismay.

under discussion, a project which must have been very distasteful to him, for he recognised from the first the possibilities of the new acquisition.

Add to all this certain private sources of annoyance; his appointment to the colonelcy of the 2nd battalion 60th (Royal Americans), dating from October 24, 1759, had not given Murray any very full satisfaction. He was pleased with the honour, but, in common with all his compeers, he desired an " old regiment." What the particular differentiation was I am not sure, but presumably an " old " regiment was one which would not be broken up at the peace, as was so frequently the case with new ones. Besides, he had succeeded Monckton, transferred to an old regiment (17th Foot), and in his own mind he classed Monckton as junior to him in age, and having been his junior in the army until " promoted over his head " (for good service at Beauséjour, be it noted).

Amherst had written hoping soon to wish him joy of the 40th regiment, but the desired transfer did not come. Lord Lauderdale had written that Pitt " is much your friend. . . . I heard him hold forth upon you in the House of Commons; he also mentioned you to me in private with the utmost regard," and both Pitt * and Lord Barrington had written to him in flattering terms and conveyed the King's approbation of his services and those of the troops, all of which was very satisfactory, but still lacked material evidence that his work, which he could not but feel had been distinguished, was duly appreciated.

In this strained frame of mind, and perhaps somewhat overwrought by the constant anxieties of a campaign in which he had been a responsible leader for eighteen months without intermission, it is not surprising that some bitterness appeared in his letters written at the time. On September 20 he wrote to Amherst, for whom he had real affection : " It is unfortunate for these gentlemen "— referring to some officers who had been, he thought, wrongly

* From Pitt, dated July 23, 1760.

passed over—" that they had not the honour to serve with you in the last two campaigns, and it may prove unhappy for the officers in this garrison that their destination is still at so great a distance from you." Which was pretty straight talk !

He reserved for his brother George, however, a more complete unbosoming of his feelings. Frankly, it is not a letter I like quoting,* and it exhibits traits which were not natural to the writer. It reminds me again of Wolfe, to whom, as I have said, Murray's character bore resemblance, and more than one of whose sentiments, written or spoken, cannot be said to conform with his true character.

The letter was in reply to one from George, dated July 12, which has already been quoted, and is dated October 19, 1760.

" You seem nettled," he wrote, " at the silence of the news writers, but if you'll coolly consider, I am highly honoured thereof.

" Mr. Townshend, Monckton, etc., etc., were in the right, perhaps, to hire these miscreants to relate feats they never performed, and to ascribe to themselves the actions of other men. I don't want any such trappings ; it is praise of my brother soldiers I am ambitious of. I have the satisfaction to know my conduct has the approval of His Majesty and the Minister. . . . It will no doubt be known hereafter to all the world who opposed the attack of the lines of Montmorency,† *and who in the beginning and to the very last of the campaign urged descent above the town at the very place where it was made,* and surely nobody is ignorant of what the left wing of the army did on September 13 ; *it* was not ' *en potence,*' it broke the enemy's line and pursued the fugitives to the gates, and would

---

* This letter is published in Fraser's work on *The Earls of Cromartie.*

† James Gibson, a volunteer serving with Wolfe, wrote immediately after the event to Governor Lawrence : " One of them of knowledge, fortune, and interest (evidently Townshend), I have heard, has declared the attack then and there was contrary to the advice and opinion of every officer." And this is admitted and justified by Townshend. I do not think Murray did more than concur with Townshend and Monckton.

have completed the destruction had it not been called off by superior authority.

"I fought a battle; I lost it.   What then?   Is every day of battle a day of victory?*   Did it be asked of any soldier if, in my situation, it was right to fight?   He will answer without hestiation, 'To be sure!'   Examine the disposition, compare it with the ground which must determine the propriety of it, and I flatter myself it will be allowed a good one.   Was not the critical moment of attack made use of?   Did it succeed?   Was not the victory gained, had the right wing been as active and vigorous April 28, 1760, as the left wing was September 13, 1759?   Was not aid instantly given during the action where it was wanted?   Were not the cannon judiciously placed?   Does not all this denote a presence of mind and a coupd'oile? (*sic*).   Where was the General in this battle?   Betwixt his own line and that of the enemy—everywhere where the enemy made a push animating his men by his presence.   He had two horses shot under him, and his clothes riddled by the enemy's musketry.   Where was he when the right wing faulter'd?   He was placing the cannon on the heights in the centre, but rode instantly to the right, and there recovered the confusion.   How did the troops retreat into town?   In tolerable order, by means of the corps the General himself posted in the two unfinished redoubts, and on an eminence.   Did he stay with the corps himself to the last?   He did; he was the last man that enter'd the gates.

"The defence of the place, as it was successful, in England (where everything is right or wrong agreeable to the decision of Dame Fortune) will answer for itself.   You are to ask the French generals what share had this campaign in the total reduction of Canada.   I am persuaded Mr. Amherst is too just to be silent on that head.   He certainly has told that I left him nothing to do, and that the Marquis de Vaudreuil insinuated terms of surrender to me, before Mr. Amherst's army appear'd, which I would not listen to, as I had intelligence of the commander-in-chief's being within six days' march of me, and I was posted at Longviel, by which the junction of the three armys (*sic*) was infallible.

"This much I have open'd myself to my brother.   It is very wrong for a man to speak of himself, but he that

* These are words used by Amherst (Chatham MSS. 96).

praises himself is unpardonable. I therefore conjure you not to show this letter to anybody but Elibank. He and you may make what use of the contents you please, provided you do not let it be known that I have trumpeted my own fame.

"I think myself accountable to my family in a very particular manner for my actions, especially as the sphere I have lately acted in has been eminent. It will be your business to dive into the truth of every sentence of this letter, but not to expose me to the reproach of vain glory. I offer my very affectionate compliments to all my relations round you, and am, my dear George," etc.

With that part of his letter in which he unbared his soul regarding the action of April, for the private information of his family, I have no quarrel. It was natural that he should put his relations in possession of the part he had taken, and inform them of the inaccuracy of the insidious statements which had appeared in print; but I can only account for his bitterness regarding Townshend and Monckton, with both of whom he was on friendly terms, from the jaundiced view of the world which, at the moment, had possession of his mind, and from the fact that these officers, and many others, had left him with very inadequate resources to bear the brunt of the trouble-filled winter of 1759–60. The statement which I have printed in italics is, however, one which I cannot reconcile with other evidence.

It is true that in the early days of July (1759) he reported that the idea of attacking at St. Michel was practicable, and, in common with others, looked upon that neighbourhood as including the Foulon; probably, too, he urged this attack rather than the Montmorency venture, yet it is as certain as anything can be that he did not maintain this view after his reconnaissance in August, and then strongly recommended a descent much higher up the river. Every act and letter of the brigadiers indicate, without possibility of misconstruction, that the orders to land at Anse au Foulon came to them as an unwelcome surprise, and the plan of operations which they put forward involved a scheme differing essentially from that which was carried out.

A bunch of home letters had arrived at Quebec after the raising of the siege. For Murray the post bag had contained much of interest. Admiral George, with his inimitable spelling, gave his congratulations on his successful defence of Quebec :

" Everything I can say must be very trifaling, as you, without doubt, have all the congratulations due to so great an action. . . . The partiality of John Bull is provocking, for notwithstanding all you have done the villains have not done you justice. . . . I am not surprised at the Monitors' being silent in regard to you, because a (I) remember your being a little rough with him at the Mount Coffee House, where he was a patriot."

The death of his younger sister " Jenny " * was announced, leaving a " guirl and a boy " †—no doubt a shock, for the two were much attached.

From his nephew, George Johnston, who was, indeed, more like a brother, for they had been boys together at Westerhall, he had a long, newsy letter, some of which will bear quoting. " I think the military have now settled that Daun ‡ is a superior General to the King of Prussia, who is quite exhausted." A remark which illustrates the danger of prophesying before you know !

" November 20 (1759) will ever stand remarkable in the annals of time, for on that day Münster surrendered to the Allies. . . . The last fleet of France destroyed by Admiral Hawke. This last affair I can speak of as a seaman. For whether we consider the critical conjunction where Duff was surrounded ; the grandeur of the two fleets ; the objects in view ; the impetuosity of the pursuit ; the heat

---

* Wife of Major Murray, afterwards Sir Robert Murray of Clermont.
† Afterwards Sir James Murray-Pulteney, who, after a distinguished military career, became Secretary at War, and was succeeded by Lord Palmerston. He married his cousin, the wealthy Countess of Bath, and died in 1811.
‡ Leopold Graf von Daun, the Austrian General who defeated Frederick the Great at Kolin and Hochkirch.

of the action ; the tempest that attended ; the studding of the scene with rocks, shoals, and darkness (*sic*) ; and the consequences of the whole, we must allow this to be the most engaging objcct (!) our element ever sustained."

Which is not a bad picture of the famous victory in Quiberon Bay, of which the sailors of the day sang :

> " 'Ere Hawke did bang
> Monsieur Conflans
> You sent us beef and beer.
> Now Monsieurs beat
> We've nought to eat
> Since you have nought to fear,"

which is rather typical of the relief in England at the unquestioned establishment of superiority at sea.

From his sister, Anne Ferguson, was a letter to her " Dearest brother," carrying a reflection of the affectionate anxiety which had followed him during the long months he had been shut off from communication with the world :

" Your letter of May 24 was most joyfully received by all under this roof. What sum would I have scrupled to have paid for it during that long time that passed betwixt our first account of the action of April 28 and the happy news of your miraculous success and safety ? God, my dear brother, has done mighty things for you. . . . The happy first of July brought us by the express the *Extraordinary Gazette*, with your letter to Mr. Pitt. The world does you justice, and your letter is thought a masterpiece. . . ." *

Womanlike, she had endeavoured to bring balm to ease the troubles which perhaps she guessed at.

* The *Gentleman's Magazine* of 1760 describes this as " his applauded letter."

T

CHAPTER XIII

In the chapters which follow concerning the commencement of British Government in Canada, I aim at tracing its evolution from the terms of the capitulation at Montreal to the passing of the Quebec Act some fourteen years later. For much of the failure and confusion during these years General Murray has received unmerited censure, but I hope to make it clear that his efforts were thwarted and rendered ineffective by the same inept administrators who caused the loss of the American colonies. This latter subject has little to do with this volume, but it will be of interest to show how the neglect of the principles of common sense and even common honesty regarding Canada had their reflections in the treatment of the settled colonies.

In a recently published work Murray is accused of having unreasonably refused to call together an elected assembly in Quebec; of having treated the British traders with contempt; by some complex process of reasoning he is even accused of giving a " main and immediate cause to the revolutionary war," by *not* bringing this same assembly of British traders into being! Yet in the same work we are told that but for Murray these British traders would have had free rein for their evil natures to oppress the Canadians.* Diversity of opinion such as this may well make the general reader wonder what is the truth, and this I hope to show by such references to the letters

* *Canada and its Provinces*, vol. xv. pp. 144–99, etc.

and other documents of the period as will enable judgment to be given.

The arrangements for the government of Canada made by Amherst pending formal orders from England were to maintain the separate Governments of Three Rivers and Montreal distinct from that of Quebec, as had been the case under the French regime.* The first-named was placed in charge of Colonel Burton, who had been Murray's second in command ; the Montreal province being handed to Brig.-Gen. Gage. Of the former, it may be said *en passant* that Murray had a high opinion. " I really have a friendship for him," he wrote to Amherst a little later.

The French civil officers were discharged—a measure which was probably instigated by the notorious want of honesty with which at that time they conducted their duties. Amherst ordained that government by martial law should replace the civil law until such time as the King's pleasure should be notified.†

Certain steps in the direction of administration had already been taken by Murray in the appointment, on November 12, 1759, of a Chief Judge in the Province of Quebec—Colonel John Young, assisted by " some of the best men I could find in the place "—and in the following January (1760) he had appointed a French Canadian, M. Jacques Allier, to execute the office of " Civil and Criminal " Judge in the parishes on the south bank of the river from Berthier to Kamouraska, and for the maintenance " of the police and good order in the said parishes." The judgments were, however, subject to appeal before Colonel Young.

On October 31 (1760) Murray issued a general proclamation of the regulations for the dispensing of justice. This document exhibits, in a great degree, the intention of

---

* Under the French regime the three districts were under lieutenant-governors, acting under a governor-general. For Amherst's orders, *see* Public Record Office, A. and W. I. vol. xcix.

† Amherst to Murray, September 23, 1760.

granting equal rights to all subjects of the King, whether new or old. I quote the preamble below:

"By His Excellency, Mr. James Murray, Governor of Quebec, etc.

"Our chief object having been, in the Government which it has pleased His Majesty to entrust to us, to ensure the administration of justice to his new subjects, Canadian as well as French, settled in the town and neighbourhood of this Government, we have likewise thought it necessary to establish the form of procedure; to fix the day of our audiences, as well as those of our military council, which we have established in this town: to the end that every one may conform to it, in the causes that they may require to have judged in our Courts, or such as we may think necessary to send to the said council." Here follows ten * "Articles," detailing the procedure.

The tenth Article of the proclamation was as follows, and was based on Amherst's "Placard," dated at Montreal October 22, 1760:

"Disputes that the inhabitants of the district may have among themselves with respect to enclosures, damages, or other provisional cases, of which we authorise the commandant of the troops to take cognisance in each locality † and try summarily, reserving appeals to the military council if the case pertains thereto and there is reason for it."

Thus, though martial law was the general basis for final decision, it will be seen that the existing French civil law was also recognised to deal with cases not referred to the military council.‡

The governors were likewise authorised to sign commissions to all vacant posts in the militia, and reinstate

---

* Printed in full in Short and Doughty's compendious report in the Canadian Archives, Sessional Papers, 1907, together with many other interesting papers on the constitutional history of Canada.

† That is in effect to continue the system of the French Government, under which the captains of the militia companies held legal powers in minor cases.

‡ In a letter dated September 23 (1760) Amherst desired that while theft and murder should be referred to military law, differences between the inhabitants should be settled amongst themselves by their own laws.

those who had enjoyed those posts under the French king.

This latter privilege, as well as a reversion to administration of justice by the militia captains of the parishes, may have been a measure of doubtful advantage, for Murray describes these gentlemen very scathingly in a letter quoted below; but at all events it was a useful preliminary to settle men's minds to the new order without too great a disruption of long-established habits, and, no doubt, care was taken to appoint men of the most trustworthy nature that could be found.

Trade under Amherst's proclamation was " to be free to every one without duty, but merchants will be obliged to take out passports (licenses) from the governors, which will be furnished them gratis."

To Pitt, Murray wrote at this time (October 22) his first " civil," as I may call it, despatch :

" Hitherto," he says, " I have given you an account of the affairs of this country in my military capacity ; now that His Majesty has the quiet possession of it, I imagine it will not be disagreeable to know what I have learnt of it in other respects."

What Murray had " learnt " he embodied in a long and very interesting report, from which I make the following extracts :

" The French inhabitants of Canada, the year before the breaking out of the present war, amounted to about 80,000, including the forty companies of the Troupes de Colonie.

" To a man they are husbandmen, and require little assistance from artificers."

The women wove the material and turned it into garments.   The system of tenure involved military service.

" The men capable of war are divided into companies of one hundred each, and all orders, civil or military, relative to ye inhabitants, are directed to the captains of those companies *who are not chose from a superiority of parts, circumstances, or knowledge, but from a depravity of heart*, which will not hesitate implicitly to execute the commands of an oppressive governor." (My italics.)

The ignorance of the people, and the power of the priesthood over them, is referred to, and the absence of a class capable of assuming the lead.

" The River St. Lawrence is the finest in the universe; the navigation is easy and now well known. Its banks produce hemp, flax, tar, pitch, masts, ships' timber, and iron enough to supply all Europe. The tide rises thirty feet, and docks may be made at small expense everywhere. That ships may winter here with as much safety as in any harbour in Holland is not to be denied."

A formidable fleet might be built, he says, without the knowledge of the European powers.

Great stress is laid on the possibilities of the fisheries and the advantage of making every Canadian a fisherman and a sailor. It is clear that Murray held the view that England's future was on the sea. He goes on:

" Had the French promoted this branch (the fisheries) with as much eagerness as they grasped at the insignificant fur trade, how formidable might their colony have proved to us. . . .

" As it is doubtful with me what will be the fate of this colony at the Peace, I apprehend it is not my duty to point out to the inhabitants the natural advantages of their country and to put them on improvements; but I am to do everything in my power to convince them how happy they would be under the influence of British laws, and therefore nothing shall be wanting in me to exert that justice and humanity which I hope will ever continue to characterise the British Government."

By this means he hoped to extinguish the prejudices of the Canadians, and cultivate connections which might be useful in case of another war—all of which was eminently sound and far-seeing.

The greater part of this document, which, it must be remembered, was written after a short experience, shows a remarkable insight into the conditions of the country, though it must be admitted that to refer to the people as being without natural leaders was perhaps an error which had undesirable consequences.   The seigneurs, or over-lords, were, in fact, leaders, not always of a good kind, who it would have been an advantage to cultivate and improve, and Murray, writing at a later date, said : " They (the peasants) have been accustomed to obey and respect their noblesse."   It is true, however, that the policy of the French Government had been to obliterate individuality. Colbert, himself a son of the people, Minister of the Grande Monarque, who declared " *l'état c'est moi*," had written :

" Rarely, or, to speak more correctly, never, give a corporate form to the inhabitants of Canada.   You should even, as the colony strengthens, suppress gradually the office of Syndic, who presents petitions in the name of the inhabitants ;   for it is well that each should speak for himself, and no one for all." *

This was written to Frontenac in 1673, but it became the settled policy, and perhaps something more might have been done by the first British Governor to eradicate it, and to have brought the seigneurs more into touch with the administration during this period of martial law and before the commencement of civil administration, when he was obliged to follow the orders received from England.

In any action to develop the colony or to improve the status of the people, Murray was greatly hampered by the uncertainty whether the British Government intended to retain possession at the forthcoming peace.   This has already been alluded to, and, quoting from Justin Windsor's *Narrative and Critical History of America*, I may add :

" As soon as Quebec had surrendered there grew a party in England who put Canada as a light weight in the scales, in comparison with Guadaloupe, in balancing the territorial claims to be settled in defining the terms of a peace."

* *Old Quebec* (Parker and Bryon).

And a number of pamphlets, which are referred to in his work, were issued arguing the matter pro and con, some of them being of a quality which gave them importance.

In this connection, however, there was another view of the case which did not fail to strike so thoughtful an observer as Murray—the effect on the American colonies which would arise from the absence of danger from their French neighbours. These colonies, continually harassed by the French claims to exclude them from any westward progress, and with their borders constantly open to attack, were very much more dependent on support from home than the same colonies relieved of all fear of aggression and rapidly developing the independence of attitude, which was their inheritance. Montcalm had foreseen this in the previous year; the loss of French Canada had seemed to him inevitable, arising from " an evil administration and an insatiable desire to rob the King " (Journal of Montcalm), and he wrote:

" But in this I console myself that the loss of this colony, this defeat, will one day be of more service to my country than a victory. . . . The English must breathe the air of freedom, and these Americans more so, and the children of these are not degenerated from the Republican principles of their parents. Their maxim is to obey as little as possible, and when their interests are touched they will revolt." *

Murray had expressed much the same view, writing to Amherst in November (1759):

" How formidable it (the colony) might be made under any other government than that of Monsieur Vaudreuil. *En bonne Politique* it should, perhaps, be destroyed ; but

---

* Montcalm to De Molé, see Doughty, *Siege of Quebec*, vi. 141. Bancroft, *The American Revolution*, ii. 203, describes these letters as forgeries; but, in any case, it is admitted that Grenville had seen them, and thus whether they truly represented Montcalm or not, they should at least have served as a warning to the English Ministers. *See also Life of William Pitt* (Basil Williams), ii. 328.

there may be reasons why it should remain, *as it is a guarantee for the good behaviour of its neighbouring colonies.*" *

These views had, as we know now, solid foundation, and they will be referred to again ; in the meantime, if questions of policy prevented all the steps which suggested themselves being taken, there was much to be done to maintain even the existence of the population of the Quebec province. We know that the stern measures adopted by Wolfe had resulted in the destruction of many of the parishes on the south and north shores east of Quebec, and though Murray's action had been more clement, still much material damage had been done by the armies, both of friend and foe, on the country immediately surrounding the capital and for some distance up the river ; but the principal causes which tended to ruin the people were, in the first place, the exactions of the French commissaries, who, though most punctilious in making paper payment for everything " borrowed," † and exacting receipts therefor, had nevertheless not only drained the country, but had left only paper money in the hands of the *habitants*, which had no value when the French Government was swept away ; and in the second place, the absence of the able-bodied men on military service almost continually for three years had caused a shortage of cultivation and of food stuffs, which threatened to produce dire results among the unfortunate people.

* The reverse view was argued in a pamphlet entitled, *The Interests of Great Britain considered with regard to her Colonies and the Acquisition of Canada and Guadaloupe.* " . . . Nor can the union of our colonies be dangerous. We have already fourteen separate Governments on the maritime coasts of the continent, which have different forms of government, laws, interests, religions, persuasions, and manners. Their jealousy of each other is so great that, however necessary an union of the colonies has long been for the common defence, yet they have never been able to effect such a union among themselves, nor even to agree in requesting the Mother Country to establish it for them." All of which the events of the next few years shows to have been a short-sighted view of what might happen if a grievance common to all should impel a union for the common defence, in circumstances relieved from other dangers.

† *See* Bougainville correspondence in vol. vi., *Siege of Quebec*, Nos. 66 and 67, for instances.

In his early letters this state of destitution was often referred to by Murray. Writing to Amherst on New Year's day, 1761, he says :

" I formerly hinted at the miserable state of His Majesty's Canadian subjects of the Quebec province. To describe it is really beyond my power, and to think of it is shocking to humanity. It has afforded the King's British subjects an opportunity of exerting that benevolence and charity inseparable from the sentiments which the freedom of our laws of Church and State must ever inspire. The merchants and officers have made a collection of five hundred pounds Halifax money, and the soldiers insist on giving one day's provisions in a month for the support of the indigent ; without these aids, many must have perished, and still I fear a famine unless a supply of corn is sent from Montreal or the British provinces."

The new Governor showed a broad-minded tolerance in regard to the religion of the country, which was much to his credit, in an age when such tolerance was very rare. Possibly the years spent in Ireland opened his eyes to the futility of forcing men to adopt a form of worship foreign to their instincts. Possibly in his own early days he had heard something of the disasters brought about by the endeavour to bring men to everlasting peace by the method of interminable war—perhaps it was merely that he had seen many countries and had the breadth of view which men acquire when they are brought in contact with all shades of thought ; whatever the reason, Murray was *persona grata* with the people, and long after his departure he continued to receive annual greetings from his friend, the Abbess of the Ursulines ; he was also on the best of terms with the Lady Superior of the Augustine Convent, and the ladies of the Hôtel Dieu—who retain more than one record of his generosity and thoughtfulness. To the priesthood, and especially the Jesuits, he was less complaisant, for he found or suspected not a few cases of trafficking with the enemy, and he was obliged to adopt severe measures ; but where he found the village curés minded their proper business, he was always ready to protect them. I have already mentioned the circumstances of his sending a donation towards the restoration of the church of Ste. Foy, and when I visited that place in October, 1915, the curé, Abbé H. Scott, assured me that Murray's memory was still green among the French Canadians.

Very possibly his action in these very matters of religion laid the foundation of the bond; but there were other and perhaps more potent reasons for the affection with which they regarded him, and this was his determination to see that His Majesty's Canadian subjects should receive equal treatment and justice with the British who flocked to his province. But for Murray's conscientious stand these British traders would have made a very strong bid to oust the *habitants* from what little was left to them. Early in January, 1761, he wrote to Amherst concerning the brutalities and many shocking things committed by the crews of the vessels trading to Quebec, both to Indians and Canadians, and hinted that the sailors of His Majesty's ships were not innocent of similar practices. He begged that a manifesto should be issued by the commander-in-chief on the subject.

In the meantime a commission as Military Governor of the town of Quebec and its dependencies had arrived, dated at Saville House, October 27, 1760, and signed by W. Pitt. This document became of some importance later on, when the delay in the settlement of regular government of the new colony took place, which will presently be adverted to. The commission ran as follows:

" . . . We reposing especial trust and confidence in your loyalty, courage, and experience in military affairs do by these presents constitute and appoint you to be Governor of our town of Quebec, and of all the lines, fortifications, and dependencies of the government of Quebec . . . and We strictly charge all our officers and soldiers who are now or hereafter shall be in the said town, lines, fortifications, and dependencies, and all other our ministers, officers, and loving subjects whom it may concern, to obey you as our Governor thereof.

" And you are to observe and follow all such orders and directions from time to time as you shall receive from Us *according to the rules of war*."

This commission was clearly a military command, and when reference is made to the uncertainty regarding the powers of the commander-in-chief in America, it will be well to remember it.

The old French custom of homage for the retention of fiefs and seigneuries, fines on alienation upon all exchanges of inheritance among the inhabitants, were continued. In a letter dated March 25, Amherst informed Murray that he had been acquainted by Mr. Gage " of the King's rights in such matters," but Murray, to whom the name of Gage was rather as a red rag to a bull, hastened to reply :

" The discovery which Mr. Gage acquaints you he has made of the King's rights in Canada he had from me. . . . I have asserted the King's rights in every respect.   Little arises from the sales of fiefs, or from exchanges of inheritance, for in the present situation of this country there are neither buyers nor sellers."

In all this there is nothing to show that under the French regime any question had arisen in regard to direct taxation for the benefit of the Mother Country.   It cannot be doubted that the fact does not indicate that hesitation would have arisen to employ such a measure, but in the then circumstances it was no doubt rightly assumed that the possible revenue would be small.

I have given this brief sketch of the early stages of the administration of the new province, partly because some of the actions taken bore fruit of great importance, but principally to bring into prominence at the outset the qualifications for government which Murray possessed. We have seen him hitherto as a soldier, prompt, severe on occasion, farseeing in his estimates of the situation, self-reliant, yet cautious in the execution of intentions decided upon.   We have now a new aspect, an administrator, seeking to rehabilitate a ruined province, determined that it shall pay its way, yet not rushing hot-headed into extortion as a means of achieving this end—seeking rather a broad basis of increasing the wealth of the individual in order, in due time, to bring in a quota to the treasury.

For the rest, the winter of 1760–61 passed happily. "Everybody, British and Canadians, are in perfect harmony and good humour." *

"Hitherto there has not, this winter, the least sign of scurvy appeared among the troops, and I believe we shall be convinced by experience that good lodging, warm clothing, and proper nourishment, will prevent the havock of that disorder in the most malignant climates." †

To Pitt he wrote :

"The inhabitants, enjoying the justice and freedom of a British Government, want nothing but that plenty which the ravages of war has deprived them of, to make them entirely happy." ‡

News of the death of King George II., "which happened on October 24 (1760) in a sudden manner," was received in Quebec on January 26 (1761) via New York—a lapse of time which gives one to think on the inconveniences of the period. The new King was proclaimed in Quebec on January 27.

In March Murray heard that the 40th Regiment, which he had hoped for, had been given to Colonel Armiger. He is evidently a little hurt, but writes :

"I am not disappointed ; soldiers of fortune should be impatient of nothing but disgrace. While the King approves of my services and you, my commander-in-chief, are satisfied with my conduct, I am very happy and doubts (sic) not of being remembered in due time."

In May (1761), writing to Pitt, Murray gives indication of another field of energy, in which he accomplished a great deal during his governorship, viz. the survey of Canada.

* Murray to Amherst, January 11, 1761 (Bath Papers).
† Murray to Barrington, January 23, 1761 (Bath Papers).
‡ Murray to Pitt, December 2, 1760 ; c.o. 42–24 in P. R. O.

The fine map which is preserved in the British Museum, and known as the King's map, or the Murray map, no doubt had its commencement at this time :

" The bearer will deliver to you a copy of the survey of Canada as far as we have yet been able to make it. The whole will be finished by the beginning of August, and I have undertaken to make myself master of the River Chaudière and the communication with our Kennebec River, and likewise the River St. John, which empties itself into the Bay of Fundy, and communicates with the St. Lawrence by a few easy portages (carrying places from one water to another), so happen what will we never again can be at a loss how to attack and conquer this country in one campaign."

A letter from Amherst at this period (May, 1761) shows the value he placed on Murray's services :

" Wherever it may be my lot to serve, if there is any real service, I shall wish to have you with me, and you may depend on it, as far as the service will permit it, I shall contrive it may be so. From present appearances I see no real service likely to fall to my share, and no place where you can so essentially serve your King in as by a continuance of your zeal and activity, and prudent conduct, in doing everything that may tend to the defence and protection and care of the very important Government of Quebec, which will so much the more require your presence, as such a number of troops are being withdrawn from it."

At home the trend of politics calls for some mention, inasmuch as changes in the Ministry and the Court occurred which were to affect affairs in Canada. A letter from Amherst, dated New York, December 5, 1761, gives the " news " :

" Lord Egremont writes me on October 9 that the King has been pleased to grant Mr. Pitt's request to retire from business and to appoint his lordship (Egremont) to be Secretary of State for the southern department. Mr. Pitt has resigned the seals ; his reason for this measure is said to be difference of opinion with the King's other ministers as to the immediate necessity of a Spanish war, which he thinks unavoidable. He goes out in good humour, and is to be handsomely rewarded. This reward appears to be a peerage to his son,* and £3000 a year pension to himself and his son for both their lives."

The accuracy of Pitt's diagnosis of the situation was speedily made manifest, and before the end of the year the Spanish Court had curtly dismissed the British Ambassador, Lord Bristol, and acknowledged the so-called "family compact," whereby the courts of Madrid and Versailles agreed to regard the enemies of the one to be common to both.

So far as we are concerned, the Spanish war, which was formally declared in January, 1762, has little in it of immediate interest, except that in the subsequent expeditions against Martinique and the Havannah Murray found a fresh source of annoyance in being retained in his Governorship while laurels were a-gathering. But the resignation of Pitt and the rise in the King's favour of Lord Bute were events of far-reaching importance, the effects of which soon made their appearance. For several years the country was a prey to ambitious politicians and to kaleidoscopic changes of policy. The Royal authority, by supporting one or other of the rival factions, made the confusion worse confounded, and no Ministry was formed of sufficient strength to enable continuity of intention to be maintained. We in our day are inclined to grumble at adhesive ministries which cling to power with limpet-like tenacity, but, at least, we are fortunate in avoiding that near balance of strength in rival parties which from 1761 to 1766 prevented any semblance of continuous government. Perhaps the essential difference in the political fabric of those days as compared with ours was that then a great speaker could influence a decision in the House ; to-day the greatest speech, and the most cogent arguments, may produce some evanescent effect on the country, but in a House shackled by what we call " party discipline," none at all.

* Actually to his wife.

During these years the seeds were sown which resulted in the loss of the American colonies, and had effects on Murray and his government of Canada which will appear. When in 1766 Pitt returned to power as Earl of Chatham, it was too late to counteract the indecision of the preceding years, nor was he physically capable of then saving the situation. " The evils," he wrote, " are, I fear, incurable. Faction shakes and corruption saps the country to its foundations."

The Government at home were fully awake to the necessity for closely examining the value of the new territories in America. Whether to be retained or not, it was desirable to form a just estimate of their value, in order that the bargaining, which the approaching termination of the war was sure to bring with it, might be conducted on sure grounds. In this view Lord Egremont called for reports from the Governors of the three provinces of Quebec, Montreal, and Three Rivers, of the general conditions of their respective charges. Murray's report is dated June 5, 1763, and is a very instructive document, to which he evidently gave great care. It is published in full in *Documents relating to the Constitutional History of Canada* (Sessional Paper No. 18 of the Canadian Archives, 1907, by Professor Shortt and Dr. Doughty), and it is unnecessary to reprint it here.

The military section of the report contained a strong recommendation for the building of a citadel on Cape Diamond, advice which was neglected at the time with serious results during the revolution. The civil section, which occupies the greater part, supplies many interesting details of the French governmental system and the customs of land tenure. The administration of justice was described, and in view of the complications caused by retaining the French system in conjunction with the English system, Murray recommended " a short and well digested code " to supersede the existing practice. Another case in which his advice was neglected with serious consequences. Trade and the expenses of government were dealt with in great detail,

For future development Murray's views were comprehensive ; the fostering of husbandry, and the abolition of those " inconveniences," such as monopolies and frequent military service, and the wastage of war which " they have much more severely felt from their pretended friends than from their declared enemies," he expected would in three or four years ensure not only abundance of home supply but " even to export *if a market can be found* " (my italics)—a remark which reads curiously to-day, when the great granary of Western Canada is a reservoir which maintains the level of the world's prices. Minerals, the fisheries, timber, flax, and hemp, all fell within his consideration, and given that no settlement unsuitable to the population would be concluded, he says :

" Convinced that this is not to be their case, and that a free exercise of their religion will be continued to them once Canada is irrecoverably ceded by a peace, the people will soon become faithful and good subjects to His Majesty, and the country they inhabit will in a short time prove a rich and most useful colony to Great Britain."

These are golden words, amply justified to-day, and if Murray's claim to a niche in the temple of fame rested on no other basis, the effect which this report of his had on the decision to retain Canada as an integral part of the British Empire would alone give him a title to remembrance.

In another letter, direct to Lord Egremont (June 7, 1762), he gave a clear indication of his views, which it is greatly to be regretted were not accepted. After saying the question of the details of the new Government was " too nice a subject for me to undertake, and I have left the same to the determination of my superiors," he adds : " One thing only I shall observe, that *the people here do not yet seem ripe for such a government as prevails in our other colonies.*" The sequel will show how correctly he gauged the situation.

Letters from Amherst in March and April of 1762 told

U

of the employment of Monckton, and, temporarily, of Burton, on service in the Spanish war, and Murray was not best pleased at being left out. Amherst did his best to console him by pointing out that his present duties did not admit of his being spared. These letters also mention that Barré, whom we last met as Wolfe's confidant during the Quebec campaign, was now an " oracle " in the Government at home. He was already Member of Parliament for Chipping Wycombe, and had made that violent attack on Pitt which Walpole, in his *Memoirs*, describes as carried out by " the bravo selected by Shelburne."

Barré, however, was no bravo, and the term was not well selected. He could attack in the open, and was a master of invective,* and if he was a bad enemy to make he certainly could be a firm friend. To Murray he stood more in the former capacity, for Murray had, in his view, opposed his idol, Wolfe. Lord Shelburne, too, who was now a power in the new Ministry (that of Lord Bute), and soon to have immediate control of American affairs, was greatly influenced by Barré's opinions. The rise of Barré to power was almost dramatic in its suddenness. In 1759 he was but a lieutenant of the 32nd Foot ; in 1761 he was Lieut.-Colonel of the 106th Regiment (The Black Musqueteers), and in 1763 he was Adjutant-General of the Forces and Governor of Stirling Castle ! Thus the inner working of the Colonial Office was little likely to be sympathetic with Murray's views, and a good deal of the mischief that followed must, I am afraid, be put down to the " New Oracle," Colonel Barré.

* Notwithstanding Macaulay's judgment, there is, I think, more to connect Isaac Barré with the " Junius " letters than was advanced in favour of Sir Philip Francis. *See* an article by the present writer in *Blackwood's Magazine* of January, 1917.

CHAPTER XIV

THE FIRST BRITISH GOVERNOR OF CANADA

ON February 10, 1763, was signed the peace of Paris, terminating as between England on the one hand, and France and Spain on the other, the state of war which had now endured officially for seven years—actually for about nine. Their Britannic, Most Christian, and Catholic Majesties declared a " Christian, universal, and perpetual peace " ; because they were too exhausted to fight any longer, and had every intention of doing so when opportunity arose. Pitt, who thoroughly disapproved of the peace as premature, and one which relinquished much of the advantage gained by victorious campaigns, besides a dishonourable desertion of the Prussian ally, declared that it could result only in an armed truce ; and Pitt's foresight was justified.

Of the twenty-seven Articles of the treaty the fourth only need be quoted ; it included the following :

" His most Christian Majesty renounces all pretensions which he has heretofore formed or might have formed to Nova Scotia or Acadia. . . . Moreover, His Most Christian Majesty cedes and guarantees to his said Britannic Majesty, in full right, Canada, with all its dependencies, as well as the Island of Cape Breton and all the other islands and coasts in the gulph and river of St. Lawrence, and in general everything that depends on the said countries, lands, islands, and coasts. . . . *His Britannic Majesty on his side agrees to grant the liberty of the Catholic religion to the inhabitants of Canada . . . as far as the laws of Great Britain admit.*"

On this foundation, the Ministry in London, now nominally in charge of George Grenville, Bute retaining the position of chief wire-puller from behind the scenes, set to work to create a form of government for the new American territories, and, incidentally, to define the governments of the old colonies, as well as to solve the knotty problem of the " mode of revenue least burthensome and most palatable " to them, to cover the additional expense of the civil and military establishments.

Lords Egremont and Shelburne, the first as Secretary of State, the latter as representing the " Lords of Trade," were in the first place confronted with the necessity of determining a geographical boundary which should include the government of Canada, and the important decision was taken that a civil rather than a military government should be established, the confines of which should be those of the original colony of New France, excluding on the west and north the territories lying about the Great Lakes. This curtailment of area was no doubt due to Shelburne, for we are told that Lord Egremont favoured the inclusion of the Great Lakes and all the Ohio Valley. But, on the ground that :

" If this country should be annexed to the Government of Canada we are apprehensive that the powers of such Government would not be properly carried into execution . . . unless by means of the garrisons at the different posts and forts in that country, which must contain the greatest part of your Majesty's American forces, *and the Governor of Canada would become, virtually, Commander-in-Chief, or constant and inextricable disputes would arise between him and the commanding officers of your British troops.*" *

Lord Shelburne's views prevailed. It would seem apparent, however, that his very argument carried its own condemnation, for " constant and inextricable disputes " were likely to arise, in any case, in a partly-settled country, should attempt be made to divorce the civil governor from all military control ; the more so that the

* Shelburne to Egremont, August 5, 1763. (My italics.)

system of government for the previous century had been
military in the strictest sense, and the people were unaccustomed to think in any other terms.   This initial mistake
was reversed within four years, as we shall see.   The form
of government which was recommended by the Lords of
Trade was " the appointment of a governor and council
under Your Majesty's immediate commission and instructions." *   In his letter of July 14, 1763, Lord Egremont signified to the Lords of Trade His Majesty's pleasure
that " The Hon. James Murray be Governor of Canada," †
and at the same time instructed them to draw up for the
King's approval a " draught " of the commission and
instructions for the governor-elect.   Lord Egremont also
stated : " With regard to the commander-in-chief of His
Majesty's forces, the king thinks that his correspondence
should remain, as it hitherto has done, with the Secretary
of State." ‡   On October 8, 1763, the draught proclamation
extending the Royal authority over the conquered territories was approved by the King.   The new Canada was
styled " The Province of Quebec."

The King's Proclamation (abridged) ran as follows :

" Whereas we have taken into our Royal consideration
the extensive and valuable acquisitions in America secured
to our Crown by the late Definitive Treaty of Peace concluded at Paris, the 10th day of February last, and being
desirous that all our loving subjects, as well of our Kingdom
as of our Colonies in America,§ may avail themselves with

* Lords of Trade to Egremont, June 8, 1763.
† It is interesting to note that the Governorship of Canada had
been in the first place offered to Pitt, though he was to be a non-
resident governor (*Life of William Pitt*, Basil Williams).
‡ There was frequent evidence of the overlapping of the business
of the public departments, and we find the Secretary of State addressing the Commander-in-Chief on the subject of taxes and quit rents
without reference to the Governors, who heard on similar subjects
from the Board of Trade, while the Chancellor of the Exchequer
framed proposals for imports and customs duties apart from either
the Secretary or the President.
§ A Report of the Lords of Trade, dated November 5, 1761,
indicates their opposition to granting free access to the colonies of
foreigners : " Our own reduced sailors and soldiers would be more
proper objects of national bounty and better colonists than
foreigners, whose ignorance of the English language, laws, and constitution cannot fail to increase those disorders and that confusion

all convenient speed of the great benefits and advantages which must accrue therefrom to their commerce, manufactures, and navigation. . . . And whereas it will greatly contribute to the speedy settling our said new governments, we have thought fit to publish and declare that we have given express power and direction to our governors that *so soon as the state and circumstances of the said colonies will admit thereof,* they shall, with the advice and consent of the members of our council, summon and call General Assemblies within the said governments ; and we have also given power to the said governors with the consent of our said councils *and the representatives of the people,* to make, constitute, and ordain laws, statutes, and ordinances for the public peace, welfare, and good government of the people and inhabitants thereof as near as may be agreeable to the laws of England, and in the meantime and until such assemblies can be called as aforesaid, all persons inhabiting in or resorting to our said colonies *may confide in our Royal protections for the enjoyment of the benefit of the laws of our realm of England, for which* purpose we have given power under our Great Seal to the governors of our said colonies to erect and constitute, with the advice of our said councils, courts of judicature and public justice, as well criminal as civil with liberty, in all civil cases, to appeal to us in our Privy Council.

" We have also thought fit to give unto the governors and councils full power to settle and agree with the inhabitants or with any other person who shall resort thereto for such lands, tenements, and hereditaments as are now or hereafter shall be in our power to dispose of, and then to grant upon such *terms as have been appointed and settled in our other colonies,* and under such other conditions as shall appear to us to be necessary and expedient for the advantage of the grantees. . . ."

Perhaps the most remarkable point in this remarkable document is the almost complete absence of any consideration of the settled inhabitants of the colony, who had grown up during the previous century and a half as a body

in our Government, which the too great migration of people from Germany has already fatally introduced in some of our most valuable possessions."   A remark which indicated that *Kultur* was not more admired in 1761 than at present !

organised with laws and customs, which even the most ruthless conqueror would hardly set aside without at least some consideration.   As was aptly said at a later period, the idea which seemed to dominate the minds of the ministers responsible for framing the proclamation was to consider only " the profit and advantage that might accrue to the King's British subjects."

On August 13 (1763) Lord Egremont had conveyed in advance the gist of the above decisions to Murray.   He wrote :

" I take great satisfaction in acquainting you that His Majesty has been graciously pleased to confer on you the Government of Canada, over which country you have already presided so long with such applause, that the King is persuaded this appointment will be received by his new subjects as a singular mark of his Majesty's Royal attention to their welfare and happiness."

These were highly complimentary terms, and in the special circumstances of the agitation carried on by Wilkes, to which reference will presently be made, indicate the appreciation of his services held by the King.   In the same letter Lord Egremont gives a word of warning regarding the activity of the religious orders :

" It becomes of the utmost consequence to watch the priests very narrowly, and to remove as soon as possible any of them who shall attempt to go out of their sphere, and who shall busy themselves in any civil matters ; for though the King has in the fourth article of the Definitive Treaty agreed to grant the liberty of the Catholic religion to the inhabitants, yet the condition expressed in the same articles must always be remembered, viz. *as far as the laws of Great Britain permit.*   But at the same time that I point out to you the necessity of adhering to them and of attending with the utmost vigilance to the behaviour of the priests, the King relies on your acting with all proper caution and prudence in regard to a matter of so delicate a nature as this of religion."

The commission of the newly appointed first British

Governor of " the Province of Quebec "—that is to say, of Canada—is a lengthy document, dated November 21, 1763, and addressed " to our trusty and well beloved James Murray, Esquire," constituting and appointing him to be " Captain-General and Governor-in-Chief in and over our Province of Quebec in America." The various oaths as to the Crown and the Protestant Succession are detailed, and the same ordered to be administered to the Lieut.-Governors of Montreal and Trois Rivières and Members of Council, and to the persons " duly elected by the major part of the freeholders of the respective parishes, or precincts," who were to form the General Assembly of the " freeholders and planters within the Government."

The powers of the Governor to make laws are contained in the following important paragraph :

" And we do hereby declare that the persons so elected and qualified shall be called the Assembly of that our Province of Quebec, and that you, the said James Murray, by and with the advice and consent of our said Council and Assembly or the major part of them, shall have full power and authority to make, constitute, or ordain laws, statutes, and ordinances for the publick peace, welfare, and good government of our said Government of our said Province and of the people and inhabitants thereof, and such other as shall resort thereunto, and for the benefit of us our heirs and successors, which said laws, statutes, and ordinances *are not to be repugnant, but as near as may be agreeable to the laws and statutes of this our Kingdom of Great Britain.*"

Laws thus made were subject to the King's confirmation, without which, received in due course, they became void. The Governor was to " enjoy a negative voice in the making and passing of all laws and statutes," and was likewise entitled to " adjourn, prorogue, or dissolve all general assemblies as aforesaid." Power to appoint courts, judges, and justices, and all other necessary officers, was granted, as was the privilege of pardon, except in cases of treason and wilful murder, which could be reprieved until the King's pleasure was known.

The military authority granted was, so far as the form of word goes, apparently full, viz.: "To levy, arm, muster, command, and employ all persons whatsoever residing within our said province," and furthermore, all officers and ministers, as well civil as military, were "to be obedient, aiding and assisting unto you, the said James Murray"; yet, as will be seen, this military structure had, in fact, no substantial reality.

To the commission itself was attached a document entitled "Instructions to Governor Murray," consisting of eighty-two clauses. In this the composition of the Council was decreed to consist for the present of the Lieut.-Governors of Montreal and Trois Rivières, the Surveyor-General of the Customs, and eight other persons to be chosen from among the most considerable of the inhabitants.

It is scarcely possible, in reviewing this creation of a new government in a colony which had grown and even prospered, at all events for a period, under a totally different system, to avoid the reflection that the ministers who evolved it lacked imagination and the instinct of statesmen. A governor, a council, an assembly, were the sealed pattern implements by which the colonies of British-born peoples, whose forefathers had been bred to parliamentary institutions, had been ruled, therefore this new possession, of which all but a fraction of the inhabitants were foreigners of different language, religion and mode of thought to the conquerors must necessarily fall into the same groove! In French Canada the doctrine of Colbert, which involved the suppression of the individual, had held sway for a hundred years. The people were voiceless, and were trained to accept the despotic powers of the rulers. To such a community the change was too sudden. To bring life and movement into a body long paralysed by disuse was a miracle likely to react dangerously, and to bring about ills not less serious than those which it remedied, and

Murray, as we have seen, clearly foresaw the unwisdom of too drastic a change, and that the people were not yet ripe for such a system.*

It is made very clear in the reports of the Board of Trade that the calling together of an assembly was intended to be a matter of early completion.

" It will be expedient for His Majesty's service, and give confidence and encouragement to such persons as are inclined to become settlers in the new colonies, that an immediate and public declaration should be made of the intended permanent constitution, and that the power of calling assemblies should be inserted in the first commissions . . . and any *temporary* power of making ordinances and regulations, which must of necessity be allowed to the governors and councils before assemblies can be called, will be better inserted in the instructions we are now preparing." †

Thus the very points which were afterwards found to be of doubtful legality, viz. temporary power to make ordinances had engaged the attention of the framers of the proclamation, and the unwisdom of the whole intention is demonstrated by the result which showed the undesirability of creating a general assembly, and even the impossibility of doing so while the religious disabilities were maintained.

But not less important than the innovations which were defined were others to which sufficient definition was not given, and in which the authority and powers of the governor and his council were left in a nebulous and unsatisfactory state, which was certain to produce unrest among sections of the community whose interests were at variance. Of these perhaps the most important was the question of religion. The fourth article of the Treaty of Paris had ordained :

" Liberty of the Catholick religion to the inhabitant of Canada . . . the new Roman Catholic subjects may profess the worship of their religion according to the rites

---

* *See* p. 291, *ante.*
† Hillsborough (Lords of Trade) to Halifax, October 4, 1763.

of the Romish Church *as far as the laws of Great Britain permit.*"

Lord Egremont had particularly drawn the Governor's attention to this limitation, and warned him that "these laws must be your guide in any disputes that may arise on this subject."

The laws in Great Britain, especially as applied to Ireland, which in many cases provided the analogy, did not recognise the possibility of any Papist holding civil office nor of taking part in any capacity in the administration of justice, and here at once arose difficulties, which brought the several factions into sharp antagonism. The number of Protestant settlers amounted to a few hundreds only, and the most of them were not persons of capacity or importance. It was subsequently held, as we shall see, that it was not intended that the literal reading of the words should be maintained, and in certain cases Murray adopted such a view, for in his ordinance establishing civil courts, he decided that " in all tryals in this court, all His Majesty's subjects in this colony to be admitted on juries without distinction " ; and in submitting this order for confirmation to the Lords of Trade, he explained :

" As there are but two hundred Protestant subjects in the province . . . it is thought unjust to exclude the new Roman Catholic subjects to sit upon juries, as such exclusion would constitute the said two hundred Protestants perpetual judges of the lives and property of not only eighty thousand of the new subjects, but likewise of all the military in the province. . . . This establishment is therefore no more than a temporary expedient to keep things as they are until His Majesty's pleasure is known on this critical and difficult point."

It should be noted that to this tentative proposal no objection was raised, nor, indeed, was any reply received.

In the Superior Court, or Court of King's Bench, Canadian advocates or proctors were not admitted, and the governor and council considered it essential to establish an inferior Court of Common Pleas, wherein minor cases could be tried according to French laws and customs, and Canadian advocates employed, whereby "the poor Canadians were enabled to shun the attempts of designing men, and the voracity of hungry practitioners in the law." Justices of the peace were appointed, but it appears that Protestants only were considered eligible, for we are told that a sufficient number of suitable persons of this religion not being available in the district of Trois Rivières the whole province should be divided into two districts only, viz. Quebec and Montreal; the holding of quarter sessions by the justices was regulated.

In all this, though the governor and his council clearly leaned towards a fair and sympathetic dealing with the Canadians and seemed determined to render their disabilities as little irksome as possible, it is abundantly evident that they were hampered by the narrow views imposed from home. The French Canadians recognised with gratitude that Murray's personal desire was to aid them, but this very fact induced outcry from that miscellaneous collection of adventurers who came on the heels of the conquest to make what they could out of a people whom they hoped to find at their mercy. It is to Murray's enduring credit that he stood between these vultures and their prey, and this though he knew it would raise against him the potent voice of the British traders, who then, as now, could bring pressure to bear in the councils of the Sovereign.

Apart from these sources of civil commotion, the military situation was not more satisfactory. The command of the regular troops within the new province was not clearly defined in the King's commission, but from other documents it was inferable that the commander-in-chief of the King's forces in America was supreme in all that concerned the King's regiments. So long as Sir Jeffrey Amherst exercised the function friction was not likely to arise, but in August, 1763, Amherst was recalled to England,* and Major-General Gage, whose post was that of Lieut.-

* He did not actually leave until the end of the year.

Governor of Montreal, was appointed to succeed him. I have hinted already that the relations between Gage and Murray were strained, and the tension was increased when the latter received the appointment of governor, and thus assumed the superior civil position over Gage, who was the senior in military rank.* Although Gage's appointment to succeed Amherst soon removed him from the anomaly of this position, yet it is certain that the soreness remained, and Gage, when he assumed the chief command of the troops was not inclined to make things smooth for an officer whose opinion of him he had probably heard.

Gage was succeeded by Haldimand as Lieut.-Governor of Montreal, and both Haldimand and Burton, who had returned to exercise the functions of Lieut.-Governor of Trois Rivières, adopted the attitude of independence of the Governor in military matters. To Murray the situation was galling, but he viewed it less from the personal than from the public standpoint. A little later (October 15, 1764) he wrote to Lord Halifax :

" When the commission His Majesty had been graciously pleased to honour me with as governor of this province arrived in Quebec, the gentlemen who had till then acted as Lieut.-Governors of Montreal and Trois Rivières chose still to continue so in their military capacitys, and declared I could have no command over the troops in their respective districts.

" The regard I have for my Royal Master's service, which must ever make me studious to obviate any real or possible motive of disagreement amongst his officers, induced me to waive a right which appeared to myself plain, incontestable, and, indeed, necessary for the governor of this province. . . . And as I plainly foresee, Mr. Gage means to divest me of all military authority, I should be deficient in my duty was I not to represent to your lordship the inconviencys to His Majesty's service which in my opinion must necessarily happen from such a step.

* Lord Halifax wrote to General Gage (November 12, 1763) : " Being informed that you will probably decline accepting the commission by which His Majesty was pleased to appoint you Lieut.-Governor of Montreal."

" It must be allowed that without a military force this lately conquered province cannot be govern'd ; there doth not exist in it above one hundred Protestant subjects, exclusive of the troops, and by my instructions, of these hundred Protestants must be composed the magistracy : But what force, what weight can such a magistracy have unless the supreme magistrate has the disposition of the military force. . . . The Canadians are to a man soldiers, and will naturally conceive that he who commands the troops should govern them. I am convinced, at least, it will be easyer for a soldier to introduce and make palateable to them our laws and customs, than it can be for a man degraded from the profession of arms. . . .

" I by no means think it right that the Governor of Quebec should be upon the American staff. . . . All I plead for is the necessity of having the disposition of the troops destined for the security of the province intrusted to my care. . . ." *

These representations were, unfortunately, of no avail, and Lord Halifax, as Secretary of State in Grenville's administration, maintained the position, formulated by Lord Shelburne, that the civil and military affairs of the colony should remain distinct, and that the military government should be directed by the commander-in-chief in America.

I have said that Murray viewed the matter as of public importance. The mutterings of the coming storm in the American colonies were already to be heard, and, not one opinion, but many, pointed to the change in the situation

---

* Governor Johnston (James Murray's nephew), speaking in the House, May, 1770, said : " If we look into the ancient historians, Tacitus particularly, we shall find that the disputes which arose between the Roman proconsuls in Africa and the military lieutenants sprung from the heterogeneous mode of giving the provinces government which was eternally at war with itself, and which, to be faithfully executed, could not but plunge the miserable inhabitants either in revolt or destruction. If the proconsul, for instance, behaved like a good magistrate, he had frequent occasions, occasions, too, as unavoidable as they were frequent, of checking the power of military lieutenants, and if the lieutenant acted like a brave soldier there was no possibility of his living on any reasonable terms with the proconsul." I quote this opinion given at a later date, to show that Murray's views as to the necessity of combining the civil and military administration in young colonies was one held by others besides himself.

which the removal of the French garrison in Canada brought about. The deeply ingrained spirit of freedom which ruled all hearts in the colonies was doubtless in no wise affected by the presence or absence of a foreign enemy on their borders. They had for years maintained themselves with varying success but with indomitable spirit against all encroachment, real or fancied, but it was not in human nature to suppose that the replacement of the foreigner on their borders by a government akin to their own, and conducted on a system which, outwardly at all events, conformed in every particular with that which custom and the lapse of time had made theirs, should not produce a disturbance in the equilibrium of the public mind.

It was no new thing for the colonial assemblies to oppose any attempts of the governors to impose measures which suggested coercion, though the gradual limitation of the political freedom, and the curtailment of privileges in later charters, which had come about since the English revolution, had been accepted. But it was one thing to accept interference from the central authority of Parliament when guardianship was extended by the same hand, and quite another to brook any dictation when the necessity for protection no longer existed. And, besides, there was an increasing leaven of men among the colonists, victims of religious persecution in Ireland, who felt no allegiance to the English Crown, though the majority was still loyal at the core.

Yet the very circumstances which freed the colonists from apprehension placed the Mother Country in the dilemma of requiring assistance from them. The expenses of the war had been heavy, and it was felt that, in justice, further contribution on the part of the colonies was due towards the cost of a conflict which had materially benefited them. It would probably have passed the wit of man to have devised a workable system which would have bound the colonies to the Mother Country in the stages of vast development which ultimately occurred, but this development lay in the womb of the future, and it certainly should not have surpassed the talents of the Home Government, at the time of which we are writing, to have treated the susceptibilities of a people who had suffered much in the cause and paid largely towards it, with a sympathy which would have attained the desired results without the appearance of too great an exercise of prerogative.

Unfortunately neither the King, in the exercise of his powerful influence, nor the chaotic character of the impotent Ministries, headed by Bute, or Grenville, or Rockingham, had perspicacity sufficient to take the broad view, or to initiate measures in such a way as to obtain the ready acquiescence of communities ready to follow, but refusing to be driven. It was even denied to the King and his ministers that they could argue themselves without warning of the results which followed. Barré had put the case powerfully : " Believe me, remember I told you so, the same spirit of freedom which actuated this people will accompany them still." Lord Shelburne had taken the same line, and Pitt had supported him in his refusal to implicate himself in the attempt to apply the right of the Imperial Parliament to dictate the financial contributions of the colonists.

Quem vult perdere Jupiter prius dementat! It remains for us to marvel that the unparalleled obliquity of vision which distorted the views of the English statesmen, and resulted in a series of measures which slowly transformed the loyal colonies of America into open insurrection, even obscured the necessity for military measures which would at least give coercion some probability of success. In Canada a weapon ready fashioned lay at hand—maintained as a military colony, following the tradition sanctioned by the system of its late masters, and guided by the sure hand of so experienced a commander as Murray, there is scarcely room to doubt that a powerful lever would have been available to force the colonies, if in the last resort, as a result of unwise measures, force should be necessary.

It may well be doubted if the Stamp Act was other than the immediate instrument which fired a train already laid, the dangerous condition of which would sooner or later have caused an explosion, and it should have been evident from the first that the prevailing spirit of a large number of the colonists was to obtain a degree of independence which could by no means be granted if the Crown was to maintain even a semblance of prerogative. In these conditions it is amazing that, side by side with such measures of conciliation as might have led the colonists into a better way of thinking, the obvious precaution of preparing for enforcement of submission should have been neglected.

In 1768, writing to the Duc de Choiseul, Francis, the French chargé d'affaires in London, gives Murray's views :

" *Le Général Murray ci devant Governeur du Canada, m'a dit hier, qu'il aurait répondu dans l'origine, d'empêcher le progrès des troubles, qu'il y avait encore des moyens certains de les arreter, mais qu'il fallait profiter des seuls instans qui restoient, par les mesures les plus vigoureuses. . . . Il avait donné le projet de faire du Canada une colonie militaire, pour tenir les autres dans la crainte et dans la soumission.*" *

That he would have succeeded in forming a military colony there is no doubt, the Canadians loved him, and would have followed his lead.

No more convincing confirmation of his views can be given than the letter of General Gage to Governor Carleton, dated at Boston, September 4, 1774 :

" The present situation of affairs in this province obliges me to collect all the force in my power. . . . As I must look forward to the worst from the apparent disposition of the people here, I am to ask your opinion whether a body of Canadians and Indians might be collected and confided in for the service of this country should matters come to extremities." †

But the demand came too late, and within a year Carleton was himself in extremities and unable to assemble

* Paris, *Min. des Affaires Étrangers*, vol. 480.
† Short and Doughty, Constitutional Papers.

Canadians in sufficient numbers to defend their own province.*   The British Government was ignobly seeking to employ a corps of Russian troops, and actually despatched a body of German mercenaries.   Had Murray's strong representations of the urgent necessity of continuing the government of Canada on a military basis, and postponing at least, the foolish London-made scheme of colonial government on the cut-and-dried methods of the Board of Trade, for which he had declared " the people do not seem ripe," what a different course the history of the American Revolution might have taken !

Even as an economic measure the maintenance of a garrison in Canada on a large scale was pressed on the Ministry in a petition from the British traders in 1765. They pointed out that the excess of imports over exports and the necessity for an adjustment of the adverse balance, which they said could be met by maintaining a larger army.   At the expense of the Mother Country, it is true, but probably for a few years only while the colony was developing.

If proof were wanting that the unwieldy military system, which attempted to govern the defence of a continent from a centre at New York, must fail, the course of events provided even this ;   and the insurrection of the Indians, headed by Pontiac, chief of the Ottawa tribes, brought home in an ugly fashion that the success with which the French had ruled the original owners of the soil was, so far, denied to their successors.   With the Indian war this story is slightly concerned, but in a land of vast distances, with means of communication of the most primitive nature, the " inconveniencys " of the system became at once apparent, and it seems astonishing that Murray's views of self-contained military authority on the part of the provincial governors met with so little consideration.

---

* " We are equally unprepared for attack or defence ;   the ancient provincial force enervated and broke to pieces . . ." (Carleton to Dartmouth, June 7, 1775).   " The King relies upon the loyalty and fidelity of his Canadian subjects for their assistance to suppress rebellion . . ." (Dartmouth to Carleton, July 8, 1775).

But, besides the Indian war, another sign was forth-coming that the military system was too unwieldy. On September 18 (1763) an order was issued that the free rations hitherto granted to the troops as being on active service should cease, and that thenceforward a deduction of fourpence for each ration should be made. This order emanated from home, and was conveyed via New York to Quebec. The result was immediate and serious The troops mutinied. There had been previous sporadic mutinies at Louisburg, and evidently the men were in a state of tension, no doubt due to the long and trying campaigns they had come through ; but one point which indicates the evil of divided authority comes out in Murray's report to Lord Egremont—the men declared they would march to New York and lay their arms at Sir Jeffrey Amherst's feet. It is clear that they looked upon the Governor as responsible for the order, which was by no means the case, and hoped for redress by appeal-ing to his military superior. For a time things wore a very serious appearance, but Murray, ably seconded by his officers, treated the situation with great firmness, and finally induced the mutinous regiments to fall in on parade, and, going personally to the head of each company, ordered the men to obey, " determined to put to death the first man who refused." This strong action overawed the men, and I cannot help dwelling upon the vigour of Murray's personality which could bring about so satisfactory a result. In a despatch of November 12 (1763) Lord Halifax (who had succeeded Lord Egremont) wrote :

" His Majesty saw with concern the account given in your letter of October 3 of the mutiny that had happened in the garrison of Quebec, and the very alarming heights to which it had risen, but observed with satisfaction the zeal and spirit which you exerted in reducing the troops to obedience, and I am commissioned by His Majesty to express to you in the strongest terms his royal approval of your distinguished conduct on that occasion."

Enough has been said to indicate that the peace of

Paris was far from bringing tranquillity to the Governor of the province of Quebec, and the effects of the blunders made must develop gradually with the course of this narrative. In the meantime, I will turn for a moment to Murray's personal concerns during the period subsequent to the Montreal campaign.

His appointment as governor was in itself a tribute to his successes and the high character he had won for himself, but it was not accomplished without a considerable opposition. In the early days of discussion on the terms of the peace of Paris the idea of governing Canada had greatly attracted John Wilkes, and, through his intimacy with Lord Temple, who became Pitt's brother-in-law, he had obtained flattering assurances from the minister.* The King, however, who liked to govern for himself, and had little affection at the time for Pitt, and none at all for Wilkes, it is said vetoed this proposal out of hand, and declared that the man who had defended Quebec was the one he wished to govern it. Wilkes' disappointment found utterance in the *North Briton* a couple of years later, and Murray did not escape his venomous pen. To be a Scot was in itself sufficient to incur the wrath of many of the political pamphleteers of the period, and Bute's rise to power as the King's confidential adviser made their bitterness fairly run over. The colonies were described as :

" Prey to the rapacity of four hungry Scottish governors † . . . as to the merits of three of these gentlemen I am a perfect stranger ; the demerit of the Governor of Quebec the world has seen, for he nearly lost the most important conquest made during the whole war—a conquest purchased with the blood of one of our first heroes, the immortal Wolfe. Among a variety of new measures which this nation must ever deplore the appointment of military men to civil governments is not the least to be lamented. . . . I will only further observe on this head

---

* Almon's Correspondence and *Memoirs of Wilkes*, 1–58.
† *Ibid.*, p. 225 *et seq.* The other three were James Grant, Governor of East Florida ; George Johnston, Governor of West Florida ; and Robert Melvill, Governor of Granada, etc. Johnston was Murray's nephew, and his eccentricity made him notorious.

that the partiality of these appointments to every new Government we have acquired plainly marks the same hand so fatal and hostile to England. . . . A gazette so late as that of Saturday, October 8 (1763) must convince every man that even now that Scottish influence is not at an end, and that all pretences of that kind whether they are made by men in or out of power, are captious and delusive." *

The " hand hostile to England," referred to Bute, and the gazette was that which contained Murray's appointment to Quebec. The Governor, however, does not seem to have been seriously disturbed by Wilkes' vituperation; indeed, the only reference I can find to him in the correspondence relates to the quality of the Highlanders who were anathema to men of Wilkes' kidney :

" Wilkes may say what he will, but every one must allow that Sandy is a good soldier, and always to be depended on. The debauched English soldier says Sandy has no more virtue than himself, for if his vice is drunkenness, Sandy's is avarice, which I am sorry to tell you, is not true, for they have spent all their money in ribbons for the Canadian girls ! "

On the political situation in England Murray had views :

" For my part I believe our young King is very capable of governing himself, and I am such a friend to our incomparable constitution that I shall be sorry ever to see him reduced to the necessity of governing by faction. All the actions of his life have hitherto shown how averse his nature is to everything contradictory to the laws of Great Britain. Happy for his people could those who oppose his Government be converted from these selfish, corrupted principle which influence their conduct, and which cannot be too soon nor too much discouraged by every well-wisher to the British Empire. These are the sentiments of an honest Briton, who blushes for the man who makes distinctions between the north and south of the Tweed, and who in place or out of place, elevated or depressed, will ever think the same and act accordingly."

* Almon's *Memoirs of Wilkes*, i. 232.

Doctor Gideon Murray, by now elevated to a valuable canonry of Durham Cathedral, was assiduous after the fashion of the day in keeping his brother's interest before the "great folks," and he writes to him of Lord Mansfield's high approval of the first acts of the Governor :

" He approves greatly of your conduct and management as a governor, and says you have acquitted that duty with much more honour, credit, and judgment than any one we have. Your lenity and kindness to the Canadians is highly commended by him, and he advises you to let them, as much as you can, see the benefits of a free British Government. It will redound to your honour and make no small *éclat* when we have a peace. These are the words of this great man—mark them well."

With Lord Bute, too, Murray stood well, though Bute's unpopularity in the country was a factor to his disadvantage. The uncertainties imposed by the want of stability in the Government is illustrated in a letter to Lord Elibank :

" It would appear from your Lordship's letter that it might have been lucky for me had Lord Bute's administration been more permanent. I wait with impatience to know what is to become of me ; but with a resolution cheerfully to receive the worst news and to persist in gratitude to those who would have served me, had it been in their power."

In his private family concerns a good deal of importance had happened. His father-in-law, Mr. John Collier, died in December, 1760, and by a codicil to his will, dated the previous April, he assigned the life interest in Mrs. Murray's share of the estate to her husband. This change in the terms of the original will was a somewhat remarkable tribute of respect to my hero, for Mr. John Collier was never very fully reconciled to the idea of trusting too much to the financial abilities of a soldier, and, indeed, he probably shared to some extent Mrs. Collier's views, that all soldiers were, by nature, extravagant. The original will had very expressly excluded James Murray from any control of his wife's fortune, and left to him, in the event of her death, no more than £500. The codicil, however, seems to indicate that Murray's gallant conduct at Quebec had turned the old man's suspicions into admiration, and it seems probable, too, from the wording of the will, that he considered it very desirable that his daughter should not be too independent of her husband. However this may be, the property, equally divided amongst the five surviving daughters, amounted to a very goodly heritage, principally in real estate in Hastings and the surrounding districts, and Murray thus became, in right of his wife, a considerable Sussex proprietor.

It would appear that when he was still in uncertainty as to the fate of Canada, he had visions of retiring to a home life in Sussex, and it was no doubt with this idea uppermost that he purchased the estate of Denham, or Denham's Folly. This purchase is alluded to in a letter from Gideon Murray, dated April, 1762, so that the date is approximately fixed. Denham was apparently immediately re-christened *Beauport*, after the French village, near Quebec, which Murray had cause to know so well. In a letter dated September, 1763, Gideon Murray hints at a change in his brother's views. Referring to the transfer of certain moneys he says :

" For your American purchases, I heartily wish you joy and good success. As you are now Governor of Canada, your money will be best laid out there. Your Excellency must be a seignior ; but I hope in time you'll transfer all and purchase in Britain, where it is more secure and less precarious in all respects. You must not therefore part with Beauport, but make it as you have designed it in due time, and if you do not chuse an absolute retirement, you may easily be chose Member for the Cinque Port."

In the early part of the year Murray had written to Mr. John Cranston, who was acting as his agent in Sussex :

" As there is now no doubt of a peace, and very little probability of my government being taken from me, I have no thought of visiting England. Indeed, I had some time ago determined to settle in America, whatever might be the consequences of a peace. I like the climate, and shall certainly never leave it unless the King's service obliges me. With this view my affairs are to be managed. . . . I wrote to your father to put a stop to all improvements proposed for Denham's Folly, and to lay no more of my money out in Sussex."

In July of same year (1763) he wrote again concerning some money affairs : " You will see I am unalterably fix'd in this American world, and that I shall as soon as possible convert into it every shilling of property I have in the earth."

This was a somewhat sudden and a very complete change of mind. It was formed before the troubles of the quasi-civil government began to mount up, and perhaps Murray was enamoured of the idea of becoming a great landed proprietor in the New World ; in this intention, I gather from another letter to Lord Elibank, his brother was apparently a partner, and some part of the money which was laid out in purchase of land in Canada was provided, or perhaps advanced, by his lordship. That he intended to go to work systematically to improve the land and farm on scientific principles is made clear from correspondence with his brother George, who was sending him two plough-men, two milkmaids, and a grieve (farm bailiff), together with seeds and a good deal of advice as to the best methods of agriculture, in which George appears to have possessed quite a store of knowledge.

It was not, however, the prospect of farming on a large scale which alone attracted him to forego the dream of a retirement to country pursuits in Sussex ; it is evident that he was thoroughly disgusted with the state of things in England, and the scant generosity with which he had been treated. The key to his feelings is given in a letter to George Murray, written in September, 1764 :

" I have of late met with so much ingratitude and harsh treatment from those whose friendship, or at least goodwill, I thought I had a right to expect, that I am determined to settle for the remainder of my days in this New World. . . . I have no natural claims to the affection and gratitude of my neighbours. If they are defective in making returns for the benevolence which I make a duty of showing to all mankind, the disappointment will not be so shocking and irksome as if it proceeded from those in whom I have a nearer concern. Besides, I really find the aborigines of the country—or savages, as you style them—less corrupt in general than the inhabitants of the most civilised nations. They lend without interest ; if a friend is lucky and kills more game, they envy him not, they rejoice at his success ; if in war fortune has favoured him, they constantly ascribe his success to his military talents, and vie with one another in singing his praises. Envy and detraction are vices they are strangers to, nor do I think them near so cruel as their more refined neighbours, now settled among them. If they dislike a man they declare their hatred, and will not fail openly to attack their adversary when an opportunity offers, but the only weapons they make use of are martial arms ; detraction and abuse they never practice, consequently they cannot be accused of cruel, cowardly assassinations of character. I tell you all this in vindication of the choice I have made ; without an explanation it no doubt must have appeared more strange than at present I flatter myself it does."

It is easy to read between the lines of this letter what was in his mind. Townshend was back in England after holding military command in Portugal, and his influence on the military situation in Canada might have been of great importance to Murray. Amherst was in England, too, but it is to be feared that he was scarcely a strong supporter of Murray's views, though, in fact, he owed a great deal of his success to him. Barré had much power, and though possibly the two men had a kind of admiration for each other, I doubt if Barré could stretch it so far as to help his former antagonist over the thorny places of his impossible military position. Burton, for whom Murray had done much, and for whom the correspondence shows

he had a real affection, was " running jealous." He had
been appointed a brigadier on General Gage's staff, and
with the latter's active connivance, was inflicting a series
of pinpricks on his former commander, which to a man of
Murray's loyal and open nature were very hard to bear
with equanimity.

In his family affairs things were not going very well.
Mrs. Murray showed an invincible dislike to crossing the
Atlantic, and Murray was evidently most anxious for her
to make the attempt. He had written pretty strongly to
his brother Gideon on the subject, and Gideon, who was
rather between two fires, did not much appreciate the task
of trying to persuade the lady : " Allow me to tell you,"
he writes, " that you were much in the wrong about your
wife. Be assured that she loves you as much as ever
woman did a man, and is determined to join you for life
next spring." But when it came to the spring of 1764
Mrs. Murray was still too delicate to face the voyage, and
Gideon writes : " It is evidently her misfortune and not her
fault, and I assure her and myself that you will not blame
her, but lament her. However, she cannot be comforted
nor easy till she receives it from yourself, so write to her
soon." There certainly seems to be a good deal of reason
for supposing that the Governor was not without good cause
for complaint, for the letters, preserved in the Collier
Correspondence, show that Mrs. Murray was well enough
to undergo considerable fatigue of a social kind, and very
probably the sea voyage would have been beneficial for the
" dizziness " in the head from which she suffered ! However, London was evidently more to her fancy than Quebec,
notwithstanding that Murray suggested " a large stock of
magnificent clothes," so that the people should see " their
Governor's lady dressed as she ought to be "; there was
also to be a " handsome showy coach * for parade, and a
strong post-chaise for common use." In short, Murray's
efforts were tinted with the most attractive colours he could
employ—all, however, to no purpose. The lady remained

* " Richly carved and gilded," as we learn from the invoice.

obdurate, very much to his natural annoyance, and poor Gideon had a difficult task as between the tearful wife, who viewed his embassy with suspicion, and the masterful brother, who thought little of anything short of prompt obedience.

CHAPTER XV

ALTHOUGH the commission of the Governor of the Province of Quebec had been executed in London on November 21, 1763, for some reason, which remains unexplained,* it was not received by Murray in Quebec until August of 1764—an extraordinary delay which was productive of much evil. A year previously Lord Egremont had informed Murray of the terms of the commission, and certainly the matter was publicly known, yet during all the ensuing months the Governor and Government were in a state of suspended animation, and his authority over the districts of Montreal and Trois Rivières was disputed and disputable. Still, more unfortunately, as we have seen, the position of the Governor in military matters was equally uncertain. During this period Murray took his stand on his military commission as Governor of the town of Quebec and its dependencies.

It will be convenient here to indicate some aspects of the confusion which had its origin in this state of affairs, and the consequent disorganisation of administration. In August (1764) Murray addressed General Gage as follows :

" . . . Mr. Haldimand (who had succeeded Burton at Trois Rivières) and some others think that Colonel Burton,

---

* The idea seems to have prevailed that the establishment of civil government should be deferred until the expiry of eighteen months from the date of the Treaty of Paris, but for this I can find no confirmation. The fourth article of the Treaty merely stipulated that French subjects might sell their estates and bring away their effects within a period of eighteen months.

being on half-pay, and now divested of his command as Governor of Montreal, can nowhere give orders to the troops. The same gentleman declares that no civil governor can have any authority in the army. . . . Neither will they allow of my military commission of Governor of Quebec and its dependencies, copy of which I have the honour to send inclosed for your information. At the same time you will be pleased to observe that I do not mean to interfere with the troops at Montreal or Trois Rivières unless idle disputes and their consequences, confusion, shall make it necessary. In that case I certainly shall assume the authority I am vested with, not only by my rank in the army, but by my military commission as Governor of the dependencies of Quebec, that good order may be preserved until directions shall arrive from you."

To which Gage replied :

" Whether His Majesty intends superseding that commission by the latter (that is, the military commission by that as Governor of the Province) or continuing you Governor of the City and Civil Governor of the Province, His Majesty alone can decide."

In theory, at least, the Government at home had decided to divorce the military from the civil functions, and the ground of the decision was that if one governor retained military command then all would have a similar claim, and yet with that readiness to distinguish between the treatment of " settled " as opposed to " acquired " colonies, which the ministers displayed when their occasion required it, they had at hand an excellent reason for exceptional treatment in the case of Canada ; a reason, moreover, which every consideration of sound statesmanship should have led them to put into practice.

Disputes between the civil and military elements had already arisen in West Florida. It is not necessary to inquire into these nor to apportion the blame, but surely the ministers were seeking trouble when Colonel Burton, who had been Murray's subordinate, and later on his equal as governor of a district, was in the first place reverted to the subordinate position as a lieut.-governor under

Murray, and then almost immediately placed in a position independent of him as brigadier commanding the troops in the northern area. Had Burton been of a loyal and open character, perhaps things would have gone better. Unfortunately, he was pompous, exacting, and jealous, and from the first set himself to impose indignities on his former commander. I have no desire to shield Murray from any share in the blame which may justly be his, but from a perusal of many of the private and semi-official letters, I cannot discern that the unhappy friction which arose originated in any action of his. On the contrary, the terms in which he wrote to Burton throughout the year 1764 seem to indicate a really friendly spirit. Such or similar homely intimacy as the following occurs frequently :

" I am happy I can supply Mrs. Burton with oil of mint, which the Doctor says is as good as that of peppermint. I beg my compliments may be made acceptable to her and my young friend Dick. I hope the young Montrealist will continue to thrive, and prove as good a woman as her mother, if so, tho' a girl, she may bid fair to put Mr. Richards' nose out of joint, hence I take the liberty to tell him he must be much upon his good behaviour."

And again :

" Now, my dear Burton, as you are on the spot, you are the best judge how far it is expedient to instruct the French people. . . . As to the discontented English traders, their conduct to you during the course of the winter proves what they are. . . . I really pity the poor French people, and think they should not from ignorance be drawn into scrapes by such restless spirits. I am persuaded you will pardon the liberty I take in so freely offering my opinion on this occasion, which can proceed from nothing but the zeal I have for the public good and the regard I shall always have for you."

And again, to General Gage, he wrote, in August, 1764, after the receipt of his commission as Governor :

" Burton is master of all your views, and has everything in the best order for the execution of them. To break in upon them at this time must certainly be productive of bad consequences, and shall not be attempted as far as I can prevent it."

Impartially viewed, I cannot but conclude that the strife which commenced during this period was not caused by Murray, who on every occasion surrendered his powers to preserve harmony; and even after he became aware that Burton had endeavoured to supplant him in the office of Governor, he was careful to avoid any reproach. Yet, as time passed, the action of the brigadier gradually exceeded all bounds of endurance, and finally culminated in a series of acts which were evidently calculated to produce an explosion. A certain Lieut.-Colonel Christie, who had been an officer in Amherst's Army, and was now deputy quarter-master-general under Burton, appears to have been the firebrand. Murray shrewdly suspected this officer of manipulating public affairs to his own benefit, and when a general warrant was applied for by Burton to enable him to impress boatmen and transport for military purposes, the Governor refused to grant it. Writing to General Gage (July 1, 1765) he says that Colonel Christie had already made improper use of such warrants, "And that gentleman is carrying on works to a very great extent for his own private emolument. Prudence will prevent me from giving him a general press warrant, and decency should hinder him from asking it." By October, 1765, the correspondence with Burton, now promoted to be major-general, had lost its old style of friendly intimacy. The subject was still the supply of transport :

" Sir, your letter of the 29th ulto. I had not the honor to receive till last Friday. Monday's post will have brought to you my injunctions to the inhabitants of the parishes, the nearest to La Chine, to furnish the men necessary for the sixteen battoes in question.

" It now remains to acquaint you that if any prejudice shall happen to the service . . . neither the government, nor the magistracy, are to be blamed. The latter have no legal power to impress men, but for services specified in the Mutiny Act : the battoe service in question doth not come within that Act, and therefore it was fortunate the magistrates disregarded Colonel Christie's menaces.   They are worthy men, who very disinterestedly give much of their time and attention to the public ; the gratitude I owe these gentlemen on that account will make me studiously avoid every unnecessary trouble to them.   Policy and justice will prevent me from imposing any task by which they may be exposed to the resentment or even the censure of their fellow citizens."

It is impossible to get away from the fact, constantly reiterated by Murray in his letters to the ministry, that his divorce from control of the troops in his province was seriously detrimental to his efforts to produce harmony and good government.   The British traders obviously took advantage of it, and the French inhabitants, accustomed to arbitrary military authority, could not fail to regard a civil governor, who had no power over the troops in his garrison, with less obedience than was good for public discipline.   They had already expressed their satisfaction with the military government which Murray had exercised up to August, 1764, and, as we shall see, were among the first to congratulate his successor, who arrived with full civil and military control.   I think it is fully borne out by incontrovertible facts that the major part of the animosity which arose between the civil and military elements in the district of Montreal originated before Murray had anything to do with that part of the province, and was the basis of the constant opposition by the British section of the community.   It was due to the two unfortunate facts, that a long delay should have occurred between the signing of the peace of Paris and the introduction of provincial government, and the division of civil from military control in a province situated as was that of Quebec.

To the Lords of Trade Murray wrote, April 24, 1764 :

" I cannot help entreating your lordships to consider for a moment the difficulties I have laboured under here,

" The people I have governed near five years without any civil jurisdiction or even instructions from home are composed of a conquering army, who claim a sort of right to lord it over the vanquished ; of a distressed people stripped of almost all their substance real and imaginary (*sic*), dreading the fate of their religion and accustomed to an arbitrary government ; and of a set of free British merchants, as they are pleased to style themselves, who with prospect of great gain have come to a country where there is no money, and who think themselves superior in rank and fortune to the soldier and the Canadian, deeming the first voluntary and the second born, slaves."

The Royal Proclamation creating the province of Quebec was published on August 10, 1764.* On the 13th Murray took the oath and administered the same to the council he had chosen, and at the same time submitted the names to the King for approval :

" Your lordships will be pleased to observe that in this (council) and in the appointment of all civil officers I must lie under great inconveniences. The British subjects in the province consist of two very different sets of people, the military and the mercantile, whom duty and interest have led here and who can only be counted as passengers."

The terms of the Proclamation were such as to create doubt and confusion ; but looking at the matter in the light of subsequent events, it would appear that much of the misinterpretation was wilful on the part of a section of the people, and had the Governor been in a position to carry out his own reading without factious hindrance the points of doubt would have been accepted in the confident spirit that in due time they would be settled or altered to their satisfaction. The special clauses which led to trouble were as follows :

" We have . . . given express power and direction to our governors . . . that so soon as the state and circumstances of the said colonies will admit thereof, they shall,

* That is, exactly eighteen months after the signing of the Treaty of Paris, and this gives confirmation to the view that the Proclamation was withheld for the reasons already mentioned.

Y

with the advice and consent of the members of our council, summon and call general assemblies . . . in such manner and form as is used and directed in those colonies and provinces in America which are under our immediate government . . . and in the meantime . . . all persons . . . may confide in our royal protection for the enjoyment of the benefit of the laws of our realm of England; for which purpose we have given power . . . to the governors . . . to erect and constitute . . . courts of judicature . . . for hearing and determining all causes . . . as near as may be agreeable to the laws of England."

It can be said at once and definitely, and as a matter which should have been apparent at the time, that it would have been wiser and more statesmanlike to have omitted all reference to a general assemby in a province hitherto unaccustomed to such a luxury, until such time as circumstances permitted its constitution. At the same time, if, as was afterwards stated, administration of justice " as near as may be agreeable to the laws of England " was intended to have a wide interpretation, then the persons appointed by the Crown to carry out the law should certainly have been apprised of such intention; failing any such instruction it is only possible to suppose that the subsequent explanation of the terms of the Proclamation (see p. 325) was a somewhat palpable attempt to shift blame on to wrong shoulders. It must also be reiterated that, in the clearest and most definite terms, Lord Egremont had written to the Governor :

" Tho' His Majesty is far from entertaining the most distant thought of restraining his new Roman Catholic subjects from professing the worship of their religion according to the rites of the Romish church, yet the condition expressed in the same article must always be remembered, viz. as far as the laws of Great Britain permit. . . . These laws must be your guide in any disputes that may arise on this subject."

In all this it was at once clear that the intention must have been to exclude Catholic subjects from all positions of a public nature which required the taking of oaths repugnant to the Catholic religion.

That the Proclamation was badly drawn up by the responsible ministers there can be no doubt, but that it should have been attempted later to throw the responsibility for its ambiguities on the shoulders of the Governor says little for the honour and credit of the persons who, as we shall see, made the attempt. It was truly said at a later date that this Proclamation " seems to have had principally in view the profit and advantage that might accrue to your Majesty's British subjects," and when it became apparent that the complete institution of British laws, which most obviously and even admittedly was the intention, was unjust to the Canadians, then the old subjects had an equal grievance by alleging, whether truly or not, that they had settled in the new province under a proclamation which assured them the " benefit of the laws of our realm of England."

On September 17, 1764, an ordinance was issued by the Governor in council, creating a system of judicature. This ordinance has been severely attacked, both for what it contained and for what it omitted. It naturally fell to the attorney-general to prepare the document, and it is certainly the case that, with the limitations imposed by the Proclamation and the Governor's instructions, it would have been difficult to have acted on different lines. The ordinance erected and constituted courts of judicature for the administration of the laws. The laws created by the King's authority were those of England, yet it was suggested afterwards that the introduction of these was not the intention, a suggestion amply repudiated by independent authority; but in issuing this ordinance the council of Quebec did in fact err in the very direction in which it was afterwards argued they should have acted, and it is strange that in the many discussions which subsequently took place on this ordinance, it was not pointed out that the Governor and his council exceeded their strict limits of authority in preserving to the Canadians certain rights which it was stated were intended, but which it is very certain were introduced by the Governor and his advisers of their own motion.

On October 16 a grand jury was " charged " for the first quarter sessions. The " charge " to the grand jury was an exhortation to be moderate and impartial, pointing out the responsibilities of the leaders of a young colony. It is tolerably clear that the spirit of the persons who alone were available needed guidance, and that but little trust could be placed in them. The result justified these suspicions, for the grand jury, taking its cue from the independent attitude of the assemblies of the neighbouring states of America, at once adopted the same line of conduct, and without any shadow of justification arrogated to themselves the right to deal, not with the causes to be brought before the courts, but with questions of general policy quite unconnected with their duty as jurors. It will be remembered that a clause of the scheme for government required the nomination of an assembly of freeholders. It had so far been impossible to set this in operation, and the grand jury claimed as the " only representative body representing the colony . . . a right to be consulted before any ordinance that may affect them be passed into law, and also to be consulted regarding taxes and necessary expenses."

All this would probably have been regarded by the Governor and his council as a contemptible exhibition of the feelings of people unused and unfit for the position in which they found themselves, but the condition of affairs in the American colonies lent more importance to this nascent spirit of revolution than it inherently deserved. We must remember that six months previously Grenville, as Chancellor of the Exchequer, had brought forward the Stamp Act, which was to be put before the House during the ensuing session. In the American colonies a number of able and sincere men at once took up the challenge, and guided the popular clamour against the liability to be taxed when not represented in the councils of state ;

but the claims which the old colonies could legitimately make of having already borne a large proportion of the expenses of the late wars, and having rights of representation, had certainly no bearing on the situation of the new colonies, which had come into being by right of conquest ; and whatever may be said regarding the disputes between the Mother Country and the settled colonies, there was no excuse for the pretentious attempt of the grand jurors of the province of Quebec to take the same position.

Besides the resolution just quoted, the grand jury presented fourteen others, the greater part of which were distinctly outside their province. The whole attitude of mind which influenced them, which clearly showed the self-seeking nature of their intentions, is made apparent by the general statement appended to their " presentments."

" Among the many grievances which require redress this seems not the least, that persons professing the religion of the Church of Rome, who acknowledge the supremacy and jurisdiction of the Pope, and admit Bulls, briefs, absolution, etc., from that See as acts binding on their consciences, have been impanelled on grand and petty juries, even where two Protestants were parties . . . we therefore believe that nothing can be more dangerous (to the King's dignity) than admitting such persons to be sworn on juries who by law are disabled from holding any office, trust, or power."

Then followed a recital of the Act of James I. against Papists and Popish recusants, all of which was artfully intended to catch the verdict of the public in England, already too much inclined to religious persecution, while at the same time concealing the real desire of the Protestant minority in Canada to rule the roost and plunder the former owners of the soil.

This document bore the signature of twelve British merchants and eight of the new subjects. The latter, however, subsequently declared that they had signed the document in ignorance of the nature of its contents, and submitted a written declaration of their views, which concludes with the following :

" That His Majesty being informed that all the subjects forming this province were Catholics, still believed them capable as such of taking the oath of loyalty, and therefore fit to be admitted to the service of their country in such a way as they shall be thought qualified for.   It would be shameful to believe that the Canadians, new subjects, cannot serve their King either as serjeant or officers ; it would be a most humiliating thought and very discouraging to free subjects who have been admitted to the privileges of the nation and their rights as explained by His Majesty. . . . The leniency of the existing Government has made us forget our losses and attached us to His Majesty and to the Government. . . ."

As may be supposed, those among the new subjects, both jurors and justices, in whose cause Murray was working whole-heartedly, entered a spirited protest against the presentments referred to, and there was also a numerously-signed petition on the same subject from the French inhabitants.   In this they asserted that :

" Mr. Murray, who was appointed Governor of the province of Quebec, to the satisfaction of all its inhabitants, has up to the present time, at the head of a military council, administered to us all the justice we could have expected from the most enlightened jurists. . . . For four years we enjoyed the greatest tranquility.   By what sudden stroke has it been taken away through the action of four or five jurists, whose character we respect, but who do not understand our language, and who expect us, as soon as they have spoken, to comprehend legal constructions which they have not yet explained ? . . ."

The petition then goes on to state the cruelty of proscribing ten thousand heads of families from authority in the State on account of religious difference.

The reply of the King to the claims of the grand jurors was to the point :

" Having taken into consideration several presentments from a grand jury at Quebec, assuming to themselves authority similar to that of a House of Representatives, against the orders and regulations of His Majesty's Government established there.   Supporting the said presentment by the names of several of the principal French inhabitants, who declare they were fraudulently drawn into signing the same, and by a representative since sent over, deny their previous knowledge or their intended approbation of the contents, which, being written in English, they did not then understand.   I am now, Sir, to signify to you His Majesty's highest disapprobation of such their proceedings and abuse of the good faith of the said French inhabitants, and by His Majesty's command I am to direct you to signify that His Majesty will give the utmost attention and consideration to all proper representations from his Canadian subjects. . . ."

Unfortunately this pronouncement was not received for *a year* subsequent to the presentments, and during all the intervening period the Governor was confronted with the ill-concealed rebellion of the jurors.

Montreal was the storm centre whence emanated these attempts to undermine the authority of the Governor. " Every intrigue to our disadvantage will be laid and hatched there." *   In truth, the course of government at Montreal had been unfortunate from the start.   From the date of the surrender (September, 1760) until the end of 1763, General Gage had been responsible, and his rule was mild and little fitted to control the disturbing elements which gathered force with singular rapidity at a critical time when all comers were seeking to profit by the opportunities of the first settlements of the new colony.   It was no time for milk-and-water politics.   After Gage came Burton, who appears to have had no capacity for civil administration, and to whom the army was the sole object of solicitude.   After Burton, who resigned in July (1764), came nobody, for Lord Halifax wrote that it was " judged unnecessary to fill up the appointments of lieut.-governors

* Murray to Lords of Trade, October 29, 1764.

at Three Rivers and Montreal.*   To this proposal Murray strongly objected, pointing out that at a distance from the capital of one hundred and eighty miles, surrounded by " nations " of Indians and the headquarters of the French noblesse, it was eminently desirable to retain, as was the case during the French regime, a lieut.-governor to control the measures ordered for the public peace.

In the Quebec district Murray had ruled sternly but justly.   The British traders were kept within bounds by an iron discipline which pleased them very little, while the *habitant* could count on support so long as he acted honestly.

Of the French Canadians of the settler class Murray held a high opinion.   Possibly his language may appear a little exaggerated, but we must remember how constantly he found it necessary to protect them against oppression, and no doubt his experience of the Ministry at home led him to believe that strong terms were needed to impel them to action.

" Little, very little, will content the new subjects, but nothing will satisfy the licentious fanatics trading here but the expulsion of the Canadians, who are perhaps the bravest and the best race upon the globe.   A race who, could they be indulged with a few privileges, which the laws of England deny to Roman Catholics at home, would soon get the better of every natural antipathy to their conquerors, and become the most faithful and most useful men in the *American Empire*." †

This term of Murray's shows that his thoughts ran in Imperial lines, and while Ministers and Members of Parliament were engaged in considering how much the supposed disunion of the colonies would act as a safeguard in preventing combined action, he and others with a wider vision would have created that Imperial senate, which in the twentieth century is approaching its birth, and by

* Halifax to Murray, July 14, 1764.   Colonel Burton was, however, appointed Brigadier of the Northern Command, and did not actually leave Montreal, though he ceased to be civil Governor.
    † Murray to Lords of Trade, October 29, 1764.

doing so might have continued the union of the American Empire with England with what results on the peace of the world one can only conjecture. To preserve these hardy Canadians, accustomed to the climate and needing only peace and equitable treatment to become good subjects, was Murray's constant care, and in August, 1764, he reported, with evident satisfaction, " that there are no more than two hundred and seventy souls, men, women, and children, who will emigrate from this province in consequence of the Treaty of Paris."

Towards the end of the year (1764) the constant petitions of the British traders against the Governor's action— forced, no doubt, on the Ministers by their correspondents in London—obliged Murray to take the step of sending his secretary, Cramahé, to England to endeavour by word to bring the real situation before the King and his councillors :

" I flatter myself," he wrote, " there will be some remedy found out even in the laws for the relief of this people ; if so, I am positive the popular clamours in England will not prevent the humane heart of the King from following its own dictates. I am confident, too, my Royal Master will not blame the unanimous opinion of his council here for the ordinance establishing courts of justice, as nothing less could be done to prevent great numbers from emigrating directly; and certain I am, unless the Canadians are admitted on juries, *and are allowed judges and lawyers who understand their language*, that His Majesty will lose the greatest part of this valuable people."

Regarding this action of the Governor in council in permitting the inclusion of Catholics on juries, it is interesting to note that the opinion of the law officers of the Crown, to whom the matter was referred, supported the view taken in Canada. This " opinion," dated Lincoln's Inn, June 10, 1765, ran as follows :

"Question: If His Majesty's subjects residing in countries ceded by the treaty are or are not subject in those colonies to the incapacities, disabilities, and penalties which Roman

Catholic subjects are subject to by the laws (of England). Answer: We are of opinion that they are not subject." *

Thus, though the action taken in Canada received this confirmation, it does not detract from the courage with which the Governor and his council faced the situation, and brought on themselves a veritable avalanche of misrepresentation from that turbulent and self-seeking section who unfortunately had the means of making themselves heard at home.

In Montreal the state of tension between the military and civil elements, abetted it is to be feared by the open action of Burton and Gage, culminated at the end of 1764 in serious trouble. The origin was in itself trivial enough to make it more worth oblivion than record, but at a period when weak government and divided councils permitted John Wilkes to absorb the interests of Parliament over several sessions and even to affect the stability of a Ministry, one might expect exaggerated importance to be given to the Canadian affair of Mr. Thomas Walker, a merchant of Montreal. Incidentally this affair brought out prominently the danger of divided authority, as between the civil governor at Quebec and the military chief at New York. Walker, it appears, was one the turbulent class who made it their business to pursue a course of disrespect to the established Government, and to set at nought, as far as it dared, the military element. During the period of Colonel Burton's government, and before the long delayed establishment of civil government, this man had, in the course of a dispute with one of his clerks, presented a petition to Burton, who had ordered the affair to be tried before a military court, there being no other available. The appellant refused to be governed by the decision, and treated the court in a disrespectful and contemptuous manner, and his behaviour met the approval and imitation of many of his fellows, producing a state of tension between the military and civil elements, which there

* Public Record Office, C. O. 42/2.

is reason to believe was not cased by any tactful action on Burton's part.   In the autumn this state of tension came to a head, when certain orders as to billeting of troops were given, to which the civilian element were strongly opposed and declared to be illegal.   A captain of the 28th Regiment was under these orders billeted on the house of one of the Canadian justices of the peace, who promptly issued a warrant for the imprisonment of the captain.   It is not very clear on what grounds this order was made or carried out, but it was quite sufficient to give the soldiers a strong incentive to show their power, and there was certainly much bitterness.   Murray, on receiving reports of this occurrence, was evidently in a difficult position.   It was impossible to repudiate the authority of the newly-made magistrates without inquiry, and they were summoned to Quebec to answer for their action, among them being Walker.   Two nights before Walker's departure to obey the Governor's summons his house was entered by a body of soldiers and he himself violently assaulted.   There is no doubt that this assault was the action of the men and perhaps some officers of the 28th Regiment, who greatly resented the magisterial action against one of their members; and it is pretty clear that Burton was less anxious to clear up the matter than to shield the military and incidentally to cause difficulties to the civil governor.

The Governor acted promptly and impartially.   It is evident from his report that he had no leanings to either side :

"On so critical an occasion I determined to go to Montreal immediately with His Majesty's council for the province. Here I found everything in confusion, and the greatest enmity raging between the troops and the inhabitants. The latter spoke and acted as if their lives were in danger. . . . From the day I arrived—how they (the military) conducted themselves *before* I shall not say—the troops certainly behaved with great submission to the civil magistrates. Every man was given up to be examined the moment he was demanded. . . . In the course of the examination before the council it was evident the army had not been very zealous in aiding the civil magistrates, and the insolent, indecent, and groundless suspicions which Mr. Walker expressed against officers of undoubted honour and reputation might have occasioned that indifference and influenced the whole army against him."

After remaining a month at Montreal and arranging, after some demur on Burton's part, for an exchange of the 28th Regiment, Murray set out to return to Quebec, but his influence had hardly been removed when the soldiers of the 28th broke out afresh and forcibly released the men of their regiment who had been imprisoned. The men were recaptured, and a second time were rescued by the soldiers. Murray's remark on this is significant : " Brigadier Burton, under whose command this result happened, had no doubt very good reasons for not inquiring into it, and for not endeavouring to find out the authors of it."

Before setting out for Montreal, Murray wrote to Burton a letter which, I think, is worth quoting, as showing his open impartiality :

" The confusion at Montreal must give every good man concern. It is my duty to do what in me lies to put a stop to it and to restore order and harmony ; to this end I shall set out as soon as possible for that part of my Government. In the meantime, as the post will reach you before I can, I write the opinions of the Attorney-General relative to the warrants and conduct of the magistrates complained of in Captain Mitchelson's letters to you.*

" I send this in tenderness to my brother officers, who, I hope, will have patience till I arrive, and then they may be assured that everything will be done with that candour and politeness which they may expect from a gentleman firmly attached to His Majesty's service. . . ."

The affair dragged on for many months with fresh difficulties cropping up. The trial originally ordered to be held at Montreal was found to be impossible, for the

* The Attorney-General's opinion was that the warrants issued for arrest of men suspected of being concerned in the attack on Walker were correct and legal.

limited choice of jurymen prevented twelve unbiassed people being found. On the recommendation of the law officers the council decided on transferring the trial to Quebec, and an ordinance was issued making the whole province open for selection of a jury. Walker refused to attend this trial, alleging fear of personal molestation at the hands of the men of the 28th Regiment then at Quebec. The *venue* was then changed to Trois Rivières. Walker still refused to appear, and the trial held in his absence resulted in acquittal of the accused. It was clear that Walker was less concerned in procuring a conviction than in creating difficulties. In June, 1765, Murray wrote to the Board :

" The examination in council . . . shows Mr. Walker in his proper colours. He had no excuse for not attending, as during the trial the 28th Regiment was to have been ordered into cantonments. His protest against Government, his seditious insinuations which prevailed with jurors summoned from Montreal to refuse their duty, the repeated complaints of his insolent overbearing temper and the impossibility of prevailing upon any other justice to act with him, are reasons sufficient for the unanimous desire of the council to have him dismissed from the magistracy. A desire I, with reluctance, yielded to in consideration of the personal ill-treatment the man had suffered and the opportunity of triumph it gave his enemies."

In London a great outcry was made by the traders, who were only too anxious to find an opening through which to attack the governor. The city, " ever the friend of those oppressed by the intruments of power," and at this period ready to hang the banner of " liberty " on any peg that would cause embarrassment to their rulers, presented memorials accusing the authorities in general, and Murray in particular, of interference with liberty. The transfer of the trial to Quebec and the enlargement of the choice of jurymen fell particularly under comment. Unfortunately the Government at home, but recently emerged from the first phases of the Wilkes' problem and its connected question of "general warrants," and already in conflict with the American colonies, had no heart to face, with justice and inquiry, the situation arisen in Canada. The results we shall hear of again ; meanwhile, it is sufficient to observe that the delay in creating a civil government, the weakness due to divided authority, and the short-sighted policy which decided to impose on a race of men alien in religious thought some part of the narrow restrictions which had already produced chaos in Ireland, were wholly responsible for the lamentable state of friction which confronted the Governor.

Murray, at all events, had nothing to reproach himself with. He had laid all the circumstances clearly before the ministers in language that could admit of no misunderstanding :

"One must be on the spot to form a judgment of the difficulties which occur in establishing the English laws in this country. The body of the people, from education and religion, are averse to them, and the few sensible men among them are still more so, being excluded from every employment they formerly enjoyed. . . . Colonel Burton, who had arrived at the government of the province and refused the lieutenant-government, is appointed a brigadier on the American staff, and remains to command the troops at Montreal. It is not natural to imagine a man will be contented with the command of a few troops in a country he had so long governed without control. . . . It may be supposed the civil establishment was by no means relished by the troops, as the new magistracy must be composed, agreeably to my instructions, of the very merchants they held so much in contempt. . . . I was aware of the disagreeable circumstances at Montreal, and remedied them as much as possible by joining with them (the civil magistrates) half-pay officers in the commission of the peace, and even by borrowing some from regiments on duty. . . . The places of the greatest business in the province have been granted by patent to men of interest in England, who have hired them to the best bidder, without considering the talents or circumstances of their representatives. *One man, for instance, who cannot read a word* *of French, is Deputy-Sheriff, Registrar, Clerk of the Council, Secretary and Commissary of Stores and Provisions. . . .* I am sensible I may displease by complaining of this, but by doing so I do my duty. While I have the honour to serve my Royal Master that shall by my only study, and the only fear I can entertain is that of being defective in it.'' *

From the private correspondence that took place during this period, Murray's views and difficulties appear. To Lord Elibank he wrote on September 16 (1764) :

'' . . . It is by the military force we are to govern this lately conquered province. . . . It is evident the brigadier must in fact be the governor, (or) that the people must be oppressed by the soldiery, that the civil governor and his magistrates must be contemptible, and in place of being the means of preserving order and promoting the happiness of the subject they must, from the natural jealousies which such an establishment will produce, become the bane of peace. . . . The reasons are so clear and simple, they should not have escaped the Ministry. If, however, they have, from the hurry of more pressing concerns, or from the artful insinuations of designing men, it is necessary they should be put right. I cannot decently write to any of them on this subject, because what I may say might be construed more the effects of ambition than zeal for the service of my master and the good of the public, and therefore I am to entreat your lordship to represent it properly, that the evil may be removed, if it really doth exist. . . . I cannot with credit to myself or satisfaction to my Sovereign govern in this province unless I have authority with the troops ; I mean not to have the chief command of them. How far that is expedient the wisdom of Government must determine, but I do insist that under the commander-in-chief I should have command of the troops, towns, and forts all over the province. It will be too hard a task for me to govern in the civil way a great populous country of a different religion, different language, different manners and customs, without the aid of troops or the assistance of the laws, *for two such ignorant needy lawyers as are sent here from England to distribute justice to the people were never before sent from any country. . . .*''

* Murray to Lords of Trade, March 3, 1765.

To Lord Eglinton * he wrote (October 27, 1764) :

" . . . . If the popular clamours in England will not allow the humane heart of the King to follow its own dictates, and the Popish laws must be exerted with rigour in Canada, for God's sake procure my retreat, and reconcile it to Lord Bute,† as I cannot be witness to the misery of a people I love and admire."

To his friend James Oswald, who at the time was Vice-Treasurer for Ireland in Grenville's administration, he wrote (October 16, 1764) :

" The necessity of the Governor of this province having the command of the troops is so evident, I conclude that will instantly be ordered, if not it will be impossible for me, or any other man, to give satisfaction. . . . If, therefore, my dear Sir, you find that His Majesty has come to a resolution to allow no civil governor to have any military command, for God's sake get me as handsomely out of this civil embarrassment as possible. The Government of this province will be a good thing for some dependant of the ministers and I am ready to resign . . . provided always that I may be continued nominal military governor of the town of Quebec, a title I own I am proud of. I therefore say nominal, for I desire no salary. . . . Every man has his hobby-horse. Mine is to die with the title of Governor of Quebec. . . ."

To his secretary Cramahé, who had been sent to England to make clear all the affairs of the province, he wrote (November 17, 1764) :

"Since you left us they have run wild at Montreal. Inclosed you have all that pretty business, the effects of Burton's intrigues, Fraser's haughtiness and weakness, and the justices' ignorance and pride, I am resolved to be cool and let the law take its course. I shall prejudge no man, so the justices will remain until I and all the world are convinced they should be removed. . . . I have appointed Monier, Mayben, and Marteil to be Judges

* Then a Lord of the Bedchamber.
† This little sidelight is interesting as showing the prominence of Bute, who was at this time supposed to be in eclipse.

of the Court of Common Pleas till you can provide better in their places. The people call so loudly for this reasonable court I cannot refuse, and sure I am it must be approved of when you represent the necessity of it, and then you will labour to find a proper person to preside there. . . . Our Chief Justice gives every day fresh proofs of his want of head and heart, and Cunningham * of his being the most thorough-paced villain who ever existed. The Attorney-General seems to understand the business he was sent here to do. Kneller is a worthy young man; his knowledge and honesty keep the other gentlemen of the law in awe, so I hope we shall rub on till things are put on a better footing. If they are not I must give it up, for I am determined to risk neither character nor constitution in attempting impossibilities and absurdities; the loss of the first must be certain, and I find the anxiety and vexation has such an effect on my health that the second will be inevitable. You know, Cramahé, I love the Canadians, but you cannot conceive the uneasiness I feel on their account. To see them made the prey of the most abandoned of men while I am at their head is too much for me to endure much longer. Take courage, therefore, my man, speak boldly the truth and let you and I at least have the consolation of having done our duty to God and our country and our own consciences. Farewell, my dear friend, I heartily pray God Almighty may prosper your labours and send you safe to me again."

On a previous page I have referred to the opinion expressed by the crown law officers on the legality of admitting Catholics to the jury. A more complete justification of Murray's policy occurred at a council held at Whitehall on November 15, 1765, when the Lords of the Committee of Council for Plantation Affairs were

" pleased to order that the Lords Commissioners for Trade and Plantations do prepare and lay before this committee a draught of an additional instruction, requiring him (the Governor of Quebec) to publish an ordinance declaring all His Majesty's subjects in the said province without

---

* William Cunningham appointed coronor of Quebec, dismissed in April, 1765, and James Potts appointed in lieu.

distinction are intitled to be impannelled and sit and act upon juries.''

For greater security it was ordained that in causes between British-born subjects only British-born jurors could sit, and in cases between Canadians only Canadians could sit—in mixed cases the jury should be equally divided. It was further ordered " that His Majesty's Canadian subjects shall be permitted to practice as barristers, advocates, attorneys, or proctors in all courts,'' though this latter concession was not to be considered as final, but until His Majesty's further pleasure should be expressed.

This decision was a triumph for the Governor. The opposition to his constant endeavour to procure equality of treatment for the Canadian subjects had been, and, indeed, still continued to be, bitter and incessant, but in thus securing them fair representation in the courts of law a great step in their favour had been gained, nor is it possible to argue that it was always intended that the terms of these new instructions should have been read into the original. Had such been the case it would not have been necessary to set in motion all the machinery of a reference to the law officers, a resolution of the council at Whitehall, and a formal authority to take the proposed action. Yet the attempt was made at a later date to show that omission to do the things now sanctioned to be done was due to want of proper reading of the original commission and its accompaniments, on the part of the Governor, his council and the law officers appointed in Canada.

Enough has been said to show that Murray had represented the circumstances fully and fearlessly during the years 1764 and 1765. Possibly his letters were not politic, and it may be that his blunt statements, in which he definitely stated that " the places of the greatest business in the province have been granted by patent to men of interest in England, who have hired them to the best bidders, without considering the talents or circumstances of their representatives,'' gave offence which might have been avoided, but apart from this the whole state of colonial administration in London was in confusion. There had been friction for a long time between the President of the Board of Trade and the Secretary of State. Lord Halifax had endeavoured to free the Board of all trammels, his successors had been content with subordinate positions. In 1763 Lord Shelburne claimed full powers, but ultimately agreed to take Cabinet rank, while nominally subordinate to the Secretary of State, an arrangement which lasted only a few months. Frequent changes and a conflict of policy marked the years 1764 and 1765, and it is little to be wondered at that the result should have reacted on the colonies, whose Governors were in the unhappy position of having no clearly defined channel of communication. They were partly subordinate to the Board with an ill-defined subordination to the Secretary of State. In 1766 Lord Chatham definitely reduced the Board of Trade to a Board of Report to the Secretary of State ; a year later the Duke of Grafton altered the policy and created a third Secretary of State to deal especially with the American colonies, the foundation of our existing colonial office.

The effect of this confused state of affairs at home is reflected in a letter from General Murray to the Lords of Trade, dated February 3, 1766 :

" I blush when I find myself under the necessity of putting your lordships to the trouble of reading so many letters when ten lines might suffice, but . . . the total silence to every remonstrance, reasoning, and report which hitherto I have had the honour to make to your Board (from which I have not had a letter that was not circular since the establishment of civil government here) makes it unnecessary for me to apologise for this method of conveying my intelligence."

It is evident that the silence of the Ministry and the want of support under which Governor Murray writhed had causes more deeply seated and less honourable to the Government at home than mere confusion in the department that regulated the affairs of the colonies. The Rockingham Ministry had come into power in July, 1765, and their *mot d'ordre* was to abase or neglect all those who were, or might be supposed to be, the nominees of Lord Bute, and in this category Murray, as a Scot, who undoubtedly had enjoyed Bute's approval, to say nothing of Mansfield's, who was equally taboo, unfortunately found himself. Besides this, popularity with the people was a desirable object, and one of the first acts of the new Ministry was to raise to the peerage the popular Lord Chief Justice Pratt, who had received the plaudits of the mob by releasing Wilkes, who posed as the champion of liberty. It must not be forgotten that at this period Mr. Thomas Walker had come to London from Canada to ape the manner of Wilkes and style himself the " agent of the people," pouring into the too sympathic ear of Lord Dartmouth, the newly appointed President of the Board of Trade, false tales of Murray's " blasphemy " and oppression. It is significant, too, that Viscount Gage, the brother of the American commander, held a position in the Ministry. On October 18, 1765, the Lords of the Privy Council considered the case of Mr. Thomas Walker and the civil and military discord that reigned in Canada, and in consequence of their representations to the King the following letter, dated October 24, 1765, was addressed to Governor Murray :

" SIR,—Divers representations having been made to His Majesty in council of the disorders that have lately happened and the unfortunate divisions reigning in the province of Quebec, where you command, I am in consequence of the same to signify to you His Majesty's pleasure that you do immediately prepare for your return to England, in order to give a full and distinct account of the present state of the said province, of the nature and causes of the disorders and divisions above mentioned, and of your own conduct and proceedings in the administration of your Government.

" It is, however, His Majesty's pleasure you should not leave the province till you receive His Majesty's further orders, and till a proper person shall be fixed on by His

Majesty for the government of the province during your absence. . . ."

Quite apart from the strong suspicion that the Rockingham Ministry were guilty of weak concession to the pressure of public clamour of an obviously biassed nature, it was surely impolitic thus to weaken the authority of the Governor of Quebec at a time when it was all important that strong government should be supported by every possible means. The immediate effect of this mandate was to enable Walker and the recalcitrant traders to declare that the recall of the Governor was due to their representations, and to argue therefrom that the Government at home viewed with favour the principles of their agitation. Such an outcome was not only a serious incentive to the spirit of rebellion, which was already in evidence in the neighbouring states, but it also tended to undermine the whole structure of loyalty among the French Canadians, which Murray had so assiduously developed. They could not but argue that the recall of a man in whom they trusted, apparently at the behest of a small number of British subjects, from which they had every reason to expect injustice and oppression, indicated that the policy of the conqueror was undergoing a change. It would even appear that Walker, who went to England to lay his grievances in person before Lord Dartmouth, was informed of the recall of the Governor before Murray himself :

" I am far from doubting the recall," writes Murray to the Lords of Trade, " but I must lament that Mr. Walker should have known it before I did, and that some clerks of the offices should have communicated to him what he had no right to know. I should be defective in my duties was I not to acquaint Lord Dartmouth that Mr. Walker takes uncommon liberties with his name. Nothing can be more ridiculous to men of sense, but in a colony constituted as this is the mischief may be irreparable, unless a stop be put to the mercenary agent's career. He does not hesitate to say that he is protected by the King's servants in stirring up the people to spurn at every ordinance and regulation made by the Governor of the province. . . . I shall not, however, be deterred from doing my duty . . . the murmurs of a few British traders residing here I must expect until I can convince the colony that my letters are read at the Board of Trade with as much attention as Mr. Walker's remonstrances."

Moreover, the means to acquaint themselves of all the circumstances of the disorders which had occurred were already in the hands of the Board of Trade. Cramahé, who besides being Murray's secretary, was also a member of the council, had been sent to England for the express purpose of laying before the ministers the state of the case. Mr. Price, also a member of the council, had been sent shortly after the great fire, which had destroyed a considerable part of the town of Montreal,* to seek aid for the sufferers, and he too would be in a position to give information. That Conway, in his capacity of Secretary of State, should have signed the letter of recall to Murray had in itself a special degree of irony, for Conway was honest and the consistent opponent of oppression in the American colonies. He was, moreover, a soldier, and had no sympathy with demagogues, whether Wilkes or Walker. He had warmly denied Pitt's general accusation against the Ministry, and declared that he at least " had not made use of liberty to ride into employment." Indeed this parrot cry of liberty had brought with it ill-fortune for Murray, for we have seen that under one Ministry he had had neglect because the Westminster mob had howled themselves hoarse for " Murray and liberty," and the sins of the brother had been visited on him, and now for the opposite reason " Wilkes and liberty " had a sinister effect on his career from a Ministry anxious to conciliate the people.

It is convenient here to anticipate events by a few months, in order to describe the outcome of the agitation created in Canada by the disappointed British merchants and fostered by their representatives in London. In

* In May, 1765.

July, 1766, the Rockingham Ministry fell, the cause being the repeal of the American Stamp Act, which Horace Walpole tells us was forced by the " clamour of trade, of the merchants, and of the manufacturing towns." " Trade " saw in the positive intention of the colonists to cease all trading until their claims had been satisfied, an endless series of losses which to the merchants was of more importance than any question of political loss which might ensue from hasty legislation. This very Government, forced by one section of trade to act unjustly to the hero of this memoir, was forced to repeal the Stamp Act by another section, and thus to set themselves in opposition to the King and the Court party, which promptly commenced to plot their downfall. By July, 1766, the King had sent for Mr. Pitt, and as Earl of Chatham a new Government had been brought together under his leadership.

It is not relevant to this story to dilate upon the extraordinary state of the political world, which was at this time a chaos of individuals, each playing a personal game and no one giving more than a passing thought to the condition of the country, or the great interests at stake. Horace Walpole, for all that he records his part as the *Deus ex Machina*, who brought the wandering atoms together in ever changing groups, and uses the personal pronoun with irritating frequency, makes it clear that in such a state of ill-defined political thought it would be impossible to find unanimity in any one party. There was in practice no Ministry and no Opposition, for within the Ministry were opposing factions, and without it were those who supported one section or another of the cabinet itself ; the result tended to form unstable groups, which, like so many chemical combinations, contained the principles of explosion, and explosion was not infrequently the result.

So far as we are concerned with the matter immediately under consideration, Lord Chatham's Ministry having taken into consideration the charges brought against Murray, the following Order in Council was made on April 13, 1767 :

" Upon reading this day at the Board a report of the Right Honourable the Lords of the Committee of Council for hearing appeals, complaints, etc., from the Plantations, dated 2nd of this instant, in the following words, viz. Your Majesty, having been pleased to refer unto this committee several petitions in the names of the French inhabitants of Montreal in the province of Quebec, and of several British merchants and traders in behalf of themselves and their fellow subjects, inhabitants of the said province, together with other papers containing matters of complaint against the Honourable James Murray, Esquire, Your Majesty's Governor of that province, the Lords of the Committee did sometime since cause notice to be given to all persons concerned in personal complaints against the said Governor Murray to attend their Lordships on this day, and being accordingly attended by Mr. Joshua Sharpe and Mr. Turnbolt, solicitors for the complainants, and also by Mr. Walker, who appeared as a correspondent of some of the complainants in Canada, the said several persons were respectively called upon to declare whether either of them would enter into security to pay costs (which the committee thought in justice ought to be done) in case they should fail to make good their charges against the said Governor Murray, on a time to be fixed for hearing the same, and they having severally refused to enter into such security, and Mr. Walker as the principal correspondent having declared that the papers sent over from Canada were never intended to come before the council in a judicial way, and that he had no witnesses to support any of the charges against Governor Murray, their Lordships do agree humbly to report to Your Majesty as their opinion that the same petitions and complaints against the said Governor Murray should be dismissed as groundless, scandalous, and derogatory to the honor of the said Governor, who stood before the committee unimpeached."

Which finding the King with the advice of the Privy Council was pleased to approve.

This document delivered after proper inquiry throws into strange prominence another addressed on March 27, 1766, to Murray, before the Rockingham Ministry ceased to exist.

" SIR,—This will be delivered to you by Mr. Walker,

who had the misfortune to have met with such treatment at Montreal as is a disgrace to all government, as no material complaint has been made against him for misconduct as a magistrate, and as his general character is supported by the test of very respectable people both in Canada and in London . . . I am therefore to acquaint you, Sir, *that he should be immediately restored and put into the commission of the peace. . . ."*

This extraordinary document was written within a few months of Murray's letter, making a full statement of the character of Walker referring to his " seditious insinuations " and the " repeated complaints of his insolent overbearing temper and the impossibility of prevailing upon any other justices to act with him as reasons sufficient for the unanimous desire of the council to have him dismissed from the magistracy." *

It is not possible to avoid the suspicion that personal or political bias influenced the officials of the Rockingham Ministry in their dealings with the Governor. In complete disregard of his full report on the tumults arising from the Walker case, accompanied by all the papers that had passed, in which his opinion, and the grounds of that opinion, had been clearly put before them, such an order as that just quoted should have been impossible until after a complete judicial investigation ; when that took place a few months later the charges brought forward by this man were dismissed as " groundless and scandalous." That the ministers were little anxious to hear the evidence is made apparent from the letters which passed between Cramahé and Murray. The first, dated January 12, 1765, written a month after his arrival in England, details his various visits to the ministers and others :

" . . . Next day I went to Lord Halifax, who received me most courteously, said he was too much taken up at present to enter into business, but would send for me when at leisure . . . I could get no admittance to the Secretary at War."

The second letter available is dated August 10, though presumably there were some during the interval. The

* Murray to Lords of Trade, June 24, 1765.

Grenville Ministry was now out, but the new ministers were not more helpful :

" I waited upon Lord Dartmouth, who received me with great politeness, expressed his concern at the perplexed state of the province, and promised as soon as the Board met to take their affairs into consideration. . . . Various are the opinions about the present Ministry, and so many political lies are propagated by the friends of the several parties, it is difficult to trace the truth. . . . If they do not something for us by next mail, I shall give over all hopes of any thing being done until the session, which probably will be a warm one."

The third letter is dated October 12, 1765. The writer is evidently giving up hope of getting any attention :

" When you desired and I undertook to come over to lay the state of the province you govern before the men in power here, we acted, I believe, from the same principle, that of procuring happiness for the people, and of rendering the acquisition of that country serviceable to this. That from a concurrence of untowardly circumstances hitherto I have not been able to succeed I most sincerely regret, but am conscious that in the whole transaction I have discharged my duty, if not ably at least most faithfully, and tho' the present Ministry inquire very minutely into those affairs, yet as they do not seem to intend a speedy decision . . . I have resolved to sacrifice my own peace and quiet and stay the winter to endeavour at obtaining a final settlement of them. . . . When the present ministers (Rockingham) began to do business, as they could not know much about the province, I thought it right to lay before them the present state of it with regard to the three principal points requiring a speedy consideration, viz. church, law, and revenue. They are very diligent in their inquiries and seem disposed to put things on a good footing ; but either from embarrassments at home or broils abroad, as yet they had not come to any conclusion, tho' considering the state of that poor province, as well as that of the other American dominions, it were much to be wished administration was firmly established, that it might be enabled to act with vigour and despatch in the important matters now before them. . . ."

Which remarks of Captain Cramahé indicate an insight into the situation which it is to be regretted was not given to " the men in power."

On June 28, 1766, Murray sailed for England in the ship *Little William*, turning his back for ever on the province he had been so closely connected with for seven years. Shortly before leaving he received from James Oswald, then Vice-Treasurer for Ireland, and a man whose good opinion he valued, a letter, which no doubt gave him comfort, dated March 16, 1766 :

MY DEAR SIR,—As this letter will be delivered by Captain Cuthbert, it is needless for me to enter into any detail in respect to information on the state of your affairs here which you will have more clearly and fully given you by that gentleman himself. All I can say therefore is in general that as I remain most firmly of opinion that nobody who has deserved so much of the public as you have done has ever had such a torrent of malice and faction poured out upon them as had been upon you, so I do in my conscience believe that your own presence on the spot, which I understand is now determined, will afford you the best opportunity of disappointing the effects by setting your conduct in its true and proper light. Some of your best friends have never had any proper opportunity of either hearing or of refuting many of ye numberless calumnys which have been so industriously circulated against your conduct. But every friend of yours, and indeed, I believe, every man of common sense and honor have had ye comfort of being perfectly satisfied, that as ye greatest part of them were either frivolous or contradictory, so many others which had the least appearance of gravity have never yet been put hitherto into any way of receiving a fair and equal hearing. Whatever therefore may be the real intention of this resolution of your return to England, I cannot but be of opinion that it must be advantageous in respect to this opportunity of giving a fair and full hearing in justification of a conduct which ought not to lie under the least reproach. It would be perfectly needless in me to endeavour pointing out any of those particulars to which you should most chiefly give your attention on this occasion, for upon my soul I have never seen any of them in light of deserving

either attention or justification.   Your own perfect knowledge of yᵉ state of that country which you had the honor
to assist in conquering, and which you have had yᵉ honor
to govern with such tranquility in yᵉ most delicate circumstances, notwithstanding yᵉ utmost efforts of calumny
and faction, will enable you to give such information for
yᵉ service of His Majesty and of the public as will deserve
most serious attention of his ministers.   It will be their
duty to lay such information before their master, and I
cannot believe that under such circumstances any man
can ever be made a victim to mere calumny and malice.
Believe me, as ever, dear Sir, your most faithfully and
affectionately, JAMES OSWALD."

There were many other signs that his departure from
Canada was deemed a misfortune to the country, and of
these I will quote from but one.   A memorial to the King
from the seigneurs of Quebec, and in regard to this it should
be remembered that the Governor had by no means favoured
this class at the expense of the community, rather, in fact,
he treated their claims to lord it over the poorer classes
with little sympathy, yet it is apparent that they recognised
the justness of his aims.

" *Au Roy,*
        " *Les seigneurs dans le district de Québec tant en leurs
noms que pour tous les habitants leurs Tenanciers pénétrée
de douleur du départ de son excellence l'honourable Jacques
Murray, qu'ils ont depuis la conquête de cette province cheri
et respecté plus encore à cause de ses qualités personelles que
comme leur Gouverneur, se croiroient indignes de vivre s'ils ne
s'efforcoient de faire connoitre à votre Majesté leur Souverain
seigneur et à toute l'Angleterre les obligations qu'ils lui ont,
qu'ils n'oublieront jamais, et les régrets sincères qu'ils ont
de son départ.*
        " *Ses ennemis ne peuvent aujourd'hui nous taxer de
flatteurs. . . . Le Caball formée par un certain nombre des
anciens sujets a triomphé ; du moins elle s'en flatte, et s'en
réjouit ; ses plaintes supposeront été écoutés refusera-t-on
de nous écouter aussi, un très petit nombre l'emportera-t-il
sur le plus grand ?*
        " *L'honourable Jacques Murray, en 1759, entourré des*

Canadiens qu'il devait regarder comme ses ennemis, n'a eu pour eux que de l'indulgence . . . sa générosité et celles de ses officiers animés par son exemple, qui par les aumônes qu'ils ont répandu ont tiré les peuples de la misère dans laquelle les malheurs de la Guerre les avoient plongé nous ont forcé de l'admirer et de le respecter. . . ."

The subject of their memorial had left the country; they recognised that there was no prospect of his return or hope of favours to come. One cannot suspect insincerity in their words, and it is clear that the French Canadians recognised that Murray had sacrificed his career in Canada by supporting their cause.

It is unnecessary to add more to show the true origin of the trouble in Canada. In the next chapter I will give some brief proofs of the want of candour shown by the responsible ministers in London and some few details of the events subsequent to Murray's departure, because it is only by a consideration of them that what Murray had done for the country emerges. The conditions during his tenure of government were too confused to permit the effect of his vigorous struggle against the short-sighted measures imposed from London to come to the surface. During the period up to the peace of Paris the people regarded Canada merely as a pawn in the game to be used for barter at the peace. After that date the effects of the measures ordered by the Ministry obscured the efforts of the Governor, and when he returned to England in July, 1766, there were probably few who believed otherwise than that another " hungry Scottish Governor " had been tried and found wanting. In Canada James Murray's name is still remembered with respect and gratitude, but at home there are not many who are aware of the great work done by the first Governor of Quebec, and of those conversant with the history of Canada I doubt not that many give to Carleton, afterwards Lord Dorchester, credit for much that his distinguished predecessor was entitled to.

CHAPTER XVI

THE GOVERNMENT OF QUEBEC (*concluded*)

IN the last chapter I have dealt with the effect of the orders imposed on the Governor of Quebec by the successive ministries which dealt with the colonies from 1763 to 1766. Let us now briefly review the intentions contained in those orders and expose the pitiful attempts made to shift the blame of their failure.

The following extract from a report by the Board of Trade, dated October 4, 1763, in obedience to Lord Egremont's orders of the previous July, gives a valuable starting-point :

" And as we conceive that it is Your Majesty's royal intention that the form and constitution of government in these new colonies should be *as near as may be similar to what has been established* in those colonies which are under Your Majesty's immediate government, we have therefore prepared the commission accordingly." *

Lord Hillsborough was at this time President of the Board. At approximately the same date Lord Egremont (Secretary of State), who was in close touch with Hillsborough, had written to Murray † (August 13, 1763) :

" The necessary commission and instructions for you are preparing by the Board of Trade, and will contain very full directions not only with regard to the form of government but to your conduct in every particular. The condition expressed in the same article (fourth of the Treaty

---

* Public Record Office, C.O./43/1.
† The substance only is quoted, but the words are those used in the letter.

of Paris) must always be remembered, viz. as far as the laws of Great Britain permit, which laws prohibit absolutely all Popish hierarchy, and can only admit a toleration of the exercise of that religion. These laws must be your guide."

In view of these intentions and instructions the limitations placed on the action of the Governor are too obvious to need further comment. Yet on March 6, 1768, Lord Hillsborough wrote to Carleton, who succeeded Murray :

" I had the honour to serve at the Board of Trade in the year 1763, when His Majesty was pleased to publish His Royal Proclamation, *and whatever the legal sense conveyed by the words of that Proclamation may be*, I certainly know what was the intention ; and I can take upon me to aver that it never entered our idea to overturn the laws and customs of Canada with regard to property. It was most unfortunate that weak, ignorant, and interested men were sent over to carry the Proclamation into execution, who expounded it in the most absurd manner, oppressive and cruel to the last degree, and entirely contrary to the royal intention. The distance of the colony and the differences of opinion occasioned by various causes have prevented as yet the necessary measures being taken to correct this original and fatal mistake." *

This letter appears to me to be disingenuous. With the legal sense of a Proclamation drafted by himself, Lord Hillsborough surely should have been well acquainted. With its defects, its difficulties, and its hardships on the Canadians, Murray had repeatedly apprised the Board and been unable to obtain any instructions. With its interpretation by "weak, ignorant, and interested men," the Government, of which Lord Hillsborough was a member, having appointed these men was alone responsible. The Governor had stated their incapacity in the most emphatic terms :

---

* One is reminded of the opinion of Lord Hillsborough, given by Junius. In his despatches are " Strong assertions without proof, declamation without argument, and violent censure without dignity or moderation."

" The places of the greatest business in the province have been granted by patent to men of interest in England, who have hired them to the best bidder, without considering the talents or circumstances of their representatives."

Finally, as Lord Hillsborough must have well known, property, to which alone he refers, was not the rock on which the Government of Canada split, but religion, laws, and oppression by a military caste uncontrolled by the Governor ; and with regard to all these, the clear and definite orders of the central authority admitted of no misinterpretation and allowed no latitude to the Governor appointed to carry them out.

The only reference to property in the Proclamation ordered that it should be granted on the same terms " as have been appointed and settled in our other colonies, and under such other conditions as shall appear to us to be necessary and expedient for the advantage of the grantees." No other terms or conditions were ever referred to the Governor, though a full report of the French customs had been received from him, and the French customs had been continued until the appointment of law officers with orders to impose English law.

Apart from published documents, such as those just quoted, it is possible to learn a good deal from others which were not finally published in the form originally conceived, and to judge from them the spirit which animated the Board of Trade when dealing with the troubles of their own creation in Canada. The necessity for finding a scapegoat, a necessity common to all weak and confused bureaucracies, is evident from the following, which formed the preamble of a long document prepared by Lord Dartmouth in June, 1766, intended to be issued by the Privy Council on the amendments necessary to the constitution in Canada :

" Whereas it hath been found upon a mature consideration in our Privy Council of the provisions made for the administration of justice, both civil and criminal, within our province of Quebec, that not only the ordinances enacted and published by you (Governor Murray) for that purpose arc in themselves inadequate and imperfect, but also that the mode of administering justice under them in a language unknown to the native inhabitants of our said province and upon principles inconsistent with their ancient usages and customs, hath created great uneasiness and discontent in the minds of our Canadian subjects there, and whereas it hath been further represented to us that our royal intentions in respect of the form of government and judicature have been misrepresented and misunderstood, and that the said Canadian subjects in consequence of certain *unreasonable and unwarrantable constructions* put upon our royal proclamation of October 7, 1763, *have been excluded not only from juries of the several courts or being admitted to practice at the Bar. . . ."* *

It is sufficient to remark regarding this that the ordinances drawn up by the council of Quebec, under the guidance of the attorney-general appointed from home, were regularly submitted according to law for the approval of His Majesty in council. And if these were inadequate and imperfect, it is remarkable that they were not condemned as such at the time of their issue.

The principal ordinance, that dealing with the creation of Courts of Justice, reached England before the end of 1764, yet no question was raised regarding it for more than a year afterwards.

That the persons selected to preside in the Courts of Justice were ignorant of the French language was a misfortune which the Governor had already pointed out to the ministers, and that the principles upon which the laws were administered were opposed to the ancient usages of the French, arose of course from the base note of the Proclamation, which ordered that the laws, statutes, and ordinances should be as near as may be agreeable to the laws of England, and the lawyers sent from England to administer these were acquainted with English laws only.

It is hardly necessary to deal further with a document

* Public Record Office, vol. C.O. 43/1. A long document detailing the views of the Board of Trade as to reform of the judicature.

conceived in such a petty spirit of ignorance and rancour.
Fortunately, before it could come before the Privy Council
the Rockingham Government had ceased to exist, and in
August, 1767, the Lords of the Committee of the Privy
Council, having taken the proposed " draught of instruc-
tions " into their consideration, were of opinion

" that the same is so general and so unsupported by
any specific or particular proof of any grievances in the
judicature to which any particular and effectual reform
or remedy can be applied (except what has already been
done),* and especially since the return of Governor Murray
no governor or *locum tenens* or any of Your Majesty's law
officers have represented in this connection any grievances
(which they would have done if any existed) . . . "†

the Lords of the committee decided to take no action
but to refer the proposed reforms for opinion of the law
officers in Canada.

One of the principal objections raised in England by the
ministers, to the justice dealt out in Canada, was the action
taken by an ordinance which decreed that juries might be
summoned from the province at large, for at the time it
was strongly suspected that an unbiassed jury could not
be obtained in Montreal alone.‡ The Board of Trade held
this to be illegal, but the action of the Governor and his
council was fully justified on a reference to the law officers,
who were of opinion " that the Governor of Quebec is fully
authorised and impowered by his commission and instructions to appoint Courts of Oyer and Terminer within all
the districts of that province." § When Governor Carleton,
having reversed this ordinance, attempted to hold the fresh
trial of the Walker case by a Montreal jury, he found good
reason to understand the wisdom of Murray's action.

* Referring to the admission of Catholics to juries and to
practice in the courts.
† Public Record Office, vol. C.O. 42/6.
‡ At the time of the Walker trial a Protestant jury was demanded
and could not be procured in Montreal alone.
§ Privy Council, November 22, 1765, in C.O. 42/27, Public
Record Office.

It was unfortunately not given to Murray to see the effects of his efforts. Lord Halifax had curtly informed him that the separate military control, which, as we have seen, was productive of such serious disorders, must continue, yet his successor, Carleton, arrived with full military powers and the rank of brigadier commanding the troops in Canada, and the address of welcome presented to him by the council congratulated him on " the military command united to the civil in your person," while the inhabitants of the city and district of Quebec congratulated him on taking up " the chief command of this province, the military as well as civil." These two extracts being sufficient to show the importance attached to the subject by the people concerned, and to emphasize the disability under which Governor Murray was forced to suffer.

The exclusion of Catholics from the courts had been a frequent theme of Murray's letters. It was on the very day of his departure that the revised instructions, permitting Catholics to practice in the courts and to serve on juries, was received in Canada.* Even in this case the attempt was made to transfer the onus of blame for the narrow spirit of the original instructions.

The incapacity of the chief justice and several other officials had been reported by the Governor without effect for two years, but his successor was fortunate in commencing his career with men in the chief positions of the law of very different capacity to those first appointed. In February, 1766, Messrs. Gregory and Suckling were dismissed by the royal command, and William Hey appointed as Chief Justice, and Francis Mascres as Attorney-General. The latter, at least, was of exceptional ability, and the Chief Justice was of respectable talents.

Early in 1766 Francis Maseres † had submitted a

* Colonel Irving to Lords of Trade, July 7, 1766 (P.R.O., C.O. 42/5).

† Maseres was of French descent and spoke that language well. He was of independent means and independent views, and on this account ceased to find favour with Carleton, who wrote in October, 1769, that he had granted him leave and hoped he would not return.

memorandum " on the expediency of procuring an Act of Parliament for the settlement of the province of Quebec," which is distinguishable by its moderate tone and breadth of view from the intemperate writings of the responsible ministers :

" The difficulties that have arisen in the Government of the province of Quebec, and which are likely still to occur in it, notwithstanding the best intentions of those who are instructed by His Majesty with the administration of affairs there, are so many and so great that the officers whom His Majesty has been pleased of late to nominate to the principal departments of that Government cannot look upon them without great uneasiness and apprehension and despair of being able to overcome them without the assistance of an Act of Parliament to ground and justify their proceedings. Two nations are to be kept in peace and harmony, and moulded as it were into one, that are at present of opposite religions, ignorant of each others language, and inclined in their affections to different systems of laws."

He then goes on to point out that the Governor's commission, empowering him to call a general assembly, in reality aggravated the animosity between the old and the new subjects :

" For it is expressly provided that no person elected to serve in such an assembly shall sit and vote there till he has subscribed the declaration against Popery prescribed by the Statute 23 Car. 2. *Which would effectually exclude all Canadians* " (my italics).

This plain statement of facts contradicted very directly the attempt made by Lords Hillsborough and Dartmouth to lay the blame of misinterpretation of the commission on the Governor and his advisors. Maseres brings out in the clearest way the necessity for toleration of the Catholic religion, not only in the form of worship, but also in the practical sense of allowing the adherents of this religion equal rights in all respects with their fellow subjects.*

* Maseres was himself a Protestant.

Regarding the settlement of the pregnant question of laws he advocated an Act of Parliament, delegating to the Governor and council the power to make laws founded on the basis of including such part of the French code as they should find suitable, and thus substituting the authority of the King and Parliament for the royal and absolute government which existed in the first proclamation.

" The doctrine of the instant validity of the whole mass of the laws of England throughout the conquered province cannot be true. And if the whole system of those laws is not valid there, then certainly no part of them can be so. For if they are, then who shall distinguish which of them are valid and which are not." Thus he says, " The Parliament only have a power to make laws . . . notwithstanding that such a power may inadvertently have been delegated by a private instruction of the King alone."

He next refers to the low state of the revenue, and touches on the dangerous subject of imposing a tax to make up the deficiency of the official salaries, which, he says, would be properly imposed by Parliament. In this connection some interesting and instructive remarks are made. Referring to the recent taxation troubles in the American colonies :

" The other American colonies have internal legislatures of their own, who have been permitted ever since their first establishment to be the assessors of all their internal taxes ; and as they had not abused this privilege with which they had been so long indulged, and further, as their exercising this privilege seemed to be in no way prejudicial to the Mother Country, it seems to have been a harsh and ungracious measure in the Parliament, by the advice of the late minister, to revive and exert a dormant and inherent right of taxing them. . . . But the Canadians have no such internal legislature, no such usuage of taxing themselves by representatives of their own choosing. Unless, therefore, they have the singular privilege of not being liable to be taxed at all, they must be liable to be taxed either by the King alone or by the King and Parliament. As to the erecting an assembly in that province, *it is a measure which probably for some years will not be found expedient.*"

And he goes on to point out that if the qualifications as regards Popery are maintained :

" An assembly so constituted might pretend to be a representative of the people there, but in truth it would be representative of only the 600 new English settlers, and an instrument in their hands of domineering over the 90,000 French. . . ."

The decision is mentioned above of the Lords of the Committee of the Privy Council to refer Lord Dartmouth's proposals for amendment in the system of judicature to the Governor and his legal advisers for opinion. By the tenor of the instructions the Governor, the Chief Justice, and the Canadian Attorney-General, were to advise on the subjects referred, and the sequel was remarkable. A draught reply was prepared, evidently by Francis Maseres, which Carleton refused to approve of. The document is given in full in Short and Doughty's work on the *Constitutional Documents of Canada;* but Maseres' views, supported by clear and logical argument, were so complete a vindication of Murray's policy and so stultified the action of those ministers who had sought to condemn him, that I greatly regret its length prohibits reproduction here.

It is a frank document, the sole work of Francis Maseres, and it does honour to his independence and honesty. It confounds at once the factious and petty spirits of Lords Dartmouth and Hillsborough, who would have laid on Murray's shoulders the burden of the careless ignorance with which the original constitutional documents were drawn up. In this connection at a later date (1774) the Advocate-General of England remarked :

" It should seem as if this Proclamation (*i.e.* that relating to Canada) had been copied inadvertently, and in the hurry of office, from some former Proclamation relative to Nova Scotia or some other unsettled British colony, and that the reflection never entered the thoughts of the drawers up of this Proclamation that Canada was a conquered province, full of inhabitants and already in the possession of a legal establishment."

The whole of Maseres' document is a scathing indictment of the responsible ministers, and in some parts might almost serve for a Junius letter of admonition to the King. It was certainly a triumphant vindication of Murray's action, though strangely enough no mention is made of that part of the ordinance issued on his responsibility, which permitted Canadian advocates to practice in the Courts of Common Pleas, and thus forestalled a part of the reform recommended.

It is, nevertheless, quite certain that Carleton was not the man to forward such a report, and we are informed that :

" The foregoing draught of a report, which was prepared by Francis Maseres, Esquire, his Majesty's Attorney-General of the province of Quebec, by order of Guy Carleton, Esquire, the Governor of the said province, was delivered in to the said Governor on the 27th day of February, 1769, but had not the good fortune to be approved by his excellency. Another report was therefore drawn up by other hands agreeable to the Governor's sentiments, in which his Excellency has omitted the consideration of all public acts and instruments, whereby the English law has been introduced, or attempted to be introduced, into that province, together with some other matters contained in the foregoing report. . . ."

It would be tedious, and for the purposes of this work unnecessary, to follow further the long debate on the proposals to amend the constitution of Canada, which in its original conception has been shown to have lacked almost every element of statesmanship and forethought. This debate constantly varied in the view taken, dependent principally whether the exponents, as Hillsborough and Dartmouth had a share in the original responsibility, or whether fresh and independent minds as Maseres and Marriott, Wedderburn or Thurloe were in possession. It suffices from my point of view to make it clear that in all that followed, culminating in the passing of the Quebec Act of 1774, the advice and opinions given by Murray during his tenure of Governorship very largely found place in the new constitution. The territories formerly excluded by Lord Shelburne were now included in the " Province of Quebec," and not only this, but a vast additional area was added, showing how completely the old views had changed.* A frank admission of the unsuitable nature of the early constitution was made, and it was declared as a result of experience " to be inapplicable to the state and circumstance of the said province, the inhabitants whereof amounted at the conquest to above sixty-five thousand persons professing the religion of the Church of Rome." From which it would almost appear that the frequent references to the vast preponderance of the French popu- lation, which so often occurred in Murray's letters, had but recently sunk into the minds of the ministers ; the Romish clergy were permitted to demand their accustomed dues and rights ; the oath of supremacy was abolished, and an oath of allegiance, not repugnant to the Catholic conscience, was substituted ; property to be held in ac- cordance with the laws of Canada ; the English criminal law, which was held as more lenient than that of the French, to be maintained ; a council, without religious hindrance as to election, to control the affairs of the province, subject to the consent of the Governor, but without the power of taxation. Thus the decision of Murray that the province was not yet ripe for representative government was upheld. Against this Lord Chatham had entered a warm protest. He styled it :

" A most cruel, oppressive, and odious measure, tearing up justice and every good principle by the roots. . . . The merely supposing that the Canadians would not be able to feel the good effects of law and freedom, because they had been used to arbitrary power, was an idea as ridiculous as false. . . ." †

* Changed at a most inopportune moment, for whereas in 1763 the boundary of Canada might have been fixed anywhere within the conquered area, in 1774 the American colonists received the new arrangement with suspicion.
† See Chatham Correspondence, vol. iv. p. 351 et seq. for a full report of the speech.

But Chatham was wrong, for the Canadians set no store by representative government, the movement to this end was entirely on the part of the new settlers; as Murray had pointed out, the Canadians desired full religious liberty and permanent rights of property under their ancient charters, and both these were conceded and sufficed for the time. With the British traders and settlers, however, it was otherwise, and they had, or at least pretended to have, a grievance that the promise of representative government was withheld.

The King's ministers of the mid-eighteenth century appear to have been dogged by a fatal inability to view their measures with that degree of detachment from personal prejudice which could alone create enduring provisions. It was not that sound advice was lacking, but it did not suffice to keep them from extreme views, which, in their want of stability, possessed an additional fault. Leaving out of question the Acts relating to the American colonies, the passings, repealings, repressions, conciliations, with which this book is little concerned, we have in the Acts relating to Canada a concrete example sufficient to prove the case. In 1763–64 measures designed to place the power unreservedly in the hands of the British settlers, in 1773–74 measures designed to do precisely the reverse. Between these two, experienced men, like Murray and Maseres, urging a happy medium, and their advice falling on deaf ears. One of them, Maseres, driven to perhaps too warm an espousal of the cause of the traders; the other driven from office for refusing to allow the French Canadians to be destroyed. The Quebec Act contained much that Murray had striven for; but had his advice been followed and an equitable weighing of French and English codes been decreed, that unfortunate cleavage between the French and English settlers which exists to this day would long since have been healed. When, in 1774, the Quebec Act was in its final stages in the House of Commons, undergoing violent, ill-considered attack from one party and equally ill-considered support from the other, it was moved that General Murray should be called as a witness.   Lord North objected, for it was known that his opinions agreed in many respects with those of Masseres, who had already been examined, and the Government feared the effect that such an opinion, given by a man of Murray's intimate experience, would have on the House.* A few months later Dartmouth, the former supporter of the British minority in Canada, was condemning the movement for the repeal of the Act, as the unreasonable desire of the few to destroy the happiness of 100,000 French Canadians !

The name of Governor Carleton is probably much more generally connected with this enlargement of the liberties of the Canadian subjects than is that of James Murray. Certainly this is the case among English subjects ; but I think I am justified in stating that the French Canadians recognise, in the efforts of the latter, the true origin of their Magna Charta.   He had more than once urged the necessity of framing more solid instructions for government,† and it was a result of his initiation that the matter was first considered by the chancellor, Lord Northington, who entirely disapproved of the views on the subject expressed by the government-attorney and solicitor-general.   It is the case that the fall of the Rockingham Ministry, which had shown itself so unjust in its action regarding Canadian affairs, was brought about by this very matter of which the initiation may be fairly held to be due to Murray.   The incident is referred to in Campbell's life of Lord Northington.   It appears that after his condemnation of the procedure proposed, the Cabinet, without consulting him, decided on sending the papers to Carleton for report (July, 1766).   When Northington heard of this action of the Cabinet, it is said he remarked, " By God, they shall never meet again," and going straight to the King recommended him to send for Mr. Pitt.   His Majesty, glad of an excuse to get rid of the Ministry that had repealed the Stamp Act

---

* *Parliamentary History*, vol. xvii.
    † His letter of July 15, 1765, to the Lords of Trade, for example, C.O. 42/3.

against his wishes, was ready to accede. Probably Murray knew nothing of this. It would have been a sweet revenge if he had !

We have seen the reiterated statements of the necessity for removing the religious disabilities made by Murray, and his consistent efforts to checkmate the usurpatory endeavours of the mercantile community of old subjects, and it is remarkable how completely his foresight enabled him to gauge a state of affairs which, after ten years, was crystallised by the Act. It is also curious to note that the same British traders, led by our former acquaintance, Mr. Thomas Walker, displayed the same turbulence in 1774 as in 1764, and one wonders whether Lord Dartmouth, on receipt of Carleton's letter of November 11, 1774,* stating that this man was now taking the lead, apparently in seditious communication with the illegal congress of the United colonies, in opposing the new measures, remembered the offensive letter to Murray of March 27, 1766, ordering his immediate restoration as a justice of the peace (*see* p. 347).

Carleton was in truth a politician, and as such had the advantage of Murray, whose blunt independence secured for him little support from the King's ministers. It was enough for Murray to believe that his honour and justice required a certain line of conduct, and he was indifferent whether the politics of the hour in London lent countenance to his action or not. Carleton, on the other hand, may have conceived his duties in a different sense ; let us give him the benefit of the doubt. Perhaps he argued that he was a representative of the King to carry out the wishes of the King's Government. Thus when the " good " Lord Dartmouth positively ordered further prosecution of the Walker fiasco, in order to placate the British traders, Carleton and his *fidus Achates*, the chief justice, lent themselves with vigour to the scheme, and on the doubtful evidence of a discharged soldier arrested six gentlemen, all friends

* Printed in *Canadian Archives*, Constitutional Documents, p. 412.

of Murray, on a trumped-up charge of being concerned in the attack on Walker. Fortunately, as Murray predicted, the grand jury selected in Montreal would have nothing to do with evidence produced by so untrustworthy a person as Walker, and refused to bring a bill against the accused, and the whole affair fizzled out miserably with threats of a charge of perjury against Walker. Nevertheless Carleton found opportunity to dismiss Colonel Irvine and Surgeon Mabane from their seats on the council, ostensibly, at all events, because they had headed a deputation to secure bail for the accused in this ridiculous trial. Actually, I am afraid, this indignity was inflicted because they were Murray's friends and nominees.*

Again, when the policy at home favoured conciliation of the Canadians and a repudiation of the promises to the British settlers, Carleton is the subservient instrument of the Ministry for the introduction of the Quebec Act, and is ready to throw over his former friend Maseres, whom he reasonably suspected of strong leanings towards a much wider view than that which met approval at Westminster.

It is impossible to peruse the voluminous records without concluding that Carleton was anxious to make favour with the ministers who had appointed him, by placing Murray's actions in the least favourable light. It is not necessary to refer to this in detail except regarding one action, which drew forth a spirited protest from the Governor, who at the time was still, at least nominally, in chief charge of the province. The occasion was an ordinance published by Carleton, couched in what reads as very pharisaical language, and to this Murray replied publicly in a signed letter to *Lloyd's Evening Post*, of January 2–5, 1767.

" SIR,—In your paper of the 26th ult. I saw a paragraph, the consequence of an advertisement inserted in the *Quebec Gazette*, November 7th, 1766, in the following words :

" Whereas the numerous fees which the inhabitants of

---

* Colonel Irvine subsequently became Governor of Guernsey, and Mabane was at a later period restored to the council at Quebec.

this province have been obliged to pay have been found very burthensome and inconvenient to the said inhabitants in the low and distressed condition to which many of them have been reduced by the late wars, the public is hereby given to understand that Lieut.-Governor Carleton has resolved to release and relinquish during the time he shall continue in the government of the province, and doth hereby release and relinquish all the fees that may be due to himself by virtue of the commission or powers with which it has pleased His Majesty to invest him, excepting only the fees due from vintners and other publicans for licenses to keep public-houses, which fees shall continue to be paid. And the said Lieut.-Governor further declares that the money arising from these fees last mentioned shall not be appropriated to his private use, but shall be paid into the hands of the Receiver-General of His Majesty's Revenue in this province and considered as a part of the revenue and accounted for accordingly !

" Every person who reads the above advertisement must draw from it two conclusions : first, that the fees established in the province of Quebec were burthensome and oppressive; secondly, that these fees had yielded a considerable revenue, and in particular that the fees levied upon vintners had formerly been applied not to the public use but to that of the Governor.

" Upon this supposition the above advertisement would no doubt reflect honour upon Lieut.-Governor Carleton, and mark at the same time the Governor with blame and reproach.

" It has never been, nor ever shall be, my practice to take notice of anonymous abuse; but where anything is signed which may be construed an imputation on my conduct, I shall always think it my duty to give a fair account of the matter to my country, and I desire nothing more earnestly than that every particular of it may be canvassed to the bottom, as I flatter myself the strictest scrutiny will do me honour. (Here follows a list of eleven fees known as Governor's fees.)

" The above is a list of all the fees the Governor of Quebec can claim, and it is to be remarked that little can arise from the patents for lands, as all the valuable lands in the province were granted before the conquest by us. That as little can arise from the licenses of marriage, letters of administration, probate of wills, and licenses to purchase lands of the Indians. There are not, perhaps, 400 English families in the province. The Canadians take no licenses for marriage, make no wills that are subject to Governor's fees, have no need for letters of administration, nor is it allowed to purchase lands of the Indians, and as not more than thirty ships in one year come from Europe, very few from the other colonies, and rarely above two or three from the West Indies, the navigation being shut up six months a year, the great revenue to the Governor must proceed from certificates to go beyond the seas.

" Had I taken fees for these certificates the amount must have been very considerable, not less than £4000, as the Canadians were obliged to send them to France relative to their paper money and other affairs which were very numerous, but I never took myself, nor permitted my secretary to take, any fees from any man on any account whatever during the military government, which lasted five years, and the amount of all the fees I have taken since the establishment of civil government does not exceed £65 sterling.

" The fees for licensing public-houses for two years last past amounted to about £450 sterling, and the ordinance published November 3, 1764, which established the said fees, declares and enacts that they are to be appropriated to the public use and accounted for as part of the revenue to the Government.

" This being a true state of the case, the public may judge of the propriety of Lieut.-Governor Carleton's advertisement above recited.—Signed, JAMES MURRAY, Governor of the Province of Quebec.

Carleton's reputation would have stood higher if he had avoided this and other methods of traducing his predecessor. It is a method not infrequently exercised by people of small minds to endeavour to influence careless superiors by sneers at alleged shortcomings of predecessors in office, and such a method is the more reprehensible that those traduced are seldom in a position to hear of the allegations, or to refute them. Carleton and Murray had been in antagonism during the Quebec campaign, but I rejoice to think that in Murray there was no sign of that petty spirit that would seek to gain a secret advantage, even in such a case as his virtual supersession by a man he did not like. Murray's reply to the address of farewell from his council, already referred to, shows the high standard of honour at which he aimed :

" At leaving a country I sincerely love, it gives me pleasure to inform you, from my personal knowledge of the gentleman His Majesty has appointed lieutenant-governor, that he is disposed and qualified to render the province happy. I am sure he will find the same assistance from you which I have met with, and hope his Government will not be disturbed by resentments against the authors of the unjust calumnies which have been raised against me."

It is not possible to read Carleton's letters and despatches without recognising that he was a good soldier and a firm, if arbitrary, ruler. I doubt if he ever commanded the sympathy of the Canadians in the same sense that Murray did, but he followed him in his conciliatory method of dealing with them. To Barré, Lord Shelburne, and Lord Chatham (whose eldest son * was consigned to his care at a later date in Canada) he probably owed much, but he was without early interest and pushed his way on his own merit, doing well for his country. Had he given credit to the self-sacrificing efforts of his predecessor, on which his own fortunes were built, the future Lord Dorchester would surely have gained further honour.

It is incontestable that Murray had acquired an extraordinary influence with the Canadians. With the quickness of perception, due to their French origin, they had grasped the fact of the Governor's genuine sympathy, and there is no doubt in the troubled time yet to come they would have rallied around him to a man. In February, 1766, shortly after his departure, he was able to write to Conway, then Secretary of State, referring to the Stamp Act : " His Majesty's subjects in this province have not

---

* Then Lord Pitt, appointed as aide-de-camp to Carleton in 1773, and an ensign in Carleton's regiment, the 47th Foot (see Chatham Correspondence).

followed the example of the neighbouring colonies, but have cheerfully submitted to the authority of the British Legislature." In August of the same year, after his return to England, he wrote to Lord Shelburne :

" As the council books of the province and likewise my answer to the complaint made against my administration have been laid before your lordship, it is needless, I presume, to say anything further on that subject than that I glory in having been accused of warmth and firmness in protecting the King's Canadian subjects, and of doing the utmost in my power to gain to my royal master the affection of that brave, hardy people, whose emigration, if ever it should happen, will be an irreparable loss to this empire, to prevent which I declare to your lordship I would cheerfully submit to greater calamities and in-dignities, if greater can be devised, than hitherto I have undergone."

With this expression of his sentiments I will quit this part of the subject, trusting that I have shown that Murray was sacrificed to the whim of an unstable and narrow-minded political caucus, who were quite unfitted to see the wisdom of his policy or to supprt him in his vigorous efforts to lay a sure foundation for what has now become the greatest dominion of the British Crown. As he said himself :

" I am persuaded I shall, unheard, be made a sacrifice of, to convince the mob, that the present administration have no connection with Lord Bute. . . . If the uprightness of my conduct will not justify me, why should I trouble my friends ? If the times are so corrupt that virtue must retire, I choose to enjoy their caresses in a private corner. So here I impatiently wait a dismission which will do me honour or a justification which will confound my enemies, those of His Majesty's government and of human society." *

His government and his efforts can claim, at the least, the preservation of the Canadian population, the abolition of religious disability, and the grant of laws of inheritance

* Murray to Ross, December 4, 1765 (Bath Papers).

acceptable to the vast majority of the people, and finally that measure of trust and subordination of the Canadians which went far to retain the province for England, and which might, under better support from home, have even preserved America from the War of Independence.

CHAPTER XVII

MINORCA

MURRAY arrived in England at the end of July, 1766, to answer before a hostile Ministry the ridiculous charges brought against him by the discontented traders of Quebec —persons who he described as " the most immoral collection of men I ever knew." It is unnecessary to waste much time over the " charges " which appeared to Lord Dartmouth a sufficient reason to recall a Governor in whose favour petitions from all the most respectable members of the community poured in. All of these petitions struck one key-note.

" We pray your Majesty, if you will deign to listen to us, continue Monsr. Murray as Governor of this province, which his valour has preserved for you, and who has gained the affection of its people by his generosity and mildness, and restore him to us." And again, " We dare to hope that he will be continued in that office, where his enlightened mind and equity and prudence enable him to keep the people in a state of tranquility and obedience." *

Fortunately his arrival in England synchronised with the fall of the Rockingham Ministry, but the new Ministry, which included Lord Shelburne as Secretary of State, with Colonel Barré as a privy councillor holding office as Vice-Treasurer for Ireland, and Lord Hillsborough, whose peculiar notions of the interpretation of the King's Proclamation in Canada have already been noticed, as President of the Board of Trade, were unlikely to be favourable to him. Nevertheless, if he could not expect sympathy and

* Petitions from Quebec and Montreal respectively.

support, the new Ministry was, at least, more honest than their predecessors, and an honest inquiry was what Murray earnestly desired.

"The charges" were obviously framed to please the narrow religious views of Dartmouth, and to most of them Murray replied with scathing contempt. Accused of giving away the brandy found in the French king's stores at Quebec, he replied :

"I gave the brandy for intelligence; no man ever had better (*i.e.* during the campaign of 1760). I am sure nobody ever wanted it more, and that no nation ever paid less for it. So I displeased the little Protestant traders. . . . Quakers, Puritans, Anabaptists, Presbyterians, Atheists, Infidels, and even Jews."

Then with a touch that reminds one of Warren Hastings at a later date, he exclaimed: "Had avarice been my passion it might have been gratified without robbing the King of eight thousand gallons of brandy." * Enacting ordinances "injurious to civil liberty and the Protestant cause," "Encouraging your Majesty's new subjects to apply for judges of their own national language," "Leaving the Protestants to this day destitute of a place of worship appropriated to themselves," † were items among the "charges."

One stands astonished that any responsible statesman should have been unable to see through such trash, and much more not worth quoting; but so far as Murray was concerned, the indictment must have occasioned much anxiety and labour, and it was not until April following (1767) that the Privy Council dismissed the several complaints, as we have already seen, as "groundless, scandalous, and derogatory to the honour of the said Governor, who stood before the committee unimpeached."

Shortly after his arrival he had the honour of being

* The brandy was given to the intelligence officers, who used it for paying spies, there being no money for secret service in the garrison during the winter of 1759–60.

† There were naturally no Protestant churches. Arrangements were made to hold services in the Catholic churches.

introduced to the King (August, 1766), and "met with a most gracious reception," but there is little on record to show what reception he had from the ministers. Apparently, Murray's first intention was to return to Quebec as soon as the business of laying the state of that province before the Government could be completed. A letter from a friend in Quebec runs :

" The good news we have received by the return of the *Little William* of your excellency's agreeable voyage, happy arrival in good health, together with the prospect of seeing you here next summer, have not a little elated the hearts of your friends."

It is, indeed, extremely probable that the King, had it been in his power, would have done honour to one who could claim to be, perhaps more than any other, the instrument by which the Canadian province became a British possession ; but the King had his own troubles to contend with, and it is evident that in 1766–67 the state of political ferment in which the Government found itself, and the plotting and counter-plotting of the period, which included the passing of the Tea Tax (June, 1767), absorbed the attention of the Court. In April, 1767, the situation is summed up in a letter from Lord Charlemont :

" Lord Chatham has not been allowed to see anybody, or even to receive letters. He is still Minister, but how long he may continue so is a problem that would pose the deepest politician. The Opposition grows more and more violent and seems to gain ground. The Ministry is divided into as many parties as there are men in it ; all complain of his want of participation. Charles Townshend is at open war, Conway is angry, Lord Shelburne out of humour, and the Duke of Grafton by no means pleased. . . . In short, such is the confusion that it is impossible to guess to-day at what will happen to-morrow." *

In such a state of affairs it would be impossible to expect attention to individual cases, or even to public affairs, and

* Chatham Correspondence, under date April, 1767.

as month succeeded month, until April, 1767, when the Privy Council pronounced the decision already quoted, we may be certain that Murray's disgust at his treatment was ever deepening.

Apparently he arrived at a determination not to return to Quebec early in the new year (1767). In a letter, dated Quebec, March 15, his kinsman, Walter Murray, wrote :

" I hear Mrs. Irvine had the pleasure of a letter from Mrs. Murray last week, which mentions your being determined never to return to Quebec more. I think you are much in the right of it, for who that had your fortune would choose to leave his lady, relations, friends, London, and Sussex to waste his days in the frozen regions of Canada, to be tormented with the constant clamours of a factious discontented set. . . ."

There is nothing on record to show the course of Murray's mind on the subject. The reasons must have been of an urgent and decided kind, for we have seen his strong leaning towards fixing his lot in Canada and his genuine sympathy with the people he governed. It may be that he foresaw, in the selection of Carleton as Lieut.-Governor of the province, the probability of endless friction, with the certainty of little support from Lord Shelburne; but another, and, I think, very probable cause of his decision, was that the glamour of home life took sudden possession of him. He had left England nearly ten years before, little known, with slender prospects, and he returned to find himself a personage who had earned for himself a niche in history.

Lord Elibank, who had been far from brotherly up to the time of his departure, was now proud of his relationship, and his letters of the period frequently refer to " my brother, the General." Thus " my brother, the General, who is in perfect health, and whose conduct has been universally approved of, from the King downwards. . . ." * The two were constantly together, and it seems very

* Lord Elibank to Mr. Mitchelson, September 25, 1766 (Elibank Papers).

probable that his lordship's wishes were opposed to the return to Canada, for his health was much broken, and it is clear from the private letters that he leant much on this " newly found " brother. Lord Elibank was anxious that the General should enter Parliament, and had arranged, as he thought, that Jedburgh should return him.

The Jedburgh scheme, however, miscarried, and a letter from his brother George tells something of the reason. " I am ashamed of the intelligence I gave you of Jedburgh, but learn Lauderdale got their promise by pretending he had your interest." I cannot find that Murray made any further efforts to enter Parliament.

Another, and perhaps potent, cause of Murray's decision was his wife's invincible objection to crossing the Atlantic. Whatever reasons may have forced this on Mrs. Murray, there can be no doubt that her absence from her place during the years of his Governorship added considerably to his difficulties ; and his anger at what he believed to be wilful caprice was not to be wondered at. A woman to grace the Governor's establishment would have gone far to smooth the thorny path of a man whose temper was naturally inclined to rise when needless obstruction was met with, and it was certainly a misfortune for Murray that his beautiful and popular wife was not there to help him by her woman's arts in controlling the elements of disaffection amongst the colonists. Arrived in England it is clear that Murray's anger was short-lived. Possibly he saw for himself that her reasons were not fanciful, as he had suspected ; at all events, they resumed the old state of affection at once. Writing to her mother, she says, " You may be assured no care or attention is ever neglected in regard to me, as my dear Mr. Murray is very solicitus about me ! " In the autumn of 1767 General and Mrs. Murray went on a tour to visit the family in the new and pleasant position of distinguished and welcome guests. After a few days at Carlton with brother Gideon the pair went on to the family mansion of Ballencrief, where Murray was born.

"I have just got a minute to say we got safe here yesterday morning," writes Mrs. Murray, "and found great joy on our arrival. As to giving any account of the country, can't pretend to do that yet, only say that this is a very comfortable good house, and two fine rooms in it six-and-thirty feet long. Miss Mary Murray and Lady Bell * are here, and to continue all the time of my stay. I am quite well, and dare say shall keep so, for here is no formality—ever (every) one dose as they like and retire when they please. . . ." †

There had evidently been great doings on the return of the hero of Quebec, and a few days later the party went on to Edinburgh, where

"The Corporation of Edinburgh all came to wait on Mr. Murray to desire his acceptance of his freedom, which is lookt upon, it seems, as a great honour, so to-morrow we ladys go to see the cerimony. Lady Stewart ‡ inquired much after you, and desired I would make her compts. As to the country of Scotland I have seen, think it just like England. But I have seen no were but in the improv'd parts, and the Duke of Beauclers' (Buccleuch) house and park I think much better than Worksop. . . ."

The visit concluded with a stay with the Fergusons § (Lord Pitfour) and with Lord Adam Gordon, who had been a friend of Murray's in Canada.

Whatever the reason or combination of reasons which led Murray to forgo his right to return to Canada, a right which, in view of the decision of the Privy Council and the King's undoubted approbation of his services, he certainly could have exercised, it cannot but be regarded as a misfortune that he permitted his career to be affected. Had he returned with military as well as civil control, with the

* Lady Isabel Mackenzie, wife of Admiral George Murray.
† Mrs. Murray to Mrs. Collier, October 27, 1767.
‡ Murray's sister, Helen Murray, to whom he had given unwavering support through all the trying period of the great Douglas cause. She had married Sir James Stewart of Grandtully, and thus became stepmother to the claimant in the Douglas cause, a legal proceeding as famous at the time as the Tichborne trial of the nineteenth century, or the Slingsby case of recent days.
§ His sister, Ann Ferguson, whose husband was a Lord of Session.

éclat naturally attaching to his successful endeavours to procure civil and religious rights for the Canadians, added to their feelings of genuine affection for him, and with the clear insight he possessed as to the military value of the colony, I can entertain little doubt that his fortunes would have risen to the same heights as did those of his successor, and he would have gained the recognition of his efforts, which in the event became Carleton's. As matters fell out, he turned his hand from the plough and relinquished to another the harvest of his labour. Even as the case stood it seems extraordinary that he received so little recognition for his services. I can only suppose that the antagonistic elements in the Government and the reluctance to bestow marks of favour on a Scot who had enjoyed the protection of Bute, stood in the way of his being recommended to the King.

The years that followed were marked by little of interest from the public point of view. Murray had expressed his intention of seeking the " caresses " of his friends in a " private corner," and he carried it out by retiring to his Sussex estates, where he busied himself in building the house of Beauport. There was much to engage him in the settlement of the property which had come to him through his wife, and the division of the Collier property was not settled without a good deal of dispute and some recourse to law. Experimental farming seems to have been a hobby too, if we may judge from a letter to Lord Elibank, in which he bewails the unfortunate result of trying Canada wheat :

" I sowed no less that twenty acres of Canada wheat in March. It flourished till about a fortnight ago, when, after a thundershower, the whole was blighted, tho' in different soils and situations. I can have no doubt of this misfortune being owing to the nature of the grain, for I distributed some of it to several people here, and the disappointment is universal. . . . I hope to come near you in my turnips and cabbages. I have twenty acres of each out of all danger, in spite of scorching weather."

His military career was more or less at a standstill. He had been appointed colonel of the 13th Foot in December, 1767, thus fulfilling his ambition to command an " old " regiment, and later on he was an " Inspecting General " of the southern district, and we have glimpses of his attending reviews in various places. In May, 1772, he received the rank of lieut.-general.

It was not until the year 1774 that further active service fell to Murray. It appears that he had tired of the routine of home military service combined with rural pursuits at Beauport, and cast about him for some foreign service which might bring with it more activity. He was still titular Military Governor of Quebec city, and, according to the custom of the time, continued to draw the salary of the post. He had once expressed the hope that he would die with this distinction still his, but now in his desire for further employment he offered it in exchange for the Lieut.-Governorship of Minorca, at the time held by Major-General Johnston, who had been in this post since the Treaty of Paris restored the island to Great Britain. Murray wrote : " You do not propose to be perpetually banished to Minorca," and suggested that there should be a mutual change of governments, and that the difference in pay of Lieut.-Governor of Minorca and that of the non-resident Military Government of the town of Quebec, " shall be paid to you for your life." The exchange was apparently accepted, for the same *Gazette* of November 26, 1774, that appointed Murray to Minorca, gave Major-General James Johnston the Military (non-resident) Government of the town of Quebec.

The Governor of Minorca was at the time General Mostyn, who was already advanced in years, and, as was the custom in those days, retained the titular appointment though no longer resident in the island. No doubt it had been indicated to Murray that the lieut.-governorship was but the stepping-stone of the senior appointment, and strange as it may seem to us, Minorca was a charge which ranked much higher both in precedence and emoluments than Canada. We must remember that although the Mediterranean was not then as now the high road to India, yet the mastery of that sea was, as a counterpoise to French and Spanish pretensions, of great importance, the more so that the French were already in possession of Corsica. Malta had not yet fallen to us, and Gibraltar, though it had been a possession for seventy years, was not of the same naval importance, and had no harbour that could compare with that of Port Mahon. It had been even seriously considered by Pitt to offer Gibraltar to Spain in exchange for Minorca, when the latter place fell to the French in 1756. The nation attached as much importance to the island as we do in our days to Malta, and its loss in 1756, when attacked by the French and defended by General Blakeney, then in his eighty-fourth year, created such a popular outcry that the admiral (Byng) who was held to be responsible was sacrificed to the popular clamour; the truth being that, as has happened in days not far removed from our own, a scapegoat was necessary to cover the shortcomings of a Government which neglected preparation for war in time of seeming peace.

Murray's acceptance of the appointment was characteristic. He had an audience of the King, and had informed His Majesty that a governorship which depended for its emoluments on " perquisites " was distasteful to him. What followed is best told in his letter to Lord Rochfort, which indicates not only his straightforward independence but the little respect in which he held ministers who regarded the Sovereign as a titular authority to be treated with contempt.

The letter ran as follows :

November 20, 1774.

" My Lord,

" The reflection arising from the conversation I had with your Lordship this morning makes me very unhappy.

" The King told me his service was not to suffer, and that he had given, or was to give, positive directions to your Lordship to allow the commander for the time being at Minorca ten shillings per day for a secretary.

" Your Lordship knows of no such order, and thinks it cannot be done unless General Mostyn consents to give up his secretary. The General is to be wrote to for his consent, and refusal must be the answer. The General Mostyn merits every attention, General Murray may expect that some is likewise due to him, but I am certain the King's service is entitled to more than either of them.

" I informed your Lordship of the King's orders to me to deposit in the hands of the proper officers the sums arising from the perquisite of the commanding officer at Minorca, and of His Majesty's assurance that my salary should be fixed independent of such disgraceful emoluments.*

" Your Lordship candidly expressed your doubts of the certainty of this measure, alleging that circumstances often occur which prevent His Majesty from fulfilling what he ardently wishes and firmly intends to carry into execution.

" This being the case, and the two points in question being of so trifling a consideration, I must conclude the hesitation in fixing them must proceed from a dislike of the minister for me, more than from his disapproval of the measure, and therefore I must beg to have them fixed before I go by some authoritative document from the Treasury, since my Royal Master's will may be controlled officially. . . ."

This plain speaking, which presumably placed the minister in a predicament, apparently led to a satisfactory arrangement, for five days later Rochfort informed Major-General Johnston that Lieut.-General Murray had been appointed by the King to succeed him.

En passant it may be mentioned that this question of

---

* There is a somewhat obscure record of the Privy Council, dated April 26, 1776. " The plan proposed by General Murray for abolishing perquisites, which have hitherto constituted the income of the commander, and the emoluments arising from the monopolies of the necessary articles of life, does the highest honour to the integrity and public spirit of the General, and their lordships would with great satisfaction and readiness have lent their assistance to the carrying this plan into execution, if considerable difficulties had not occurred with respect to the bread contract " (P.R.O., C.O. 174/9).

the perquisites had evidently been notorious before General
Murray took it up, and it is evident that General Mostyn
when Governor had not been above profiting by it, which,
indeed, as it was the custom of the time, is not to his discredit.

Accompanied by his wife and niece,* Miss Maria Murray,
the General left England early in December, and landed at
Port Mahon on December 24 (1775). Very unfortunately
they experienced a bad storm between Marseilles and
Minorca. General Johnston, writing to the Secretary of
State, mentions it as almost without precedent, and says
that the landing was effected with great difficulty and some
danger. The private letters tell us that Mrs. Murray had
to be lowered into a boat blindfolded, and considering her
extreme delicacy and nervous condition, it is easy to suppose
that this *contretemps* had a bad effect on her health.

The first years of his command were passed in strengthening the fortifications of Fort St. Phillips, which dominated
the harbour at Port Mahon. On his arrival he reported
that he was " much pleased with the aspect of things ; "
but he soon found that great preparations for war were
going forward at Carthagena and Barcelona and Toulon,
nominally with a view to attack the Emperor of Morocco,
but actually, as Murray strongly suspected, as preliminary
to renewed demonstration of the " family compact " against
England. Louis XV. was dead, but the French ministers
saw their opportunity in the embarrassments of England
in America, and only the depleted treasury and the chaotic
state of all departments of Government which the late king
had left for his grandson and successor prevented earlier
rupture of the peace. In America, after four years of sullen
quiescence, open revolution was in progress, and during
Murray's first year at Minorca, British troops found themselves arrayed against the " Continental Army " raised by
British colonists.

One seeks in vain in perusing the more intimate histories
of the policies of the period 1775–1780 for any indication

* The illegitimate daughter of his brother, Lord Elibank.

that the ministers were alive to the urgent necessity for maintaining the armament of the nation as the only sure foundation for retaining the position bequeathed by the victorious wars concluded in 1763. The whole intervening period had been one of decadence and little effort. As with us in the years preceding the Great War, infatuated politicians drowned the clamour of foreign war preparations by the tin-pot rattle of Irish dissension and exuberance in parochial legislation. In 1914 shameless ministers had squandered the nation's resources by ill-digested measures of social reform, and the nation's time by promoting discord in Ireland, setting class against class, and destroying the preparedness of the country by reducing its armaments and closing its workshops. Then with unparalleled effrontery posing as saviours by doing in haste at ruinous expenditure what should have been done gradually and with consideration during peace.

So in the decade ending with the loss of America and of sea power in the Mediterranean, Lord North's Ministry, and the Rockingham party that followed, had deliberately abolished the magnificent legacy of superior armament bequeathed by Pitt. The armies, the fleets, the armaments brought to the lowest ebb of numbers and efficiency.* The people distracted and rendered unstable by lack of firm continuous government, a mixture of weak concession and hesitating harshness. Ireland in open rebellion, harbouring the king's enemies and demanding concession as the price of peace. Squabbles over parliamentary duration and representation overshadowing the doings across the channel, which were destined to drive the final nail into the coffin of American empire. It was fortunate for England that the decadence of both France and Spain was not less pronounced than that at home.

Murray, from his point of vantage in Minorca, could see very plainly the direction in which events were shaping,

---

* As early as 1770, Chatham had deplored the weak condition into which the fleet had been allowed to fall, and stated the necessity of a fleet to cover the communications with Minorca (*Life of William Pitt*, Basil Williams, ii. 274).

and his despatches to Rochfort and Weymouth, who succeeded him as Secretary of State, contain frequent reference
to the necessity for preparation.   It seemed, however,
that the Government at home cared little for the danger
which threatened.   Five battalions had been allotted for
the garrison of Minorca, and of these two were removed
(2/1st and 13th Foot) in August, 1775, and replaced by two
Hanoverian regiments of no more than 471 men and
officers each, an exchange which we may be sure Murray
did not approve, though it would have been thought
disloyal to say so.   The three British battalions left were
the 25th, 51st, and 61st, and a little later the 25th was
removed on being replaced by 400 " invalid drafts," who
were to be incorporated in the two remaining battalions.

It is plain that Murray regarded this weakening of his
garrison as dangerous.   Writing to Weymouth at the end
of 1776 he says :

" This letter will be put in your Lordship's hands by
Captain Robinson, and therefore I take the liberty to put
you in mind how unequal the troops I have here are to the
defence of the extensive works of St. Phillips' castle, and
that there appears to be an absolute necessity for sending
another company of artillery."

In the same letter he asks for a supply of " pease and
oatmeal," equal to six months' supply, for 3000 men, this
provision being desired for storage as a preventive of scurvy,
of which he had had such dire experience at Quebec.

He was evidently filled with anxiety as to the prospects
of defence and with misgivings as to the degree of support
he would receive from His Majesty's ministers.   He knew,
no doubt, that the neglect of the Duke of Newcastle, when
Minister in 1756, was much more the cause of the loss of
Minorca than any shortcomings of Admiral Byng, and he
saw in the action of Weymouth the same absorption in
party politics to the neglect of external affairs ; thus when
that minister ventured to warn him against the danger of
surprise, while at the same time denying him the means of

resistance, he administered a well-deserved snub, which, if it showed unwisdom from the point of his own advantage, at least indicated his splendid independence.

" I trust your Lordship, from your own feelings, will allow me to have those natural to a man descended from noble ancestors. Such feelings will not admit of the existence of a soldier who will allow himself to be surprised."

This thrust at Weymouth is very characteristic, and if, as I say, it shows a splendid independence, it also shows that excessive pride from which I am afraid I cannot deny Murray suffered.

By March, 1778, hostilities with France had commenced at sea. Lord Stormont had retired from Paris * " without taking leave." So far as Minorca was concerned, however, this made little difference. The French naval armaments were no more ready to attack than were the English ships in a position to defend, and Murray's activities were confined to keeping General Elliot at Gibraltar apprised of the enemy's movements and endeavouring to reinforce his garrison.

" I am very sensible," he writes to Weymouth, " there can be no men spared from England to reinforce us, but I wish to be allowed to avail myself of the powers I have within my reach. It is now too late to think of a Minorquin Militia,† had they been formed in time of peace I might have made them soldiers capable of good service. The war being now declared I fear I shall not be able to get a volunteer among them, especially as Spain is to join in the contest."

Murray's project was to enlist 1000 Corsicans, but Weymouth dealt with the plan as he had dealt with the Minorquin Militia proposal, and gave indefinite answers to the suggestions made. It seemed sufficient to convey to Murray the King's gracious " approval of the distinguished diligence in providing everything necessary for

---

* Murray to Weymouth, March 28, 1778 (P.R.O., C.O. 174/11).
† An addition to his means of defence which he had endeavoured to form, but had received no support from home.

defence of the important fortress committed to your care, and of the zeal for his honour and for his service which has on every occasion distinguished you."

As the year passed the French cruisers became more and more numerous. All regular communication ceased, except through neutral vessels.

" Some may think our situation not very agreeable ; we are, however, in good spirits, ready to repel and desirous, indeed eager, to attack the King's enemies, who must have suffered much from the efforts of this island long before this, had the commissions for reprisals reached us in due time."

The commissions referred to by Murray were those for the issue of letters of marque, and in September, 1778, authority to fit out privateers was issued, though the commissions did not reach the island. However, without delaying any longer, Murray issued his own commissions, and he says, " If the mode is defective the idea is at least pious, and therefore if I have erred I rely on the King's forgiveness."

By the end of November he had so far succeeded in waking the enthusiasm of the Minorquin sea-faring population that fourteen vessels of a total of 435 tons, having 56 carriage guns and 170 swivels, had been fitted out, and these had already captured eight prizes of a value of £25,000. By the end of December the number of prizes was eighteen, and the value £58,900 ; 25 privateers being at sea. However, though around the island his command of the sea was considerable, Murray was none the less practically blockaded. He had had no communication with Gibraltar or with England by sea for months, and the only route by which letters could be sent was via Leghorn.

The year was a very unhealthy one. A sickness called " tertiano " played serious havoc with the garrison, and he described his two British battalions as

" totally worn out. If we are besieged I can expect no service from them. In short, if in the month of March or

April I can muster 1400 able men, including artillery, fit to undergo the hardship of a siege, we shall be stronger than the present situation of the garrison promises."

It was due to this sickness that he suffered the serious loss of Colonel Mackellar, the chief engineer, who died in January, 1779.   I have no doubt he felt his death, not only on account of his professional value, but because they were old comrades, and had served together throughout the Louisburg and Quebec campaigns.

In these circumstances the chances of relief by a naval force began to be discussed.

" We hope soon to see the King's flag commanding this sea, or a reinforcement to this sickly garrison.   In the memory of man there never was known here so unhealthy a summer and autumn as we have had.   The inhabitants have suffered equally with the troops.   We hope when the northerly winds take place, which is not yet the case, the sickness will abate."

By February, 1779, he apparently had less hope of assistance.   He says, referring to the French :

" They have not more than five ships of the line at present, which is enough, as we have *none* in these seas. They cannot be ready before May, and then may have ten or twelve.   If a squadron equal to that can be spared for our relief, well ; if not, it will still be well ; as individuals we have nothing to lose.   As soldiers we have a field of glory in which every man of the garrison seems determined to reap as much as he possibly can."

And in another letter in the same month, he says :

" I am confident we can hold the place until His Majesty can send a fleet sufficient to destroy the naval power of France in the Mediterranean.   I can say no more than that I am sure this must be the case if the exertions elsewhere are equal to what I expect my brave garrison will show on this occasion."

These words may, I think, be read to imply some doubt whether the " exertions elsewhere " would be all they should be.

In February (1779), in addition to his anxieties regarding

2 c

the military situation, Murray had to face domestic trouble. His wife was, no doubt, affected by the tertian ague in common with so many others, and he decided to send her to England, taking the opportunity of a neutral ship going to Barcelona. No details of this journey are preserved, but evidently the unfortunate lady was seriously ill before starting, and no doubt the rough journey aggravated her complaint. She reached the Sussex home at Beauport just before she died. Her family attributed her illness to going abroad. In this I think they were mistaken. She seems to have enjoyed the life on the island during the four years of residence there, and the misfortune of the unusually sickly season was one which could hardly be considered otherwise than as an accidental cause. Mrs. Murray was certainly tenderly attached to her husband, and I believe there is no shadow of doubt that he guarded and tended his delicate wife with every care.

In April, 1779, Murray received his commission as Governor of Minorca in place of General Mostyn, deceased. Lord Weymouth, in communicating the information, wrote, " This distinguishing mark of favour, unsolicited by you, will prove His Majesty's approval of the zeal and attention you have constantly shown in his service." Murray was honestly delighted with the King's favour, and wrote to express his joy and thankfulness. Reading between the lines of the correspondence, it is evident that he anticipated that the politicians in power, who were certainly not inclined to bestow favours on any one so independent in his views as our General, would jockey him out of the appointment, and he was surprised and proportionately grateful that the King should stand by him firmly.

At the same time another appointment was made which resulted in much trouble. To succeed Murray in the post of lieut.-governor of the island the Government appointed Sir William Draper. The King's commission was dated May 28, 1779, and a less suitable appointment could hardly have been made.

It was not that Sir William was not worthy of any

honours in the King's gift, for, indeed, his record was a distinguished one. He was an example of a somewhat rare combination—a soldier-scholar. At Madras he had acquired a reputation as a gallant officer, but his principal claim to military fame came a few years later, when in command of the land forces in the attack on Manilla in 1762. Here his personal example, energy, and soldier-like instinct had won an important and intrinsically valuable acquisition, which was, however, restored to Spain at the treaty of Paris.

It was not, however, his reputation as a soldier which is likely to be longest remembered, for Manilla, like many others of the distant posts, conquered for England by the valour of her sons, has been long forgotten. It is as an opponent of the famous *Junius* that Draper is best known. Perhaps it is doubtful if he would have ventured to cross swords with so redoubtable an opponent if he had been fully aware of the strength which lay behind the first Junius letter, but Draper plunged all unwitting against " a writer who signs himself *Junius*," and brought on himself a castigation of which, perhaps, the hardest part was the contemptuous lenity with which he was handled.

Nevertheless, to have fought four rounds with *Junius*, and though worsted to have received commendation, albeit of a somewhat scornful kind from the victor, was sufficient to place him in a position of a certain eminence in literary circles, and there can be no question that long before his appointment as Murray's subordinate his head was fairly turned by his various claims to importance and his " blushing ribband," which *Junius* described as " the perpetual ornament of your person." Could it be expected that such a star qualified in fact, and doubly qualified in his own estimation, to form the central body in a solar system, could consent for long to follow the controlled orbit of a mere planet. At all events, as the course of this story will show, the inevitable collision occurred, and if it resulted in the destruction of the planet, the ruling body did not escape serious injury. Draper, be it noted, held the same military rank of lieut.-general as Murray, though he was junior in that rank by some five years. In age they were practically equal. For the moment all went well. Murray welcomed his new colleague. He was never the man to forejudge his subordinates, but his own imperious nature would exact and be satisfied with nothing short of obedience.

The year 1780 did not bring the long expected attack. The French and Spanish, now acting in concert,* were contented with a blockade; but Murray, writing to Mr. William Green,† in May, mentions that the Spaniards were building 48 vessels at Majorca, each to carry 250 men, and that a large force was assembling at Barcelona. " We cannot conceive these vessels can be for any other purpose than the invasion of this island." A little later (July 9) he gave an opinion which reads curiously to-day :

" Both French and Spaniards have abandon'd us, (as) we have done the Mediterranean, all parties judging that Gibraltar and Minorca may be conquered in America. To say truth, when the insignificant trade we enjoy in this part of the world is considered, our two mighty fortresses seem calculated more for pomp and ostentation than utility. The parade of them is a prodigious expense, and I wonder in all the proposals for economy it has not been hinted to abandon both."

There is another letter of this period which I must quote as laying further emphasis on the almost exaggerated strictness with which the Governor adhered to the standard of purity he had laid down. It concerned a certain Doctor Olivar, a Minorquin, who had apparently, on payment of the usual fees, been appointed by General Mostyn to a position known as the Rectorship of Port Mahon. Murray had formed a bad opinion of the man, and positively refused to confirm the appointment. Writing to the agent and secretary for Minorca in England, he says :

* A formal declaration of war on the part of Spain was handed to Lord Weymouth by the Marquis d'Almodovar on June 16, 1779.
† Who had married Miss Jane Collier.

" I am impatient to know why the appointment to the Rectorship of Mahon has not arrived, and when I know, I hope I shall find the delay has not proceeded from any intrigues of Doctor Olivar. I repeat to you, once more, that I never will have any intercourse with that man, and that I cannot conceive what you did mean by saying that it would be better for both if I recommended him to the vacant living. As you and I are likely to have much business together, it is necessary that you shall think I am a plain honest man, totally unacquainted with the intrigues of the offices in London, and entirely incapable of conniving at anything which can have the smallest semblance of chicane. I cannot distinguish between a fee and a bribe, nor can I undertake the defence of any man unless I am convinced he is in the right.*

Another letter, addressed quaintly to " The Honourable George Murray,† Uncle to the Duke of Athol, Captain in His Majesty's Navy, at Messrs. Drummonds, Bankers, Charing Cross, London," gives us an insight into the writer's state of mind as well as some views on naval matters :

" We have just received the accounts of Rodney's fight.‡ It is not a pleasing one ; we must get such men as you in our line of battleships, that our admirals may not give more praise to the enemy's captains than our own. . . . If the accounts we have from France are true, Clinton will not succeed in Carolina. If he is baffled we shall hardly recover America. Everything here is as you left it. We thought we were certainly to be attacked, or at least invested, till very lately. They have given up all thought of it at present. To say truth, I imagine they do not think us worth the blood and treasure the conquest of this island would cost them. . . . The insolence and disregard of the Moores, since our fleets have abandoned the Mediterranean,

* Letter to Mr. Henry Sayer, who had married Miss Sarah Collier.
  † Second son of Lord George Murray who was " out " in both the '15 and the '45, and died in exile in 1766.
  ‡ Rodney's action against a French fleet under the Count de Guichen, off Martinique, is referred to. This was accounted a victory, but from another letter of Murray's it would appear that the behaviour of some of the captains led to its being less complete than it might have been.

is not to be wondered at. It is now plain they like the French better than us. . . . I find myself very happy to have Sir William Draper's company, but I shall be happier to give up the command to him when the times will allow me with decency to kiss your hands in London, but when that will be God only knows ; at present it looks as if I may broil here four or five years more, if I can hold out so long. You know I never repine at being at my post, be it where it will. I confess, however, I wish in these hustling times to have a more active one, for I have recovered my health wonderfully. . . . You cannot think how I amuse myself sometimes by building castles in the air. I very often in these reveries have you at Beauport. Happy ! happy ! shall I be to chat over all our adventures in reality in that pleasant retreat. It may happen sooner than appearances promise at present ; one lucky blow in the West Indies will give us peace, for I judge the enemy finds the expense of the war as intolerable as we do."

The correspondence includes letters to his old opponent, the Marquis de Levis, to whom he writes in affectionate language, and, illustrative of the easy-going customs of the day, asks for a passport through France if he should obtain leave to go to England.

" The heat of this climate and a wore-out constitution will make it necessary for me to leave the command to my lieut.-governor, Sir William Draper. Nothing but the idea of being attacked could have kept me here this summer."

Several letters are addressed to a brother Scot, the gallant George Elliot, then engaged at Gibraltar, in withstanding a blockade in very similar conditions to that at Minorca. Elliot, however, was more fortunate than Murray in being twice provisioned by incoming fleets, which also brought reinforcements to his garrison. In Murray's case the months rolled on without any alleviation of the situation, and Fort St. Phillips was not a delectable spot in which to be inclosed. It is no wonder that he sighed occasionally for his pleasant retreat at Beauport, or for some activity on the part of the enemy which would break the present monotony. To Elliot he afforded all the assistance in his power, both as to provisions and in intelligence of the enemy movements.

The year 1781 opened with no early prospect of any activity on the part of the French or Spanish, but the number of England's enemies was increased by the participation of the Dutch in the war, brought about by that extremely delicate question, the right of neutrals to handle trade of benefit to the enemy. In July Murray wrote: "A rumour says the Spanish have raised the siege of Gibraltar, and next month we are to expect 8000. I fear it is too good news to be true."

Some small reinforcements, a few Corsicans, were landed—on one occasion fifteen men, on another thirty-four. Among them was a nephew of the famous General Paoli, and it was stated that many more of his compatriots were anxious to offer their services to England against the French, whom they still regarded as the common enemy. It is a curious reflection that among these recruits Napoleon Buonaparte might conceivably have found a place. Friendship had long existed between Paoli and Carlo Buonaparte, and the latter, supported and even urged by his wife, Maria Letizia, had warmly supported the cause of Corsican liberty, until, believing the struggle to be useless, he had recognised the French ascendency and carried his sons to France for their education. In those days boys began their soldiering earlier than is the fashion now, and Napoleon Buonaparte, unhappy recluse at the military school at Brienne, jested at by his companions, because he knew but little of the French language, nicknamed *Paille-au-Nez*, because he pronounced his name Napoleoni, might well have joined his friend, the younger Paoli, in his expedition to join Murray, had he been a little older—perhaps twelve years of age—even with a character so remarkable as his, was rather young to take so decisive a step!

On August 19 all doubt was at last set at rest, and a Spanish army landed on the island. The landing was practically unopposed. The small garrison was quite insufficient to hold an extensive coastline, and in point of fact the Spanish commander, the Duc de Crillon, having already an overwhelming force of 8000 men and no naval attack to dread, divided his landing operations into several sections, and simultaneously disembarked in the bays of Biniancollar and Alcansar to the west and La Merquida to the east. Both forces could then advance on the town of Mahon, which they occupied at once, thus isolating Fort St. Phillips on the land side.

As was usual with him, Murray's fighting spirit was rising at the prospect of activity. He was at his best when, depending on himself, he faced an enemy. Victory, no doubt, meant as much to him as to most men, but far more than victory, honour for his country and an unsullied reputation for himself were the high pinnacles of his striving, and I believe if he gained these all else mattered little. At Fort St. Phillips he could hardly in his inmost heart have hoped for escape. Naval assistance, which alone could save him, was unlikely to be forthcoming, and he had little faith in ministers who gave freely of fair words with little of strong action. He was now about to commence the last act of his military career, and to end it in " a blaze of glory," as Mr. Lord says in his book.* Probably Murray had never heard of Schiller, then beginning to emerge into light, but his views were certainly those of the poet, " Of all life's joys, the highest is fame."

Before closing this chapter, it is necessary to record two important events which occurred in Murray's private affairs during this period. The first was the death of his brother Patrick, Lord Elibank, which took place at Ballencrief on August 2, 1778. George Murray, now become sixth Lord Elibank, announced the fact. The late baron disposed of a large part of his property among his illegitimate children, but James Murray was generously dealt with, with a bequest which amounted to £15,000, debts due to the late lord to that amount being cancelled. This money evidently represented the sums advanced for

* *The Last Possessions of England*, by Walter Frewin Lord.

purchase of the properties in Canada.   In a letter on the subject to the family solicitor he says :

" I cannot express how much I think myself obliged to you for your attention to me in transmitting to me the last settlement of my poor brother Elibank.   He certainly was a very great man, and did honour to the age he lived in.   I have personally no reason to find fault with the settlement of his effects, but as his memory must be ever dear to me, I wish he had left me nothing, and showed more attention to my brother George ; may I say, likewise, that I wish George and my other relations had paid more attention to him.   You know how much they used to teaze and torment him, which behaviour of theirs . . . turned the overflowings of his warm heart into an un-natural channel to the great loss of his legitimate heirs. I have done all I can to make the present lord some repara-tion by settling £15,000 upon his two daughters.   This is about the sum I actually owed to the late lord, including the interest, and really I have no use for it, being richer than I ever expected to be, and in a way to increase my fortune.   May I entreat you, my dear sir, to get from amongst my late lord's papers the original title deeds to my estates in America.   They, with mortgages he had upon my estates, were deposited with him, and I know he carried them with him to Scotland,"

Murray's generosity, indeed, went further, for he gave orders to purchase for the " title " the whole of books, plate, and pictures, which under some perverted influence his brother had willed away.

The second event referred to was his second marriage, the lady being Miss Ann Whitham.   This event took place at Minorca on June 1, 1780.   The bride was not yet nineteen, and there was, therefore, a considerable disparity of age ! Her father, Abraham Whitham, member of an old English family, held an official position on the island in the Consular service.   A brother, also Abraham, was serving at Gibraltar, as an officer of the artillery, who afterwards greatly dis-tinguished himself during the famous sortie on November 27, 1781, as aide-de-camp to the Governor.   From this marriage a daughter was born before the siege of Fort St. Phillips commenced, on March 16, 1781. The name chosen for the newcomer was Cordelia, presumably after Cordelia Collier, his first wife, which perhaps showed a degree of complaisance on the part of the new Mrs. Murray! On August 19, the day of the landing of the Spanish army, Mrs. Murray, with her infant, was sent off to Leghorn in a small vessel. They reached their destination after an adventurous voyage, eluding the enemy ships. At Leghorn she remained awaiting the events of the siege.

CHAPTER XVIII

THE DEFENCE OF FORT ST. PHILLIPS

THE closing scene of Murray's active service was approaching. The long expected attack on the fortress, which for the past three years had been constantly expected and even eagerly desired, was now about to take place. The fortress of St. Phillips stood on the southern side of the harbour of Port Mahon, accounted one of the best harbours in the Western Mediterranean. The town of Mahon was about four miles distant, and higher up the deep waterway which constituted the harbour.

Across the harbour, opposite to the castle, was Cape Mola, with its signal tower, and the small fort of Philipet, guarding the entrance to the cove of the name ; scattered along the harbour-way were the islets known as Quarantine Island, Bloody Island, the Naval Hospital, Round Island, and others. To the south, within range, a line of low hills covered with short bushes obscured the view. The rocky nature of all the foreshore, cut by water action into steep scarps and ravines known as barankas, and indented by a number of coves or small bays, gave an unpleasing aspect to the scene, while the lack of trees and the stony nature of the country made it almost unendurably hot in the summer months. The outermost or seaward defence was a small semi-detached work known as Fort Charles, and from this, stretching along the harbour, ran a long line of defences, surrounding the central keep, known as St. Phillips Castle.

Unfortunately Murray's garrison was far short of the complement he had stated to be necessary, and what is worse, the men had been kept for over long in the unhealthy confinement of the fortress and were already weakened by disease. The enemy strength, on the other hand, was from the first overwhelming ; the allied commanders were determined to leave nothing to chance, and evidently had a wholesome respect for the prowess of the defenders.

The spirit in which the two commanders entered on active hostilities was almost an exaggeration of chivalry, which might have served as the theme for a new Cervantes. De Crillon relates that when inspecting his troops Murray's gunners had narrowly missed hitting him, and Murray in reply was

" extremely sorry for the behaviour of our artillery officers ; they protest they had no intention to point the guns at the Duc de Crillon . . . the thing happened when I was at breakfast. I soon perceived by your attendants and the running footmen that it must be your Excellency, and I was unhappy. I perceive your Excellency was not mounted as well as you would wish to be, and therefore take the liberty to beg you to accept of a mare I had from Grand Cairo, which I know to be of the first breed in Egypt."

De Crillon, in reply, accepts the present with gratitude : " *Mais point du tout l'attention de ne point tirer sur moi . . . je vous estime trop pour ne pas vous traiter en ennemy tant que la guerre durera j'espère que vous me ferrey le même honneur.*" Such communications and others of a like nature convey a strange picture of war as we know it ; but " the world went very well then," and one can hardly avoid thinking that the civilisation of the twentieth century has not improved the culture of the race.

Although Murray had advised Lord Hillsborough that a small fleet of six ships of the line would suffice to relieve his garrison and effect the destruction of De Crillon's host, it is very evident that there was no intention of sending any help. What remained of the English naval power was, indeed, fully occupied ; but it would have been more honest to say so at once, instead of uttering vague promises of succour as was the case. Murray soon found that Minorca was left to its fate.

It was during this period, when the Spanish commander, urged on the one hand to effect something decisive which would enable his Court to commence peace negotiations with something in hand, and on the other finding the fighting qualities of his soldiers unequal to the emergency, that he made the attempt to bribe the Governor to hand over the fortress. If this story of James Murray's career has realised its object, the indignation and horror which such a proposal would excite in him can be imagined. I have endeavoured to picture his character as almost supersaturated with notions of military and personal honour, and here was a proposal repugnant to both in the highest degree. The age in which he lived was one in which bribery and corruption was winked at, and one might almost say connived at, by sanction of the highest officers of State. Placemen, and the sale of official posts, out of which the purchaser was openly allowed to profit, had tainted the whole community, and it was the more to Murray's credit that he was prepared to quarrel with his nearest friend, or to dismiss any subordinate, if he suspected practices not in accordance with his ultra strict ideas of propriety.

It was in October (1781) that De Crillon made the attempt, which, if he had known his man better, he would have refused to carry out. The incident has been often quoted, but Murray's reply was of so lofty a nature that I must be forgiven for giving some detail of it. It appears that on September 18 a certain Mr. John La Rivière, who was Murray's confidential clerk, was sent under a parlementaire to take some payments to the officers' ladies left in the town of Mahon. The Duc de Crillon sent for this man, and telling him that he knew him to be poor, he would make his fortune.

" I replied," says Mr. La Rivière, " that those who had informed him of my finances had not been mistaken, but at the same time they had omitted to acquaint him I was born and brought up with the principles of an honest man, from which I never would deviate.''

La Rivière returned to the fortress, but did not report the matter of the bribe, fearing that vengeance might be taken on his family which was living at Mahon. Nothing further happened until October, when on the 15th of that month Captain George Don, adjutant-general of the garrison, was sent by Murray with a letter to De Crillon. Captain Don relates :

" On my arrival at Mahon I was conducted by the Count de Crillon to the Duke's private apartment. A little after the Count had retired the Duke locked the doors of the room and asked me if Mr. La Rivière had communicated anything particular to me or my General. . . . My answer was in the negative regarding myself, and that I did not believe he had acquainted General Murray of anything extraordinary. The Duke said he had only thrown out general hints to that gentleman of what he would hereafter communicate to me. . . . I then told the Duke that he need not be under the smallest uneasiness about anything which he had communicated to Mr. La Rivière, as I knew him to be a young man of great honour and integrity. . . . The Duke then said, I perceive, Sir, by General Murray's letter, that you are his relation, and I understand you are his confidant, I shall therefore openly declare to you that I am authorised to treat with General Murray. If you choose it, Sir, I will show you the minister's letter ; in short, your General may have what sum he pleases and one million at first. I then interrupted him, and told him it was unnecessary to proceed further on that subject, and that both the minister and him were egregiously deceived in the character of General Murray. His Grace said he was charged with the negotiation of this affair, that he was confidently informed that General Murray had a strong party against him at Court, that he was ill-treated by some people at home, and that he might expect soon to be relieved (of his command ?). I told him, on the contrary, tho' he might have some enemies, I believed he was very well at Court, and imagined his Grace to be misinformed. The Duke said that the fiscal, Don

Peter Surtas, had been intercepted and the paper he was charged with seized, by which great discoveries were made. He said that our nation was undone, that it was impossible for any succours to be sent to us, as he was informed by the minister that the combined fleet, double the force of ours, had orders to give battle to any British fleet which might attempt getting into the Mediterranean. He said that peace would not be made till Fort St. Phillips was taken, and assured me, tho' he had but twenty battering cannon, he should soon have 180, a great army and the best miners in Europe, and that the place would certainly be warmly attacked, that it would be humane to save the effusion of blood, that General Murray had already acquired enough glory and a great reputation in arms, that there were modes of giving up places honourably . . . and that it was a pity to sacrifice so many brave men. I told him that whatever might be the event, it was the duty of a soldier to submit to his fate ; that I knew there was not any place impregnable, and that he might ruin our works with a numerous train of artillery ; yet I was sure our defence would be such as would always entitle us to an honourable capitulation, but not to flatter himself with the hopes of obtaining the place by any other means, and that a siege was what General Murray ardently wished. The Duke said that if I thought the negotiation would not succeed I need not mention the affair to General Murray. I begged to be excused, and said it was my duty to lay his proposition before General Murray, and to communicate to him every word which had passed betwixt his Grace and me, which I assured him I would accordingly do. . . . The Duke hinted that there were some private transactions carried on when St. Phillips Castle was taken by the French in '56, and that Admiral Byng had not deserved so cruel a fate. . . . The above I communicated to General Murray on my return from Mahon."

Murray was not an even-tempered man, and his wrath had been felt by many delinquents who had aroused it ; but whatever explosion may have been caused by this communication, it did not prevent his sending a reply on the following day, which for measured, haughty, reproof could hardly have been excelled.

" Monsieur, Lorsqu'il fût proposé à votre brave ancêtre par son souverain d'assassiner le Duc de Guise, il rendit la résponse que vous auriez dû faire quand le Roi d'Espagne vous chargea d'assassiner le caractère d'un homme dont la naissance est aussi illustre que la vôtre, ou celle du Duc de Guise.*

" Je ne puis à l'avenir avoir d'autre communication avec vous qu'avec les Armes.

" Si vous avez de l'humanité, envoyez les hardes de vos pitoyable prisoniers.   Laissez les à une certaine distance, ou ils seront ramassées par mes gens parceque d'or en avant je ne permettrai point le moindre contact avec vous, hormis ceux d'une hostilité dans le degré le plus invétéré."

That the Duke was an unwilling actor in the affair is probable, at least his reply possessed a certain dignity.

" Monsieur, votre lettre nous remete chacun à notre place, elle me confirme dans l'estime que j'ai toujours eu pour vous."
" J'accepte avec plaisir votre dernière proposition."

This correspondence was immediately laid before the King, and Lord Hillsborough, under date November 5, writes :

" The spirited contempt with which you have received the offer and unworthy attempt of the enemy upon your fidelity and character is a strong confirmation of your title to that reputation of zeal for the King's service which you have always enjoyed, and the manner of your rejecting the mean and degrading offer is much applauded and admired."

---

* This reply must be considered as extraordinarily apt. Possibly this story of De Crillon's ancestor was better known then than now, at all events, I searched many contemporary accounts of the assassination of the Duc de Guise without finding it.   In the *Biographie Universelle* (Paris, 1813) an account of it is given.   Louis, Comte de Crillon, was a noted soldier, " L'homme sans peur," " le Brave des braves."   When Henri III. plotted the removal of his too powerful subject, he applied to De Crillon to be the instrument, and offered him the Sword of Constable of France as a reward. Crillon replied : " Sire, la preuve, que me donne votre Majesté, que ma conduite, jusqu'à ce jour irréprochable, n'a pu me gagner son estime, m'engage à me retirer dans ma famille ; je ne flétrirai point son nom par une infamie . . . permettez que j'aille rougir, loin de la cour, d'avoir entendu mon roi . . . me demander le sacrifice de ma gloire."

Throughout October and November the siege continued with little that was remarkable. Deserters reported the arrival of 6000 French troops, and that the Spanish forces were now not less than 10,000. An overwhelming force to encompass so small a garrison, and one that Murray felt it did him honour to confront! No less than seventeen separate batteries had been constructed, some of them mounting 15 guns—in all 168 guns, besides several mortar batteries. The whole place was practically surrounded by artillery, and the determination to capture the fortress was obvious, even if the means employed seemed excessive.

It was on December 28, the siege then having lasted four and a half months, that the first note of disaster occurred.

"Everybody," wrote the Governor, "is alert and in spirits, but unfortunately the scurvy has made its appearance. The experience I have so often had in the course of my service of its dreadful effects alarms me, when I consider that one-half the troops has lived eleven years on salt provisions, the other half not less than six."

It is probable that one cause of the appearance of this terrible disease was the unwholesome life in the subterranean casemates of the fortress. These defences formed a feature of the place, and were hewn out of the rock, but they were both damp and doubtless saturated with germs of disease. Yet for the most part, when not on duty, the garrison appears to have occupied them, probably because they were sheltered from the enemy's shot and shell.

Reference must now be made to an occurrence which was to have a marked effect on this story, namely, the unfortunate differences which arose between Murray and Sir William Draper, the lieut.-governor of Minorca. There is nothing to show what caused this trouble. In several of his letters Murray expresses himself as happy to have Draper's assistance, and I do not find any indication that my hero was given to any display of superiority that would justly have annoyed a man of Draper's distinguished record. On the contrary, there are many indications that

2 D

Murray had in a considerable degree the habit of introspection and a frank estimation of his faults. As an instance I may quote from a letter written at this period to the Secretary of State :

" His Majesty may depend upon my caution and circumspection, and that those who formerly blamed me for being deficient in these necessary endowments will find that altho' the fire still burns it is moderated by old age and the experience of forty-five years' service."

He certainly had a warm, frank admiration of Draper as a soldier, and describing himself as having " carried arms from his youth and as not educated for any of the learned professions," he felt the superiority of a man of whom *Junius* had written : " You are a scholar, Sir William, and, if I am truly informed, you write Latin with almost as much purity as English."

It is remarkable that Draper took his first step a few days after the incident of the Duc de Crillon's attempt to buy Murray's fidelity. So far as I can gather, it was taken without any warning and without the victim being even aware of it. Whether it was merely a coincidence cannot be certainly said, but Draper's action, taken at the time when proposals were being made to win the fortress by unfair means, certainly played into the hands of the enemy and weakened the hands of the Governor very considerably. The action referred to was the following letter to Lord Holderness, dated October 29, 1781 :

" My Lord, I am sorry to be obliged to inform you that I think Lieut.-General Murray in his capacity as a magistrate has acted so very ill that I hold it incumbent upon me to bring him to trial for the same, and I must beg the favour of you to inform His Majesty therewith." *

The curious thing about this letter is that it seems to have no connection with the charges subsequently raised by Draper. It seems vaguely to hint at civil misdoings,

* Public Records Office, C.O. 174/14.

and it seems astonishing that a subordinate should consider himself entitled to forward so indefinite a statement concerning his superior, or that he should dream of putting a document of this kind unsupported by a shred of evidence before a former Secretary of State with any hope of effecting his desire. There seem to be only two possible explanations, the one that Draper's excessive vanity had literally turned his head, or that De Crillon's offer had been extended to the Lieut.-Governor with more success than it met with in the case of the Governor. As a matter of fact, this letter did not reach London until January 27, 1782, and it appears to have ended then and there. At the time it was written the records show that Murray entertained no suspicion of Draper. He had been placed in command of the outward defences of the fortress, and Murray's correspondence with him, preserved in the Record Office, shows a most friendly disposition. A long memorandum addressed to Draper, and written at the end of September, gave the Governor's views on the possible methods of attack and the best defence in various circumstances.

The first recorded note of the quarrel appears in a letter dated October 4 :

"Sir William Draper presents his respects to the Governor, and begs the favour to be informed what his *Definition* of the *Outline* is. Sir William Draper thought it comprehended the outworks in general ; on that supposition, as he was charged with their defence, he imagined some traverses in the covered way necessary for that purpose. He finds they are forbid, therefore desires to know the extent of his command. . . ."

It is not possible to express an opinion on the question of the necessity for the works in question, or whether in countermanding them Murray had given unnecessary offence to his touchy subordinate. But the matter was certainly trifling, and it argues a very complete absence of the sense of subordination, that Draper should presume to cavil at instructions issued by his commander. Murray, in his reply, was firm, but courteous :

" Lieut.-General Murray presents his respects to Sir William Draper. . . . Lieut.-General Murray will for ever think himself obliged to Sir William Draper for his exertions. He would be happy now to be assisted with his advice, as would the chief engineer, but 'tis uncommon for a Governor to have works carry on when he is present on the spot, without his knowledge. . . ."

This view of the case can only be considered correct and moderate, and I think it is clear that Draper assumed an attitude of complete independence, which even a milder man than Murray would hardly have accepted.

A month later (November 11) a message was sent by Captain George Don, asking the reason certain changes were made in the guards without the knowledge of the Governor. From Don's written statement it appears that when he had delivered part of the message, Sir William stopped him,

" and said he was deprived of all command . . . which was such an affront shown him that he would insist on a general court martial to decide who was in the right or wrong in regard to that as well as other things. That a General upon the staff and in his situation here to be obliged to apply for permisson to fire a gun was a thing unheard of and extremely insulting to him. . . ."

Murray replied on the following day (November 12):

" It gave me infinite concern to receive the enclosed to a message I had the honour to send you yesterday. I am conscious I have never done anything to give you offence. I told you before I would do all in my power to please you, but that of divesting myself of the command which His Majesty has been pleased to confer on me. I gave you a very large share of it, and for the sake of peace and harmony, which should subsist in the garrison, I did and would have continued to wink at the contempt and neglect you have shown by your never reporting to me the changes you have made and the occurrences which have happened in the department confided to your charge as Lieut.-Governor. I judge the orders of the 15th of last month to be both proper and necessary, and therefore cannot retreat from them.   At present it is necessary to know if it is your pleasure to act as the Lieut.-Governor of this garrison, because if you will not I must make other arrangements."

In reply to this Draper stated that he owed too much to the public and his own character to decline acting in his post, and there the matter rested for a short time.   It is obvious that the tension was great, and the ill-effects of such division between the leaders must have had serious results on the well-being of the defence.

Early in January, 1782, it became necessary, in order to strengthen some of the defences, to abandon others, and Murray, choosing what was known as the inner covered way and the Marlborough battery, decided to withdraw the men from them.   This decision produced a fresh out- burst of insubordination from Draper, who declared :

" I should never have thought myself equal to the defence of the out line, unless I had flattered myself with a certainty of support from the inner.   That support being withdrawn, I confess myself unequal to the task and by no means responsible."

Murray replied : " I wish to avoid all altercation with you at present.   I, and I alone, am responsible to my King and my country for the defence of this place."   He then detailed his reasons for the action ordered, and adds :

" In short, I will not, with so pitiful a handful of worn- out men, undertake the defence of the inner covered way, and give the enemy the opportunity or rather the certainty of entering upon the place pell-mell.   To attempt this would be having a short siege indeed.   I mean it shall be a long one, which will do honour to the troops and the officers commanding them.   Every attempt to take the command of the garrison from me will be ineffectual.   If you, Sir, decline the part of the defence I have assigned you, I shall appoint another."

Draper, in his reply on the January 16, demanded a council of war, failing which he declined to act any longer in his capacity as Lieut.-Governor.   The harassed Governor probably welcomed this final act of insubordination, as getting rid of his troublesome enemy within the gates, and promptly appointed Colonel Pringle of the 51st and Colonel Linsing of the Hanoverians to divide the command of the outer line.   To Draper he wrote :

" As you decline the execution of the command I assigned to you, and will not obey your Governor, it is better for the service that you should be taken at your word ; such an example of disrespect and contempt of a Governor is inexcusable at all times.   In the present state of affairs here I think it cannot be justified. . . . As to personal abuse, I shall do justice to myself you may be assured when the time arrives."

In this state of affairs the Governor considered it desirable, as a measure of evidence, to obtain the written views of the senior officers, and the question was put whether the inner covered way should be defended or not. The reply, dated January 18, given was, " The state of the garrison is such that we apprehend it could make but a feeble resistance in manning the whole internal covered way ; " but a rider was added that an armistice should be asked for, and that if succour should not arrive within a month capitulation should follow.   Murray's reply to this evidence of faint-heartedness among his leaders betrayed a spirit of which we may be proud.   Let us remember that he was one facing a crowd of men ready to give in— men whom he strongly suspected of having yielded to the arguments of the mutinous Lieut.-Governor.   That he was worn out with constant work himself and worried by the recalcitrance of one who should have been his principal support.

" Brother officers," he wrote, " with great attention I have examined the paper in answer to what I had the honor to propose and lay before you.

" Your answer takes in a latitude I never meant to give you, that of the prudential measures for entering into terms of capitulation with the enemy.   The state of the siege can by no means, in my opinion, admit of that. Our only course is how to prolong our defence. It was on that point and that point alone I consulted you. The idea of capitulation to me seems a very distant one indeed. . . . It is mortifying that the experience I have had in the service has so little weight. The reputation I have acquired in it will not admit of my consent to propose any terms to the enemy for the surrender of the place till we are wore to the last extremity. I have promised so to His Majesty; I told his ministers we looked upon ourselves as a forlorn hope, who would glory in doing our utmost for the honor of our master's arms. To think of any reinforcements from England would be chimerical. All we have to be solicitous about is our own glory. . . . Believe me, I mean to be prudent but intrepid. Some confidence I expected would have been put in me; but as it is the opinion of the principal officers of the garrison (that we should treat with the enemy), for without their confidence I can expect little from the troops, I can only demand their obedience in the execution of my orders, which in the most solemn manner I do. If it is not to be granted I am no longer Governor, I resign the command to the Lieut.-Governor, who is a better officer, I sincerely believe, than I am; I am sure he is a better politician, so there may be no demur or uproar on the subject."

This appeal shows a gallant spirit, and at the same time the bitterness of the situation into which Draper had forced him. The Governor was ready to cast all question of precedence to the winds, so long only that the defence be continued. It is a pleasure to record that the officers' reply shows them touched by the attitude of the commander.

"We beg leave to assure your Excellency, notwithstanding our unanimous opinion is not so happy as to meet your Excellency's approval, that we are perfectly satisfied and at all times determined to obey your Excellency's views."

The mutiny, for it was scarcely less, was ended, but Murray, who had strong suspicions of the origin, placed the following on record:

" George Don, Captain 51st Regiment, swears : That the Governor went to Colonel Pringle's quarters in the Caroline Lunette and asked to see a paper wrote by Sir William Draper, which the colonel had had. I did not see the paper, but from conversation I gather it contained Sir William Draper's ideas of the then situation, and that he, Sir William Draper, was of opinion that propositions ought to be made to the Duc de Crillon, desiring a cessation of hostilities for a certain period of time, and that in case of no succours arriving, to capitulate. The paper was wrote on or about the 14th inst."

In the sequel, Colonel Pringle was directed to obtain Sir William Draper's assent to handing the paper to the Governor, but Draper objected to this course and withdrew it. There was enough, however, to show pretty clearly that Sir William Draper, not content with open contempt of the Governor's position, had attempted to form a combination among the officers with the object of forcing a capitulation. Here for the present we will quit an unpleasant subject, but when, after Murray's return from Minorca, he had to undergo trial on charges brought by General Draper, one can only be astonished that the prisoner before the Court was not Draper himself, rather than the man whom he had done everything in his power to injure and to thwart.

It is unnecessary to detain the reader much longer with the affairs of the siege of Fort St. Phillips. The enemy's artillery, formidable as it was, was not destined to prove a determining cause of the capture of the fortress. During January the sickness amongst the troops increased rapidly and alarmingly, and several cases of what was described as a " putrid fever "—no doubt typhus—occurred amongst the numerous cases of scurvy. The terrible debility accompanying the latter disease dominated the spirits of the garrison. On February 1 the Physician-General, Dr. George Monro, reported :

" From the extraordinary increase of the sick in the garrison, and the little progress we make in reducing the evil, we judge it necessary, both on account of the public service as well as our own credit, to inform your Excellency that the prevailing disease, the scurvy, amongst the troops is got to such an alarming height as seems to us to admit of no remedy in our present situation. Every means has been tried to palliate this formidable malady; but the daily, and we may say hourly, falling down of men baffles our endeavours. . . . We are sorry to add that it does not appear to us that any one now in hospital will be able to do the smallest duty under present circumstances, where no vegetable food is to be had, or free air."

The number of men doing duty in the four regiments was reduced to 766, which shows that nearly half the infantry force available on January 1 (1502 men) had been taken into hospital during the month. Of the men fit for duty on February 1, 106 were carried to hospital in the first three days of February, leaving only 660 soldiers available. Of this remnant 560 were reported to be scorbutic, evidencing symptoms of the oncoming of the disease. The surgeons reported that these last-mentioned men " will in all probability be in a few days incapable of performing any duty." The garrison had practically ceased to exist in one month since the disease first showed itself, so rapid had been the spread of the complaint.

In view of this disastrous state of affairs, the Governor assembled another council on Sunday, February 3, at which he addressed the members as follows :

" Brother officers, the candour and openness with which I have conducted myself with regard to you, makes it impossible for you to reproach me, or for me to reproach myself in any respect.

" Sixteen days ago, when you thought it necessary to advise a suspension of arms from the Duc de Crillon for a time, till succours might arrive from Britain, my experience dictated to me that time was in our own possession. For sure I am, that had we men we have nothing to apprehend from any attempt of the enemy.

" Sixteen days ago, when the ravages of the scurvy had not taken place. Now the desertion of one man may alter the case, for this day we have only 741 men of the four regiments, 389 sailors, 95 of the Royal Artillery, now doing duty, of which 600 are scorbutic.*

" It now only remains for me to apologise for not concurring in your first opinion, of immediately treating with the Duc de Crillon, agreeable to your first opinion given to me unasked.†

" In the first place, I am to observe to you that although I expected no succours from England, I thought we had the means of making a glorious defence for our numbers. That the asking for a suspension of arms was a poor artifice easily seen through by the most ignorant enemy, and if granted was only a matter of parade calculated to amuse the shallow politicians of St. James' coffee-houses. . . . I abhor ostentation as much as I detest regulating my actions with the view only of pleasing the English populace. Thank God, I am above such low artifices. . . .

" That the officers almost to a man are determined to obey their commander and depend on his prudence and experience, I have had assurance from the mouths of most of them. That the soldiers are animated by the same sentiments is evident to every man. Rather than yield and succumb under their present malady they consent to be lifted up to go on sentry ; and, having performed that office, are found dead in their beds when called upon to take it again in turn.

" All this calamity, brother officers, has rushed upon us since January 18. The question now is whether or not we should capitulate directly. The parade of a suspension of arms appears to me idle. An immediate remedy for the relief of our most brave, distressed soldiers, is what we should obtain."

Details of the medical opinion here followed. The council unanimously concurred that capitulation was the only course remaining to be pursued.

It is superfluous to refer to what must have been Murray's feelings when submitting this last proposal to his brother officers. He was himself affected by the prevailing epidemic, and no doubt the fact lent additional

---

* The figures are somewhat different to those quoted, and were based on an earlier return.

† An apology seems to have been unnecessary, as the new conditions had altered the case.

difficulty to bearing with equanimity so shattering a blow
to all his high hopes of a gloriously continued defence, but
a word regarding the heroism of the men will not be out of
place. The private soldiers of those days differed in very
many respects from their descendants of to-day. In
general they were men enlisted for long service, and the
regiment was their home and their pride. There are
countless instances of the collective gallantry of battalions
in those days, and it is not too much to say that that
subtle camaraderie, which we know as *esprit de corps*, had
its birth during these wars of which we have been treating.
Under the old system the battalions were known by the
names of the colonel commanding, and he had wider
powers and a more intimate connection with the well-
being of his men than is now the case, when every detail
is drawn up in regulations beyond which the commander
dare not go. Of comfort for the men there was little;
they lived hugger-mugger in horrible surroundings; married
men and their wives and children in the same barracks
with the unmarried, with little or no privacy; but the age
was not one when comfort, as we know it, had penetrated
to the lower classes, and the private soldier found, in his
military surroundings, what was almost luxury compared
to what he left. When an officer was appointed to the
staff he was technically taken into the "family" of his
commander, and this term describes the general feeling.
The men were rough and uneducated, but they looked up
with respect to officers, who were also gentlemen, and for
the most part they were so. A commanding officer who
saw to it that the men had the best of what was to be had
was fairly worshipped, and his soldiers would do anything
for him. Murray was such an one, and he had achieved
that greatest mark of popularity which the rank and file
could bestow—an affectionate nickname. We have all
heard of the "Petit Caporal," and what that name nerved
the French soldier to do a few years later; to his men at
this time Murray was "Old Minorca," and they relied on
him to see them through, whatever happened. Perhaps

we may smile at Old Minorca, his reiteration of the " Glory of His Majesty's arms," and his superlative notions of the pre-eminence of things military; but there is something enviable and admirable in a commander for whom his rough soldiers will do and dare to the end. If Murray's character rested on nothing else, I think this picture of soldiers enduring the distressing symptoms of scurvy, suffering themselves " to be lifted up to go on sentry, and when having performed that office are found dead in their beds when called upon to take it again in turn," would suffice to indicate that he was a man with a hero's heart. But if we draw such a conclusion of the commander, what praise is too much to give to the heroism of the men ? They, at least, had little or nothing to gain from endurance ; for it was not the custom to do anything for the soldier " broken in the wars." In the opening of this story I have told of the fortitude of the men who faced the disasters of the Carthagena campaign, later on I have told you how the starved, frozen, sickly garrison of Quebec kept the flag flying, on neither of these occasions did the British soldier show a greater spirit than that which filled the garrison of Fort St. Phillips.

On Monday, February 4 (1782), the Governor sent his proposals for capitulation to the Spanish General. He wrote:

"SIR,—As the succours I expected from England have not come, and to save blood of brave men on both sides, humanity bids me not obstinately to persist in defending a place which in the long run must yield to the superiority of your force. At the same time national honour, and my own feelings, dictate to me the necessity of expiring with our arms in our hands, unless the articles of capitulation, which I have the honour to enclose to you, are granted by your Excellency."

The " Articles " included : " That the garrison be allowed the honors of war, to march out with drums beating, shouldered arms, colours flying, twenty-four rounds per man, matches lighted. Four cannons and two mortars with twenty-four rounds for each piece."

The granting of these terms would have meant that the garrison was free to rejoin the army in England or elsewhere, and it is not surprising that the Duc de Crillon, who knew the desperate condition of the troops, should have seen through the bluff contained in Murray's letter. The orders of his Court, he replied, prevented his accepting any terms but that the garrison should yield themselves prisoners of war !   On the same day, at ten o'clock at night, the inevitable result followed, and fresh articles were sent out, in which the one already quoted was changed :

" As his Excellency, the Duc de Crillon, by the express orders of his Sovereign, cannot receive the garrison but as prisoners of war, his Excellency, the Honble. Lieut.-General James Murray, consents to surrender the garrison agreeable to the Duc de Crillon's instructions from his Court, but he expects the Duc de Crillon will allow the garrison to march out with all the honours of war he has required in the second article of those sent to the Duc de Crillon, which is by no means incompatible with his Excellency's instructions, and will tend more to his glory, for certainly no troops ever gave greater proof of heroism than did this poor worn-out garrison of St. Phillips Castle, who have defended themselves almost to the last man."

To this the Duke replied :

" The garrison shall be prisoners of war, but in consideration of the constancy and valour which General Murray and his men have shown in their brave defence, they shall be permitted to go out with their arms shouldered, drums beating, lighted matches, and colours flying, till having marched thro' the midst of the army they shall lay down their arms and colours."

To this was added that the other conditions, chiefly in regard to transport of the troops, were accepted :

" For the courage and firmness of his Excellency M. de Murray add further to the esteem that I have already for him, and that which the Spaniards and the French together with all Europe accord to the valour of the English nation and of the Hanoverians."

We can close this distressing scene by quoting Murray's despatch to the Earl of Hillsborough, which he sent home by the hand of his adjutant-general, Captain George Don, dated Minorca, February 16, 1782:

"My Lord, I have the honour to acquaint your Lordship that Fort St. Phillips was surrendered to His Catholic Majesty the 5th instant. The capitulation accompanies this. I flatter myself all Europe will agree the brave garrison showed uncommon heroism and that thirst for glory which has ever distinguished the troops of my royal master. Our necessary guards required 415 men the night before the capitulation ; the whole number able to carry arms amounted to 660 only. Of course there were none for picquet, and a defect of 170 to relieve the guards, as is evident by the return. The most inveterate scurvy which I believe has ever infected mortals reduced us to this situation. The reports of the faculty fully explain the dreadful havoc it made, and that three days' further obstinacy on my part must have inevitably destroyed the brave remains of this garrison, as they declare there was no remedy for the men in hospital but vegetables, and that of the 660 able to do duty, 560 were actually tainted with scurvy, and in all likelihood would be in hospital in four days' time. Such was the uncommon spirit of the King's soldiers that they concealed their disorders and inability rather than go into the hospitals ; several men died on guard after having stood sentry ; their fate was not discovered till called upon for the relief when it came to their turn to mount again. Perhaps a more noble, or a more tragical scene, was never exhibited than that of the march of the garrison of St. Phillips through the Spanish and French armies. It consisted of no more than 600 old decrepit soldiers, 200 seamen, 120 of the Royal Artillery, 20 Corsicans and 25 Greeks, Turks, Moors, Jews, etc. The two armies were drawn up in two lines, the battalions facing each other, forming a way for us to march through ; they consisted of 14,000 men, and reached from the Glacis to George Town, where our battalions laid down their arms, declaring they had surrendered them to God alone, having the consolation the victors could not plume themselves in taking a hospital. . . ."

CHAPTER XIX

THE REWARD OF CONSTANCY

Murray remained long enough at Minorca to complete the arrangements for embarking the remains of his garrison to England, and to see that every possible care was given to the large number of invalids. He sent his adjutant, Captain Don, direct to England with his despatches, and the other officers were permitted to return on parole not to serve again during the war. By Don he sent the following letter * to Lord Hillsborough, which explains the situation which had arisen very completely :

Minorca, Feb. 16, 1782.

" Private. To be laid before His Majesty if Lord Hillsborough shall think proper.

" My Lord, I judge it was better not to mention in my public letters a word of the unhappy differences betwixt Sir William Draper and me. They commenced the moment the enemy invested the place, and at last he refused to act as lieut.-governor, because I would not consent to call a council of war. . . .

" After Sir William resigned, or rather refused to act, I ordered the field officers of the garrison to meet and give me their advice how to defend the fort. In place of that they to a man declared it impossible to resist longer, and advised to require a cessation of arms from the besiegers for a month, and then to capitulate if no succours arrived to us from England—an idea which appeared to me absurd and malicious. . . . All this will appear evident to your Lordship by the authentic papers which I will have the

* The quotation from the letter only includes the points of importance.

honor to present to you. . . . Although great honor must result to me from a publication of the facts, I am far from wishing it, if the least inconveniency to His Majesty or any of his servants should proceed from it.''

It is unfortunate that he did not himself make all speed to get to England. Probably he did not foresee the power which the malignancy of Draper could exercise, and it was but natural that his first thoughts were towards his wife and a desire to see his newly-born son and heir, who had arrived on the scene on January 25.

In his own interests it is certain that no family question should have detained him. He did not arrive in England until the beginning of June, and the time was little propitious to his affairs. Much mischief had already been done by the start given to Sir William Draper, and the very causes which militated against Murray favoured the other. The Government of Great Britain was again in confusion. The Ministry of Lord North had but recently fallen, and that of the Marquis of Rockingham which followed was unstable. The Marquis himself was dying, and the dissensions of the principal officers of State was soon to lead to fresh changes. In the Rockingham Ministry Lord Shelburne had a leading position, and, of course, his *fidus Achates*, Colonel Barré, had a place.* The views and consideration which might have obtained under the advice of Lord North were likely to be much less favourable under Shelburne, and it is more than probable that Barré would do nothing to lessen the scandal of Draper's attack. Apart from this, the long-drawn negotiations over the terms of peace with the revolted colonies were in full progress, and the disasters of the war had even served to throw into the background the whole question of Minorca. The feelings of the nation were numbed by reverses, and if the loss of Minorca had caused a shock, it was but an additional wrench to nerves already so torn as to be scarcely capable of further feeling.

* At first as Vice-Treasurer of the Navy, subsequently as Paymaster-General.

Probably the first inkling of the state of affairs was conveyed in a letter from Captain Don, dated London, March 24, 1782:

" I arrived here the 19th inst. at six o'clock in the evening, and immediately delivered your despatches and the private letter to Lord Hillsborough.* He read them in my presence and expressed his entire approbation of the contents. . . . I went to the levee. His Majesty inquired particularly about your health, wished it might soon be perfectly re-established, and seemed desirous to see you in England. . . . The dispute between you and Sir William is a good deal talked of. In general he is greatly condemned and looked upon as a madman, yet I can perceive he has some friends. Last night a total change of the Ministry was announced. The Rockingham party comes in. The Marquis in place of Lord North; Shelburne and Fox, Secretaries of State; Burke, First Lord of Trade; Conway, Commander-in-Chief; Barré, Secretary at War.† The Greys have been vacant for some time. . . . it is said his Majesty intends to give you the regiment as a distinguished mark of his approbation of your conduct. . . ."

On the April 10 Captain Don reported further :—

" Sir William Draper has had an audience with the King. He has done his utmost to prepossess His Majesty against you, and daily endeavours to injure your character and reputation as an officer; but both, thank God, are established on too firm a basis to be shook by his infamous stories, with which he tries to fill the ears of ignorant people of this country. All he says and does tends to his own ruin and destruction, which his friends foresee. . . ."

On receipt of the first of these letters, Murray wrote to the Secretary at War (Thomas Townshend), dated Leghorn, April 22, 1782:

" I am informed letters have been wrote by Sir William Draper arraigning my conduct in the defence of Fort St.

---

* When Murray wrote his despatches Hillsborough was still a Secretary of State in Lord North's administration ; by the time they arrived Lord Hillsborough was out.
† This was not correct, *see* above.

Phillips, and that his accusations are talked of to ruin my reputation.

" His Majesty is too just to allow the character of an old faithful servant to be hurt by whispers of his enemies. I do, therefore, in the most humble manner, throw myself at the King's feet, to beg that a public inquiry may be made into the conduct of his Governor and Lieut.-Governor during the late siege of Fort St. Phillips, that not only His Majesty, but all the world may judge whether or not my behaviour and proceedings on that occasion are liable to any degree of censure."

Enclosing a copy of this letter to the Commander-in-Chief, General Conway, he said :

" My friends tell me His Majesty means to confer the command of the Greys on me, but that letters from Sir William Draper arraigning my conduct occasions a delay of that intended honour. Certainly the delay is very just and proper. Of course nothing can be more reasonable than my desire to have a most rigid and most public scrutiny made into my conduct.

" No honour or emolument which the King and my country can bestow can make up for the uneasiness I feel while there is the least shadow of doubt regarding my reputation, either as a soldier or a citizen. I therefore flatter myself General Conway will promote my wishes to procure the inquiry I apply for through the Secretary of War, which, I presume, is the proper channel. . . ."

Conway replied, dated May 11 :—

" . . . I have at the same time the pleasure to inform you that the cause of His Majesty disposing of the Greys, which had been some time kept open, as, I understand, in the idea of their being offered to you on your return, was now disposed of from no prejudice in His Majesty's mind arising from anything personal to you, or any idea of disapprobation, but from the long and as he foresaw necessary delay."

Captain Don wrote on the same date that :

" General Conway commanded me to acquaint you that His Majesty still entertained the highest and most favourable opinion of you, and that after inquiry he would most certainly bestow on you the great honour which your conduct justly deserved."

These letters indicate that if he had returned to England direct from Minorca and put the case in person before the King the course of events would have been very different. His Majesty was evidently well disposed towards him, and it is impossible to suppose that he would have permitted the evident malice of a subordinate to bring discredit on a gallant commander, had that commander been present to state his case.   In his absence, the publicity given to the statements of Draper, whose literary ability and journalistic fame gave him an immense advantage over Murray, probably left the King no choice but to bring the matter to trial.

We live in happier days, and it would be difficult to suppose that a subordinate officer, who had been relieved of his post during active service for refusing to carry out his orders, would have the power under King George V. to bring his commander to trial.   At all events, whether the commander were tried or not, it is pretty certain the subordinate would be tried first.   Under King George III. this did not take place.   There seemed to be no disposition to bring Draper to trial, and perhaps Murray had no course open to him but to press for a public examination of the statements published broadcast by Draper.   Murray maintained silence, preferring, as he said, to suffer the attacks of his enemy rather than publish matter which might be inconvenient to the Ministry.

On arrival in England he addressed the Commander-in-Chief from Beauport, dated June 11, 1782.

" When I arrived here, two days ago, I had the honour to receive your Excellency's letters of May 11 and 29.* I am perfectly sensible the only favour my royal master can grant me at present is a public trial and investigation

* Conway's letter of May 29 conveyed the positive orders of the King : " That you do on no account think of calling on him (Draper) personally for anything that has passed."

of my conduct by a general court martial. His Majesty's justice assured me of obtaining that, which is the only thing I wished for.

" The zeal I profess for the service of my country, the obedience I owe the King, and the regard I have for my own honour and reputation, must stifle the resentment I severely feel, until the world is convinced and can determine who has been faulty. If I shall be proved in that predicament I must be unworthy of receiving any commands from His Majesty or living in a country I have dishonoured."

To Lord Mansfield he expressed himself from a more public point of view :

" My royal master's affairs have suffered much from the disagreements and caprice of his admirals and generals. I judge it high time to correct such abuses. Minorca, the beginning of the last war, occasioned the reformation of the British admirals ; it may now be productive of that of its generals. If Sir William Draper and I are to blame, we both should suffer, and be made examples of, to deter others from forming factions and intrigues, the prevailing spirit of the times, so destructive to the welfare and honour of our country."

Murray's expressed desire for a court martial was granted, but owing to various delays, the trial did not take place until November (1782), commencing on the 12th of that month and continuing with various adjournments until January 20, 1783. The cause was something of a *cause célèbre*, and attracted much public attention. The loss of Minorca had stirred the popular imagination, and the gallant unaided struggle had brought the defenders prominently to notice, while at the same time it had lent powerful incentive to the opponents of the late Government. The tragedy of Admiral Byng was still a recent memory, and the gossips and scandalmongers of the coffee-houses laid wagers that the Minorca trial of 1782 would bring the same excitements as had followed its loss in 1756.

General Sir George Howard, K.B., was President of the court, and among the members, most of whom were distinguished officers, was the name of General Thomas Gage, and to have this old enemy sitting in judgment upon him must have added a drop to Murray's bitter cup. The general charge, formulated at the instance of Sir William Draper, was :

"Having antecedent to the siege but after certain notice of the preparation making by the enemy for the purpose—as also during the siege and subsequent thereto —been guilty of flagrant misbehaviour in the exercise of his command, as well as of culpable neglect, particularised in full instances."

The particularised instances comprised in all twenty-nine items, of all degrees of importance, from having permitted officers to reside outside the fortress before the siege, and making a road between the fortress and the town of Mahon, to orders published to the troops, which in the opinion of the accuser, tended to " cool the zeal and ardour of the garrison." Of these charges Draper attempted to withdraw several, but Murray insisted on everything remaining on the sheet and declared his strong desire that every item should be fully examined. The proceedings of the court are contained in a bulky volume (War Office Records 71–100 in the Public Record Office) of 600 or 700 pages. It is unnecessary to do more than very briefly summarise the result.

It was not until December 9 that the prosecution completed the evidence tendered, and General Murray was called upon to make his defence. He was much broken, and had hardly recovered from the fatigues and ill-health of his late experiences. It is recorded by the court that " by reason of his voice being feeble " his defence was read by the judge advocate-general. This moving statement, which he had prepared himself, was a long document, of which a few extracts must suffice to indicate its character.

" Sir George Howard, and the other general officers on the court martial ! I am brought a prisoner before you after forty-three years' service in various stations, under all the different climates where His Majesty's arms have been employed in the extensive operations which will fill the page of history during that period, without ever having been the author or the object of any military dishonour, nor the prosecutor of any officer to a public trial, much less a prisoner myself at the bar of justice.

" As it is not my wish to conceal or perplex anything, it is my desire to have every accusation sifted to the bottom. It was this motive that induced me to apply for a court martial to decide on my conduct. Some of my friends have thought I did wrong in pressing such a decision : it certainly is not a situation wantonly to be courted. For although I have made no complaints that no assistance was sent to me during so long a siege ; and although I have endeavoured to avoid every imputation of blame upon others, and to confine the justification of my own conduct to the best disposition of the means put in my power, yet I hope the peculiar circumstances attending my garrison in this respect will never be forgotten, for their honour and my own, by those who consider the final catastrophe.

" In a scene so trying, with a feeble garrison, a defective fortification, and little hope of relief when attacked by the combined forces of such powerful enemies, I must consider it as a very unfortunate circumstance, notwithstanding the little regard I can now possess for General Sir William Draper, that a man of his rank, station, and reputation for abilities saw all my actions through a medium which appears from the charges he has exhibited, I will show from a previous report I made to the King that I acted in all things from deliberate resolves drawn from my conception of the fortification and the probable attack and the best mode of defence which could be adopted under the circumstances in which we stood.

" That the Duc de Crillon did attempt acquiring possession of the fortress I commanded by corrupt means is known to all the world, as well as the answer I made him at the moment while I proclaimed the disgraceful proposal. I claim no merit from this behaviour. I hope the meanest soldier in my garrison would have equally rejected such an ignominious offer ; but I beg, while I claim no merit from such conduct, that it may not subject me to any malicious insinuations. . . .

" I might, indeed, justly complain of Sir William Draper for endeavouring to prejudice the public opinion against me by a number of charges which he had not even professed or attempted to establish in proof. . . .

" If in such a complaint of a public accuser there are any, much more if there are many, charges evidently dictated by malice or gross prejudice; if there be found a number of articles which he must have certainly known from the beginning to have been incapable of the slightest support from evidence, which could therefore be introduced for no other reason than to prejudice my defence, and which he himself seeks even to abandon and retract, the presumption in the minds of just and sagacious judges is that the same temper pervades the whole accusation, and thus the innocence of the accused derives support from the injustice of the accuser. . . .

" One of the heaviest charges against me, and which has made the greatest impression on the public, is giving out in public orders on the 8th day of January last (being the third day of the siege) that ' the enemy's battering train was such as had never been brought against any place of the first magnitude since the invention of gunpowder, and that the garrison of Fort St. Phillips had little or no dependence upon its artillery,' which orders tended to augment the terror of the enemy's attack and to cool the zeal and ardour of the artillerymen of the garrison, and from the date of which order the fire from the place became almost extinct in the day time, and the enemy redoubled their efforts.

" Now, is it possible for any man to read the entire original order and pervert the plain and obvious meaning of it to such an accusation as is stated above, or to believe that a man could suppose that this order should have the effect of dispiriting the corps of artillery as described in the charge. . . . I do not pique myself on being an elegant writer. I have carried arms from my youth, and was not educated for any of the learned professions, neither did I ever study the words of any military order with the view of parade. I wish at all times to make my meaning intelligible, and I can only declare to this court that I never was more unfortunate in conveying my sentiments or less understood, if my words contained in that order can bear the interpretation which my accuser has put on them, for my intention was to rouse the vigilance of the garrison and to dissipate some little alarm which the opening of so unusual a train of artillery against us had occasioned. . . .

" The fortress of St. Phillips was besieged in the last war. The garrison then consisted of 3252 men, of which 2951 were regular troops. The army of the Duc de Richelieu was 14,000 men. The place was taken in 72 days, after an effort was made to relieve it, and the Governor was made a peer.

" My garrison consisted of 2692 men, of which number only 2016 were regular troops, including 400 invalids from England in 1775. The army under the Duc de Crillon was 16,000, and from the time of his landing to the time of my surrender was 171 days.

" I had no relief sent to my assistance; my unfortunate worn-out soldiers suffered every hardship incident to the want of vegetables and to foul air.

" I suffered many of these calamities in common with the rest, and did not surrender my garrison until all the principal officers of the fort were unanimous in their opinion that no further effective defence could possibly be made, and in reward I am a prisoner before this court loaded with imputations of the foulest and blackest kind, drawn up by a man who seems to have been harbouring malice against me from the year 1780, and couched in language the most opprobrious and reproachful to a soldier. . . ."

After this address Murray proceeded to examine each charge. I shall only notice three of them :

" Giving out in public orders on January 8 that the enemy's battering train was such as had never before been brought against any place of the first magnitude since the invention of gunpowder. . . . Tending to cool the zeal and ardour of the garrison."

In reply to this charge the whole original order was submitted to the court, and the effrontery of trumping up a charge on the extract is so apparent that one marvels that the accuser was not then and there tried himself. The whole order ran thus :

" The Governor is highly pleased with the alacrity and zeal which has hitherto been shown by the artillery in their profession. He desires they will accept his hearty thanks. It is true the defences have been hurt by the superiority of such a battering train as was never before brought against any place of the first magnitude since the invention of powder, but the garrison may be assured that the defence of Fort St. Phillips has little or no dependence on its artillery. That branch has already done more than he expected. It is certain that at least 1000 men of the besieging army suffered before its batteries were opened. When our well-timed and well-served fire upon them, while they were exposed so much in opening their batteries, is considered, great havock must have been made. Our artillery is still vigorous, our mines, subterraneous and underground defences, with our outline and glacis, are inaccessible ; it is by a vigorous defence of them we are to get the glory the world expects from us. They cannot be disappointed by so brave a garrison. . . ."

These words may not have been so clear or so elegant as the scholarly Draper would have chosen. As General Murray stated to the court, he had served from his boyhood, he had little opportunity of learning to turn nice phrases ; but the intention cannot be mistaken, and the scandal of permitting his subordinate to bring the charge referred to can hardly be forgiven.

The judgment of the court on this article was " not guilty," and they added a rider :

" The court think it incumbent on them to remark that this article of charge contains a partial quotation from the order in question, the whole whereof, although injudiciously worded in the part alluded to, collectively taken bears a very different construction."

The eighth article of charge ran thus :—

" Giving out an order, dated October 15, 1781, ' No gun or piece of ordnance is hereafter to be fired in daylight without orders of the commanding officer of artillery, who can upon the smallest notice communicate with the Governor, who is ever watchful ' ; which order greatly tended to invite and facilitate the enemy's approach, and numerous opportunities of obstructing their movements were thereby lost."

The instant comment of a modern soldier on such an order would be that if the commander considered it necessary to issue it, it was certainly not for a subordinate to find fault. I imagine very similar orders were not uncommon during the early days of the struggle on the Aisne in our own Great War.* General Murray explained that " the young officers wasted rounds on insignificant objects, and finding remonstrance ineffectual he issued the order," and he had no difficulty in showing that the rate of expenditure of gunpowder gave serious cause for alarm that a shortage would ensue before the critical state of the siege arrived. The real trouble arose from the fact that Draper considered himself insulted by having his authority in this respect subordinated to that of an artillery officer of junior rank. Strangely, as it seems to me, the court adopted this view ! " The court are of opinion that Lieut.-General Murray is guilty, although it does not appear to the court that the order was issued with any intention of inviting the enemy's approach."

The only other charge I intend to mention is one of " exacting large sums on auctions held in the prize court of the vice-admiral, notwithstanding that he had agreed to take a fixed allowance in lieu of all perquisites." It appears that the rule formerly in vogue was that the officials of the Vice-Admiralty Court were entitled to a perquisite of $2\frac{1}{2}$ per cent. on the value of the sale of prizes captured from the enemy. Murray considered this rule oppressive, and in the particular circumstances likely to give rise to ill-practices, and altered it to one of public auctions, in which the auctioneers' fees should be reduced to $1\frac{1}{2}$ per cent. Some correspondence had taken place on the subject between the secretaries of the Governors of

* I remember that a precisely similar order was issued to the officers of the Naval Brigade during the siege of Ladysmith. Gun ammunition was not plentiful, and permission had to be sought by telephone before a round could be fired.

Minorca and Gibraltar, and the evidence showed that Murray had been told that, at the latter place, the fees were at the disposal of the vice-admiral. It appears that he did not trouble himself much about the matter, but permitted some person, whom he refused to name, to draw one-half of the fee, the auctioneer retaining the other half. In doing so he stated :

" I imitated the Governor of Gibraltar, who is on the same footing with the Governor of Minorca with regard to having a fixed salary. . . . The court, after what I have candidly said and avowed, are to judge whether or not this half of the auctioneers' fees was not a fair and ostensible perquisite of the Vice-Admiral of Minorca and Gibraltar. If I had not thought it such I certainly would not have claimed it. I do not think it proper to say just how I disposed of it. It is sufficient to assure the court I did not put it in my own pocket."

Perhaps it may have caused some sense of shame to Draper when Murray declared that he had communicated this matter to him, as there was a proposal for him to succeed to the governorship, and he (Murray) did not wish him to lose. The whole affair was trivial, but the court saw fit to adjudge the Governor as guilty. I have little doubt that to the man who had refused to take up the post of Governor, so long as it depended for emoluments on perquisites, and who had written to Lord Rochfort of " His Majesty's assurance that my salary should be fixed independent of such disgraceful emoluments," such a decision was bitter. The very order on which the court relied, which ran, " The revenue arising from monopolies of shops, canteens, corn, oil, tobacco, fines, etc., which formerly composed part of the emoluments of our commandants at Minorca, be abolished," had been published by Government at the instance of Murray himself !

On the remaining charges the court declared the accused to be not guilty ; and a general summary stated :

" Upon the whole it appears to the court, from the evidence, that Lieut.-General Murray did conduct himself with great zeal, courage, and firmness in the defence of Fort St. Phillips, that the place was not half garrisoned, had no prospect of relief, and was not given up till it became, from the enfeebled state of the garrison, no longer tenable, also that several of the articles of charge which have been preferred against Lieut.-General Murray are frivolous and ill-founded."

In addition to the direct charges, Sir William Draper had preferred four others of a personal nature, in which he claimed that he had been " offended." From the court he got very little satisfaction, but out of them arose a secondary question which became important. Murray was alleged to have accused the lieut.-governor of trying to take the command into his own hands, Draper had replied that such an allegation was " false and infamous," and to this the Governor had replied that " he would do justice to himself, he (Draper) might be assured, when the proper time arrives." The court scented the probability that a duel was intended, and there is not the least doubt that the irascible Governor was looking forward to meeting his subordinate on the " green at twelve paces." Such a *dénoûment* was apparently highly scandalous to the court martial, though why they should all through have had so much regard for Draper's safety is not apparent. His conduct had been unsoldierly to a degree, and he should certainly have been tried himself, and if Murray had succeeded in putting the contents of a pistol into him it was no more than he deserved. In the event, however, in placing the proceedings of the court martial before the King, His Majesty's attention was drawn to the offensive words, and the court suggested that of his royal authority an injunction should be issued " to prevent the most serious consequences between the parties."

The King's award on the court's finding was announced by the judge advocate-general. He declared the

" Royal approbation of the opinion of the court martial *upon every point*, but that in consideration as well of the zeal, courage, and firmness with which Lieut.-General

Murray appears to the court to have conducted himself in the defence of Fort St. Phillips, as of his former long and approved services, His Majesty had been graciously pleased to dispense with any other reprimand in respect of the misdemeanours whereof he has in two instances been found guilty, than that which the sentence of the court martial itself virtually conveys. And that His Majesty had at the same time expressed *much concern* than an officer of Sir William Draper's rank and distinguished conduct should suffer his judgment to be so far perverted by any sense of personal grievance as to view the general conduct of his superior officer in an unfavourable light, and in consequence to exhibit several charges which the court martial, after a diligent investigation, have deemed to be frivolous or ill-founded."

The court was further instructed to take such steps as they considered adequate to compose the personal question between the parties.

Sir William Draper at once declared his willingness to make the apology which the court prescribed, and to comply with their injunction to its full extent. It seems, indeed, obvious that he was being treated with a leniency which almost inferred partiality. With Murray the case was far different. The court first decided that Draper had not " sustained any grievance," and then called upon his commander to " express concern," in other words, to apologise for using words that hurt his feelings ! This was more than our stout Scot could *thole*. He replied to the court that he was ready to abide by the injunction of the court with respect to the matter not having any further consequence, " *so long as he continued a soldier*," at the same time " remonstrating against and objecting to that part of the declaration . . . which is expressive of concern that he should have made use of any words which could have hurt Sir William Draper's feelings " ; and on explanation being demanded " he plainly intimated he should not hold himself bound to such compliance beyond that period (of being a soldier), and that he trusted he should not be compelled to serve during life."

Here was a deadlock ! The court offered conciliatory arguments, and recommended the outraged General to retire and consult with his friends.

" After some time elapsed, Lieut.-General Murray returning, declared that he still retained the same sentiments, and that he might not be misunderstood, had committed the same to writing, which he read to the following effect : ' In all private concerns I conceive I am master of my own actions, and I choose to keep my honour under my own preservation. In every military point I am under the orders of the King, whose commands are sacred. If Sir William Draper has been guilty of any military offence the department to which it belongs will do justice to this country, as to what respects me privately I seek for no interference.' "

I hardly think any one can read this reply without a thrill of approval at the attitude taken by this gallant old gentleman. Let us remember that he was broken in health and worn by what was a shameful attack on his reputation ; but though he could not control the judgment of the court or of a Sovereign who valued so lightly the services which he had rendered, he was adamant when the placing of his personal honour in pawn was in question. The court was non-plussed, and remanded Murray in close arrest to communicate the position to the King. The result was that His Majesty, who, perhaps, appreciated the difficulty, sent by Sir Charles Gould a positive order to Murray, that he should comply with the injunction to refrain from violence towards Draper, and to this he felt forced to submit.

" His orders it is as much my inclination as it has ever been my ardent desire immediately to comply with, I therefore in obedience to His Majesty do not hesitate to give my solemn and explicit assurance that the matter in difference between Lieut.-General Sir William Draper and myself shall not have any adverse consequences originating from me . . . "

But to the further point of apologising to Draper he could not yield. He wrote to the King :

" Your memoralist finds himself truly miserable that he cannot prevail upon himself to express in the words prescribed to him by the court martial the reply to Sir William Draper's apology to him.   That being conscious he never did say or write a word which was meant to hurt the feelings of Sir William Draper, to declare to the world that he did, would be loading himself with the blame of having originated the unhappy difference . . . which was so unbecoming and might have been so hurtful to His Majesty's service. . . .

" That if it is necessary that he should make some declaration before the court martial, he will most cheerfully make the following one : ' I do in deference to the sense of the court martial accept this acknowledgment as a sufficient and full apology for the words used by Sir William Draper in his letter to me, and I think it very unfortunate if any words of mine should so much hurt the feelings of Sir William Draper, who I never did mean to offend while he was under my command at Minorca as I have often declared both in public and in private.' "

This form of words was accepted by the King.   On February 8, 1783, the court having by this time been constituted for nearly three months, it was formally tendered by General Murray, who was then released from arrest and the court dissolved.

I turn from this closing incident of Murray's military career with indignation at the gross injustice meted out to him.   Blakeney, who, bedridden and senile, had nominally defended Minorca in 1756, during a resistance which might well have led to inquiry, was created a peer ; Amherst, whose successes in Canada had resulted far more from Murray's exertions than his own, was a peer and had several high offices ; Carleton, who had tried to fasten envenomed shafts in Murray's reputation in Canada, had been forced to follow his policy, and, in fact, owed much of his success and his subsequent peerage to the solid foundation built by his predecessor ; Keppel, who had been tried three years previously by court martial, like Murray, at the instance of a subordinate, was acquitted, the charges against him pronounced *malicious and ill-founded.* He received the thanks of both Houses of Parliament, was subsequently made a peer, and his accuser brought to trial.

Murray, who more than any one leader, had aided in adding a great dominion to the empire, who had added glory to the King's arms by a defence which obtained honour and respect from abroad ; against whom charges were brought by a subordinate which were pronounced *frivolous and ill-founded ;* whose accuser escaped anything but a mild censure, while the accused received neither reward nor honour. Rather, indeed, he had received reprimand on a petty charge, which, to a man who had scornfully refused a fortune in return for the betrayal of his trust, and whose whole life had been evidence of a standard of lofty altruism and official integrity, must have been singularly galling. It happened to him, as it has happened to others, that men rose to place and power through his courage and ability, while he who had done much was left without recognition.

I cannot forbear recalling the story of his ancestor,* recorded in an early chapter of this history, who was brought to trial at the instance of a malicious enemy, and who " taking impatiently that his fidelity, whereof he had given so great proof, should be called in question, did contract a deep melancholy . . . and so after a few days departed this life." The analogy is almost complete, for though James Murray did not " depart this life," there is no doubt that the consciousness of injustice affected his remaining years. One wonders if King George III. did, like King James VI. of Scotland, " Sore forethink that he should have given ear to such dilations."

I am afraid not, for His Majesty did not possess the wisdom of the " wisest fool in Christendom," though, if a predilection for favourites and an exaggerated idea of prerogative are sufficient basis for comparison, the two were not unlike.

* Sir Gideon Murray.

CHAPTER XX

CONCLUSION

So far as events of historical importance or of public interest are concerned, I have done. What remains to be recorded relates only to Murray's private life, when, after the episode related in the last chapter, he retired to his Sussex estate, there to reflect on the inconstancy of princes and the unwisdom of those that put trust in them. The King did not easily forgive what he deemed obstinacy on the part of a subject, who had refused to accept the royal advice in a matter which concerned his honour, and, without friends at Court to support his cause, and no inclination to push it himself, the gallant defence of Minorca and the insult that followed by way of reward were soon forgotten. On February 19, 1783, Murray was promoted to the rank of full General. This could scarcely be called a recognition of his services, for it was merely a promotion, following the custom of the time, of a batch of lieut.-generals of the same date of rank, of whom he was one, but at least it served as an indication that the court martial had not found him wanting. His ambition to command the Scots Greys was never fulfilled. The King had promised it, but when two years later the regiment became vacant it was given to Lieut.-General James Johnston. At the same time Murray was appointed Governor of Hull—one of those military governorships which at the time were numerous, and served as rewards for officers of meritorious service, without necessitating residence or any very active duties. Possibly this appointment

instead of the Greys was made with his concurrence ; *
there is nothing to show, but in 1789 he obtained his desire
to command a Scots regiment by being transferred to the
21st, then known as the Royal North British Fuzileers,
now the Royal Scots Fusiliers, a famous regiment which
had borne an honourable share in all the battles of Marlborough's campaigns and many that followed.

It is recorded of Lord Shelburne, when at about this
period he was forced from office, that he found himself
"immersed in idle business, intoxicated with liberty and
happy in his family." In very similar mood Murray wrote
to his friend Dr. Mabane in Quebec :

"I, at the age of sixty-six, enjoy perfect health and
happiness, truly contented with my lot of independent
mutton. I enjoy the comfortable reflection that I have
ever zealously acquitted myself a faithful friend to my
country and its Sovereign. Having laid aside every
ambitious view, and as great a farmer as ever, I never
think of St. James', and am only anxious for the prosperity
of my two delightful children and the cultivation and
increase of my fields and garden, all which objects are due
to my heart's content."

Truly, I think, this unconscious picture of a mind
undisturbed by a life, which had had a big share of stirring
events, is a tribute to a loftiness of character which requires
no better illustration.

On Beauport he expanded all his care and energy. To
increase the beauty of that already beautiful home became
to him a sufficient aim, which served to obliterate the disappointments of the past. From here he could revel in
vistas of wide land and sea-scapes—the Bay of Rye, the
Romney Marshes, Dungeness Point ; on a fine clear day
Cape Grisnez and the high ground surrounding Boulogne ;

* I think that the probable course of events was that this General
Johnston, who was the same General whom Murray succeeded as
Lieut.-Governor of Minorca, was given the command of the
Greys in agreement with Murray, the latter then ceasing to pay
him the £300 a year that had been arranged when the exchange of
governorships took place.

THE MANSION HOUSE OF BEAUPORT.

From an architect's design found among General Murray's papers.

westwards the coast-line as far as Beachy Head could be traced, with the long ridges of the South Downs; northward the horizon is bounded by that high upland known as the backbone of Kent, and, traditionally, occasional views as far off as Sevenoaks—a place for an artist to rejoice in, and, in fact, J. W. M. Turner in later years spent much time in the neighbourhood, and has left sketches of Battle Abbey, Ashburnham Place, Crowhurst Place, and also one called "Beauport, near Bexhill," though certainly Turner's "Beauport" is not the Beauport of reality. The house itself he greatly enlarged. In this pleasant home Murray spent the remaining twelve years of his life, and here his many friends enjoyed his hospitality and talked over stirring times or discussed the prospect of the farms, for the owner of Beauport was always a keen farmer. Here several children were born to him, and altogether there were six children of the second marriage, of whom four survived him, the last having been born in 1793, when Murray was nearly seventy-four years old. It is interesting to note that among the visitors to Beauport, but after James Murray's time, was Isaac Disraeli, accompanied by his famous son Benjamin, Lord Beaconsfield. Sixty years later, meeting the present owner of Beauport, he remembered these visits at once, saying, "I used to visit the house with my father. It had a very pretty garden and a splendid view of the channel towards Dover."

Besides Beauport, he was Lord of the Manor of Ore, and the property of Ore Place was in his possession; but I believe he had only a life interest in it, through the first Mrs. Murray. In this old house he had resided in former years while Beauport was being rebuilt, and he retained a lasting affection for it. Tradition has it that the Manor House was built by John of Gaunt, and it may be that Murray's feelings towards it were prompted by his own descent from that old-time hero, whose record of battles and sieges would be sure to inspire his admiration. It was in the old church of Ore that he erected the family vault, and here he himself was buried.

In the New World, too, Murray had considerable possessions. The record is not very clear, but he certainly possessed a large estate situated on the shores of Lake Champlain, which he purchased in 1764 from M. François Foucault.

The other principal property was the estate of Lauzon or Point Levis, purchased from a M. Cherast in 1765. This would be a valuable property to-day, extending for six leagues along the St. Lawrence, and including the parishes of St. Joseph, St. Henry, St. Nicholas, and part of St. Charles, that is to say, the area from the old landing place at Point Levis up to and including the parish of St. Nicholas, which lies opposite St. Augustin beyond Cap Rouge. This is now a well-populated area, with many important mills, dockyards, and factories, and would be a princely possession; but in Murray's time the annual value of the property amounted to no more than £358 13s., and out of this had to be deducted " all expenses attending collection of rents and the wear and tear of the mills."

There appear to have been other properties in Canada, but the record on this head is very obscure. By his will, dated September 6, 1793, he left these properties to his son James Patrick Murray, who was born at Leghorn on January 25, 1782, subject to a life interest in Beauport to his wife, and a charge of £5000 each to his three surviving daughters, the executors having power to raise any defect of these sums by mortgage on the American estates, the widow to receive an allowance of £400 a year besides an allowance for each child. There are, unfortunately, no details available in the will or elsewhere as to the property, and practically no information as to why or when it was sold; but the probability is that the executors, of whom there were three—his two nephews, Sir James Murray and William Young, being two of them—were obliged to sell the lands in order to provide the daughters' portions.

James Murray died at Beauport on June 18, 1794, in his seventy-fifth year, and was buried, in accordance with his desire, in the old church at Ore. In the foregoing chapters I have endeavoured faithfully to portray the achievements and character of one who was a maker of history at a time when the foundations of the British empire were being laid. If I have been successful I have given the impression of a man who was generous to an extraordinary degree, even perhaps to an extent which savoured a little of ostentation. He undertook, with a readiness which rather outran his means, the education of his nephews and provision for relatives not well endowed. It was customary for men of his position to affect a magnificence which many could not afford, and he was certainly no whit behind them. It cannot be denied that he was autocratic and hot-tempered—he quarrelled with many; but if he found himself in the wrong he made the best amends he could think of, and it must be admitted that in the majority of cases the enemies he made were of persons of little worth, with whom his ultra strict notions of honour permitted no friendship. With those of his opponents in war, who proved themselves worthy, he was on terms of friendship when circumstances permitted. For De Levis, for instance, whom he regarded as *preux chevalier*, he had the greatest regard and frequently corresponded with him. For Vaudreuil, on the other hand, he expressed the bitterest contempt as of a man who had betrayed his trust. Of political acumen I have given proof that he possessed a singular gift; but as a politician, that is, one capable of securing his desires by opportunism, he was defective—he was too blunt and downright, too honest, in fact, to please minds accustomed to reach their goal by roundabout methods. Thus he often failed to secure a successful issue where he had pointed the way, and others of less merit secured the applause and the honours which were his due. He lived in a corrupt age, and one which, according to our standard, was immoral. When he sent his brother George's natural son to Amherst, the latter had replied : " I shall be very glad to see Mr. Patrick Murray, and do anything for him that you desire, and if you will send me one or two of your own I will convince you what a regard I have to Marshal Saxe's scheme ! " Yet in all the papers I have been through there is nothing to show that he had occasion to take advantage of Amherst's offer. He had, however, been elected a Knight of the Ancient Order of the Beggar's Benison,* a society of wits whose foundation was on much the same lines as the famous club at Medmenham Abbey, and whose morals were on about that level. He lived long enough to see an immense improvement in public life, the reform of parliamentary representation, and the abolition of that worst form of misgovernment, the sale of offices to the highest bidder. In this great reform, Lord Shelburne, to his honour, led the way, but before he had enunciated his principles Murray had, so far as his opportunities admitted, taken action in the practical application of them.

There was a certain genius, almost of eccentricity, in all the children of Alexander Lord Elibank and his wife, Elizabeth Stirling, and none showed it more than the eldest, Patrick, Lord Elibank, of whom even Dr. Johnson could speak with admiration, and James, the youngest, who should be better known as one of the makers of the Dominion of Canada, if not as the chief builder. His greatest glory was that he sacrificed himself to befriend the Canadians, oppressed by a Government too short-sighted to see the immense part which Canada could play as an integral part of the empire—a part, which the event of 1914 to 1918 has demonstrated to the full. If James Murray lived his life as an aristocrat, he was ever the friend of the people, without indulging in that excess of championship which,

---

* The Order of the Beggar's Benison was established at Anstruther in Scotland about the year 1739, and included in its membership eminent men of all classes, even some members of the royal family. Its motto—" Be fruitful and multiply "—serves to indicate the hedonic nature of its orgies. Apparently the " Hell-Fire Club," installed at Medmenham Abbey in 1742, with the motto, " Fay ce que voudras," was a foundation following the same lines, where a group of brilliant wits, among whom, by the way, was John Wilkes—Murray's bitter detractor—carried on a secret ritual of blasphemous revelry. Both orders were, no doubt, an attempt to put in practice the Rabelaisian conceptions of the Abbey of Théléme. As Murray's biographer, I must add that I do not think he ever had opportunity of taking up his membership.

in many cases at this period, was not without a suspicion of selfish motives. It was never his method to belittle others, or to harass the men in power that he might gain credit for himself. He lived as a gentleman should, and acted up to the motto of his family, " Virtute Fideque."

INDEX

ABERCROMBIE, General, defeat at Ticonderoga, 70, 78; recalled, 79

Abraham, Heights of, 158; survey of, 215; Plains of, 135; battle, 219

Adams, Captain, 150

Adventures of Roderic Random, 32

Agnew, Major, 247

"Agriculture in Scotland, Society of Improvers in the knowledge of," founded, 16

Agriculture, methods in Scotland, 21

Aigle, Cap à l', 101

Aix, island of, captured, 55

Aix-la-Chapelle, peace of, 49, 53

Albany, 251

Alcansar, bay of, 394

Allenson, Ensign John, 39

Allier, Jacques, 277

Almodovar, Marq. d', 390 *note*

Almon, John, opinion of the Germans, 242 *note ; Memoirs of Wilkes*, 310 *note*, 311 *note*

America, colonies of, insurrection, 304–308; revolution, 382

Amherst, Jeffrey, Lord, 95; in command of the expedition against Louisburg, 59; at Halifax, 63; Boston, 70; Commander-in-Chief, 70, 79; instructions 71, 72; characteristics, 79; despatch from J. Murray, 199, 210, 213, 238, 240, 246–249, 284; campaign against Montreal, 250, 257; attack on Fort Levis, 259, 261; crossing the rapids, 262; terms of surrender, 264; despatch to Pitt, 268; tribute to J. Murray, 288; recalled, 302; in England, 315; peerage conferred, 433; offer to J. Murray, 439

Ann Elizabeth, the, 139

Anne, Queen, 17

Annual Register, the, 23 *note*, 201, 237

Anse au Foulon, 114, 141, 142, 168, 273; landing of the British troops at, 152–155; mystery of, 170–187

Anse Demers, 111, 113

Anse des Mères, 111

Anse St. Michel, 114, 141, 144

Anson, Lord, voyage round the world, 18; destruction of the French fleet, 46

Anstruther, Colonel, 95

Anticosti, island of, 98

Archibald, Captain, attack on Brulé, 215

Arethuse, the, 66, 243 *note*

Armiger, Colonel, commanding the 40th Regiment, 287

Atalante, the, 96 *note*, 122 *note*, 244

BAILIE, Captain, killed, 65

Balfour, Sir James, 11

Ballencrief, 13, 20, 24, 377; inventory of, 14

Bancroft, G., *The American Revolution*, 282 *note*

Barré, Colonel, Deputy-Adjutant, 93, 95, 140, 172; wounded at the battle of Quebec, 167; M.P. for Chipping Wycombe, 292; career, 292; relations with J. Murray, 315; Vice-Treasurer for Ireland, 372; Paymaster-General, 418

Barrington, General, 91 *note*

Barrington, Lord, 59 *note*

Barton, Colonel, 146

Bath, Countess of, 274 *note*

"Bath Papers," vi

Beachy Head, 437

Beaconsfield, Lord, at Beauport, 437

Beaton, James, 4

Beaton, John, 4

Beaton, Mary, 4
Beaumont, 105, 109, 196
Beauport, 106, 137, 195
Beauport, 313 ; view from, 436
Beggar's Benison, Ancient Order
    of the, 440 ; motto, 440 note
Bell, Captain, 95, 103
Bell, Lieut. John, 38
Bell, Lady, 377
Bell, Ensign Robert, 39
Belleisle, 46
Belleisle, M., Minister of War,
    88, 97
Bergen-op-Zoom, fall of, 46
Bernier, Commissary, on the
    character of J. Murray, 193
Bernis, Abbé, Minister of Foreign
    Affairs, 80, 81
Berryer, M. de, Minister of
    Marine, 86, 89, 255
Bethune, Grizel, marriage, 2, 4.
    See Murray
Bethune, Janet, marriages, 2.
    See Scott
Bethune, John, 2
Bic, Isle de, 72, 112
Bideford, 53
Biggar, H. P., vi
Bigot, François, intendant of
    New France, 83 ; dishonest
    practices, 83–87 ; Commissaire
    de la Marine, 84 ; surrenders
    Louisburg, 84 ; intendant of
    Quebec, 85 ; creation of La
    Friponne, 85 ; mistress, 86
Biniancollar, bay of, 394
Blackbarony, 2
Blackwood's Magazine, 170 note,
    191 note, 292 note
Blakeney, General, 29, 33, 380 ;
    peerage conferred, 433
Blau, Sieur de, 184
Bloody Island, 397
Bocachica Lake, 34, 36
Boroihme, Brian, 2
Boscawen, Admiral, captures
    French ships, 53 ; voyage to
    Louisburg, 62
Bothwell, James, 4th Earl, 3
Bougainville, M. de, mission to
    France, 81, 86, 97 ; return
    to Canada, 87 ; in charge of
    the defences of Quebec, 122,
    131 ; headquarters, 133, 135,
    174 ; at the battle of Quebec,
    157, 160–167 ; treatise on
    the Integral Calculus, 157 note;
    absence from Cap Rouge,
    181–184 ; relations with

Madame de Vienne, 183–185 ;
    at Île-aux-Noix, 187
Boulogne, 436
Bourlamaque, Brig. de, 225 ;
    captures Dumont's Mill, 234 ;
    at St. Francis, 258
Bowling, Lieut., verses, 99
Boyd, Major, 25
Braddock, General, defeat at
    Fort Duquesnes, 78
Brage, Colonel, 95
Branxholm, 4
Brest, 30
Brewer, Colonel, 95
Briscow, Ensign Musgrave, 39
Bristol, Lord, Ambassador to
    Madrid, 289 ; dismissed, 289
British Army, condition, 28 ;
    eulogy on, 36 ; at Quebec,
    229 ; appearance, 229 ; at
    the battle of Dumont's Mill,
    232–235 ; retreat, 235 ;
    casualties, 235 ; expedition
    against Montreal, 253–263
British Fleet, voyage to Quebec,
    96–104 ; three divisions, 99 ;
    transports, 100 ; at Tadoussac,
    101 ; leave Quebec, 201 ;
    result of the removal, 222 ;
    condition, 383 note
Brown, Lieut., attack on Louis-
    burg, 65
Brulé, attack on, 215
Buccleuch, Lord of, 4
Buchanan, Master George, 3
Buonaparte, Carlo, 393
Buonaparte, Maria Letizia, 393
Burnet, Archbishop, 14
Burnet, Elizabeth, 14 note
Burton, John H., History of
    Scotland, 11 note
Burton, Colonel Ralph, 253 ;
    advance on Dumont's Mill,
    229 ; Governor of Three
    Rivers, 277, 305 ; relations
    with J. Murray, 315, 320–
    323 ; character, 320 ; Briga-
    dier of the Northern Command,
    320, 330 note ; promotion,
    321 ; administration of Mon-
    treal, 329 ; resignation, 329
Burton, Mrs., 320
Bute, Lord, 289, 294 ; Colonial
    policy, 306 ; unpopularity, 312
Butler, Lieut., mission to Am-
    herst, 209, 210 ; failure, 212
Buttes-à-Neveu, 162, 223
Byng, Admiral, 384, 422
Byron, Commodore, 243 note

CADET, Joseph, munitionaire-général of New France, 83, 85 ; on the despatch of a convoy, 174–176, 181 ; treachery, 176
Calvaire, attack on, 215
Campbell, Captain Charles, 38
Canada, conquest of, 57, 135 ; history, 75 ; government, 276 ; map, 288 ; report on the development, 290 ; civil government established, 294 ; Royal Proclamation, 295–297, 353 ; need for a military government, 306–308 ; amendments on the Constitution, 354, 360–362 ; legislative measures, 363
Canada and its Provinces, 276 note
Canadians, French, 302, 330, 364 ; opinion of J. Murray, 285, 369
Canardière, the, 183
Cantley, Colonel Thomas, vi
Cape Breton Island, 76 ; restored to France, 50 ; export of coal, 252
Cape Horn, 18
Captain, the, 155
Cardin, Captain, 152 note, 154
Carleton, Colonel Guy, Deputy Quartermaster-General, 93, 95 ; commanding Grenadiers, 116 ; raid on Pointe-aux-Trembles, 118 ; at Orleans, 141 ; wounded at the battle of Quebec, 167 ; Governor of Quebec, 351, 356, 364 ; character of his rule, 351, 357, 369 ; a politician, 365 ; method of traducing J. Murray, 366–368 ; peerage conferred, 433. See Dorchester
Carthagena, capture of, 31 note; fleet at, 33
Cartier, Jacques, 74
Cathcart, Lord, in command of the expedition to the West Indies, 29–32 ; death, 32
Centurion, the 155
Chadds, Captain, 138 note
Champlain, Lake, 58, 251, 438 ; Point, 256
Champlain, Samuel de, 74 ; at Tadussac, 75
Charlemont, Lord, 374
Charles Edward, Prince, 43
Chatham, William, Earl of, Prime Minister, 290, 341, 345 ;

dismisses charges against J. Murray, 346 ; opinion of the constitution of Canada, 362
Chatham Correspondence, extract from, 374 ; Papers, 127, 128
Chaudière River, 111, 151, 152, 196, 288
Cherast, M., 438
Choiseul, Duc de, Minister of Foreign Affairs, 81
Choméwy, Paul de, founds the Ville Marie, 113 note
Christie, Lieut.-Colonel, 321
Cibber, Mrs., 47
Coal, export of, 252
Cocoa Tree Club, 18
Colbert, J. B., 76, 281
Coldwell, Captain, 95
Collier, Cordelia, 42 ; in London, 46 ; attentions from J. Murray, 46–48 ; marriage, 48. See Murray
Collier, James, 42
Collier, Jane, 390 note
Collier, John, justice of Hastings, 41 ; at Bath, 48 ; exercises influence for his son-in-law, 52 ; death, 312 ; legacy to J. Murray, 313
Collier, Sarah, 391 note
Colville, Lord, 240 ; appeal from J. Murray, 216
Conflans, victory of, 197 note
Connecticut, 29
Constitutional Documents of Canada, 290, 360
Contrecœur, 260
Conway, Major-General, 51 ; Secretary of State, 344, 369 ; letter from J. Murray, 420
Cornwallis, Major-General, 54
Courtemanche, M. de, 104 note
Cramahé, Captain Hector Theophilus, 202, 258 ; mission to England, 331, 344 ; correspondence with J. Murray, 347–349
Cranston, John, agent for J. Murray, 313
Cranston, William, 46
Criech, 2
Crillon, Duc de, 23 ; commanding the Spanish army, 394 ; at the siege of Minorca, 394 ; relations with J. Murray, 398 ; attempt to bribe him, 399–402 ; terms of capitulation, 415

Crown Point, 250, 251, 257
Culloden, battle of, 43, 62
Cumberland, Duke of, 92
Cunningham, William, Coroner of Quebec, 339 *note*
Cuthbert, Lieut., killed, 65

Daily Advertiser, the, 269 *note*
Dalling, Major, 152 *note*, 229 ; attack on Point Levis, 213 ; at the battle of Dumont's Mill, 233 ; wounded, 233
Daniel, Colonel Samuel, attack on Fort St. Lazarus, 35 ; death, 38
Danks, Colonel, 95
Dartmouth, Lord, President of the Board of Trade, 342, 348 ; amendments to the constitution of Canada, 354, 360
Davies, Ensign Thomas Davenport, 39
Daun, General Leopold Graf von, 274 *note*
Dawson, Rev. Eli, thanksgiving service at Quebec, 195
Dawson, Captain George, death, 38
Dawson, W. Bell, Superintendent of the Tidal Survey of Canada, 136
Deane, Captain, 247 ; commander of the *Lowestoft*, 253 *note*
Delaune, Captain Henry, 38
Delaune, Captain William, 152 *note*, 153
Denham estate, purchase of, 313
Dennett, Captain John, death, 38
Deschambeau, 243, 256 ; attack on, 123 *note*
Diamond, Cape, 105, 107, 188, 195
Diana, the 98, 99, 116, 242, 253 *note*
Disraeli, Isaac, at Beauport, 437
Dobson, Lieut., 95
Don, Captain George, 400, 406, 410, 416 ; letters from, 419, 420
Dorchester, Lord, 351
Douglas, Colonel, 29 *note*
Douglas case, 377 *note*
Doughty, Dr., vi, 112, 118 *note*, 182 ; *The Siege of Quebec*, 156 *note*, 174, 282
Doutelle, the, 43
Draper, Sir William, appointed Lieut.-Governor of Minorca, 388 ; opponent of *Junius*, 389 ; relations with J. Murray,

403 ; charges against him, 404, 410,419,423–433; insubordination, 407–410, 417
Drucour, Chevalier de, Governor of Louisburg, 58
Drummossy Muir, 43
Duchambon de Vergor, 88
Dumont's Mill, battle of, 231–235
Dungeness Point, 436
Durrell, Admiral, commanding the naval force at Halifax, 72 ; orders, 72 ; at St. Lawrence, 96 ; Île-aux-Coudres, 103
Dyce, William, school in Selkirk, 24

Eden and Mary, the, 138
Edinburgh, "Select Society," 18
Eglinton, Lord, letter from J. Murray, 338
Egremont, Lord, Secretary of State, 288 ; colonial policy, 294 ; on the government of Canada, 297
Elibank, Alexander, 4th Lord, 14 ; education, 15 ; marriage, 15 ; financial losses, 16 ; children, 17 ; death, 24
Elibank, Elizabeth, Lady, character, 16 ; children, 17
Elibank, George, 6th Lord, 18, 394
Elibank, Gideon, Lord, 7
Elibank, Patrick, 1st Lord, 13 ; death, 13
Elibank, Patrick, 2nd Lord, 13 ; death 14
Elibank, Patrick, 3rd Lord, 14 ; marriage, 14
Elibank, Patrick, 5th Lord, 17 ; military service, 17 ; marriage, 17, 25 ; literary career, 17 ; founder of the "Select Society," 18 ; member of the Cocoa Tree Club, 18 ; Lieut.-Colonel of Marines, 29 ; attack on Fort St. Lazarus, 36 ; return, 37 ; estrangement with his brother James, 48 ; letter from him, 337 ; pride in him, 375 ; death, 394 ; character, 440
Elibank, Viscount, v
Elizabeth, Queen, death, 9
Elliott, George, 392
Elliott, "Gibby," 7

Elliott, Major, 188, 214
Elliott, Mary, 7
Elphinstone, Lord, 14 note
England, war with Spain, 26, 289, 390 note; ultimatum, 28; war with France, 53, 385; sea power, 77
Entick, Hist. Late War, 63 note
Eriskay, island of, 43
Etchemin River, 114, 116, 130, 132, 173, 196, 214

FENDIE, Meggie, 7. See Elliott
Ferguson, Anne, 377; letter from, 275
Fergusson, Captain, commanding the Prince of Orange, 63
Finnisterre, 46
Flanders, 44, 62
Fletcher, Andrew, 22
Fletcher, Henry, 21
Flitner, Zachariah, Provost-Marshal, 241 note
Florida, West, 319
Foligné, M., extract from his diary, 177
Foot, the 15th, 29, 35, 43; casualties, 38; expedition to L'Orient, 44; at Limerick, 52; Halifax, 59; Maidstone, 59 note
Foot, the 16th, 43 note; the 24th, 29, 35; the 27th, 29; the 34th, 35; the 36th, 35; the 58th, 59; the 64th, 91
Forbes, Margaret, Lady, 2, 3
Fort Charles, 397
Fort Duquesne, 78
Fort Levis, attack on, 259; capture of, 261
Fort St. Phillips, 382, 392, 394; attack on, 397; siege, 397–414; garrison attacked by scurvy, 403, 410; capitulation, 414–416
Fort William Henry, 78
Fortescue, on the attack of Fort St. Lazarus, 35; History of the British Army, 165
Foucault, François, 438
Fowey en route, 201
France, war with England, 53, 385; condition of the navy, 76; colonial policy, 77, 79; corruption of the Court, 80
Francis, Lake, 261 262
Francis, M., 307
Francis, Sir Philip, 292 note

Fraser, Malcolm, 102
Fraser, Colonel Simon, 95, 152, 154, 207; raises the Highland Regiment, 102; attack on the French, 214; advance on Dumont's Mill, 229; commanding the garrison at Quebec, 254
French army, defeated at Louisburg, 65; number of the troops, 108, 131, 220–222; at the battle of Quebec, 162–166; flight, 163, 166; reassemble at Jacques Cartier, 167; advance on Quebec, 216; land at Cap Rouge, 217; at Pointe-aux-Trembles, 224; advance on Lorette, 224–226; at the battle of Dumont's Mill, 232–235; casualties, 235; condition, 254; prisoners, 266
French fleet, sails from Brest, 30; return, 33; destruction, 46, 66; captured, 53; capture Minorca, 53; at Quebec, 201; strength, 215
Friponne, La, creation of, 85
Frontenac, M., 74
Fundy, Bay of, 288

GABARUS BAY, 63
Gable, Benjamin, hangman, 241
Gage, General Thomas, Viscount, promotion, 67, 69; Governor of Montreal, 277; appointed commander-in-chief, 302; relations with J. Murray, 303; letter to Colonel Carleton, 307; letters from J. Murray, 318, 320; administration of Montreal, 329; member of the Ministry, 342
Garrick, David, 47
Gaspé, 71; Bay, 243 note
Geerke, H. P., Napoleon, 27 note
Gentleman's Bay, 112, 124, 135
Gentleman's Magazine, 232, 275 note
George II., King, 17, 26; instructions to Amherst, 72; death, 287
George III., King, 311; reply to the Quebec grand jurors, 328; appreciation of the services of J. Murray, 388, 402; award on the court martial, 430; letter from, 433

Germans, characteristics, 242 *note*
Ghent, 43
Gibraltar, 380
Gibson, James, 271 *note*
Good Intent, the, 252 *note*
Gordon, Lord Adam, 377
Goreham, Colonel, 95
Goreham's Point, 133, 134 ; Post, 141, 172, 196 ; meeting at, 141, 144
Gould, Sir Charles, 432
Grafton, Duke of, 341
Graham, Mr., *Social Life in Scotland*, 15
Grant, Colonel Alexander, 17 ; attack on Fort St. Lazarus, 35 ; killed, 36
Grant, James, Governor of East Florida, 310 *note*
Grant, Lieut. John, 39 ; attack on Louisburg, 65
Green, William, 390
Gregson, Lieut. Thomas, death, 39
Grenville, Rt. Hon. George, Chancellor of the Exchequer, 294 ; Stamp Act, 326
Grisnez, Cape, 436
Guichen, Count de, 391 *note*
Guienne, Regiment of, 161, 178–181
Gwillam, Captain, 95

HADDINGTON, 24
Haldimand, Lieut.-Governor of Montreal, 303 ; of Trois Rivières, 318
Halifax, 57, 59, 63, 72, 96, 240
Halifax, Lord, letter from J. Murray, 303 ; tribute to, 309 ; Secretary of State, 341
Hamilton, Captain, 116
Hardy, Admiral Sir Charles, 58 ; expedition against Gaspé, 71
Hastings, mayor of, vi
Hastings, smuggling at, 46
Haviland, Brig.-General William, advance on Montreal, 251, 257 ; attack on Île-aux-Noix, 259 ; captures it, 261
Hawke, Edward, Lord, captures French ships, 46, 53 ; victory in Quiberon Bay, 99 *note ;* of Conflans, 197 *note*
Hazzar, Colonel, 95
" Hearts of Oak," 99 *note*
Hell-Fire Club, motto, 440 *note*

Hey, William, Chief Justice of Quebec, 357
Hide, John, commander of H.M. *Swift*, 41
Highland Regiment, the 63rd, 102 *note*, 207
Hillsborough, Lord, President of the Board of Trade, 352, 372 ; on the Proclamation to Canada, 353 ; despatch from J. Murray, 416, 417
Holderness, Lord, 141
Holley, Ensign Robert, 39
Holmes, Admiral, in command of the naval force, 115, 122 ; voyage to Quebec, 96 ; naval movements, 133 ; leaves Quebec, 201
Hooper, William, master of the *Good Intent*, 252 *note*
Hopkins, Lieut., attack on Louisburg, 65
Hopson, General, 91 *note*
Horde, Ensign Allan, 39
Howard, General Sir George, President of the court martial on J. Murray, 422
Howe, Colonel the Hon. William, 253 ; commanding light infantry, 152
Hume, David, 17
Hungary, Queen of, subsidy to, 46
Hunt-Walsh, Colonel, failure of his expedition against Pointe-aux-Trembles, 206
Hunter, the 130, 134, 135, 137, 145, 146, 149, 150, 152, 153
Hussey, Major, 152 *note*

ÎLE-AUX-COUDRES, 103
Île-aux-Noix, 187, 216, 250 ; attack on, 259 ; capture of, 261
Indians, treaty with J. Murray, 262 ; insurrection, 308
Interests of Great Britain considered with regard to her Colonies, 283 *note*
Ireland, 50 ; condition, 52 *note*
Ireland, Primate of, 51
Irvine, Colonel, member of the Quebec council, dismissal, 366 ; Governor of Guernsey, 366 *note*
Irvine, Mrs. 375
Isle of Wight, 29, 54

JACQUES Cartier, 124, 167, 223, 226, 243, 255

Jamaica, 33, 37
James I., King of England, 5; accession, 9
James I., King of Scotland, 12
James II., King of Scotland, 12
Joan, Queen Dowager, 12
John of Gaunt, 12, 437
Johnson, Dr., opinion of Lord Elibank, 18, 440
Johnston, Barbara, Lady, 24
Johnston, Chevalier, *Dialogue in Hades*, 154, 180; on the battle of Quebec, 158, 167; on the policy of J. Murray, 267
Johnston, George, letter from, 274
Johnston, George, Governor of West Florida, 310 *note*
Johnston, Governor, 304 *note*
Johnston, Sir James, 24
Johnston, Major-General James, Governor of Quebec, 379; commanding the Scots Greys, 435
Johnston, Lieut. Theophilus, death, 39
Jordan, Colonel John, commanding the 15th Foot, 50
Journal tenu à l'Armee, 162
Junius, letters of, 389

Kames, Life and Writings of Lord, 16
Kanon, Jacques, commanding French transports, at Quebec, 96
Kennebec River, 288
Kennedy, Colonel, 95
Kennington Cove, 64
Keppel, Admiral, court-martial on, 433; peerage conferred, 434
Ker, Robert, 5. *See* Somerset
Kerallain, M. de, *La Jeunesse de Bougainville*, 182 *note*
Knox, John, extracts from his Journal, 129 *note*, 132 *note*, 133 *note*, 142, 156, 205, 207, 208, 214, 228, 239, 257

Lamb, Sir Archibald, vi
Lane-Sayer, Charles, vi
Lascelles, Colonel, 95
Lauderdale, Lord, 270
Lauffeldt, battle of, 46, 62
Laurel, the, 138
Laurentian Mountains, 196
Lauzon estate, 438
Laurence, Brig. Charles, 59, 95

Leghorn, 396
Lery, M. de, 109
Leslie, Captain, 95, 208
Lestock, Admiral, 44
Letter to an Honourable Brigadier-General, 130, 189
Levis, Chevalier de, Journal, 157, 160, 264, 267; advance on Quebec, 201, 216–218; force, 220; attack on Lorette, 224–226; on St. Foy, 227; at the battle of Dumont's Mill, 232; besieges Quebec, 239–243; criticism on his tactics, 244; despatch to the Marechal de Belle-Isle, 257; on J. Murray's strategy, 262; letter from him, 392; friendship with him, 439
Ligonier, Lord, 70
Limerick, 52
Little William, the 349, 374
Livingston, Lord, 4
Lloyd's Evening Post, 366
Lockerbie Lick, 5
Loftus, Major Simon, death, 38
Longue Pointe, 263
Longueuil, 262
Lord, Walter Frewin, *The Lost Possessions of England*, 394
L'Orembeck, 64
Lorette, 159, 196, 205; advance on, 224–226
L'Orient, proposed capture of, 44; attack on, 62
Lotbinière, 256
Lotbinière, M. de, 158
Loudon, General, expedition against Louisburg, 78
Louis XIII., King of France, 75
Louis XIV., King of France, 75, 76
Louis XV., King of France, 75, 76; corruption of his Court, 77, 89; death, 382
Louisburg, capture of, 24, 44, 57 *note*; restored to France, 50; position, 57; fortifications, 58, 76; expedition against, 62–64; attack on, 64–66; capitulation, 66
Louisburg Grenadiers, at the battle of Quebec, 156
Louisiana, 76
Lowestoft, the 99, 130, 145, 146, 242, 253 *note*

Mabane, Dr., member of the Quebec council, dismissal, 366;

restored, 366 *note* ; letter from J. Murray, 436

MacCartney, Captain, 240

Machault, the, 122 *note*, 243 *note*

Mackellar, Colonel, death, 387

Mackenzie, Lady Isabel, 377 *note*

Mahon, Lord, *History of England*, 28 *note*, 30 *note*, 37 *note*

Mahratta War, 22

Maidstone, 59 *note*

Mainwaring, Captain Arthur, death, 38

Maitland, Major John, 39, 95, 247

Malartic, Captain de, negotiations with J. Murray, 245

Malta, 380

Mansfield, Lord, opinion of J. Murray, 312 ; letter from him, 422

Mante, *History*, 130

Marie, the escape, 244

Martinique, expedition against, 289 ; victory of, 391 *note*

Mary, Queen of Scots, 2, 3

Mary, the capture of, 86

Maryland, 29

Maseres, Francis, Attorney-General of Quebec, 357 ; memorandum on the administration of Quebec, 358–361

Maupassant, Jean de, *Les deux Expéditions de P. Desclaux au Canada*, 96 *note*

McAlpin, Lieut., 246

McDonald, Captain Donald, 152 *note*, 154 ; attack on Calvaire, 215 ; killed, 215 *note*, 234

McKellar, Major, 105, 217 ; at Gorcham's Post, 141

Meadows, Mr., vi

Medway, the, 190, 201

Meech, Lieut., lands on the Island of Orleans, 104

Melvill, Robert, Governor of Granada, 310 *note*

Mereci Convent, 233

Merquida, La, 394

Miller, Captain, blown up, 206, 210

Minorca, Island of, 379 ; capture of, 53 ; garrison, 384 ; blockade, 386 ; outbreak of tertiano, 386 ; Spanish army land at, 393

Miramichi Bay, 71

Mississippi valley, 76

Mohawks, the, 262

Mola, Cape, 397

Molé, M. de, 199 *note*

Monckton, General Robert, 61, 95 ; promotion, 67, 92 ; commanding the 2nd Battalion Royal Americans, 91 ; voyage to Quebec, 99 ; occupies Point Levis, 109 ; at Gorcham's Post, 141 ; at the battle of Quebec, 162 ; wounded, 167, 189, 191 ; at New York, 201 ; serves in the Spanish war, 292

Moncrief, Major, 154

Monro, Dr. George, 410

Mons, 43

Montcalm, Marquis de, on the siege of Louisburg, 58, 65 ; the position of Gaspé, 71 *note* ; takes Oswego, 78 ; death, 81, 83, 167, 168 *note* ; charges against, 82 ; extracts from his journal, 82–86, 104, 107, 137, 151 *note*, 176, 184 *note*, 186, 282 ; on the dishonesty of the officers, 82, 88 ; at the battle of Quebec, 157–167

Montmorency, 114 ; evacuation, 130, 133 ; falls of, 104 ; river, 105, 110, 196 ; attack on, 118

Montreal, 107 ; campaign against, 58, 250, 253–263 ; surrounded by British troops, 263 ; terms of surrender, 264–266 ; administration, 277, 329 ; tension between the military and civil elements, 332–335 ; fire at, 344

Montressor, Lieut., mission to Amherst, 213, 248

Montreuil, Major-General, at the siege of Quebec, 158–161 ; adjutant-general, 178

Moravia, William de, 2

Mordaunt, General Sir John, commanding the expedition against Rochefort, 54 ; court martial on, 55 ; acquitted, 55

Moreton, Colonel, 29 *note*

Morris, Lieut., death, 39

Morris, Major, attack on St. Foy, 226

Mostyn, General, Governor of Minorca, 379 ; death, 388

Mount Murray, 101, 102

Münster, surrender, 274

Murray, Agnes, marriage, 6. *See* Scott

Murray, Lieut.-Colonel Alexander, 94, 95 ; occupies Quebec, 188

Murray, Alexander, 18 ; character, 19 ; Jacobite views, 19 ; imprisoned, 19 ; in France, 19 ; title of Count, 20 ; at the Westminster elections, 51

Murray, Sir Andrew, 2 ; second marriage, 2, 4

Murray, Ann, 395 ; birth of a daughter, 396 ; at Leghorn, 396 ; birth of a son, 418

Murray, Cordelia, 48 ; attack of small-pox, 49 ; at Waterford, 50 ; refuses to join her husband, 316, 376 ; at Ballencrief, 377 ; Minorca, 382 ; illness, 388 ; return to England, 388 ; death, 388

Murray, Hon. Dudley, v

Murray, George, naval career, 18 ; letters from his brother James, 200, 271–273, 315 ; letter to him, 274

Murray, Lord George, 391

Murray, Dr. Gideon, Canon of Durham, 18, 312

Murray, Sir Gideon, 2, 4 ; career, 5–8 ; councillor to King James VI., 5 ; knighted, 6 ; story of, 6 ; Treasurer Depute, 7 ; Lord of Session, 7 ; member of the assembly at Perth, 7 ; charge against, 8 ; death, 8, 434 ; eulogy on, 9. See Elibank

Murray, Grizel, 2, 4

Murray, Helen, 377 note. See Stewart

Murray, General the Hon. James, ancestors, 1–14 ; parents, 14–17 ; brothers, 17–20 ; birth, 20 ; characteristics, 23, 60, 193, 222, 365, 380, 385, 439 ; education, 24 ; death of his father, 24 ; cadet in the 3rd Scots Regiment, 25 ; second lieutenant, 26, 29 ; expedition to the West Indies, 31–37 ; attack on Fort St. Lazarus, 37 ; captain in the 15th Foot, 37 ; at Hastings, 40, 47 ; friendship with the Colliers, 42, 47 ; Jacobite views, 42 ; wounded at Ostend, 43 ; expedition to capture L'Orient, 44, 62 ; attentions to Cordelia Collier, 46–48 ; marriage, 48 ; at Waterford, 50 ; loyalty to King George, 51 ; lieut.-colonel of the 15th Foot, 52, 59 ; expedition against Roche-

fort, 53, 62 ; against Louisburg, 59, 62–66 ; relations with Wolfe, 61 ; tributes to, 67, 288, 297 ; on his claims to preferment, 67–69 ; promoted colonel, 69 ; commanding troops at Halifax, 73 ; brigadier, 91 ; voyage to Quebec, 99–104 ; instructions from Wolfe to reconnoitre, 111, 114, 118, 122 ; ordered to Montmorency, 114 ; at St. Anthony, 123 ; plan of a night attack, 134, 138 ; at St. Nicholas, 144 ; at the battle of Quebec, 162–168 ; strategy, 169, 262 ; appointed Military Governor of Quebec, 191, 285 ; adminstration, 193–195, 199, 202, 207, 276, 284–286, 302, 330 ; manifesto, 202–204 ; stern measures, 205, 209 ; method of borrowing money, 207 ; despatch to Sir J. Amherst, 209–211, 213, 238, 240, 246–249, 284 ; appeal to Lord Colville, 216 ; occupies Cap Rouge, 216, 222 ; measures of defence, 223 ; attack on St. Foy, 227 ; gift to the church, 227 note, 285 ; retirement, 228 ; at the battle of Dumont's Mill, 232–235 ; criticisms on his action, 236, 269 ; appeal to his men, 238 ; in the siege of Quebec, 239–244 ; colonel of the 2nd Battalion of Royal Americans, 247, 270 ; expedition against Montreal, 253–263 ; despatch to Mr. Pott, 254 ; disarms the inhabitants, 258, 267 ; treaty with the Hurons, 262 ; return to Quebec, 268, 334 ; feelings of bitterness, 270–273, 315 ; proclamation, 277–279 ; report to Pitt, 279 ; tolerance to religion, 284 ; qualifications, 286 ; map of Canada, 288 ; report on the development of Quebec, 290 ; Governor of Canada, 295, 297 ; commission, 297–299, 318 ; relations with Gage, 303 ; on the need for military government, 304, 308, 323 ; checks the mutiny of the troops, 309 ; opinion of George III., 311 ; legacy, 312 ; purchases Denham estate, 313 ; decides to settle in Canada, 315 ; treatment by his friends, 315 ; refusal of his wife to join him, 316, 376 ; relations with Colonel Burton, 320–322 ; takes the oath, 323 ; ordinance creating a system of judicature, 325, 355 ; admission of Roman Catholics on juries, 330–332, 339 ; at Montreal, 333 ; on the difficulties of administration, 336–339 ; order of recall, 342 ; charges against, 346, 372, 404, 410, 419, 423–433 ; dismissed, 346, 373 ; return to England, 349–351, 372 ; letter to *Lloyd's Evening Post*, 366–368 ; influence with the Canadians, 369 ; result of his administration, 370 ; received by King George III., 374, 380 ; at Ballencrief, 377 ; decision against returning to Canada, 377 ; experiments with farming at Beauport, 378, 437 ; colonel of the 13th Foot, 379 ; lieut.-general, 379 ; lieut.-governor of Minorca, 379 ; on the system of perquisites, 380 ; at Minorca, 382 ; blockaded, 386 ; death of his wife, 388 ; Governor of Minorca, 388 ; death of his brother Patrick, 394 ; second marriage, 395 ; birth of a daughter, 396 ; in the siege of Fort St. Phillips, 397–414 ; relations with the Duc de Crillon, 398 ; rejects bribe, 399–402 ; insubordination of Sir W. Draper, 403–410, 417 ; appeal to his officers, 408, 411 ; nickname, 413 ; capitulation, 414–416 ; birth of a son, 418 ; court martial on, 422–433 ; defence, 423–426 ; General, 435 ; appointed Governor of Hull, 435 ; commanding the Royal Scots Fusiliers, 436 ; life at Beauport, 436 ; children, 437 ; Lord of the Manor of Ore, 437 ; properties in Canada, 438 ; will, 438 ; death, 438 ; generosity, 439 ; Knight of the Ancient Order of the Beggar's Benison, 440 ; chief builder of Canada, 440

Murray, Sir James, 438
Murray, Rev. James Arthur, vi
Murray, Mrs. James, v
Murray, James Patrick, birth, 418, 438
Murray, Jenny, death, 274
Murray, Maria, at Minorca, 382
Murray, Mary, 377
Murray, Sir Patrick, 11 ; services to King James, 11 ; peerage conferred, 13. *See* Elibank
Murray, Patrick, 439
Murray, Sir Robert, death of his wife, 274 *note*
Murray, Walter, letter from, 375
Murray, Sir William, 94 *note*
Murray, Colonel William, career in the Dutch Service, 25
Murray Bay, 101, 102
Murray-Pulteney, Sir James, Secretary at War, 274 *note*
Musgrave, Sir William, 168 *note*

NAIRNE, John, 102
Namur, siege of, 25
Napoleon, Emperor, 22, 393
Naval Hospital, 397
Navy, condition, 28
Neptune, the, 55, 95, 197
Newcastle, Duke of, 41 ; letters from J. Murray, 67–69, 199
Newcastle Papers, 127, 128
New England, 74 ; administration, 77 ; population, 78
New England Rangers, 59
New France, 74 ; French colony in, 75 ; administration, 77, 87 ; population, 78 ; Grande Société, 85 ; ceases to exist, 265
New Netherlands, 74
New Scotland, 74
New Spain, 74
New York, 29
Nicholson, Lieut., killed, 65
Noire river, 101
North and Grey, Lord, 17, 25
North, Lord, Ministry, 383 ; fall of, 418
North Briton, the, 310
Northington, Lord, 364

OGLE, Admiral, 34
Ohio valley, 76
Oleron, Island of, 55
Olivar, Doctor, appointed rector of Port Mahon, 390

Ore, Manor of, 437; church at, 438
Orford, the, 98, 201
Orleans, Island of, 103, 104, 196, 201, 252
Ostend, siege of, 43
Oswald, James, Vice-Treasurer for Ireland, correspondence with J. Murray, 338, 349
Oswego, 250; capture of, 78
Otway, Colonel, 95

PALLISER, Captain Hugh, occupies Quebec, 188
Paoli, General, 393
Paris, Peace of, 293, 295, 322, 351; treaty of, 293, 300, 318, 323, 352
Parry, Memoir of the Rev. Joshua, 61 *note*
Particular Transactions, 152, 154
Pauchot, M., surrenders Fort Levis, 259
Pause, Chevalier de la, on the battle of Quebec, 158, 160; at Jacques Cartier, 223
Péan, Madame de, 86
Peasantry, in Scotland, 22
Pelham, Rt. Hon. Henry, Prime Minister, 41
Pelham, Thomas, 41
Pennsylvania, 29
Penzance, the, 253 *note*
Pepperel, Sir William, captures Louisburg, 44, 57 *note*
Perrot, Isle, 262, 263
Perth, assembly at, 7
Phipps, Sir William, 197 *note*
Pie, La, 96 *note*
Pitfour, Lord, 377
Pitt, Lord, in Canada, 369
Pitt, Rt. Hon. William, Prime Minister, 22; policy, 27, 78, 306; plan of an expedition against Rochefort, 54; Secretary of State for Foreign Affairs, 57; plan for the Conquest of Canada, 57; reports from J. Murray, 279, 287; commission appointing him Military Governor of Quebec, 285; resignation, 288; created Earl of Chatham, 290
Point Levis, 105, 109, 132, 137, 196, 201, 438; attack on, 213
Pointe-aux-Pères, 105, 111, 196
Pointe-au-Pie, 101
Pointe-à-Puiseaux, 113, 116

Pointe-aux-Trembles, 117, 123, 133, 138 140 142, 143, 170, 171, 172, 224, 243; raid on, 118; tide movements, 136; expedition against, 206
Polwarth, Lord, 7
Pomonc, the, 96 *note*, 122 *note;* burned, 244
Pompadour, Madame de, intrigues, 80; extravagance, 89
Pontiac, chief of the Ottawa tribes, 308
Porcupine, the, 172, 201, 222, 253 *note*
Port Mahon, 380, 382
Port Royal, 33, 37
Pott, Mr., despatch from J. Murray, 254
Potts, James, coroner of Quebec, 339 *note*
Poularies, colonel of the Royal Roussillon Regiment, 158, 167
Prairie, La, 261
Pratt, Lord Chief Justice, peerage conferred, 342
Prevost, Colonel, resignation, 68
Price, Mr., mission to England, 344
Prince of Orange, 63
Pringle, Lieut. Andrew, death, 39
Provoked Wife, 47
Prussia, King of, retains Silesia, 50
Public Record Office, Chatham Papers, 127, 128
Puiseaux, M. de, 114
Pulteney, W., 27

QUADRUPLE Alliance, 43
Quarantine Island, 397
Quebec, campaign against, 16, 72, 90, 135, 156–167; condition, 88; surrender, 89, 167; view from, 105, 195–198; bombardment, 121; tide table, 136; position, 164; convoy at, 174; Union flag hoisted, 188; destruction, 191, 194; fuel supply, 194; thanksgiving service, 195; garrison measures, 205; sufferings of the men, 207–209, 212, 214, 224, 242, 252; number of deaths, 219, 220; siege of, 239–244; administration, 276, 284–286; proclamation, 277–279; destitution of the people, 283; Province of, 295; Royal

Proclamation, 295–297, 323–325, 353; commission, 297–299, 318; change in the administration, 299–303, 305; mutiny of the troops, 309; disorganisation, 318; system of judicature, 325, 340, 355; attitude of the grand jury, 326–329; petition from the French inhabitants, 328; memorial from the seigneurs, 350; memorandum on the administration, 358–361; Act of 1774, 361, 363
Quiberon Bay, victory in, 99 note, 275
Quimperle Bay, 44

Racehorse, the, 201, 206, 222, 240, 253
Ramezay, De, Governor of Quebec, 159; surrenders Quebec, 167, 244
Ramsay, John, Scotland and Scotsmen, 15
Rangers, the, 111, 153; raids, 133
Rapids, crossing the, 262
Recher, Abbé, extract from his Journal, 179
Reivers Wedding, 3
Remigny, M., 141 note; reports, 144, 173; commanding the Sillery Post, 178
Repentigny, De, commanding the garrison at Jacques Cartier, 255
Revenge, the, 18
Reveryns Point, 152
Rhé, island of, 55
Rhode Island, 29
Richardson, Ensign Daniel, 39
Richelieu, Cardinal, 76
Richelieu River, 122, 251, 258; rapids, 255
Richmond, the, 104, 240
Rivière, John de la, 399
Robaud, Jesuit missionary, 82
Robinson, Colonel, 29 note
Robinson, Captain, 384
Rochefort, expedition against, 53–55
Rochfort, Lord, letter from J. Murray, 380
Rockingham Ministry, policy, 342; fall of, 345, 356, 364, 372, 418, 419
Rodney, Lord, action off Martinique, 391 note

Rogers, Colonel, 95
Rollo, Lord, at Louisburg, 112; at Sorel, 259
Roman Catholics, inclusion on juries, 330–332, 339, 356
Romney Marshes, 436
Rouge, Cap, 111, 113, 118, 133, 135, 153, 155, 181; tide table, 136; French army land at, 217; river, 164
Round Island, 397
Rous, Captain, 116, 117
Royal Americans, the 2nd Battalion, 91; 60th Foot, 59
Royal Scots Fusiliers, 436
Royal William, the, 98
Rye, Bay of, 436

SACKVILLE, Lord George, 52, 63; correspondence with Wolfe, 66
Saguenay River, 243 note
St. Augustin, 118, 133, 223, 225
St. Antoine, 256
St. Anthony, 123
St. Charles River, 105, 106, 120, 156, 164, 165, 178, 195, 196
St. Clair, General, 44
St. Croix, 256
St. Dominica, 32
Ste. Foy, 159, 196, 198; post at, 205; church at, blown up, 227
St. Francis, 258
St. Helen's, 59, 63, 96
St. John, Height of, 127; river, 288
St. Lawrence, Gulf of, 57, 76, 97; river, 70, 106, 164, 195, 201, 216, 250, 280, 288, 438
St. Lazarus fort, 34; attack on, 34–37
St. Louis gate, destruction of the block-house, 239
St. Louis fort, 34; attack on, 37
St. Martin, M. de, 177
St. Michel, 111, 113, 126; story of, 113 note; burned, 214
St. Nicholas, 144, 146
St. Ours, Brigadier, killed, 167
St. Peter, Lake of, 256 note, 258
St. Roch, 156
St. Rupert's Bay, 32
Salmon, Edward, Makers of National History: Wolfe, 128 note
Samos battery, 155
Sardinia, King of, subsidy to, 46

Saunders, Admiral, 72 ; at Halifax, 96 ; ascent of Montmorency River, 116 ; leaves Quebec, 200

Saxe, Marshal, victories, 43, 46

Sayer, Henry, letter from J. Murray, 391

Scatari, Island of, 97

Schomberg, Captain, 116, 247

Schuyler, Colonel, 106 note

Scotland, feudal system, 1 ; result of the suppression of the border warfare, 10 ; characteristics of the people, 10 ; religious controversy, 10 ; conditions in the eighteenth century, 20 ; methods of agriculture, 21 ; peasantry, 22

Scots Regiment, the 3rd, 25

Scott, Agnes, 7

Scott, Grizel, 4. See Murray

Scott, Abbé H. A., 227 note, 285 ; Une Paroisse Historique de la Nouvelle France, 113 note

Scott, Janet, 2 ; " Auld Witch of Buccleuch," 3

Scott, Major, commanding the 40th Foot, 64, 95 ; attack on Louisburg, 65 ; commanding the Rangers, 111, 153

Scott, Mary, " Flower of Yarrow," 7

Scott, Sir Walter, Lay of the Last Minstrel, 3

Scott, Sir Walter, " Auld Watt," 6

Scott, Walter, " Wicked Watt," 2 ; murdered, 2

Scott, William, 4

Scott, William, of Harden, 6

Seahorse, the, 112, 130, 134, 145, 172

Sedieres, Lieut. Gabriel, death, 38

Selbie, Captain William, death, 38

Selkirk, 24

Senezergue, Brig.-General de, at the battle of Quebec, 158 ; killed, 167

Senneterre, the, 122 note

Seven Years' War, 53

Sevenoaks, 437

Shads, Captain, 138

Sharples, Lieut. George, death, 38

Shelburne, Lord, 292 ; colonial policy, 294 ; President of the Board of Trade, 341 ; letter from J. Murray, 370 ; Secretary of State, 372 ; retirement, 436

Silesia, 50

Sillery Point, 113, 116, 149, 152, 153, 178, 196

Sissenhurst, 59 note

Smollett, Tobias, 21 ; description of the ship hospital, 32 ; History of England, 46

Smuggling, custom of, 40

Smyth, Captain, 95

Somerset, Robert, Earl of, 5 ; Lord High Treasurer, 7

Sorel, 258, 259 ; destruction, 260 ; river, 215, 222

South Downs, 437

South Sea Bubble, 16

Spain, war with England, 26, 289, 390 note ; ultimatum, 28

Spanish army, land at Minorca, 393 ; at the siege of Fort St. Phillips, 397–414

Spies, payment of, 373 note

Spital, Captain, 95

Spithead, 31, 33

Spottiswood, Archbishop, History of the Church in Scotland, 8

Squirrel, the, 116, 122 note, 133, 145, 146

Stair, Earl of, 18

Stamp Act, 306, 326, 369 ; repeal, 345, 364

Stark, Colonel, 95

Stewart, Helen, Lady, 377

Stewart, Sir James, 377 note

Stirling Castle, the, 155, 172

Stirling, Elizabeth, marriage, 15 ; character, 15. See Elibank

Stobo, Major Robert, escapes from Quebec, 112 ; Memoirs of, 113

Stone, Andrew, 41 note, 51, 59 note

Stormont, Lord, 385

Strachy, Lieut. William, death, 38

Stuart, Elizabeth, marriage, 12

Stuart, James, 8, 12 note, 20

Stuart, John, 12. See Traquair.

Suete Marsh, 225

Suette, 196 ; river, 224

Sussex Archæological Journal, 42

Sutherland, the, 116, 117, 118, 122 note, 130, 133, 142, 146, 149, 183 note

Swanton, Commodore, 135, 242, 247

Swift, H.M., 41

TADUSSAC, 75, 101
Tea Tax, 374
Temple, Lord, 310
Teresa, Island of, 260, 263
Tertiano, outbreak of, 386
Thompson, Captain Robert, death, 38
Thorp, Dr., 42
Three Rivers, 257, 277, 318
Ticonderoga, defeat at, 70, 78
Tide table, at Quebec, 136
Tindal, Matthew, *History*, 33, 44
Toulon, naval action off, 18
Tourmente, Cap, 103, 195, 196
Townshend, Colonel Sir C. V. F., *Life of his Ancestors*, 98 *note*, 100, 127
Townshend, General George, commanding the 64th Foot, 91, 92; relations with J. Wolfe, 92, 115; voyage to Quebec, 96–104; diary, 98, 100, 135 *note*, 138 *note*, 143, 151 *note*, 172; at Montmorency, 114; at Goreham's Post, 141; at the battle of Quebec, 162–167; Commander of the forces, 163, 166; decision, 189; attacks on, 189–191; return to England, 191, 201, 315
Townshend, Thomas, Secretary at War, letter from J. Murray, 419
Trade, Lords of, letter from J. Murray, 341
Traquair, John, Earl of, 12; Treasurer Depute, 12; death, 13
Tremain, M. Querdisien de, mission to Canada, 87
Trent, the, 99
Trentham, Lord, candidate for Westminster, 51 *note*
Trois Rivières, 257, 277, 318
True Briton, the, 253 *note*
Turner, J. W. M., sketches, 437

UTRECHT, Treaty of, 76

VANDEPUT, Sir George, 51
Vanguard, the, 242
Varennes, 261
Vaudreuil, Marquis de, character of his rule, 80; letters to Abbé Bernis, 81; jealousy of Montcalm, 82; at the battle of Quebec, 157–167; orders to the troops, 158 *note*; charge

against, 179; retreat, 188; surrenders Montreal, 265; criticism on, 439
Vauquelin, De, commander of the *Aréthuse*, 66, 201, 243; taken prisoner, 244, 247.
Vergor, Captain de, wounded, 154; in charge at Anse-au-Foulon, 177; character, 177
Vernon, Admiral, 28, 34
Vesuvius, the, 138 *note*
Vienne, Madame de, 183–185; flight, 184
Vienne, Sieur de, 183
Virginia, 29

WAGER, Sir Charles, on the preparations for the expedition to the West Indies, 30
Walker, Sir Hovenden, 197 *note*
Walker, Ensign Job, death, 39
Walker, Thomas, case of, 332–335, 356, 365; in London, 342; character, 347
Walpole, Horace, opinion of Lord Elibank, 18, 19; extracts from his *Memoirs*, 28, 42, 91 *note*, 202, 269, 292, 345; opinion of J. Wolfe, 61
Walpole, Sir Robert, 41; policy with Spain, 27
Walsh, Colonel, attack on St. Foy, 226
Ward, the, 139
Waterford, 50
Watson, Captain, on the attack of Fort St. Lazarus, 34
Watson, Ensign Justly, 39
Webb, Colonel, 95; at Point Levis, 132
Wellington, Duke of, 22
Wentworth, Major-General, 29; in command of the expedition to the West Indies, 33; at Jamaica, 33; attack on Fort St. Lazarus, 34; incapacity, 36
West, Benjamin, "The death of Wolfe," 24
West Indies, naval reinforcements, 28; expedition to, 29–37, 62
Westerhall, 24
Westminster election, 51
Weymouth, Lord, Secretary of State, 384; policy, 384–386
Wheeloch, Captain, 109
Whitham, Abraham, 395

Whitham, Ann, marriage, 395.
See Murray

Whitmore, General Edward, 59;
Governor of Louisburg, 91,
252

Wilkes, John, 332; extracts
from his *Memoirs*, 310; poses
as the champion of liberty,
342; member of the Hell-
Fire Club, 440 *note*

Williams, Basil, *Life of William
Pitt*, 282 *note*, 295 *note*, 383
note

Williamson, Colonel, commanding the artillery, 94, 95

Windsor, Justin, *Narrative and
Critical History of America*,
281

Wolfe, Colonel, 29 *note*

Wolfe, Edward, death, 60

Wolfe, General James, 22, 59;
tribute to J. Murray, 24,
67; member of the expedi-
tion to capture L'Orient,
44; quartermaster-general, 54;
characteristics, 60; ill health,
60, 124, 126; gift of organisation, 61; relations with J.
Murray, 61; career, 62;
wounded, 62; voyage to Halifax, 63; attack on Louisburg,
64; correspondence with Lord
G. Sackville, 66; expedition
against Quebec, 72, 90; want
of tact, 92; army, 93, 95, 132;
voyage to Quebec, 96–104;
survey of Quebec, 105–107;
plan of attack, 106, 110–120,
125, 134, 141, 146, 173;
extracts from his diary, 110,
117; correspondence with his
brigadiers, 125, 126, 147–
149; captures Quebec, 135;
orders for the attack, 135,
138–141, 144, 150; postpones
attack, 137; last despatch,
141; at Goreham's Post, 141,
144; change of plan, 142–144,
170, 186; indomitable spirit,
150; attack on Quebec, 156–
167; killed, 167, 168 *note;*
advice from his brigadiers,
171, 176; receives a " packet,"
172

Wolfe-Murray, General Sir
James, 94 *note*

Wood, Colonel William, 112;
Logs of the Conquest of Canada,
57 *note; The Fight for Canada*,
156

Wright, *Life of Wolfe*, 94
note

Wrong, Professor, *A Canadian
Manor and its Seigneurs*, 102

Wynyard, Colonel John, 29;
attack on Fort St. Lazarus,
35

Yonge, Cornelius de, 25

Young, Colonel, 139; Chief
Judge at Quebec, 204, 277

Young, William, 438

THE END

PRINTED BY
WILLIAM CLOWES AND SONS, LIMITED,
LONDON AND BECCLES, ENGLAND.

CPSIA information can be obtained at www.ICGtesting.com
Printed in the USA
BVOW02s0407261213

340115BV00012BA/193/P